WONDER
GIRL

ALSO BY DON VAN NATTA JR.

First Off the Tee: Presidential Hackers, Duffers,
and Cheaters from Taft to Bush

Her Way: The Hopes and Ambitions of
Hillary Rodham Clinton (with Jeff Gerth)

WONDER GIRL

The Magnificent Sporting Life of

BABE DIDRIKSON ZAHARIAS

DON VAN NATTA JR.

LITTLE, BROWN AND COMPANY

New York Boston London

Little, Brown and Company
Hachette Book Group
237 Park Avenue, New York, NY 10017
www.hachettebookgroup.com

First Edition: June 2011

Little, Brown and Company is a division of Hachette Book Group, Inc. The Little, Brown name and logo are trademarks of Hachette Book Group, Inc.

The publisher is not responsible for websites (or their content) that are not owned by the publisher.

Library of Congress Cataloging-in-Publication Data
Van Natta, Don.
Wonder girl : the magnificent sporting life of Babe Didrikson Zaharias / Don Van Natta Jr. — 1st ed.
p. cm.
Includes bibliographical references and index.
ISBN 978-0-316-05699-1
1. Zaharias, Babe Didrikson, 1911–1956. 2. Women athletes — United States — Biography. 3. Women golfers — United States — Biography. I. Title.
GV697.Z26V36 2011
796.092 — dc22   2010041794
[B]

10 9 8 7 6 5 4 3 2 1

RRD-C

Printed in the United States of America

For
Isabel and Sofia,
my wonder girls

I don't see any point in playing the game if you don't win.
Do you?

— Babe Didrikson Zaharias

If we have that one shot in us, we must have thousands
more — the problem is to get them out, to let *them out.*

— John Updike

Contents

Contents

WONDER
GIRL

Prologue
Matinee at the Palace

They began lining up for the early matinee at the Palace Theater not long after dawn. Blazing in block letters on the theater's marquee were the names Fifi D'Orsay, a B-movie actress usually cast as a saucy French girl, and a musical group called Bob Murphy and the California Collegians. But no one had scrambled out of bed on a frosty Chicago winter morning for them. No, the people had come to witness the unlikeliest of vaudeville debuts, the invitation glowing high atop the theater's marquee: "BABE" DIDRIKSON — IN PERSON — WORLD'S GREATEST WOMAN ATHLETE. High above the Palace roof, a single gigantic word — BABE — shimmered in golden lights, an electric carnival barker shouting the name into the sky.

It was January 27, 1933, and the people had come to find out the answer to a peculiar question: *Is there anything Babe Didrikson cannot do?*

Practically every sports fan in America could recite the highlights of Babe's all-sport résumé: how she could run fast and far and jump high and long. They knew she could throw a nasty curveball and smash a baseball into the next county. They knew she was an all-American basketball player, outfoxing defenders with quickness and guile, head fakes, and stutter steps. She could swim with speed and endurance, scamper across a gridiron wearing pads and a helmet, and outhit and outwit the sharpest billiards hustlers. They knew Babe had stormed her way into the worldwide sports pantheon at the 1932 Olympic Games in Los Angeles, winning two gold medals and a silver medal while etching her name in the record books.

But...*this?*

At the age of twenty-one, just five months after her Olympic triumph, Babe suddenly had the audacity to spin the roulette wheel of her athletic career, letting it ride on a vaudeville stage, of all places. In those pretelevision years and earliest days of films with sound, the vaudeville stage was still one of America's leading entertainment tickets. Wedded to its tradition of quick-witted improvisation, vaudeville was renowned for its ruthless and often lethal unpredictability. It had a way of chewing up the ill-prepared or fainthearted, and the audience relished whatever disastrous moment awaited a jittery performer. Nothing was more intoxicating for a vaudeville crowd than the chance to deliver a harsh comeuppance to some ham-and-egger and then watch him or her slink offstage, leaving behind the footlights for some two-bit career unloading trucks or sweeping floors. Some in the audience no doubt hoped that kind of embarrassment would befall Babe Didrikson. Everyone knew she had earned a place among the biggest names in sports, right up there with Red Grange, Jim Thorpe, Bill Tilden, and Babe Ruth. But this seemed beyond her reach.

Here, in the final somber weeks of the Herbert Hoover Presidency, many Americans took comfort in the thought that Hoover was busy packing and would move out of the White House soon. President-elect Franklin Delano Roosevelt was assembling his cabinet and preparing for his inauguration just five weeks away. Many Americans doubted that FDR—or anyone else, for that matter—possessed the know-how to lift the country out of a deep ditch. The Depression was going to last forever, and, like a natural disaster, it discriminated against no one, handing out calamities in equal portions to street sweepers and bank executives, stockbrokers and stock buyers, dress designers and seamstresses, theater owners and theatergoers.

The owners of the Palace were especially worried. Built just six years earlier to take advantage of all the shrillness of America's giddiest and gaudiest decade, with embellishments designed to evoke the royal palaces at Versailles and Fontainebleau, this monument to Roaring Twenties excess was now struggling for survival. Formerly the tough-ticket showplace for headliners such as Mae West, Jimmy Durante, Sophie Tucker, and Bob Hope, the Palace had been relegated to featuring also-rans performing before a valley of vacant maroon seats. It seemed that everyone in Chicago was hoarding their nickels and dimes for the city's new movie houses or staying home to listen to Eddie Cantor and Bing Crosby on the radio.

George P. Emerson, a Chicago advertising man with an eye for a good stunt, decided there was one woman who just might pump life into the Palace: Mildred Ella "Babe" Didrikson, a genuine American sports heroine *and* a vaudeville novice, onstage—*for one week only!*

Sure enough, around the Palace that wintry day, there was reason for hope. By late morning, hundreds of people had formed a raucous three-block line stretching down Randolph Street. Rainy-day nickels and dimes stashed in coffee cans and beneath mattresses were pushed through the ticket windows. Every ticket was sold for the early matinee.

At noon, the Palace's wide doors swung open, and the boisterous crowd surged into the theater's sumptuous lobby. Ticket holders paused to gape at the glittering designs leaping up the walls in gold leaf and oak. A few women stopped to touch up their hair and makeup in the oversized mirrors framed by sweeps of violet and ivory marble.

After settling into their seats, audience members buzzed with anticipation: Why would Babe agree to do such a preposterous thing? Is she dead broke? Will she bomb? The prognostications were divided almost evenly along gender lines. The men guessed at the number of minutes that would elapse before Babe fell flat on her face. The women just smiled, hoping and half-certain that the men would be counting until kingdom come.

With her eyes squinted into slits, Babe peeled back the maroon velvet curtain just enough to spy on the buzzing crowd filling the two thousand seats. She had always suffered pre-performance jitters, and manic stomach pains often kept her awake the night before a big athletic competition. As she peeked, she felt the usual riot of butterflies. Losing a competition was one thing, but nothing could be worse than facing an orchestra of ridicule from a sold-out vaudeville crowd. Babe inhaled deeply and, not for the first time that day, whispered, "My Lord, I can't go through with this…"

"Two minutes to curtain," the stage manager said. "Quiet, everyone…Babe, go to the lobby." No time for second thoughts. Babe stepped out a side door and sprinted down a long corridor toward the front of the Palace.

The theater lights dimmed, the crowd hushed, and the curtain raced skyward. The audience cheered until they noticed that Babe was not on the stage. A swirling white spotlight landed on a trim, middle-aged man dressed in a sensible gray business suit and sitting behind an ebony baby grand piano. The man introduced himself as George Libbey, a vaudeville veteran from New York City. A restless murmur rippled over the filled seats, and he responded with a be-patient half smile.

The piano player asked the audience if they were ready to meet Babe Didrikson. The crowd roared yes. Without another word, Libbey started to play a fast-paced tune. The audience began to clap along with the music, and then a woman's voice shot out from the back of the house.

The music stopped, and everyone turned around in their seats to see the purposeful young woman striding down the left-hand aisle toward the stage. It was Babe, chattering in her unmistakable Texas twang about having just arrived in icy Chicago after a glorious Florida vacation. She wore a long green swagger coat, high-heeled spectator shoes, and a Panama hat. As she approached the footlights of the stage and the crowd got a good look at her, Babe's chatter was drowned out by a lusty cheer. She beamed, waved, and grabbed an oversized microphone.

"As I was saying...," Babe said, and the crowd laughed.

Babe was not glamorous, but her face was striking and intelligent, with impish hazel eyes, a hawk nose, and a slightly crooked, thin-lipped grin—all framed by closely cropped chestnut hair. She stood 5 feet 6½ inches tall, weighed 132 pounds, and walked with a champion athlete's loping gait. Unlike most of the great, blocky male athletes of her era, Babe was lean and smoothly muscled, and she glided with leonine grace. With her head held high, she moved with a striking economy of motion. Something about her steely confidence and her audacious attitude made it impossible to take your eyes off her. Slumped in a third-row seat, George Emerson watched Babe beam at the audience and thought, *She's the real thing.*

The piano player asked Babe a few questions about her trip north before playing the introduction to a popular tune, "Fit as a Fiddle (and Ready for Love)." Babe raised the microphone to her lips and began to sing, toying with the lyrics:

> *I'm fit as a fiddle and ready to go.*
> *I could jump over the moon up above.*
> *I'm fit as a fiddle and ready to go.*
>
> *I haven't a worry and haven't a care.*
> *I feel like a feather just floating on air.*
> *I'm fit as a fiddle and ready to go.*

Her voice was smooth, on-key, and remarkably buoyant. She even dropped an improvised "boop-boop-a-dee-dee," in an exaggerated baritone, bringing the crowd to its feet.

Babe then kicked off her high heels and quickly slipped on a pair of rubber-soled track shoes. She peeled off her coat, revealing a red, white, and blue Olympic team warm-up jacket emblazoned with the initials *U.S.A.* and satin shorts. Babe bounded onstage and began running on a treadmill. Behind her was a large, white-faced clock attached to a black velvet backdrop. As she ran, the clock's long arm kept time. Another woman ran onstage, jumped on a second treadmill, and simulated a race against Babe. The treadmills had been rigged, making it look as if Babe rushed through a white-tape finish as the winner. The crowd cheered as Babe smiled and ran a victory lap onstage, her fists thrust above her head. She then teed up a few plastic golf balls and used a nine-iron to smack them into the crowd, her grin widening as audience members lunged for the souvenirs.

As the crowd pleaded for another trick, Babe craned her neck to look at a large sign on an easel at the foot of the stage. The sign usually carried the name of the current act. Today it featured her name. As she studied it with a puzzled expression on her face, George Libbey asked, "What are you looking at, Babe?"

"Oh, I'm just looking to see who the hell's on," she said, and the audience laughed.

Someone offstage tossed Babe a harmonica for the show's grand finale. She played "Jackass Blues," "When Irish Eyes Are Smiling," and "Begin the Beguine," her harmonica swinging and singing.

She was onstage for just eighteen minutes, but it was long enough to establish her as vaudeville's brightest new star. The next day, in the *Chicago Daily Tribune,* a stage critic named Clark Rodenbach wrote, "Friday afternoon was the 'Babe's' first time behind footlights, and the girl from the Lone Star state took the hurdle as gallantly as she ever did on the track."

Babe was paid $1,000 for a single week of shows — four or five performances each day. It was a preposterous sum of money at a time when some women were making 6 cents an hour for muscle-wearying work. Just a few months earlier, Babe was earning $75 a month from the Employers Casualty Insurance Company of Dallas, where she worked as a clerk.

Within several days, Babe's show had become the most sought-after ticket in Chicago and the talk of the vaudeville circuit across the nation. Jack Dempsey, the former heavyweight boxing champion, sat in the VIP section for a performance. Babe was so popular that George Emerson scheduled vaudeville appearances for her in Manhattan and Brooklyn. Performing onstage was "beginning to get in my blood," Babe recalled.

In New York, Babe's pay would increase to $1,200 a week. (She later claimed that her salary was going to be $2,500 a week.) But the money could not make up for the fact that the vaudeville stage was not the place for an athlete to make a living. Despite the show's glowing reviews, the fit wasn't quite right.

Before long, Babe's routine had become routine. Chicago audiences came to her show knowing the outcome, applause was all but guaranteed, and there was no longer even the threat of embarrassment. Babe began to complain about being forced to apply "that grease paint" before each show. Worst of all, she had to spend all her time indoors, either at the theater or in her hotel room.

She missed the joy of competition, a longing that was underscored each time she ran a fixed race on a rigged treadmill against a stagehand. Babe wanted to win again for real.

Part I

———•———

LET ME

1

Poppa's Fables

The girl would close her eyes and try to remember the hurricane—the black, rolling clouds, sideways rain, and a roar so loud you could feel it in your bones. She would try to remember the sudden way that the storm banged on the door and then took its time and lingered, assaulting her ears for hours until it was suddenly quiet, the calm like the wake of an uninvited guest who had worn out his welcome, but not before leaving behind a big mess. She was four years old when the killer storm barreled into her hometown, arriving just a few hours after her mother gave birth to her baby brother. Too young, she couldn't remember anything about her brother's arrival or the howling storm that followed. But she would never forget her father's telling and retelling of the hurricane story and the way hearing it made tiny goose bumps stand up on her skinny arms and the back of her neck.

Perched atop her father's knee, young Babe spent many hours listening to stories—some true, some imagined, some a blend of both. Her father, Ole, was a seafarer who left Norway with his family to become a furniture maker in East Texas, where he found fine pay and finer weather. She called him Poppa, and to Babe and her brothers and sisters, no one could cobble together a better tale, even if much of it seemed, at first, almost impossible to believe. "What a bang we used to get out of his stories about his experiences," Babe recalled years later. "We'd huddle around him and listen like mad."

Poppa's fables were genially preposterous. Most of his stories featured himself as the swashbuckling star, a kind of Viking Huck Finn of the Seven Seas. In one, he was stranded for weeks on a deserted island, where he was forced to hunt wild monkeys to survive. In another, one of his seventeen trips around Cape Horn ended when a storm shattered his ship into a million pieces. He bobbed atop the ocean surface clinging with one hand to a mast rope tied to a jagged shard. With the other hand, he saved a man from drowning.

But it was the hurricane story that young Babe asked her father to repeat again and again, mostly because she was the littlest hero in a tale full of frightened grown-ups.

Poppa always started the same way. He said it was a rare thing for a family to lose a home but gain a baby boy on a single box on the calendar. The newest member of the family was born in the early-morning hours of August 16, 1915, in Poppa and Momma's bedroom in the family's two-story wood-and-cement-block house at 2230 Seventh Street in Port Arthur, a town nestled on Texas's Gulf Coast. Not long after the baby woke up hungry after his first long nap, a hurricane suddenly swamped the coast. Poppa said that the wind sounded like a giant freight train had jumped off its tracks and soared upward, careening around the sky in crazy half circles like a cut-loose helium balloon.

"We was so scared," Babe's older sister Lillie, who was six at the time, recalled. But not everyone was flat with fear.

The way Poppa told it, as the gale-force storm approached, Babe danced in the tumult, running happily in circles as neighbors fled or hunkered down deep inside their shuttered homes. Her father liked to say that Babe was the only person on Seventh Street to laugh at the wind.

The hurricane hit so hard that floodwaters filled the first floor of their house, and the family was forced to retreat to a second-story bedroom. Poppa had no choice but to sweep Babe up in his arms and carry her to the bedroom closet, where everyone, even the baby, rode out the storm. Wind gusts exceeded 120 miles per hour, and the rain fell for nearly 24 hours, killing 275 people and causing an estimated $56 million worth of damage. Never once during the storm, not even for a moment, did Babe take on the worried expression creasing her momma's face, Poppa said.

"Everything was gone in the flood—ducks, chickens, trees, beds, money, dishes, everything," Lillie explained. "We didn't save nothin'. We just got out of town."

Poppa had a more poetic way of putting it. He liked to say that the storm blew the family seventeen miles inland, to the town of Beaumont, where they moved in late 1915. As a young girl, Babe imagined an invisible force powering the family into the air and carrying them that distance. Poppa and Momma christened the baby boy Arthur Storm, but the name didn't stick; he would always be called Bubba.

As a teenager, Babe convinced herself—and tried to tell anyone who would listen—that she could remember everything about that day's drama, even the sound of Bubba's first breath as the storm was bearing down on them. In reality, one of the most important pieces of the story—the fact that Poppa was there, in the middle of the action— wasn't even true. Poppa had been at sea, on a tanker that didn't bring him home until nine days after the storm. The story's real hero was Momma, who gave birth to Bubba, assisted only by the family doctor, with her six young children surrounding her. Momma then crawled out of bed and protected those children, and the baby, from the whipping winds and the rising floodwaters. There was nothing malicious about the way Poppa told the story. After all, he always talked about how brave Momma was, too. Perhaps Poppa told the story that way to impress and flatter Babe, Lillie later said, but also to ease his own conscience about not being there to comfort Momma in childbirth and protect his family.

Babe didn't hold a grudge against her father for the fib. The truth merely increased her already immense respect for her mother, who doted on her youngest daughter in a way that Poppa never did. But Poppa's fables taught Babe a lesson: no matter how improbable a story may sound, if you tell it right, people will savor every word. Tell it well enough, and no one will ever doubt even the tallest tale.

By the end of the nineteenth century, Beaumont, Texas, was a slow, quaint town without much ambition besides maintaining a sleepy status quo. Its main street, such as it was, had a not-quite-finished feel, as if the town's forefathers had run out of supplies or had fled to avoid the moneymen. The dense, humid air was hardly the right motivator to get people to do much of anything. Residents took their time with the simplest tasks — strolling along the dusty streets, ambling off to school, sipping a hot cup of joe in front of the Black Cat Coffee Shop. They never felt the need to rush. Hurrying just encouraged the sweat to cascade down their backs or seep into their eyes. Besides, anyone who had lived in Beaumont for a spell knew there was no point hurrying anywhere. Even if you were inclined to hurry to one of the town's few hospitable places — the Alamo Café, where men shuffled up the back stairs to buy a lady's companionship, or the Hotel Beaumont's Rose Room, which offered a variety of fine whiskeys — you were just going to lie down or sit down when you got to wherever you were going, in the shade, if you were lucky, or better yet on a porch. There was plenty to complain about, too, but few bothered. Even if someone listened, it wouldn't change anything.

The town was built on cattle, lumber, and rice milling. After word got out that Sam Houston once took a long, restorative bath in the mineral waters of Sour Lake, just outside town, a few folks took the trouble to try to lure tourists to Beaumont, but that hope depended on Beaumont being something other than Beaumont. A more durable way to earn a living was making moonshine. Distilleries quickly multiplied along the hardscrabble outskirts of town. Meanwhile, horseback preachers christened those outskirts the Alligator Circuit because of the dangers lurking in the swamps along the west bank of the Neches River: water moccasins, alligators, and the occasional human hazards, mostly bootleggers with a low tolerance for a man on a horse reading Scripture and peddling salvation.

In 1900, fewer than ten thousand people lived in Beaumont, and less than half that number lived in Port Arthur, to the southeast. People preferred just keeping to themselves. Indeed, staying out of your neighbor's business was a matter of civic pride in Jefferson County. This was still as fine a place as any in Texas to lay low, go on the lam, or sit in the shade with a tall glass of lemonade and watch the world slide by. To awaken an area from that kind of slumber, you'd need a big-bang kind of attention grabber. Sure enough, in January 1901 a gusher of oil erupted from the earth three miles south of Beaumont. Within a week, a black lake stretched over an area more than three hundred acres across. The Lucas Gusher, produced by the prick of a nearly worthless patch of land known as Spindletop, was soon churning out 100,000 barrels of oil a day.

Practically overnight, everything—and everyone—in East Texas changed. Old cattlemen became oil wildcatters, and refineries were built on top of lumberyards. Beaumont started hustling. It seemed as if everywhere you looked, new drill holes, followed by new pipelines, were being carved out of the ground. Men and women who used to shuffle lazily along the streets began rushing everywhere, perspiring furiously in the scorching heat. No more dawdling — there was a boom to catch.

Nothing moved faster than the price of land. A man who could not get $150 for a small chunk of scrubland back in 1898 sold it for $20,000 after the gusher. Fifteen minutes later, the buyer of the same piece of scrubland turned around and sold it for $50,000. It was crazy money, made crazier in just the time it took to change your overalls.

In 1905, when Ole Nickolene Didriksen stepped off a Norwegian tanker docked at Port Arthur, just west of the Texas-Louisiana border, he explored the cluster of new towns busily pursuing the big oil hustle. He listened eagerly to the locals chattering about fresh oil and fast money. He soaked up the humid air, imagining that the warmth would allow his three small children — Ole Jr., Dora, and Esther — to spend most of their time outdoors. ("Get plenty of exercise," Ole would tell his children, "and keep your bowels clear.") Like the rest of the people in this newly minted patch of East Texas, Ole rushed toward a new and better life. Everything he saw was irresistible. East Texas was about as far from Oslo as you could get, but it did not take long for Ole to see that this was the perfect place to start over.

The nation's immigration rules required him to live and work in the United States for three years before his family could join him, so the Didriksen family stayed behind in Oslo. Ole began working as an odd-jobs carpenter based at the port. His father had taught him how to transform wood into objects that were as beautiful as they were useful — a mahogany chassis for the frame of an old Model T Ford or a miniature sailing ship moored inside a small-mouthed bottle. The oil money made it possible for the wealthy to have a lot of things built or rebuilt for them. Even the working class felt more secure knowing that there was oil in the ground nearby.

Within days of setting up shop at the port, Ole considered himself blessed. After work and on weekends, he built a sturdy wooden house for his family on a small patch of land on Seventh Street, in a development of homes owned by Gulf Oil. The house, with a long porch and tall windows, eight on each side, was meant to resemble the interior of a ship, with built-in walnut cabinets and hidden mahogany cupboards. He used the finest wood: the two-by-fours were marked with the letter *B,* indicating that they were made of the best material available. Beneath an eave, extending from the front porch, Ole put a metal flagpole, and each morning he unfurled the Stars and Stripes in the breeze. "I'm a Norwegian," he liked to say, "but nobody's a prouder American than I am."

By the summer of 1908, Ole Didriksen was making enough money to support his family — barely. His wife, Hannah, and his three children arrived in Port Arthur on a muggy August afternoon. Hannah shielded her eyes from the hazy sun and looked suspiciously at the oil tankers belching fumes and the black oil rigs poking the big Texas sky. She smelled the stench of petroleum and listened to the gears grumbling inside the enormous refineries. Standing on the dock, surrounded by her children, her husband, and half a dozen travel cases, Hannah began to cry.

"My Momma, she told me that she couldn't believe what she seen — nothin' but oil, oil, oil, and she just couldn't stand it," Babe's sister Lillie recalled years later. "My Momma, she cried and cried and cried to think she had left beautiful, beautiful ol' Norway for this."

Hannah Marie Olson was the daughter of a Bergen shoemaker. She stood about five feet four inches and moved with the effortless gait of an athlete. Later, Ole was convinced that he had given Babe her athletic gifts, but Babe always attributed them to her mother. "When I was grown up," Babe recalled, "I once got her to try swinging a golf club. She had the prettiest swing you ever saw for someone who'd never done it before."

During her first few months in Port Arthur, Hannah tried to make the best of it, but nothing came easily. For one thing, she struggled to speak and understand English. For another, she never seemed to have enough money to pay all the bills. Ole had good months and bad months, but when things turned bad, he struggled to make even $100 a month — the minimum the family needed to survive. The most important thing to Hannah was giving her children a happy home. When money was tight, she worked hard to keep up her spirits and to hide any sense of hardship from her children. But keeping a lid on those troubles, like everything else about their new life in America, was not easy.

Lillie and her twin brother, Louis, were born in 1909, the first Americans in the Didriksen family. At 5:30 a.m. on June 26, 1911, another girl, the Didriksens' sixth child, arrived. They named her Mildred Ella. For the next four years — until Bubba and the storm arrived in Port Arthur — Mildred was the baby of the family, and Momma doted on her. "Min Bebe," she would coo to her, or just "Bebe."

When Mildred was just six weeks old, Momma noticed that she knew exactly what she wanted and never hesitated to tell you. When she was tired or hungry or just fussy, she let you know, ferociously. "How is it with this girl, Hannah, I'm afraid no crib I can build is going to hold her," Ole said. Bebe was eventually shortened to Babe, the name Mildred would be called for the rest of her life. "When Babe was born we all called her the Baby, and later when Bubba was born, we kept it up," her oldest brother, Ole Jr., explained. "Bubba couldn't say Mildred, and in some way Bubba shortened the Baby to Babe, and the whole family took it up and it stuck." No one — not the children or Poppa or even Momma, who had named her — believed that "Mildred" was the proper thing to call this little girl.

2

The Only Girl

Whenever anyone saw Babe, she was running, usually barefoot, and always pretty fast for a girl who couldn't have been more than eight or nine. And the observant residents of Beaumont's South End figured Babe wasn't running to get somewhere on time; they figured she was fleeing the scene of her latest act of mischief.

When she was no more than ten, a dare from a boy made Babe jump off the unfinished roof of a half-built house. Her fall, if it could be called that, was one of those awkward crashes, broken, thankfully, by a giant pile of soft sand. The children watching laughed as if the fall were another of Babe's staged pratfalls, until they heard her shriek with pain. A piece of wood had punctured her right leg, eventually leaving a jagged scar shaped like a golf driver. The next day, with her leg still wrapped in bandages, Babe performed the same stunt again. This time, there was an even larger audience. Babe crashed into the sand just as hard as she had the day before, but with more painful results: three cracked ribs. News of the double jump flabbergasted the neighborhood parents, who informed their sons and daughters that any kid willing to dive off the roof of a house two days in a row was just wild for the sake of it or, worse, dumb as a brick.

It didn't take long before most folks in the South End began referring to Babe as "that Didriksen girl" or "the worst kid on Doucette Street," where the Didriksens now lived. Each phrase was delivered with either an annoyed frown or a grim roll of the eyes. The labels were not applied just because Babe appeared determined to find new ways to endanger herself, as she did when she climbed the flagpole in front of Magnolia Elementary School to balance herself on top like a curious crow—just to see what it would be like to have the world at her feet. ("One day I heard the kids outside yelling for me," recalled the school principal, Effie Piland. "I went outside and there was Mildred, sitting on top of the flagpole. She had climbed to the top and I told her to come down.") Instead, the neighborhood's residents were concerned that Babe's antics would endanger the safety of others. Babe often encouraged her big sister Lillie to join her in a dangerous game of hitching a ride on a slow-moving freight car, then jumping off as the train accelerated. "Sometimes we got skinned up," Lillie said, "but we never got hurt no worse than that." More than once, the game came close to ending tragically when Babe slipped while running alongside the train and barely escaped being yanked beneath its churning wheels.

Led by Babe, the neighborhood kids engineered an annual Halloween prank that targeted the motormen responsible for driving the streetcars up and down Doucette Street. A ride cost 6 cents for adults and 3 cents for kids, a price that was out of reach for Babe and her pals. So they sought revenge by lathering up the tracks with Octagon laundry soap, bedeviling the drivers when they applied their brakes. After a streetcar finally eased to a halt or regained its proper path, one of the kids—usually Babe—shimmied up to the car's roof and yanked the trolley pole off its wire. This forced the sweaty motorman to get out, scramble to the roof, and struggle to reinstall it. To the neighborhood kids, there was no more entertaining sight than that.

One Halloween evening, Babe made the mistake of targeting a streetcar that just happened to be carrying her father home after work. A few blocks from home, the streetcar began to slip and lurch on the soap-slicked tracks. In the dusk, Ole saw a kid running and laughing alongside the car. Without the benefit of good light, he mistook the culprit to be Babe's older brother Louis. Ole's horror doubled when the troublemaker stumbled and slipped in the mud, nearly getting dragged under the car's wheels. When Ole called Louis's name, Babe, dressed in Louis's old shirt and slacks, turned and dashed home, sliding beneath the porch to avoid the sting of Poppa's belt. After hiding there until nearly midnight, she confessed that it was she, not her brother, who had soaped the tracks. She figured it just wouldn't be right to let Louis take the blame for her prank. As was often the case with her father, her honest confession, given with a slight cock of her head and a big smile, spared her the whipping she had coming. Although her father tried not to play favorites among his seven children, the girls usually won the benefit of the doubt.

Suffice it to say, Babe's behavior was unusual. In the early 1920s, girls were taught to be little ladies, seen and rarely heard, and the parents of Beaumont had never seen a girl quite like that Didriksen ruffian. Babe was rambunctious because that's how boys behaved. She learned that her acts of derring-do were a way not only to attract the boys' attention but also to win their respect—and that's all that mattered to her. Winning their respect meant she'd be included in their games.

Parents began assuming that Babe was the chief instigator of every neighborhood mishap—a window smashed by a baseball, a bed of daffodils crushed by a football, a house pelted with a few dozen rotten eggs. Even when she was not responsible, she got the blame. "Babe was known as a little tartar and the neighborhood pest," recalled Emma Andress, a Doucette Street resident and childhood acquaintance. Another classmate proclaimed Babe "a tomboy with no manners."

The neighborhood children were warned not to emulate "that Didriksen girl," and the parents reached an easy consensus: Babe should be sent away to reform school, for her own good and everybody else's—a recommendation that Momma and Poppa chose to ignore (in part because there wasn't enough money to pay for it). But among the children, Babe could always be counted on to navigate her way—and theirs—out of the worst pickles. "If we got into trouble," recalled one of Babe's pals, Frances Mazolla Hughes, "we would go to the Babe and she would always take care of us. She was always for the underdog. We clung to her." Even the boys—*especially* the boys—thought that anyone called the worst kid on Doucette Street was someone to keep an eye on, maybe even show a little respect to, even if she was just a dumb girl.

Doucette was a straight ribbon of dirt and mud that connected the South End's two unsightly but necessary landmarks. At one end of the street was the Magnolia Oil Refinery, southern Beaumont's largest employer and one of the largest refineries in Texas. It was perpetually encased by a thick oily haze belched from its cluster of wheezing smokestacks and humming, crisscrossing pipes. At the other end was the town's bustling train yard. The lattice of tracks served as a launching pad for the convoy of northbound freight trains loaded with freshly refined oil and headed for Houston, Dallas, and points beyond.

This was Beaumont's ugly industrial southern backside, a neighborhood that was a one-hour hike from the tourist welcome center near the downtown railway station, which, not coincidentally, faced north. Magnolia Oil wasn't concerned with creating a leafy neighborhood fit for young families. It wanted to shoehorn as many employees as possible within walking distance of the refinery. Even if each house on Doucette had been painted a different color, they all would have looked the same — shotgun-style houses with two bedrooms, a kitchen, a dining room, a living room, and a small front porch. (The shotgun house was so named because if you stood on the front porch and fired a shotgun through the door, the pellets would travel through the house and clean out the back door.) The houses were built on cookie-cutter lots divided by low green hedges that stood just above knee-high on an adult.

In the Didriksens' house at 850 Doucette Street, there was not nearly enough space for a couple with seven children. Poppa yearned to live in a big, wide-open, rambling country house, and he tried to execute that dream with his toolbox. He built a wraparound, enclosed porch that ran along one side of the house and went around back. After he installed a partition down the middle of the porch, the girls slept on one side and the boys on the other. This gave the kids a chance to enjoy "real fresh-air sleeping," Babe said.

More space for more beds translated into more space to clean. Every Saturday, twenty-eight tall porch windows had to be washed by hand, a chore that usually fell to Babe and Lillie. The girls were also asked to scrub the linoleum floors, a job that would be backbreaking for an adult. Hannah told them that the proper way to get the job done was to get on their hands and knees and scrub until the floors gleamed. "Don't let that dirt in the corner laugh at you," she said. "Get it out."

Babe used the chore's drudgery to invent a new indoor sport. With soapy water an inch deep on the linoleum, she ran and slid the full length of the floor, once falling and splitting her knee wide open. She also used shoelaces to fasten scrub brushes to her bare feet so that she could skate around on the soapsuds. It was no surprise that the job usually did not get done right, and Hannah, whom Babe called "strictly sweet," would have to enforce the rules.

"Babe, look at that," she would say, pointing at a patch of dirt lurking in some corner. "Is that right?"

"No, ma'am, that's not right, but I had to leave. The ball game was going to start."

"Well, you go do it now. And do it right."

Do it now and do it right. This became the Didriksen family motto. Babe soon applied this lesson to the way she competed on the South End's playgrounds and sandlots. For Babe, the games of baseball, football, and basketball took priority over homework and household chores, even if it meant getting a whipping.

Babe wasn't tall, but she was lean and lanky and had long, skinny legs. Her brown hair was cut in a Dutchboy style. She had the rough-edged mannerisms of a boy, even down to the way she thrust one leg in front of the other when posing for a picture. At that time, it wasn't enough for Babe to look like a boy and act like a boy. She wanted to *be* a boy. Then she'd be able to play all the games that boys played, no questions asked. And she wanted to *beat* the boys. She tried playing ball with the girls, but there was nothing challenging about that.

Before anyone had figured out what Babe was capable of, the boys on Doucette Street—including Babe's older brothers—rolled their eyes whenever she and Lillie showed up on the sandlot, demanding to join their football game. Hannah told the boys to let Babe, Lillie, and a few other neighborhood girls play with them, but on one condition: "Don't tackle the girls." So the boys had no choice but to play touch football, although Babe grumbled that she'd rather play tackle.

Led by Babe, a few of the girls eventually became regular players in the boys' baseball games, which were often played inside the tight confines of the Didriksens' backyard. There was more than one hazard to avoid in the yard, such as Momma's clotheslines whipping in the humid breeze and Poppa's big toolbox. Beyond the imaginary outfield fence, there were rosebushes, so hitting a home run was often a good thing that turned into trouble. Momma kept telling the boys and girls to keep the baseball out of her roses. Then one day, Momma joined the game and smashed a ball into the middle of her flower bed, crushing a few of her beloved roses. "We never heard any more complaints from her about our ball playing after that," Babe said.

Even in less physical arenas, Babe's superiority was quickly demonstrated. At the age of seven, she took up marbles, practicing for hours after school until she was better than anyone in the neighborhood. "She could out-do all the boys," recalled Effie Piland.

In the Didriksens' mud-splotched backyard, Ole built an outdoor gymnasium, with metal bars forming a tricky obstacle course. In the garage, he made a barbell out of an old wooden broomstick with a flat-iron tied to each end. "He put it there for the boys, so they could strengthen their muscles," Babe recalled, "but my sister Lillie and I would get in there and work out with it too." Ole often didn't have any money to spare for picture shows or ice-cream sodas, but he decided he'd give his children something even more valuable that didn't cost anything: "I'll build good bodies for them."

It worked. By the time she turned ten, Babe was no longer considered a nuisance on the sandlots and ball fields of Doucette Street. She could run, pass, throw, and hit. Almost always, she won. And she didn't mind razzing you about it. The boys noticed. "All the boys in the neighborhood would come and Babe was always there," said Raymond Alford, one of the boys who became a close friend of Babe's. "Let me tell you, she was the only girl, but she was among the first to be chosen. . . . Ordinarily we didn't have anything to do with girls then. Babe was different. Once you saw her play, you didn't mind having her around."

*   *   *

One afternoon, Momma sent Babe down the block to the grocery store to buy some ground beef for dinner. It was a special night: Lillie was graduating from Magnolia Elementary School, and Hannah and Ole were expecting half a dozen dinner guests. "Hurry," Hannah told Babe, who ran to the store and bought the meat. On her way home, Babe saw some boys playing baseball in the park behind the school. "I stopped to watch for a minute," Babe recalled, "and the next thing I knew I was in there playing myself. I laid the package of meat down on the ground. I was only going to play for a couple of minutes, but they stretched into an hour."

While in the outfield, Babe heard Momma's frantic screams. Then she saw her mother hunting for her. Babe ran off the field to assure her mother that she had stopped to play for just a moment. "I got the meat, Momma," Babe said. "It's right here." Momma pointed to a spot along the third-base line, and that's when they were startled to see a big dog chomping on the last few bits of hamburger.

Babe didn't bother to wait for her mother's reaction; she turned around and ran. Hannah ran after her. "Poor Momma," Babe recalled years later. "She couldn't quite catch me, so she picked up an old piece of rope that was sitting on the ground and swung it at me. She whipped me all the way home with that rope. I was running as fast as I could to stay ahead of her, but she could run fast too."

Another time, Momma had sprained her ankle by catching her foot in a streetcar's door. One evening, Babe came home covered with filth. She also had torn the pretty new dress that Hannah had made for her by hand. Momma took one look at Babe and started hobbling after her on her badly sprained ankle. Babe dashed away, as always, then stopped. "Momma, don't run," Babe said. "I'll wait for you."

Hannah raised her right hand to spank Babe, then stopped, tilted her head back, and laughed. "I can't whip you," she said. Momma hugged Babe, whispering, "Min Babe."

Something about the way Momma hobbled after her, wincing in pain, bothered Babe. She wasn't really sure what it was. Perhaps it was the weary way that Momma shook her head when she realized Babe had let her down again. Or the plain fact that it hurt Momma physically to try to discipline Babe. Or just the way Momma set her lips in that grim line as she listened to Babe rattle off another far-fetched excuse. All that mattered was Babe vowed to herself that she would never disappoint Momma again.

3

The Big Blue Sugar Bowl

As Babe figured it, there was one sure way to make good on her secret vow to stop disappointing Momma: she'd get a job—a *real* job. Without telling anyone, Babe decided she'd begin working after school. For incentive, she needed only to imagine Momma's look of surprise when she heard that first fistful of nickels rattling into the big blue sugar bowl, the family piggy bank kept on the kitchen counter.

To Babe and her siblings, it seemed as if all Momma and Poppa talked about was how to make what little money they had stretch a bit further. They always spoke in a rush, sometimes in a rat-a-tat-tat mix of Norwegian and English, as if they were trying to talk faster than the money was being spent. The kids usually had to strain to hear their fast-talk chatter. Sometimes, however, Momma's and Poppa's shouts were heard out on Doucette Street, even a ways up the block. In a good month, Poppa brought home more than $100, but it was barely enough to pay the bills. The family's weekly supply of groceries, pulled home in a wagon by Lillie and Babe from the store near the Magnolia Oil Refinery, cost $16 or $17. "My Gosh," Babe would say, "all that money for this."

Momma and Poppa argued often about how they should spend their money. Hannah believed that Ole should give up his two indulgences — a well-stuffed pipe that was usually fired up and a few cold beers with his pals in a tavern not far from the house. She lost that battle. Ole believed that Hannah's job was to raise the children, because that's what women were supposed to do. Hannah wanted to do her part to help pay the bills. Ole lost that argument. Hannah took in mountains of laundry, scrubbing it all by hand on an oak washboard and then carefully hanging it on a crisscross of clotheslines to dry. On occasion, she worked as a nurse's helper. Ole said that the few extra dollars she made were hardly worth Momma being exhausted and unhappy, but Hannah insisted, even if the extra money made only the smallest difference.

Babe noticed how the creases in Momma's forehead and along the sides of her mouth deepened whenever she was tired or unhappy. Babe's job, she figured, would erase those lines on Momma's face. As Momma said, everyone had to do his or her part. But it didn't occur to Babe that the shopkeepers, merchants, and factory foremen of the South End might not be overly eager to hire a thirteen-year-old, smart-mouthed, barefoot girl, especially one with a reputation for inventing new kinds of trouble. All of the shopkeepers within walking distance of Babe's house said thanks for the offer, but no thanks — and then they kept their eyes fixed on Babe to be sure she didn't swipe a candy bar on her way out the door. Finally, a job came looking for Babe. A classmate told Babe that a lot of teenage girls worked on the assembly line at a figs factory.

"A pigs factory?" Babe asked.

"No, *figs*," her friend said.

"Oh, OK, swell," Babe replied. Years later, Babe said, "I guess they didn't have any child-labor laws in Texas then."

For 30 cents an hour, Babe sorted figs, separating the bruised and discolored ones from the good ones. She did this until small white blisters appeared on her fingertips, and even afterward.

From there, Babe moved up to a better-paying job sewing up potato gunnysacks for a penny a bag. She sewed quickly, until her hands and wrists were so sore she could barely make a fist. But for a kid not yet in high school, the money was good — four or five dollars a week. Each payday, Babe kept a nickel or dime for herself and took the rest home to Momma, who dropped the coins theatrically into the sugar bowl. Momma not only smiled at the sound, but she gave Babe a bear hug and a kiss on the cheek. "Min Babe," she whispered.

"Momma," Babe said, "I don't want you to spend it on groceries or anything like that. I want you to buy little things for yourself." But Hannah would never dream of it; that money wasn't hers. If Babe wanted something — a new doll, a whistle, or a chocolate bar — Hannah would take some change out of the sugar bowl and say, "You go buy what you want, Babe. It's your money. You earned it."

But Babe always said no. She accepted the fact that the family's life on the edge of poverty meant that she'd never get most of the things she wanted. The one exception was a shiny harmonica, which Babe bought for $1.75 after saving up enough nickels and dimes. And she learned to play it well, mimicking the musicians she heard on the radio, during long evenings practicing on the family porch.

Babe figured that once the money was in the sugar bowl, it was family money, and she had no more right to it than a stranger did. The money was meant for food and clothing for her brothers and sisters and, of course, for Momma and Poppa. Babe later recalled that it was easy to turn down Momma's offers of a few extra nickels to buy treats. After all, what right did Babe have to dip her hand in the sugar bowl when Momma never did? Besides, there weren't enough nickels in that bowl to buy enough fun for seven children.

Babe was an observant girl, and she was especially sensitive to the things left unsaid between her parents when it came to money. Babe winced every time she heard Poppa quietly cursing himself when he couldn't spare a nickel for Louis to go to the movies with his friends. And she saw Momma's face darken when there wasn't enough money for necessities such as a new pair of shoes. "I wore mine to school," Babe recalled, "but I was barefoot the rest of the time, except on Sundays." Keeping good shoes on seven growing pairs of feet was enough to bust the budget of any family in Beaumont.

"We went barefoot all the time," Raymond Alford recalled. "Some of us never did have shoes. Everyone was poor. We weren't collecting any relief checks, but we were poor."

Relief checks? Handouts? Out of the question, Hannah insisted, though perhaps that rule could be bent a bit. Her best friend, a Norwegian woman named Laura Hanson, was well-off, the wife of a well-paid chef on a luxury liner. During her husband's frequent voyages, Mrs. Hanson was often invited to dinner at the Didriksens', and she never arrived empty-handed. She brought enough food to feed the family and always insisted on cooking it herself. Once a week, she brought a big roast. Hannah didn't see that as charity because, as Babe put it, "it was a sociable occasion among friends," and, well, that just didn't count.

Indeed, Hannah did not want the family to be viewed as a charity case. "Don't you ever dare take any old clothes from anybody," she told the children. This edict was a matter of pride. When Babe was no more than twelve, a friend from across the street, an older girl named Anna Louise Mansfield, gave Babe an old houndstooth wool skirt that didn't fit her anymore. One afternoon, while Hannah was working, Babe ran a pair of scissors through the skirt and used the family sewing machine to add a row of wide, fancy pleats. Before it got dark, Babe put on the skirt and then darted around the neighborhood, twirling fast so that the skirt flared. Babe was so proud of herself. With her own hands, she had made something special out of something that someone didn't want anymore. That could hardly count as charity, could it?

When Hannah got home that night, she asked Babe, "Where did you get that skirt?"

"Momma, this is Anna Louise's old skirt," Babe said. "I made me a flare skirt out of it."

Hannah thought for a moment, then said, "All right, that's fine. You did a good job on it."

Years later, Babe still remembered the infrequent Saturday matinees and the cheap shoes her father bought for her. Not having enough was a childhood ache she never forgot. "I can remember them hamburger days," Babe often told friends. "Where I go now I gotta have mink."

"As far back as I can remember," Babe told a reporter as an adult, "I played with boys rather than girls."

Dolls and tea parties, jacks and hopscotch didn't interest Babe. "I preferred baseball, football, foot-racing, and jumping with the boys," she explained. "I guess the habit of playing with boys made me too rough for the girls' games. Anyhow, I found them too tame."

When Babe was twelve, an older and bigger boy named Red Reynolds, a freshman football player, confronted her at Magnolia Elementary School. While a throng of classmates watched, Red told Babe that she wasn't so tough, and he stuck out his chin, daring her to hit him. Without saying a word, Babe landed a punch on his chin and knocked him "squarely to the floor." When the principal, Effie Piland, heard about the incident, she didn't punish Babe, but she warned Babe that if she did it again, she'd be expelled. Piland then did something else, which was a surprising and bold act for 1923: she permitted Babe to play sports with the boys after school. This was no punishment; this was a gift. "She was too good to compete with the girls," Piland explained to parents astonished by the decision. "They couldn't interest her for she was too far ahead of them." And it went without saying that, as Babe's knockout punch proved, she was as tough as *some* of the boys, even some who were older than she was.

Just because Babe was permitted to play on the boys' teams, that didn't mean the boys necessarily liked it or easily accepted it. She *was* different, more like a boy than a girl, a phenomenon that was unsettling for most boys. (Babe was so sensitive about those differences that in high school, she looked for other ways to fit in, changing the spelling of her last name from "Didriksen" to "Didrikson." "I didn't want people to think I was a Swede.") Most of Babe's new teammates teased her mercilessly, and the audacity of her knockdown punch increased peer pressure among the boys to test her toughness. They tapped her on the arm, thumped her back, clawed at her hair, and dared her to take another poke at another thrust-out chin. Often two or three boys would gang up on her. Babe might walk away, but she eventually sought payback on the playground, cornering a boy, stepping on his heels, and kicking him until his shins turned blue. "If we didn't do as she wanted us to," classmate John Lockhart said, "she'd chase us down and sit on us until we promised to play by her rules."

Babe also instigated fights with black boys and girls. When asked to explain the bruises on her face at school one morning, Babe said, "Oh, some niggers wouldn't get out of my way and I had to cold-cock 'em." It was the ugly language and bigotry of her neighborhood and of the era, but to some friends of Babe, she seemed to relish any chance to pick on the black boys and girls.

"She really did hate blacks in those days," said a physical education teacher of Babe's. "I think she went out of her way to antagonize them and truly, to *hurt* them."

For the impoverished kids of the South End, a racist attack was a crude way of proving their toughness. And proving their toughness, in sports and in life, was the fastest, surest way for them to communicate. For Babe, beating up and antagonizing blacks also were ways for her to impress the crowd.

Babe was attracted to both fisticuffs and organized sports for a lot of reasons. They were fun, of course, and she was good at them. But excelling in sports also was a sure way to stand out and, with any luck, get out. "I knew that winning in sports was the only way I'd ever be recognized," Raymond Alford explained. "Babe and I were both from poor families. If you did not have a car or if you did not have money, you were unacceptable. I thought that I might get to be the same as the richer people if I were good at sports; I figured I'd be asked to their parties. Sports were a way of getting to be equal, and I think that's what carried Babe through and made her work so hard."

Of course, the difference between Alford's prospects and Babe's was enormous. It had everything to do with gender. Alford could dream of college sports stardom, maybe even a shot at playing professional ball. No young girl growing up in the early 1920s had any reasonable chance of living such a charmed life. But that didn't stop Babe from trying.

4

The Highest Hedge

Before I was even into my teens," Babe wrote near the end of her life, "I knew exactly what I wanted to be when I grew up. My goal was to be the greatest athlete that ever lived. I suppose I was born with the urge to get into sports, and the ability to do pretty well at it." She may have been born with the urge, but she found the inspiration in the miniaturized type of the sports section of the *Beaumont Journal*. Ole adored the sports pages, and he passed on that affinity to Babe, who read them every day even before she entered high school.

Babe's first impressions of the world of sports were formed at a fortuitous time — the apex of the Golden Age of Sport, which was boosted in large part by the public's love of newspapers. Newspapermen's mythmaking and outright lies transformed star athletes into sun gods. Each year, the papers dished out ever more sensational reporting, led by the tabloid the *New York Daily News,* born in 1919. Within a decade, the *Daily News* boasted one million devoted readers. Dozens of new tabloids tried to match that success, racing to give readers the gaudiest headlines about the era's most sensational stories — the Lindbergh kidnapping, the shooting murders of Winnie Ruth Judd, the Leopold and Loeb murders. Readers relished articles about outlandish sporting events and flash-in-the-pan fads. Marathon dancing, rocking-chair derbies, and pea-eating contests vied for column inches with the major-league box scores. In 1924, a national flagpole-sitting craze was launched by a thirty-one-year-old daredevil named Alvin "Shipwreck" Kelly, who sat atop a flagpole above a Hollywood theater for thirteen days and thirteen hours straight. He later proposed to a shopgirl from the top of a flagpole. She said yes. (Their divorce six years later was covered even more gleefully.) It was Kelly's stunt that inspired hundreds of children, including Babe, to climb flagpoles. Sometimes the stunts were even more absurd. A high school senior from Warsaw, Indiana, made an impression on a United Press writer: "Clarence Tillman, 17, a local high school student, put 40 sticks of chewing gum in his mouth at one time, sang, 'Home Sweet Home,' and between verses of the song drank a gallon of buttermilk." The biggest stunts won the biggest headlines.

It was not a coincidence that the most famous and influential sportswriter of the time wrote the prettiest prose poems. Tennessean Grantland Rice described a sporting event as if he were writing a few verses of the Gospels. On an overcast October afternoon in 1924, Rice hunched over his typewriter in the press box at New York City's Polo Grounds and watched a college football game between Notre Dame and Army. But the next day, in the *New York Herald Tribune,* his readers saw something else.

"Outlined against a blue-gray October sky, the Four Horsemen rode again," Rice wrote in one of the most famous lead paragraphs written about a sporting event. "In dramatic lore they are known as Famine, Pestilence, Destruction and Death. These are only aliases. Their real names are: Stuhldreher, Miller, Crowley and Layden. They formed the crest of the South Bend cyclone before which another fighting Army team was swept over the precipice at the Polo Grounds this afternoon as

55,000 spectators peered down upon the bewildering panorama spread out upon the green plain below."

Rice described his favorite athletes as gods on earth. And God Himself? He was the Official Scorekeeper of Life: "For when the great Scorer comes to write your name, He writes not that you have won or lost, but how you played the game." Rice's superlative-spiked columns helped athletes such as Babe Ruth and Red Grange become heroes, earning them far bigger paydays than the President of the United States.

Through such filters and megaphones, Babe's sporting heroes acquired an almost supernatural combination of grace, grit, and guts. Most of these stars were men; there were only a handful of female athletes at the time. Babe was a fan of the era's finest woman golfer, the willowy British champion Joyce Wethered, but there were few other women atop podiums.

Whatever Rice had written about "the great Scorer," Babe thought that how you played the game mattered only if you won. On the philosophy of winning, Babe agreed with General Douglas MacArthur, who opened the Olympic Games in Amsterdam in August 1928 on behalf of the American team by declaring, "We are here to represent the greatest country on earth. We did not come to lose gracefully. We came here to win — and win decisively."

Soaking up every detail in the *Beaumont Journal* articles about those Olympics, Babe and her father cheered on the women athletes who, for the first time, were permitted to compete in five track-and-field events — the 100-meter and 800-meter races, the 4 × 100-meter relay, the discus, and the high jump. Not everyone believed that women should be allowed to compete. Some experts were convinced that most athletic events could be harmful to women, while historical purists declared that women should be prohibited because they did not compete in the original Olympic Games in ancient Greece. These arguments were bolstered when some female runners collapsed at the end of the

800-meter race. Some men also ended that race exhausted, but nevertheless many journalists argued that women lacked the stamina to compete in such strenuous athletic events.

Amid the hubbub, the Canadian women's track-and-field team dominated the action, winning two gold medals, two silver medals, and one bronze. Still, women's track and field was only on trial in Amsterdam, and it was doubtful that women would be permitted to compete in the next Olympics.

None of that controversy mattered to Babe, who began envisioning a gold medal adorning her chest. "Next year," Babe told her father, "I'm going to be in the Olympics myself."

"Babe, you can't," Poppa said. "You'll have to wait four years."

"Well, why?" she asked. "Why can't I be in it next year?" Ole explained that the Olympics were held every four years, which to his daughter only made the games sparkle even more. "It sounded like the greatest thing in the world to me — that free trip across the ocean and everything," Babe recalled. She didn't know that the next Olympics, in 1932, would be held in the United States, in Los Angeles.

Babe was not alone in her dreams. With the heroics of the Amsterdam games still fresh in their minds, she and her sister Lillie, like a number of American children at the time, set out to become Olympic athletes. They had no idea how to train, no coach, not even an idea about what events they might compete in. When Poppa told them there was no baseball or basketball in the Olympics, the girls settled on track and field. Lillie decided to be a runner, and Babe decided she'd be a hurdler and jumper. "I never was too good at straightaway running," Babe said. "I didn't seem to want to stay on the ground. I'd rather jump some obstacle." And she already had a head start, thanks to years practicing on Poppa's backyard obstacle course.

From the Didriksens' porch to the corner grocery store, there were seven hedges marking the property lines of the houses on Doucette Street.

Most were cut at about the same height, except one unruly hedge, which had grown taller than Babe. Most kids would have skipped that hedge and just jumped over the other six, but Babe figured that six was not as good as seven, and besides, she'd have to jump ten hurdles at the Olympics. The highest hedge marked the property of the King family. Babe knocked on their door and asked if Mr. King would mind trimming those hedges. Sure enough, he said OK, and he trimmed it to match the others.

"I'd go flying over those hedges," Babe said later, "and Lillie would race alongside me on the pavement."

A hurdle used in competition is nearly two inches thick, but the hedges that Babe was clearing were nearly two feet wide. It was impossible to clear them straight-legged, so Babe hurdled by crooking her left leg—the one that she always used for her first step. It looked awkward, but Babe's crooked-leg hurdling style allowed her to clear the hedges without scratching her legs.

In their races down Doucette Street, Lillie, whom Babe praised as a worthwhile "competitor," had an obvious edge because she didn't have to jump over the hedges as she rushed toward the imaginary finish line. But the advantage didn't stop Babe from trying to beat her big sister. "I worked and worked," Babe recalled, "and finally got to where I could almost catch her." Lillie simply "had too much fight in her to want to lose." But, Babe added, "I was a pretty competitive type myself."

Babe and Lillie stumbled upon another way to prepare themselves for lives as athletes, but it was as preposterous as it was dangerous. The circus, of all things, came calling.

Across Doucette Street lived a fifty-three-year-old woman named Christine McCandless. She doted on the Didriksen children, who called her Aunt Minnie. To a daredevil like Babe, Aunt Minnie had a dream job: she worked as a butterfly girl for the Barnum and Bailey Circus, which barnstormed across the country. While the circus was "hibernating" during the winter, Aunt Minnie regaled Babe and Lillie with tales of her life performing under the big top. Near the peak of the tent, as Minnie hung from a trapeze by her teeth, with her arms spread out wide, her frilly costume made her look — to a youngster's eyes, at least — like a fluttering butterfly. "She really did hang by her teeth, Aunt Minnie did," Lillie recalled decades later.

In the late winter of 1925, when Babe was a few months shy of fourteen, Aunt Minnie pitched a wild idea to Hannah and Ole: what if Babe and Lillie went with her on the road, just for a few weeks, to perform in the circus? There was always a need for youngsters under the big top, especially to do things such as ride the elephants, Aunt Minnie explained. Children had more natural balance than grown-ups, and their unexpected appearance was a guaranteed crowd-pleaser. Besides, Aunt Minnie said, Babe and Lillie would make perfect butterfly girls. Babe even had enough promise to make a very good trapeze artist.

"Naturally, the girls were beside themselves with delight over the thought of it," Babe's brother Louis recalled. "They clamored to go. They said it would make them feel like some kind of pioneers, at their tender ages." Momma and Poppa would have none of it — at first. But Babe "was an awfully hard child to refuse," Louis said, "when she wanted something."

Somehow, Aunt Minnie and Babe "talked my Momma into lettin' Babe and me go along for a while," Lillie said. Perhaps the prospect of having two fewer mouths to feed, just for a few weeks, appealed to Hannah and Ole. And the girls wouldn't be gone for long.

The weeklong car ride to California terrified Babe and Lillie, who huddled in the back of Aunt Minnie's open-air, ramshackle automobile as it wheezed its way along the winding back roads through the mountains and across the desert. Once in California with the circus, Babe and Lillie learned how to walk the tightrope without an umbrella. Babe hung upside down from a trapeze and turned flips, both forward and backward. These things came more easily to Babe than learning how to keep her balance on the back of an enormous elephant — claimed to be the world's largest — as it lumbered around the center ring. "I loved being on that ol' thing," Lillie recalled, "but for some reason Babe was scared. That's the only time I ever seen her afraid of somethin' that I wasn't." When Babe finally conquered her fear, she even stood on her head on the elephant's back when the beast was standing still.

As the trip that was supposed to last only a few weeks extended into months, Hannah and Ole grew worried that they would never see Babe and Lillie again. "All of us became frantic," Louis recalled. Ole figured out that the girls were in California, and he demanded that the circus pay for their train tickets home. The men running the circus sent word that "they would be happy to get rid of" the girls, Louis recalled, but Ole had to come get them. Although the Didriksens had been a hit with the other circus workers at first, now, for some mysterious reason (perhaps because the girls had big appetites), they weren't.

"It sounded to me mighty like the circus had become disenchanted with my little sisters," Louis said. "Frankly, I always will believe that the big tent entertained the fear that Babe would start turning the wild animals loose on the towns."

By train, Poppa caught up to the circus in northern California and collected his two daughters, who were ready to go home. When Babe returned to school in Beaumont, her teachers could tell that she had done almost no schoolwork while she was away, so they held her back a full year in school. But circus life had taught Babe at least one valuable lesson: the more outlandishly you behave, the more the crowd will applaud.

At the age of sixteen, Babe arrived at Beaumont High School with a reputation among her classmates that if you tried to get in her way, you should expect her to knock you down, or at least try. Because she had been held back a year, Babe was a year older and bigger than most of her classmates, a physical advantage that she would often exploit. The phrase that her classmates used to describe her was "the rough and tumble type." "She had great confidence," one classmate said. "She believed she could do anything—and she could."

Babe cared little for academics. All she wanted to do was play sports. This placed her among a handful of girls who were looked down on by the other girls. Babe wore the uniform of the girl athlete—a denim skirt with pockets, gym socks pulled up to the knees, and flat oxford shoes. Her short, straight hair and bangs were plastered down. In contrast, most of her female classmates wore silk stockings, blouses, and high heels, and their hair was waved. These were the daughters of Beaumont's middle class, and they looked at Babe and laughed. She was an oddity, a tomboy, whose boyish looks and coarse manner made her an instant outsider. And while the girls didn't like Babe, she didn't like them either, calling them "sissy-girls."

"She should have been a boy," said Sigrid Hill, a classmate. "Lots of people thought she was a boy, but she wasn't. She was a girl. She was tough." That toughness—and her tart tongue—became Babe's armor against taunts and barbs.

One afternoon, Babe sat in the bleachers watching the boys' football team practice. Raymond Alford, the team's star and a South End neighbor of Babe's, was kicking extra points. "I can beat Raymond all to little bits and pieces at kicking," Babe told coach Lilburn "Bubba" Dimmitt. "You got to let me come out and kick those points for you."

On a lark, Dimmitt told Babe to show him her stuff. "And, you know," Alford recalled, "she was better 'n I was—lots better. Bubba really wanted to let Babe try it, but there was no way the school board would let her in the games. The Texas high school rules were flat against letting a girl play a man's sport. Babe's poor old heart was broken, but there was nothing to be done."

Babe's official first team sport was basketball. Her coach was Beatrice Lytle, the school's lone female physical education instructor. "Babe was the most teachable person I have ever known," Lytle recalled years later. "You could explain the rudiments of a golf swing, a basketball movement, and Babe could do it." Playing for the Miss Royal Purples, Babe was one of the team's stars. For three years, the team went undefeated, drawing even bigger crowds than the boys' team. After one of her early games, she met the sports editor and columnist for the *Beaumont Journal* Bill Scurlock, who would become Babe's full-time local booster and biographer. Scurlock's nickname was "Tiny," although there was nothing small about him: he weighed nearly three hundred pounds. He liked Babe, and she liked him.

"Babe is her nickname," the editors of the 1928 *Pine Burr* yearbook wrote. "She plays with an ease and grace rivalling that of a dancer to tally goal after goal for the Purple during the season." The following year, Babe was called the "star...who very seldom misses the basket. When 'Babe' gets the ball, the scorekeeper gets his adding machine, and then he sometimes loses count."

Babe didn't just play basketball; she was a member of every girls' team: swimming, volleyball, tennis, baseball, and golf. In yearbook photographs, Babe is always deadly serious, squinting at the camera and wearing a grim expression beneath that mop of dark hair. Even then, all business.

On the field or court or in the swimming pool, that is. In the classroom, her grades were Cs and Ds with the occasional B. "She was sports, nothing but sports," said Pee Wee Blanchette, a teammate of Babe's. She was never seen reading a book, unless it was a rule book. She devoured the sports page but had little interest in anything else.

Her sister Lillie agreed that if it had not been for athletics, Babe wouldn't have known what to do. "Babe *had* to succeed as an athlete," Lillie said. "Her physical equipment was so much better than her mental equipment at the time. She never had a vision of herself as being anything but an athlete. Babe just did what she had to do."

5

Letters to Tiny

Inside the humid Houston high school gymnasium on a gloomy February afternoon in 1930, no one looked more out of place than the Colonel. He wore a slate gray suit and a smart Stetson atop his graying head of closely cropped hair. Several rows up the wooden bleachers, among the exuberant students, he sat impassively as the two girls' high school teams raced around the hard court. Behind round glasses, his steel blue eyes followed the action while his hard-set expression hinted at nothing.

The wiry, middle-aged stranger was Melvorne Jackson McCombs. A few folks called him M.J., but because he had served as a colonel in the U.S. Army Reserves, nearly everybody else just called him "the Colonel." He was the manager of the department of safety of the Employers Casualty Insurance Company in Dallas. The company had begun as a workers' compensation firm before branching out to sell life, health, fire, and auto insurance. But while the Colonel's department was safety, his mission was publicity. A 1904 graduate of Texas A&M, where he lettered in four sports — football, baseball, track, and tennis — McCombs had been hired by Employers Casualty in 1925 to manage the company's athletic department, including its semiprofessional basketball team for women, the Dallas Golden Cyclones. Teams such as the Cyclones served as traveling advertising campaigns for the companies that sponsored them.

For two decades, McCombs had coached independent and school football, baseball, basketball, and track teams across Texas, Oklahoma, and Louisiana, an experience that honed his ability to recognize and recruit winning talent. But in his first season at the helm of the Cyclones, the team was the winless laughingstock of the league. The Colonel never raised his voice in anger over the taunts directed at his team. This measured response was in large part a necessity: a heart condition had disqualified him from the army, and he was careful to maintain his composure. But he was a determined man, and quietly he decided that the Cyclones would win the national championship.

By 1930, "basket ball," as it was called in the papers and on posters, still had the feel of a newfangled invention. Nearly forty years earlier, in Springfield, Massachusetts, a Canadian physical education instructor named James A. Naismith had invented the game with a soccer ball and peach baskets. In less than four decades, basketball's popularity had swept America, and women's basketball had attracted nearly as many fans as the men's game. Women in their late teens and early twenties played on company-sponsored teams under the auspices of the Amateur Athletic Union (AAU). The women worked for these companies, usually as typists, stenographers, mailers, or filers, but on the court, they were considered amateur athletes. This designation was a technicality—everyone knew that most of the companies hired the women, some of whom were semiliterate, to play basketball. The twenty-game season concluded with a single-elimination tournament, held each year in a different city, to crown a champion. The team that won the national title wrapped its corporate sponsor in a winning glow that the flushest advertising budget could not buy.

McCombs used the newspaper sports pages as tip sheets. If a girl consistently led a team in scoring or caught the eye of the local newspaper, he'd write her name on an index card. With help from the insurance company's personnel department, McCombs maintained index cards on dozens of the best high school prospects, each carefully marked with the highlights of her performance. But the only way he could know if a girl was qualified to be a Cyclone was to watch her play. Because the games were usually low-scoring contests, the Colonel placed a premium on a girl's ability to play a smothering defense, including her willingness to deliver fouls with hard slaps and pointed elbows. Far more important than shooting or passing skills was a player's willingness—even eagerness—to take and land a punch.

As shrewd as the Colonel was at recognizing talent, he was even smarter at filling gymnasium seats. He was one of the first coaches in Texas to change his team's uniform. Women's basketball players typically wore baggy woolen bloomers that extended past the knees, long thick stockings, and flapping middy blouses. Their uniforms were so cumbersome that it looked as if they were running underwater. A debate in the United Kingdom was currently raging after female tennis players had run onto the grass courts at Wimbledon in shorts revealing their upper thighs. In some cities in the northeastern United States, women's basketball players had begun wearing shorts, although such revealing dress had not yet come to Texas.

When McCombs took over the Cyclones in 1925, he told the women that they would be much quicker if they traded their bloomers for shorts—the shorter, the better. He also advised them to wear sleeveless, lightweight jerseys that would make it much easier for them to shoot. Sportswriters also knew that the flimsier dress would attract more men to the games. The passionate, moralistic debate about McCombs's decision filled hundreds of column inches, with most commentators weighing in against the change. For the Colonel, the pressure to return to bloomers was easy to resist. The less restrictive clothing dramatically improved the girls' level of play. Even more important, attendance figures that had averaged in the low hundreds in 1925 sometimes exceeded five thousand in 1930. The industrial league had become a big, cash-generating business. The publicity bonanza for the sponsoring companies was enormous.

That February afternoon in the Houston gym, the Colonel had intended to scout the star center of the Houston Heights High School team. But after the game, it was the young woman wearing Beaumont High's number 7, who had scored a game-high 26 points, that he hurried to meet. Outside the Beaumont locker room, the Colonel introduced himself to Babe.

"How'd you like to play on a real big-time basketball team?" he asked.

"Boy, would I," Babe said. "Where?"

"At the Employers Casualty Company in Dallas," the Colonel said. "We're getting ready to go into the nationals in March."

Babe told him she'd need permission from her parents. "My Dad's right here," she said. McCombs and Ole huddled together as Babe paced the floor out of earshot. Then Ole told Babe, "We'll have to talk this over with Momma. If you get up there in Dallas, that's a long way from home. You'd best talk to Momma about this."

Inside the Rice Hotel that night, Babe's teammates kept chattering about her sudden moneymaking opportunity. Babe attended to more pressing matters. "She was too busy leaning out the window trying to see how many people she could spit at and hit on the head when they walked below on the sidewalk," teammate Thelma Hughes recalled.

The next day, the Colonel drove Poppa and Babe down to Beaumont in his big yellow Cadillac. At the Didriksens' dinner table, over plates of Hannah's steaming Norwegian meatballs, the Colonel made his pitch. He explained that a year earlier, the Cyclones had been knocked out of the national tournament in the quarterfinals, losing by one point to another team from Dallas called the Scheppes Aces. The Cyclones needed Babe to help them win the national tournament, which would begin in a few weeks in Wichita, Kansas. At the end of dinner, McCombs made a bold prediction: if Babe joined the Cyclones, she would become a national champion, an all-American, and, quite possibly, the finest lady basketball player in the land. *Champion...all-American...the best*—the words put a flutter in Babe's chest. By the way, McCombs added, he knew a little something about all this: four Cyclones were all-Americans.

No sooner had McCombs driven off for the long trip back up to Dallas than Babe began pleading with her parents for permission to join the Cyclones. Babe said that she wouldn't have to drop out of high school; she'd just leave for the remainder of the season before returning home in the late spring to graduate. The Colonel had offered Babe $75 a month to do clerical work, an enormous sum in Depression-era America. The average American household in 1930 earned $1,970 a year. Babe would be making nearly half that and wouldn't be expected to do much work: she didn't even know how to type or take shorthand. And she offered to split her paycheck with Momma and Poppa, who desperately needed the money.

"Min Babe," Momma said, "do you want to go way up to Dallas?"

"Yeah, Momma, I want to go."

Hannah turned to Ole: "What do you think?"

"I think it might be good for Babe," he said.

Momma felt sure that Babe was still too young to be on her own, even for six weeks. Poppa offered to escort her to Dallas. Reluctantly, Momma agreed. Babe hugged her and couldn't stop smiling. She was going to hop a train for the big city to play a game for a paycheck. What could be better than that?

The next evening, Babe arrived at the Beaumont railroad station clutching a one-way ticket bought for her by Employers Casualty. "Here I was," she wrote years later, "just a little old high-school girl, wanting to be a big athlete." She was dressed as if she were going to Sunday services, in a sky blue silk dress with box pleats, spit-polished black patent leather shoes that matched her black patent leather purse, and a little cream-colored hat she'd worn to her junior high school graduation ceremony. Inside her purse was "an entire fortune"—$3.49, the change remaining from the money the Colonel had sent to buy her ticket for the 275-mile northbound trek to Dallas.

For the overnight trip, Babe clambered into the upper half of a sleeper compartment. Ole settled into the lower half, puffing on his black pipe while perusing the newspapers. At daybreak, the train pulled into Dallas, and McCombs welcomed the two Didriksens. A redcap loaded their bags into the wide trunk of the Colonel's Cadillac. McCombs tipped the redcap a quarter. "Look at that," Babe whispered to Poppa. "He gets a quarter just for carrying those bags out."

The shiny, sharp edges of the city stung Babe's eyes. She marveled at the company's lavish headquarters in downtown Dallas, a city that was much bigger and better developed than Houston. Inside Room 327, home of the company's engineering department, McCombs introduced Babe to her colleagues, many of whom would also be her teammates. "Practically all the basketball players worked there," she said of Room 327. "I guess that was to make it easier to round them all up and take off when there was a basketball trip."

Babe was astonished at the height and bulk of many of the players, especially their oversized hands and feet. "They were really husky," she recalled. One of the girls, Lalia Warren, asked Babe, "What position do you think you're going to play?"

Babe shot back, "What do you play?"

"I'm the star forward," Lalia said.

"Well," Babe said, "that's what I want to be."

The Colonel just rolled his eyes. He could see that Babe was going to cause him all kinds of trouble.

But she would be worth it. That night, the Golden Cyclones played the Sunoco Oilers, the defending national champions. Babe started at forward, her high school number 7 emblazoned on her sleeveless, tight-fitting, orange satin jersey, which she had grabbed from a box of surplus uniforms. The Cyclones cruised to a 48–18 win. Babe led all scorers with 14 points, despite enduring a barrage of bruising fouls. "They started hitting me that night, and they kept it up the whole season," she recalled. "If one guard fouled out against me, they'd send in another one. But I broke away for my share of shots."

The Cyclones were talented, but they won mainly because they practiced for at least three hours every day on a court at Bryan High School in Dallas. They often scrimmaged against boys' teams (and sometimes won). The Colonel pushed the girls hard, benching any player who coasted through a practice session.

Each month, Babe separated $40 from her $75 paycheck and sent the money to Momma and Poppa. Five dollars a week paid for her modest room in a house in the Oak Cliff section of Dallas, a placid neighborhood where most of her teammates lived. After paying for meals — breakfast cost 15 cents; dinner was never more than 35 — Babe had about $5 a month for herself. Babe ate lunch at a drugstore, the same thing every day — toasted cupcakes washed down with Coca-Cola. It wasn't so long ago that she had been hoarding a spare nickel or dime that didn't land in Momma's sugar bowl. Extra folding money felt like a fortune, and in that first full year of the Depression, it was.

*　　*　　*

The press noticed. How could they not? Babe almost always led the Cyclones in scoring, and she once scored more than the entire opposing team. And what she lacked in beauty she more than made up for with a fresh mouth. Indeed, Babe was a reporter's dream: you never knew what kind of quote was going to come your way.

Within three weeks, as the team prepared for the season-ending national tournament, Babe had become the Cyclones' most bankable star. A typical headline read, "Beaumont Girl Plays Tonight in Cage Meet." One paper ran the banner "Mighty Mildred" above a large cartoon of a grinning, winking Babe. On the eve of the tournament, one of the Dallas newspapers featured Babe's picture "in the center, blown up way big," she said. "There were just little head shots of the others. Man, I just loved that!" Babe cut out the clipping and sent it to Beaumont, where Hannah carefully pasted it into a new scrapbook.

Because the Cyclones' games were broadcast live on local radio stations in Texas and Oklahoma, Babe became an instant regional celebrity. She savored her newfound fame, but it would mean more to her if news of her success reached her friends and neighbors back in Beaumont. With that in mind, Babe sat down the morning after her successful debut as a Cyclone and wrote a letter to Tiny Scurlock, the sports columnist at the *Beaumont Journal*. She stuffed a newspaper clipping describing her 14-point performance against the Oilers inside the envelope with the Employers Casualty Insurance return address. On company letterhead, she wrote:

Dear Tiny: Played my first game last night the 18, and I never before practice with them and they say that I was the girl that they have been looking for. They put me to start and kept me in until the finish. Tiny I am a working girl and have got to get busy. Please keep this write up for me please or send it back when you get a chance. Thanks so much, Babe.

This was the first of a series of letters that Babe would write to Tiny over the next two years. Two nights later, Babe scored 16 points in a 46–15 victory against Seagoville. The triumph didn't seem real until she could describe it for Tiny:

Dear "Tiny" — The games are coming in pretty fast here lately. We played Seagoville again last night and tomorrow at Cisco, Texas, and Monday night we play the champs of city. They have beaten the Cyclones but if I can help it they won't do it anymore. I am sending two write ups & my box score. They don't give you any write ups here. Well Good by Babe P.S. Please save write up for me.

In early March, the Cyclones played in the Southern Amateur Athletic Union tournament, an important precursor to the national championship to be held later that month in Wichita. The Cyclones demolished their first two opponents, Western Union, 62–9, and Evary, 82–5. Against Evary, Babe scored a game-leading 36 points. This time she typed her letter to Tiny:

Dear "Tiny" — Boy I am still knocking them cold. . . . We started in the S.A.A.U. tournament this week and are stilling holding out very fine and hope we keep on. . . . We have two All American guards and two All American forwards on our team and Mr. McCombs said that he would have three All American Forwards and Three All American Guards before the season is over. So Tiny I am up here now and that is what I am going to be, just watch and see. I will be home I guess about April 3rd or the 5th somewheres around there, that is after the National A.A.U. is over and I get that All American Badge to put on my left sleeve of this hot orange sweater that I have. "Tiny"—I have had two more offers and they are from the Sun Oil and the Sparkman of Ark. The Oil Man said they could use me in the national this year but I am going to stay with the Golden Cyclones until this season is over.... Maybe in the national I will be able to send to Beaumont a picture of me in the newspaper about the national A.A.U. Hope so anyhow. Well to be frank with you I am going to make an All American cause I have got my mind set on that. Well Tiny I have to close. Good by. Babe.

There was nothing subtle about the way Babe played—me first, team second—or how she played Tiny. "I have a whole lot of fans now," Babe said not long after arriving in Dallas, "and they are all going for the 'Golden Cyclones' and betting on them." She was obsessed with making all-American; that goal became more important than winning. Her teammates didn't much appreciate that, and they were even more annoyed that Babe openly ordained herself the team's best player within days of arriving in Dallas. Who did she think she was? "We had some pretty good players in those days," center Belle Weisinger later said. One of those stars was Agnes Iori-Robertson, the team's center, who would be selected an all-American a record six straight years. Worst of all was Babe's showboating with the fans and the press. On the court, Babe hogged the ball, shooting often and rarely passing. Off the court, she regaled fans and reporters with recaps of her own fine play without saluting the contributions of her teammates. "She was out for Babe, honey—just Babe," one teammate said. "We played as a team, we played as one. But I don't know how her mind ran. She was not a team player, definitely not. Babe, she was out for fame. There were lots of players on the Cyclones more popular than Babe was. But she got to be famous. And that's what she wanted."

Babe overheard many of the girls' catty whispers. She saw their eyes roll. She knew they had aired their complaints and resentments to the Colonel, who chose to remain neutral (for the time being). She wanted to be popular and always hoped that being a winner would make people like her. But Babe also had figured out that being the best at something usually didn't win you any popularity contest with someone who wasn't.

The Cyclones rolled to the regional tournament title. Next up: the national championship. This was the prize the Colonel wanted most of all. Babe was joined by her sister Lillie on the train ride to Wichita. At each stop, the two girls were too frightened to step off the train, convinced they'd end up stranded in some cow town. Hannah had instructed them to wash their underwear on the train and let it dry overnight. So the girls washed their underpants by hand in a small sink, then hung them out the window to dry. The next morning, they woke up to discover their intimates blackened with soot. Quickly, they rewashed them, but they spent their first day in Wichita squirming in their wet underwear.

The Cyclones crushed their four opponents, setting up a dream rematch for the title against their archrivals, the Sunoco Oilers. It was a seesaw battle; neither team kept the lead longer than a few minutes at a time. With less than a minute left to play, the score was tied. According to the rules of the time, when a player was fouled, the coach was permitted to choose any player to shoot the foul shot. With the Cyclones trailing by one point, Babe was selected to shoot. She missed the free throw. "It turned out that we lost the game by one point," Babe recalled. "I really felt bad about the whole thing."

Nevertheless, Babe's tournament play—she scored a total of 210 points in five games—clinched her selection as an all-American forward, an amazing accomplishment after just six weeks of play. Her teammates were livid, whispering among themselves that Babe had gotten her secret wish—no title for the team, but the all-American title for herself.

Almost immediately, rival coaches attempted to lure Babe to their squads. In a letter filled with glittering promises, R. C. Martin, the coach of the Kansas City Life Insurance Company team, told Babe that he was trying to turn "a mediocre girls' basketball team" into a national champion. His offer was $80 a month—a $5 raise—plus bonus money for each tournament game the team won. Her job at the company could be anything, and the coach assured her that workplace expectations were low. "If you have had no experience," Martin wrote, "do not hesitate to say so as that will have no bearing on your opportunity." The aggressive wooing of Babe, coming after and in spite of her missed free throw, deepened her teammates' bitterness and resentment.

Babe had promised her parents that she would return to Beaumont to graduate high school after the season, but she never did. Her high school records say simply, "Withdrew, Feb. 14, 1930." Hannah saw the broken promise as a betrayal, but with Ole working less, both parents put aside their anger because Babe continued to send home money. After cashing a few Employers Casualty paychecks, an enormously proud Babe also bought her mother a new radio.

Now that the basketball season was over, Babe played on the Employers Casualty softball team, smacking two home runs in her first game. But softball was not nearly as popular with the public as basketball, and Babe quickly became bored. On a hot spring afternoon, the Colonel took Babe and a few of the other girls to Dallas's Lakeside Park to watch several track-and-field teams practice. There had been no track-and-field team at Beaumont High, and Babe's own experience was limited to hurdling hedges on Doucette Street. She was awestruck by the swirl of competitive events. Shot puts soared; girls jumped high and long and cleared hurdles; they ran hard on the outer track, handing off bright blue relay batons. Everywhere you looked, someone was doing something amazing.

Babe pointed toward a long stick lying on the ground. "What's that?" she asked the Colonel.

"It's a javelin," he said. "You throw it like a spear."

The Colonel demonstrated the mechanics of a javelin throw. Babe tried it and "got pretty good distance, but it was so heavy — it was a men's javelin," she recalled. Each time she threw it, she poked herself in the same spot on her back, raising a welt.

From the stands, Babe watched mesmerized at the athletes' solitary pursuit in most events: it was just you and the event. She liked that. Babe asked the Colonel if he would be willing to start an Employers Casualty women's track-and-field team. The company had disbanded its team two years earlier, due to the high cost ($5,000 a year) and the lack of interest among the company's women athletes. McCombs recognized a couple of compelling reasons to reorganize the team: there wasn't much to keep the women busy during the long Texas summer, and the national women's track-and-field championship was coming to Dallas on the Fourth of July, the first time the tournament would be held in the South. The more the Colonel talked about a new team, the more excited he became about its chances. He told Babe he'd raise the possibility of forming a team with the company's president, Homer R. Mitchell, under one condition: she would go with him.

The following Monday morning, Babe and the Colonel pitched the idea to Mitchell. It was an easy sell. "Babe," Mitchell said, "whatever you all want, you can have."

When the Colonel asked the women who were interested which events they'd like to specialize in, each picked one or two.

"Colonel, how many events are there in this track and field?" Babe asked.

"Babe, I think there are about nine or ten," McCombs said.

"Well, I'm going to do them all," Babe said. Everyone laughed, but her teammates later whispered among themselves: *What gall. What an ego. There aren't enough sporting events in the world to satisfy Babe.*

The allure track and field held for Babe was obvious: you depended on yourself to win. If you set a record, your name went into the record books. *Just one name. Yours. Alone.* Nearly all of Babe's sporting experiences had been as a member of a team, whose fate depended on the play of other girls who Babe believed were not as talented and disciplined as she was. She despised having to depend on anyone else to win. She liked the idea that she'd get all the credit if she won, all the blame if she lost. Sure, it was pressure, but the good kind.

Each company's track-and-field team amassed points as it competed against other teams. If Babe won her events and the team also won, that would be good. But as Babe saw it, if she won and the team lost, that wouldn't be any less good. *Just one name. Yours. Alone.*

Each late afternoon, Babe practiced with her track-and-field teammates. The Colonel pushed the girls hard. He set the high-jump bar at five feet three inches—the women's world record at the time. After Babe finally cleared it, he rewarded her with a chocolate soda. Babe's teammates called it a day after a couple hours of practice, but after dinner, Babe returned to the field, alone, and stayed until after dark. Then she ran, with her legs lifting high, up and down a steep hill. "Practice makes perfect," Babe wrote to Tiny.

In the Cyclones' first meet, Babe *was* perfect, winning first place in four events—high jump, shot put, javelin, and baseball throw.

In late June, the team prepared for the Texas state championship. Two days before the meet, Babe stepped on a large piece of glass on the floor of the bathhouse inside Southern Methodist University's Ownby Stadium. She visited a doctor, who roughly removed the glass from her left foot, but the foot was still sore. Babe only practiced harder, working for two hours on the evening before the meet, concentrating on the timing of her steps for the high jump and broad jump, then capping it off by running the 440-yard dash. McCombs had advised her to pace herself and save her energy for the meet, but Babe ran all-out and ended up sprawled on the grass, facedown, seeing stars.

Oddly, McCombs, who had initially pushed Babe nearly as hard as she pushed herself, was becoming disenchanted with her rigorous pace. "Her only fault, as I have found it, is that she unconsciously and unknowingly overtrains," he later said. He blamed the unruly rigorousness of Babe's workout regimen on her "juvenility and nervous energy," saying the two sometimes combined to undermine her performance. "She has a tendency to brood over coming events and even though she is not training on the field, her thoughts and tenseness generate her whole being into a seething fervor and unless continually cautioned she loses the spark that has carried her like a sweeping meteor to the very pinnacle of success."

Perhaps the only tendency Babe revealed was a tendency to win. The way she aggressively attacked her four events at the Texas championship, it was impossible to tell that she was nursing a serious foot injury. On a steamy day with temperatures in the mid-nineties, she set a U.S. record in the high jump (5 feet 1½ inches) and broke southern records in her other three events — the shot put (37 feet 1 inch), baseball throw (264 feet ½ inch), and javelin (119 feet 7 inches). Babe put up 20 of her team's 78 points, leading the team to an easy victory. The local newspapers were flabbergasted by her performance, dubbing the team "Babe Didrikson and Her Employers Casualty Girls." She liked the ring of that.

Dear Tiny. Had the Texas A.A.U. Track meet Saturday. We have had 4 track meets so far, and Tiny I have made first place in all four of them and have been high pointer in all. I have a record in every meet and every thing that I have ... Oh! Yeah! Right after the Track season I am gonna train for the Olympics in 1932 on the Broad Jump, High Jump true Western roll, Baseball and Javelin Throw.... Boy at the National and Olympic gonna show everyone I have ants in my pants. By — Babe

On the Fourth of July, another cloudless, unseasonably hot day, nearly two hundred track-and-field competitors congregated at Southern Methodist University for the AAU national women's championship. Before a crowd of two thousand people, the hometown, two-month-old Cyclones stood as an enormous underdog to the nation's perennial powerhouse, the Illinois Women's Athletic Club, an elite squad that enjoyed advantages measured by medals and confidence. In a span of just ninety minutes, Babe broke three world records in the javelin, which she threw 133 feet 3 inches; baseball throw, 268 feet 10½ inches; and the broad jump, 18 feet 8½ inches. Babe's first jump was even longer — 18 feet 11 inches — but she was whistled for a foul when her foot crossed the line. Her record lasted only a few minutes; Stella Walsh beat Babe's jump by seven-eighths of an inch. The Cyclones finished second to the Illinois Women's Athletic Club, but Babe had scored 15 of her team's 19 points. From the sidelines, McCombs could see that the gap between Babe's talent and that of her teammates was widening.

"I have broken 6 American records, 7 or 8 Southern records and 4 world records," Babe told Tiny in another letter. The tally of her debut season in track and field was impressive, and her confidence soared higher. She reported that officials had told her that she "had a berth on the Olympic team in 1932 ... without a doubt." Twice she asked Tiny to put "a big write up" in the Beaumont paper. And just in case Tiny had somehow missed the purpose of these horn-blowing letters, Babe signed off, "Yours for a big headline, Babe."

Babe had no idea that a berth on the 1932 Olympic team was very much in doubt.

6

Where She Did Not Belong

The founding father of the modern Olympic Games was a French aristocrat named Baron Pierre de Coubertin. In the 1890s, he made it his life's mission to create a world-class competition of nations that would continue the grand tradition of the ancient games at Olympia: amateur athletes from rival nations settling their differences on playing fields rather than battlefields. As the baron envisioned it, the modern games would emulate the Olympic ideal established during the ancient games that had commenced in the eighth century B.C. The modern Olympics would begin and end with lavish ceremonies and, as at Olympia, the centerpiece contests would be in track and field. Also as in the ancient games, women athletes would be prohibited from competition. "The Olympic Games," Coubertin declared, "must be reserved for men," and the winners should look forward to "female applause as their reward." Women competing in sports "violated the laws of nature," he said, adding that a sweating female athlete was "the most unaesthetic sight human eyes could contemplate."

The modern games were revived to worldwide fanfare in Athens in

1896 and were quickly recognized as the world's most prestigious sporting event. Women—or, more precisely, one woman—refused to remain on the sidelines. A thirty-year-old Greek named Stamata Revithi was determined to run the inaugural 40-kilometer marathon. She left her hometown of Piraeus, on foot, for Marathon, traveling with her seventeen-month-old son. Revithi's determination to compete against the men—and her boast that she'd outrun more than a few of them—captured the attention of the press and captivated the Greeks. But Olympic organizers denied her permission to compete, ruling that her application had been received past the eligibility deadline, although gender was in fact the sole reason for her exclusion. (Even a local priest, instructed to see only sanctioned athletes, refused to bless her.) On the eve of the race, a male runner teased Revithi, telling her that by the time she staggered into Panathinaiko Stadium, all the spectators would have gone home.

To protest being barred, Revithi decided to run the marathon a day after the official event. In Marathon, she asked several local people, including the mayor and the magistrate, to sign a paper attesting to her departure time of 8:00 a.m. Five and a half hours later—about two hours longer than many of the men the day before—Revithi, drenched in sweat and covered in dust, arrived, panting with fatigue, outside the marble stadium. When several police officers denied her access to the stadium, she ran a spiteful single lap around the perimeter, securing her place in history as the first unofficial female Olympian.

Four years later, women debuted on the farthest fringes of the modern Olympics, competing in Paris in a one-time-only lawn tennis tournament. Only eleven women participated, but the precedent was enough to anger Coubertin, who declared that women athletes were constitutionally incapable of conquering any sporting event played by men. "Women have probably proved that they are up to par with almost all the exploits to which men are accustomed, but they have not been able to establish that in doing so, they have remained faithful to the necessary conditions of their existence and obedient to the laws of nature," he said.

The Olympic creed — "The most important thing in the Olympic Games is not winning, but taking part" — was introduced at the 1908 London games. Women, however, were permitted to take part in only a few events, including, for the first time, archery and figure skating. Swimming, platform diving, and gymnastics were added at the 1912 Stockholm games, though only as exhibition events and only because the Olympic committee declared those sports to be "ladylike activities and aesthetically pleasing."

To the baron, even this chauvinistic standard granted women too much freedom. Of the 2,407 athletes competing in Stockholm, only 48 were women. If 11 had bothered the baron in Paris, 48 infuriated him in Stockholm. He sensed that it would not be long before women would be granted access to most, if not all, Olympic competitions, including track and field — a prospect that he viewed as unacceptable. On the eve of the Stockholm games, Coubertin issued his first lengthy statement against women's participation in the Olympics. Written on behalf of the International Olympic Committee (IOC), the baron's declaration was intended to stop the gradual march toward gender equality for Olympic athletes:

We feel that the Olympic Games must be reserved for men.... As the saying goes: a door must be open or closed. Can women be given access to all Olympic events? No?.... Then why permit them some and bar them from others? And especially, on what basis does one establish the line between events permitted and events prohibited? There are not just tennis players and swimmers. There are also fencers, horsewomen, and in America there have also been rowers. Tomorrow, perhaps, there will be women runners or even soccer players. Would such sports practiced by women constitute an edifying sight before crowds assembled for an Olympiad? We do not think such a claim can be made....

Impractical, uninteresting, inaesthetic, and we are not afraid to add: wrong; in our opinion this is what this female semi-Olympiad would be. Such is not our idea of the Olympic Games in which we feel that we have tried and that we must continue to try to achieve the following definition: the solemn and periodic exaltation of male athleticism with internationalism as a base, loyalty as a means, art for its setting and female applause as reward.

Despite Coubertin's steadfast opposition, female athletes pressed for acceptance into more sporting events. They were able to gain access to a gradually increasing number of sports because host cities' Olympic committees were persuaded to add such events, usually as experiments, despite the lobbying by Coubertin and others.

The strongest push for women's inclusion in the Olympics was in track and field, but the baron stubbornly barred them from participating in the marquee event. (Coubertin relished his autocratic hold on the IOC, which usually voted as he wanted.) Instead, women were forced to stage their own separate track-and-field competition. Dubbed the International Ladies' Games, the inaugural event was held in Paris in 1922, the second in Göteborg, Sweden, in 1926. Both events were popular, attracting enormous, boisterous crowds. Proponents of women's athletics argued that the success of these events had proved that female track-and-field athletes were ready to compete in the Olympics, and the public was ready, too.

After the Paris Olympics of 1924, Coubertin retired as the leader of the IOC, but not before firing a parting shot at the growing momentum for allowing female track-and-field events in the Olympics. Once again, he declared that women athletes did not belong on a track or field. "As to the admission of women, I remain strongly against it," he said. "It was against my will that they were admitted to a growing number of competitions."

It was not a coincidence that women at long last won permission to compete in track and field at the Amsterdam games in 1928. Although there were thirteen track-and-field events for men, women were allowed only five—the 100-meter and 800-meter races, 4 × 100-meter relay, high jump, and discus. The main rationale for limiting the events was the widespread worry that women's bodies were incapable of enduring any more than five events in a single week. Leaders of the British women's track-and-field team, considered the favorites to win the most gold medals, were so annoyed with the partial schedule that they boycotted the games. (The British men did not join the boycott.) No other women's team followed suit, pleased at least to participate in what was portrayed as an experiment—a test of female endurance, even if the test itself was limited.

On a humid early August day in Amsterdam, some of the women failed that test. After passing the finish line of the rigorous 800-meter race, six of the nine women runners collapsed from... *something*. Several of them had to be assisted off the hot track. The sixty thousand spectators could not tell whether the women were overcome by exhaustion or had died in front of their eyes.

The world press dwelled on the calamity, vividly describing stricken women being carted off the field by male attendants like damsels in distress. At least one observer, an official timekeeper on the track, reported a different reason for the women's collapses. "There was nothing wrong with them," the official said. "They burst into tears thus betraying their disappointment at having lost the race, a very feminine trait."

Many sportswriters demanded that women's track and field be permanently barred from the Olympics, a position embraced by the incoming IOC president, Count Henri de Baillet-Latour, who declared in 1929 that there be no women's events at the Los Angeles games. That year, the executive committee of the IOC banned women from "the Olympic Games except in the events of gymnastics, swimming, lawn-tennis and skating."

Babe was unaware of any of this. All she knew was that the U.S. women's Olympic track-and-field team had only a limited number of places, and she intended to get the chance to win a gold medal in Los Angeles.

The year 1931 began with another Golden Cyclones basketball season, Babe's second. With more time to learn one another's strengths and rhythms, the Cyclones defeated some opponents by as many as 50 points, combining a smothering defense with a quick-draw scoring attack. In March, the Colonel realized his dream when the Cyclones won their first AAU national championship. Babe led the team in scoring, accumulating 195 points during the six-game tournament and securing a spot on the all-American team.

McCombs was ecstatic. He was stunned by Babe's rapid growth as an all-sport athlete. She was also excelling in softball, swimming, and diving. She'd even played a handful of games for a men's sandlot baseball team. He'd never seen anything like it. Nobody had. Yet the happier the Colonel became with Babe, the more disenchanted she became with him. Two all-American teams, one national basketball championship, a dozen track-and-field gold medals, including several national records—and yet, over the course of that glittering year, Babe's monthly salary of $75 had not increased by a single dime. The way Babe saw it, McCombs kept taking, taking, taking—and giving nothing for all she had done for Employers Casualty. The publicity that the company had won from its basketball title alone was worth big money. Why shouldn't Babe and her teammates share in that windfall? Seventy-five dollars a month—still a fine salary in the Depression's second full year, when teachers didn't earn much more—seemed like a pittance. Worse, the Colonel had persuaded the AAU to pass a rule that athlete-employees could not leave their employers until one year after playing in the national tournament. This rule was designed to keep companies from entering into bidding wars for a tournament's top players, but it made Babe feel imprisoned by what suddenly felt like a barely livable wage. The earliest she could leave for another company's team was the spring of 1932. A year felt like a lifetime.

So she had an idea. She'd pretend she had received an unsolicited offer to join another team for $125 a month or even $150. When McCombs learned that another team was trying to steal her away, he'd have no choice but to do the right thing—pay her more to keep her, maybe even double her wages. Babe tried to recruit Tiny to help her get that raise—first as her "manager," then as her coconspirator.

Dearest "Tiny" Why hello old top, how in the heck are you getting along. Now this is the time that I need a manager. Tiny I think that I should be making more money so I am asking you to write me a letter telling me of a better job that I can get and more money—about $125.00 a month, you see they have us under a twelve month rule, that is if you played in the national tournament with one team you can't change clubs until one year after the date of the last game that you played with this one team. So if you will tell me it's a better job as professional and more money. You know kinda shake 'em up a little.

They wouldn't want to let me go for nothing.

Colonel McCombs made that twelve month rule so that he could keep us in the Co., and make us work for nothing. But he has another *thing coming. I know good and well I am worth $150.00 and I am gonna get it out of this company, with your help.*

All I want is a letter from you telling me about a keen proposition that you have found for me. And kinda stretch it, see, cause when I show it to him he will raise my pay to about what you say in the offer. This is just to make them break loose and pay me a little more dough.

Put the price and everything. Make a keen contract form, and make it plenty real — Tiny don't tell anyone about this will you, because I couldn't have it get to Dallas —

The president is giving me free Golf Lessons out at Dallas Country Club, and they are plenty nice so they won't have to raise my pay. When I get your letter I will take it in to Mr. McCombs and show it to him. I am the only prospect of him winning the National and he knows that, plenty of teams want me, but can't get me on account of the 12 months rule. The only way out is to turn Professional and that will make them chirp up and pay me what they ought to. All the rest of the teams get paid keen and lots more than any of us do. Tiny will you please do that for me. Write just as though I had never written to you — so they won't suspect. Love Babe Didrikson.

Tiny pitied Babe's predicament, but not enough to write a phony letter. Babe never proposed the scheme again.

The question of women's eligibility for track and field at the Los Angeles games was at the top of the IOC agenda when its leaders met in Barcelona in April 1931. The memory of the 800-meter debacle in Amsterdam was still fresh in the minds of opponents. But supporters of women's track and field had been encouraged by a nearly flawless international exhibition of women's events in Berlin in 1930. Foremost among these proponents was Avery Brundage, the newly installed president of the AAU, who was embarking on an influential role in the Olympics that would stretch across forty years. At the meeting in Barcelona, there were murmurs of boycotts if women's track and field was excluded. Such threats turned out to be unnecessary, as the IOC voted overwhelmingly to allow fencing, swimming, and track and field for women at the 1932 games.

When news of the decision reached Dallas, McCombs was pleased. But he was disappointed that Amsterdam-like restrictions had been imposed. Only six track-and-field events would be held for women, and no woman would be allowed to compete in more than three. The Colonel knew that Babe derived far more pleasure from track and field than from basketball. Sure, basketball had made her a fan favorite in northern Texas, but the bigger stage of track and field promised national stardom. If given the opportunity, Babe could compete in all five events.

McCombs decided that Babe's road to qualifying for the U.S. Olympic team had to begin in Jersey City, New Jersey, site of the ninth annual women's track-and-field championship in late July 1931. On a humid, cloudy day, more than fifteen thousand people filed into the makeshift stands at Pershing Field, a 13½-acre park that was barely a decade old. The overflow crowd had come to see the most impressive collection of women's track-and-field athletes ever gathered on a single field in the United States. Of the 235 women on teams from each state, 11 were defending champions and 8 were veterans of the 1928 Olympics. And yet the star attraction, Babe Didrikson, had won almost nothing. Most of the fans — and all of the writers in the press box — wanted to see if this young woman from Dallas, who had made the trip north with a dozen Employers Casualty teammates, was worthy of all the hype and headlines. A few members of the New York press had heard of her success in Texas and had already proclaimed her a phenomenon, but she had not done much to earn the title. Now she had her chance.

Before the afternoon's first event, the giant crowd—far more people than there were seats—surged onto the fringes of Pershing Field. Mounted police had to be called to restore order, and the horses' hooves chewed up wide swaths of the track. One of the athletes called the scene "Bedlam."

Even from a seat high up in the stands, it was impossible not to iden-tify Babe, clad in her bright orange Employers Casualty uniform and pacing in semicircles with a slightly nervous gait as she loosened up her limbs. Her boyish looks matched her rough-edged manner, which some of the other women found intimidating. A shock of short, straight brown hair was perched above Babe's bewildered—and bewildering—expression. She wore a half grin that was equal parts friendly and cocky, conveying a mix of mirth and contempt.

First up was the 80-meter high hurdles, Babe's favorite event. The gun sounded, and Babe bolted off the starting line, beginning nearly last but quickly catching up. She swooshed over the hurdles with grace-ful, loping strides, taking three steps between barriers while her com-petitors needed four. The crowd gasped at her seemingly effortless fluidity. When she hit the tape, five of the six officials' stopwatches clocked her at 12.0 seconds, two-tenths of a second faster than the world record. One official's watch read 11.8 seconds, four-tenths of a second better than the record. The final times stunned the officials, who decided to check the 80-meter distance with a steel tape measure. They discovered that the distance was indeed wrong—it was precisely two feet four inches *too long.*

Next was the broad jump. Babe won easily, jumping 17 feet 11½ inches, nearly a foot better than the runner-up, Nellie Todd of the Illi-nois Women's Athletic Club. Finally, Babe hurled the baseball 296 feet, shattering her own world record by an amazing 27 feet 2 inches.

Babe's three wins overshadowed the performance of the nation's reigning track-and-field star, Stella Walsh, of the New York Athletic Association, who, like Babe, was expected to win three events. In 1930 in Dallas, Walsh had defeated Babe in the long jump. For Walsh, Jersey City was a meet to forget. Earlier in the day, warming up for the discus throw, she tossed a discus toward a teammate and accidentally struck a twenty-eight-year-old Jersey City man named James McBride, who fell to the ground unconscious with a skull fracture. A police officer immediately prepared to arrest Walsh, but tournament officials persuaded him to allow her to run in the 220-yard dash, which she won. It was the only event she won that day. Although Walsh was arrested, she was released several hours later.

In the high hurdles, Babe faced off against another competitor from the national meet in Dallas, Evelyne Hall, of the Illinois Women's Athletic Club. In Dallas, Hall had won the 80-meter high hurdles, an event that Babe had sat out. But at Pershing Field, Hall finished second to Babe. Over the past year, Hall had noticed an off-putting shift in Babe's demeanor. Back in Dallas, Hall had found Babe to be "a modest, likeable girl," whose teammates were "very proud" of her. But in Jersey City, "Babe was pretty cocky," Hall said. Babe's other competitors also found her changed, and not for the better. She was aloof, the only member of the Employers Casualty team lavished with useful perks, special amenities, and constant attention. "Everyone was doing things for her," Hall recalled. "If she wanted a drink of water, someone got it for her. She seemed to have managers; her teammates waited on her. She didn't snub me, but she was not nearly as friendly to me as the year before."

Hall also noticed that Babe had another advantage: she wore the best track shoes of any competitor on the field. "We didn't have any money," Hall said. "We were poor. We each had a pair of track shoes, but the points were worn down to nothing. I remember Babe had the longest spikes of anyone, and they were very sharp. I remember I didn't have the money to get mine sharpened."

With 19 total points—15 scored by Babe—the Employers Casualty team finished second to the Illinois Women's Athletic Club, which compiled a total of 26 points. But it was Babe's three-event sweep that seized the headlines. "It was my medal hunting in this event that started the sportswriters' keys clattering," Babe said years later.

Indeed, in the next day's *New York Times,* the superlatives leapt off sportswriter Arthur Daley's typewriter: "A new feminine athletic marvel catapulted herself to the forefront as an American Olympic possibility at Pershing Field." Daley ticked off the highlights of Babe's record-shattering day, saying the "crowd of 15,000 looked on in amazement" at "this remarkably versatile girl." He saved his flashiest accolades for Babe's world-record performance in the 80-meter high hurdles: "Her timber-topping effort was far and away her finest performance. She streaked over the sticks with the utmost finesse.... The crowd fairly gasped as she flew over the barriers."

Daley's description of Babe's versatility was limited to her track-and-field résumé, but other writers were also beginning to grasp her cross-sport abilities. Fresh off her success in Jersey City, Babe returned to Dallas and posed for a newspaper photographer as she played half a dozen sports, including baseball, golf, and boxing. Below photos arrayed across the top of the page, a *Dallas Morning News* headline blared, "Dallas Girl, Noted All-Round Athlete, Is Proficient in All Sports." The caption read, "She has been hailed as the world's outstanding all-round feminine athlete." This was the first time the press portrayed Babe as an athlete who could excel in any sport, even boxing. She meticulously cut out two copies of the photo spread and mailed one to Momma, who pasted it in Babe's scrapbook, and the other to Tiny, whom she urged, as usual, to write a version for the hometown fans.

Even then, it was unusual and inappropriate for a sports reporter to manage an athlete's career, but Tiny needed Babe as much as she needed him. They quietly signed a business contract to make it official, though nothing much came of it — the Colonel saw to that.

Babe wanted at least $50 more a month but would have been happy with anything. In just eighteen months, she had established herself as Employers Casualty's star, helping the team win its first basketball championship and setting world records in track and field. She also was one of the leaders on the company's softball team, hitting multiple home runs in several games. (Babe claimed to have hit thirteen home runs in a doubleheader, an obvious exaggeration. One newspaper account does say that she hit three in one twin bill.) And she led the company's swimming and high-diving team.

Weeks after signing the contract with Tiny, Babe realized that as long as she worked for the Colonel, she wouldn't have much use for a manager. The Colonel had a simple rule when it came to a player being recruited by a rival team: *You are paid what you are paid, and if someone wants to pay you more, well, there's the door.* So what could a manager do except break the bad news to his client? Furthermore, the Colonel advised Babe that she would violate AAU amateur rules if she employed a manager "unless it was a team manager." Babe told Tiny to tear up their contract.

Babe was only twenty years old in the fall of 1931, yet she already felt that her time to cash in on her talent was fleeting. "I got to make something on my athletic ability now or never — I'm not gonna be good always you know," she told Tiny. She was so annoyed with the Colonel that when the new basketball season began, she "shut down" her game in protest. He benched her, but it didn't bother her. "I don't care whether I play basket ball anymore or not," she wrote to Tiny. "I'm sitting on the bench most of the game now because I won't try to play ball — I play about a half or more and won't make a shot. I miss every one of them cause I don't want to play with them for nothing." This was a startling strategy for the era. Rarely, if ever, did an athlete—especially a woman athlete—refuse to play as hard as possible or even threaten to go "on strike" for better pay. In this way, too, Babe was half a century ahead of her time.

She began plotting an exit strategy. She daydreamed about quitting Employers Casualty and hitting the road, though she wasn't sure what she could do to make a consistent living. One possibility was to move out to California and "go to school and be a gym teacher." A more attractive, though less likely, option was to get Tiny to enlist a Beaumont oil millionaire to bankroll a traveling team of some kind, maybe basketball or softball, that would feature Babe and other young women.

In an October 5, 1931, letter to Tiny, she wrote:

Dearest Tiny, Heck I'm tired of this old Burg. Wish I could get out of it as soon as possible. Saw an advertisement in the Billboard wanting "Girl Athletes" and that they would give good salary at this place in Ohio.

Heck, "Tiny" if I get me another letter from Wichita, Kans. I'm Gonna take it. Because I would like it better up there. These girls here are just like they were in Beaumont High School. Jealous and more so because they are all here and trying to beat me. But they can't do it.... What you say "Tiny" lets get into some action and try and get me out of this place. And then maybe someday I'll come back and whip the socks off the whole bunch. I remain, yours very truly, Babe Didrikson.

As 1932 approached, the Depression had squeezed out many Americans' capacity for hope. President Herbert Hoover, a derided symbol of the country's overwhelming poverty and dejected mood, assured Americans that life was slowly improving, though few could see it or feel it.

Everywhere Babe looked, there was evidence of the country's hard times: homeless people, including hungry children, camping out in shantytowns called Hoovervilles; unemployment lines stretching down city blocks; a thousand applicants for a single job. An empty pocket turned inside out was called a Hoover flag. Babe mailed more than half her paycheck to Momma and Poppa, and with Poppa barely working, her family depended on that money. If she could nudge a raise out of the Colonel, it would mean more for them and more walking-around money for herself.

To Babe, the Colonel seemed incapable of expressing his appreciation, and not just with money. He was a dour man who used three words when seven or eight would have been nice. Babe was expected to perform, and when she did, she received no praise from him. When she did not, however, he let her know it, and usually not in private. He never mentioned the incalculable benefit that Employers Casualty had enjoyed just by having Babe wear its name splashed across her bright uniform. She kept threatening to quit, but not once did he try to stop her.

In January 1932, Babe asked the Colonel for a week off with pay. He refused, and she impulsively quit the basketball team and went home. Back on Doucette Street, Hannah and Ole urged Babe to apologize to the Colonel and ask for her job back. Babe knew that they needed her to continue earning money as much as she needed to continue competing. After several days, she called the Colonel in tears and begged for her job back. He agreed.

Babe returned to Dallas and began exerting herself again, rejoining the team's starting lineup but continuing to grate on her teammates' nerves with her selfish play and on-court spats with the Colonel. Despite the festering tensions among the players and their increasingly erratic play, the Golden Cyclones managed to make it to the AAU tournament final, which they lost. For the third straight year, Babe was named to the all-American team, though never before had there been a more recalcitrant all-American.

"Is it necessary to say that Miss Didrikson expects to win all of the individual track and field events for women in the Olympic Games at Los Angeles next summer?" asked *Amateur Athlete* magazine in a feature story on Babe. "She claims that she can throw the discus 140 feet. The Olympic record is 129 11⅞. She has reached a height of 5 feet 4 inches in the high jump. The Olympic record is 5 feet 3 inches. She already holds the world record in the 80 meter hurdles and threw the javelin 133 feet 5½ inches for a world record last year. She has run the 100 yards in 11 flat. With only five individual events for women in the Games, will 'Babe' win them all?"

But first, Babe needed to qualify for the Olympic team. Two weeks before the Los Angeles games, the tenth annual AAU national women's track-and-field championship would be held in Evanston, Illinois. It would serve as the qualifying event for the second U.S. women's track-and-field team in Olympic history. Most of the local teams planned on sending a dozen women or more to the meet, with specialists in one or perhaps two events. But McCombs had an idea: what if Babe competed in all ten track-and-field events, from the 100-meter dash to the discus throw? It wasn't as far-fetched as it sounded; the Colonel felt certain she had a legitimate chance of winning at least half of them. What better way to persuade the world of the folly of the three-event limit placed on women in the Olympics than to have Babe compete in six, seven, eight, or even ten events in a single afternoon? Imagine the publicity for Employers Casualty!

AAU rules explicitly prohibited the Colonel's plan: "No woman shall be allowed to compete in more than three events in one day, of which three events not more than two shall be track events.... The relay shall count as one track event."

The creator and enforcer of the three-event rule was a stickler named Fred Steers, the AAU rules committee chairman and manager of the U.S. women's track-and-field team. Steers believed that the prohibition safeguarded the health of the women and that waiving the rule, even for a woman who was the favorite to win multiple events at the AAU's national championship, wasn't up for negotiation. The issue was fraught with controversy and emotion because of the collapse of the 800-meter runners in Amsterdam. If something happened to Babe, Steers thought, the AAU would be blamed. Finally, it wouldn't be fair to give Babe eight or ten chances to qualify for the Olympics when all the other women were given one or two.

McCombs wasn't in the mood to talk about fairness. As the chief of one of the South's most powerful AAU members, whose pioneering ideas had helped attendance surge in recent years, the Colonel knew he had clout. He decided to combine his public declaration that Babe was going to compete in eight to ten events with an ultimatum to Texas-based AAU officials: if Babe was denied access to these events, Employers Casualty would withdraw from the AAU and McCombs would lobby other Texas teams to withdraw as well. The cost to the AAU in money and prestige would be incalculable.

Local AAU officials listened grimly to the Colonel's ultimatum, but they made no promises. They told him they didn't think Steers would agree to such a radical idea. Whether the officials had spoken to Steers at that point is unknown, but such a conversation would have been unlikely. Still, the AAU probably gave McCombs reason to believe that his ultimatum had worked. As a result, he began telling the local press that Babe was going to compete in as many as ten events at the national championship in Evanston.

Then McCombs came up with another idea, one that was even more radical than the first. One morning while Babe was sitting at her desk, her phone buzzed. It was the Colonel, summoning her to his office. When she walked into his office, she said, "Colonel, will I get to go up to Chicago for the nationals this year?"

"Yes," McCombs said. "That's what I wanted to talk to you about. I've been studying the records of the girls on the other teams that will be in the meet. I think if you enter enough different events, and give your regular performance, you can do something that's never been done before. I believe we can send you up there to represent the Employers Casualty Company, and you can win the national championship for us all by yourself."

7

The Cyclone

"A nybody traveling to Chicago to win a track meet ought to wear a hat," Onie Wood, the team mother of Employers Casualty, told Babe. "Team mother" was the appropriate title for Wood, a company bookkeeper who cared for the Golden Cyclones as if they were her own daughters. She planned travel itineraries, accompanied the team on overnight trips, and accounted for meal money per diems. More important, she dispensed advice, soothed egos, and served as a sympathetic ear for complaints about the Colonel's domineering demeanor. Babe didn't wear hats and didn't much care for them, but because of Wood's advice, she scoured the shelves of a Dallas department store, where she found and bought a lovely pink felt hat.

Staying behind in Dallas were Babe's Cyclone teammates, who were livid about being excluded from the national championship that was doubling that summer as the tryouts for the second-ever U.S. women's Olympic track-and-field team. Their fury was directed squarely at the Colonel. He explained as diplomatically as possible that the company could afford to send only those women to Evanston who had a legitimate shot at making the Olympics. All the other coaches intended to send squads of at least ten women; one was sending twenty-two. The Cyclones who were forced to remain in Dallas saw through the Colonel's Olympic-worthy standard. They knew he had one motive for keeping everyone but Babe home: the bonanza of publicity that would come Employers Casualty's way for attempting to win the national track-and-field championship with one woman.

At the last minute, the Colonel decided not to accompany Babe to Evanston. His decision was motivated in part by the desire to stay home and try to quell the mutinous mood among the demoralized Cyclones. McCombs was also quite concerned that his presence on the sidelines would hinder Babe more than help her. By the summer of 1932, he and Babe had cobbled together a delicate peace. The hurt feelings caused by McCombs's slights and Babe's quicksilver temper simmered just below the surface of their fragile relationship. Often what wasn't said was more hurtful than what was. A misinterpreted sigh or roll of the eyes usually triggered a fresh argument over a sore subject.

The Colonel's disenchantment with Babe had nothing to do with her performance, which had continued to be stellar. "I have been coaching athletes of all kinds for 28 years," McCombs told Tiny that summer, "but never before in my life have I seen a man or woman to compare with Babe Didrikson for natural ability. In grasping, understanding and executing the most technical details of what she is taught, she has no equal." Babe's toughest opponent was herself. Despite her rawhide cockiness, she worried pathologically about her competitions. And she doubted her ability to live up to the high expectations that she and others had set for her. She tried to overcompensate by training herself weary, far exceeding the Colonel's own gargantuan demands. McCombs knew that he was powerless to stop this cycle of under-confidence and over-preparation, but he worried that it would lead to physical or even psychological injury.

In the weeks leading up to the national championship, the Colonel did all that he could to prepare Babe. At the Southern Methodist stadium, he designed a rigorous, six-day-a-week training program emphasizing the events in which she had the least experience, particularly the shot put and discus throw. The Dallas newspapers reported that she intended to compete in all ten events at the national meet—javelin, discus, 80-meter hurdles, 100-meter run, high jump, 50-yard and 200-meter dashes, broad jump, baseball throw, and shot put. The tone of the coverage was a kind of giddy bewilderment. A one-woman team competing in every track-and-field event? At a time when women were limited to compete in no more than three events in a given week? It had never before been done. The idea wasn't just presumptuous—it was preposterous. McCombs confidently predicted that Babe would win at least five of the events and smash a handful of records.

With the Colonel staying home, Onie Wood inherited twin responsibilities, serving as both chaperone and de facto coach of America's "one-girl track team," a phrase Babe had coined for herself. The title had an infectious sound, particularly with the local press corps, who quickly adopted it.

On the platform at the Dallas train station, just after 5:00 p.m. on a sticky July afternoon, Babe was treated to a star's send-off. She wore a freshly pressed pink dress complemented by a white leather purse. The only thing out of place was her new pink hat, which sat slightly askew atop her head. Her frilly clothes startled the crowd, which included the Colonel, her teammates (who kept their anger in check), and dozens of other Employers Casualty employees and fans. As Babe waved from the train car's bottom step, the crowd roared its approval. She "radiated confidence," one writer observed.

Few fans or writers knew that Babe's cockiness was a kind of armor. As she settled into her seat in the Pullman car, tiny beads of sweat appeared on her brow. Her stomach began a riot of somersaults that did not subside as the northbound train rumbled across the Texas prairie toward the big city.

Babe was feeling no less anxious, despite Wood's attempts to calm her down, as the train glided into Chicago's Union Station. Her nervousness increased when she looked through the passenger-car window at the congregation of serious-looking men in smart suits, apparently waiting to welcome her. Behind them a platoon of photographers were readying their cameras.

With flashbulbs popping, the first man to welcome Babe to Chicago was Avery Brundage, the AAU's top man. All week, America's 250 elite women track-and-field athletes had streamed into Chicago by train, bus, and automobile. Brundage chose Babe—and only Babe—to receive his official handshake. Some of her competitors saw the photograph of Babe and Brundage, both with wide smiles, in the next morning's newspaper and felt it smacked of favoritism. They'd find much in the coming days to reinforce that impression.

As the reporters huddled around her, Babe declared that she planned on competing in eight events on Saturday. McCombs had decided at the last minute that she should skip the 200-meter and 50-yard dashes. Neither were Olympic qualifying events, and they'd sap her strength for the other events. Also, McCombs concluded, Babe was too slow off the starts to have a shot at winning either race. A few of the reporters snickered at Babe's brashness, but she promptly raised the ante by declaring that she intended to win all eight events, a result that would allow her to single-handedly seize the AAU national team title for Employers Casualty.

The next day's papers showcased Babe's arrival as the unofficial start of the national meet, as writers piled up the superlatives with a single story line: the star had arrived. Even the *New York Times,* an infrequent chronicler of women's sports, agreed that the meet was Babe's to lose: "Miss Mildred Didrikson, the sensational young lady from Dallas, Texas, is expected to be the standout."

The Chicago area was enduring a weeklong record heat wave, with 100-plus-degree temperatures and smothering humidity. The combination made it difficult to breathe, even if you weren't jumping over hurdles. The site of the meet—cinder-surfaced Dyche Stadium, on the campus of Northwestern University in Evanston, just north of the city—was sweltering, and worry about injury kept the athletes from doing much more than light workouts and modest run-throughs. Babe, however, took long, brisk walks, endured a rigorous gymnasium workout, and careened around the field, taunting her opponents with bravado. "Ah'm gonna lick you single-handed," she told more than one woman. Babe's mind games had begun.

Her braying and needling were having their intended effect on many of the athletes. Babe felt sure that nothing stood in the way of her success, except perhaps Fred Steers. Steers confronted Babe on the practice field, informing her that she would be permitted to compete in a maximum of three events and that she should choose the three and tell him before Saturday. He was furious that Babe had plans to compete in eight events and that McCombs had apparently struck some kind of deal with AAU officials in Dallas.

Wood advised Babe to ignore Steers—whom they called "the old man"—and continue to practice for the eight events that she and the Colonel had chosen. But Steers harangued Babe all week, and his threats heightened her anxiety. It was hard enough preparing to compete as a single-woman team. The possibility that Steers might bar her from doing so made it even worse. Nothing, not even losing all eight events, would be more heartbreaking than being barred from the competition.

On the eve of the national championship, Babe was more nervous than Wood had ever seen her. Filled with excitement, she could not sit still, chattering endlessly while circling their hotel room. Worried about what Steers might do, she found it impossible to fall sleep; the harder she tried, the more she tossed and turned. Of course, Wood couldn't sleep either. After midnight, shooting pains began ricocheting around Babe's stomach. The pain was so severe that when Babe placed her hand atop her stomach, her hand would "just bounce up and down." Certain that Babe was suffering from an appendicitis attack, Wood summoned the hotel doctor.

After examining Babe, the doctor told Wood, "There's nothing wrong with her. She's just all excited. The excitement is affecting the nerve center in her diaphragm." The diagnosis calmed Babe somewhat, and just before dawn, she and Wood managed to fall asleep. "When we woke up," Babe said, "there was hardly time for us to get ourselves ready and make it out to Evanston for the start of the meet."

Without a moment to spare, Babe and Wood arrived on the sidewalk in front of the hotel. The sun was blazing hot, the humidity oppressive. They climbed into the backseat of a taxicab and asked the driver to hurry them to Dyche Stadium. He refused, telling them that he operated only in Chicago. They jumped out and hailed another cab. The midday traffic was heavy, and "it began to look like there wouldn't be time for me to dress out at the field," Babe said. "There was only one way we could make sure. Mrs. Wood held up a blanket around me and I changed into my track suit while we were riding along in the cab."

They arrived outside Dyche Stadium just before the meet's start time of 2:00 p.m. The Evanston American Legion post's drum and bugle corps was accompanying an Olympic-style procession of athletes into the concrete stadium with five thousand people packed into the bleachers. When the Illinois Women's Athletic Club was introduced by the public-address announcer, twenty-two women clad in bright yellow uniforms ran onto the field to the cheers of the hometown crowd.

Then the announcer's voice boomed over the loudspeaker: "Representing the Employers Casualty Company of Dallas, Texas—Mildred 'Babe' Didrikson." Babe dashed onto the field, grinning and wildly waving her arms. When the crowd realized that just one athlete was representing the team, its roar of surprise and approval was so loud that Babe instantly got goose bumps. It was a moment she would cherish the rest of her life.

Arriving just before the start of the competition gave Babe an immediate, unexpected advantage: it was virtually impossible for Fred Steers to try to enforce the AAU's three-event rule. Because each event had qualifiers, semifinals, and then the final, Babe had to compete in at least twenty-four separate events—on average, one every six minutes. So even if Steers had wanted to stop her after the competition began, there was no time. "Some of the events that afternoon were Olympic trials," Babe explained. "Others were just National A.A.U. events. But they all counted in the team point scoring. So they were all important to me if I was going to bring back the national championship for Employers Casualty." Babe saw Steers glowering, but he did nothing to stop her.

Babe's eight-event afternoon created an unprecedented logistical nightmare for meet officials. As soon as she finished one event, officials called for her to compete in another. "For two and a half hours I was flying all over the place. I'd run a heat in the eighty-meter hurdles, and then I'd take one of my high jumps," she recalled. "Then I'd go over to the broad jump and take a turn at that. Then they'd be calling for me to throw the javelin or put the eight-pound shot." Over and over, judges and officials delayed starting events to give Babe the chance to finish another event or catch her breath, even for just a minute or two. Moments before several events, Babe taunted her competitors, some of whom had been kept waiting a long stretch for her to join them. She bragged about a recent victory and predicted another win. "I'm going to win everything I enter," she kept telling the other athletes.

The first event was the 80-meter high hurdles, a much-anticipated rematch of the Jersey City confrontation between Babe and Evelyne Hall. In the qualifying heat, Hall edged Babe out by a tenth of a second. In the semifinal, Babe won with a time of 11.9 seconds. But the final was something else. Babe and Hall took off on opposite sides of the track so they were as far from each other as possible. Babe started slowly, as usual, but by the midpoint she had caught up. Their movements appeared synchronized as they ran side by side and cleared each hurdle with mirrorlike precision. In a blur, they hit the white finish-line tape together. As Hall slowed down, she turned to catch a glimpse of Babe thrusting her arms above her head in triumph. Hall had done no such thing because she didn't know if she had won.

Two judges were charged with determining the winner, and two other judges were focused on second place. The first-place judges said "Hall." But then the second-place judges also said "Hall." The discrepancy confused the clerk of the course.

"Where's Didrikson?" asked the clerk.

"Well," one of the first-place judges said, "she must have been first."

This flip-flop satisfied the clerk, who declared Babe the winner — in 12.1 seconds, the same time as Hall. "I don't know what happened," Hall recalled years later. It was no easy thing to get second place after hearing the two first-place judges say you were first and then have one change his mind and say you were second. "They took first place away from me and gave me second," Hall said. "They put Babe in first. I was too shy and modest to complain, but I think since she was expected by the judges to be the star, it was a foregone conclusion that she won it. There was never a film of the race. I don't know where she really finished."

For her part, Babe admitted that her performance was below her usual standard, "but my time of 12.1 seconds was good enough to win." She said nothing in her autobiography about the judges' decision. Babe,

Hall, and the third-place finisher, Simone Schaller, won the three slots on the Olympic 80-meter high hurdles team.

From there, Babe raced to the baseball throw, winning the event for the third straight year with a toss of 272 feet 2 inches.

She next hustled over to the 100-yard dash, changing from cleats to track shoes. Babe "drew a blank there," as she put it, finishing in the top three in the first heat but missing the final after finishing fourth in the semifinal. "But that was the only thing I got shut out in," she said later. "Even in the discus, which wasn't a specialty of mine at all, I placed fourth to pick up an extra point."

The event that Babe had the least amount of experience in was the shot put, but she stunned everyone by winning with a throw of 39 feet 6½ inches, defeating the big favorite, Rena McDonald. Then, with a jump of 17 feet 6 inches, she won the broad jump.

By 3:00 p.m., the temperature had nudged up past 100 degrees. One of the athletes ordered a 100-pound block of ice, and the women took turns sitting on it. Babe had the most to do of anyone on the track, but she looked to be the least bothered by the heat. "It was one of those days in an athlete's life when you know you're just right," Babe said. "You feel you could fly."

Babe's principal high-jump rival was a veteran of the 1928 Olympics in Amsterdam named Jean Shiley. At the age of twenty, Shiley, who lived in poverty in the rural township of Haverford, Pennsylvania, west of Philadelphia, was considered the favorite to win the gold medal in Los Angeles. She and Babe had more than a little in common. Like Babe, Shiley was an all-sport dynamo, making her name as a basketball star but also playing tennis and baseball before she turned to track and field. In sharp contrast to Babe, however, Shiley, who at nearly 5 feet 9 inches towered over most women, was almost painfully shy and unassuming.

"I really never went out with any expectations," she explained. "I just loved what I was doing and went out and did the best I possibly could." If she won, it didn't mean she was the best; it meant she was the luckiest. Her father had no use for his daughter pursuing athletics; he not only discouraged her from competing, but he never once watched her compete.

Shiley was the star forward on the Haverford High School basketball team. Perhaps as evidence of Shiley's good luck, a reporter for the *Philadelphia Inquirer* named Dora Lurie happened not only to have a good eye for talent but also to have been a former high-jumping specialist at Temple University. Lurie encouraged Shiley to take up track and field, and the young woman quickly established herself as one of the nation's best high jumpers.

In the final of the event, Babe and Shiley tied for first at 5 feet 3¾₆ inches, an AAU record, sharing the gold medal. Their rivalry would be revived at the Olympics.

As the shadows lengthened across the field, it was time for Babe's final event: the javelin. She won with a record throw of 139 feet 3 inches, smashing her own record of 133 feet 5½ inches set in 1930.

With sweat soaking her navy blue Employers Casualty uniform, Babe dashed off the field and found Onie Wood in a crowd of athletes and officials. With tears streaking her cheeks, Wood grabbed Babe's hands and said, "You did it! You won the meet all by yourself!"

It was true. Altogether, her amazing performance amassed a total of 30 team points for the Golden Cyclones. She did just what the Colonel had predicted she would do. The second-place team, the Illinois Women's Athletic Club, scored a total of 22 points — with twenty-two athletes. Babe won the gold medal in five events: broad jump, baseball throw, shot put, javelin, and 80-meter hurdles. She tied for first in the high jump. In the process, she qualified for three Olympic events: 80-meter hurdles, high jump, and javelin.

With the crowd standing and cheering, Babe jogged a lazy victory lap around Dyche Stadium, whistling at a few young men and lifting her clenched fists above her head. After the noise began to subside, she grabbed her harmonica from Wood and began to play. Standing on the hot cinder surface, Babe was jubilant.

As the reporters watched upstairs in the steamy press box, their eyes darted between Babe's impromptu celebration and the paper spooled in their typewriters. Filling a blank page would never be this easy again.

The morning after the national meet, America woke up to the front-page, banner-headline coronation of a woman whose sport and gender were usually consigned to single columns in the back of the sports section. "The most amazing series of performances ever accomplished by any individual, male or female, in track and field history," declared United Press reporter George Kirksey.

"Didrikson, Unaided, Wins National Track Championship; Babe Lands Thirty Points to Outclass Nation's Best Feminine Teams," blared the *Dallas Morning News*.

"Implausible is the adjective that best befits the Babe," observed Arthur Daley in the *New York Times*. "As far as sports are concerned, she had the golden touch of Midas."

"Gangway!" the *Chicago Tribune* gushed. "Here comes a real woman athlete. With the speed and grace of an antelope."

Years later, Paul Gallico, the famous sportswriter who as sports editor of the *New York Daily News* turned the tabloid's sports page into a must-read for knowledgeable sports fans, equated Babe's feat that afternoon with the greatest performances in the male sports pantheon. "I cannot think of any male athlete, with the possible exception of old Jim Thorpe, who has come even close to spread-eagling a track meet all by himself in that manner," Gallico wrote.

The Associated Press dispatch, published in newspapers across the country, introduced the sports-crazed nation to the young woman athlete whose domination of a single sport was undisputed: "Miss Mildred Didrikson of Dallas, Texas, who prefers to be called 'Babe,' will lead the American women's Olympic track and field team. Such assistance as she may need against the foreign invasion will be provided by [sixteen] other young ladies."

Whether those other young ladies liked it or not, America's team was Babe's team.

8

"Iron-Woman"

Stretched across the side of the Pullman car preparing to leave Chicago's Union Station was a red, white, and blue banner emblazoned with the words U.S. OLYMPIC TEAM. It was Sunday evening, July 17, and the train was bound for Los Angeles, site of the Tenth Olympiad. Sixteen of the American team's newly christened members climbed the sleeper car's steps and surveyed the luxurious accommodations, which they had to themselves. They were all wowed by the magical seats that could be converted into upper and lower sleeping compartments—everyone, that is, except Babe, who had already traveled in a sleeper car. This was not quite the transoceanic voyage to the Olympics that Babe and her sister Lillie had imagined when they started hopping hedges along Doucette Street. "But a trip to Chicago, and then to Los Angeles, was almost the same as going overseas to me," she said years later. "I was as thrilled as any kid could be."

As soon as the train departed from Chicago, Babe began expressing that thrill by running her body and her mouth, usually at the same time. While most of the women were content to pass the time quietly playing cards or watching the countryside whoosh by, Babe turned the car into her own gymnasium. She hurdled over her teammates' legs stretched out in the aisle. She did calisthenics until sweat cascaded down her face and neck. Several times a day, she jogged the full length of the train and back. ("Here she comes again!" passengers would say as Babe rumbled past them.) She invented annoying ways to stay in shape, such as yanking pillows from beneath her sleeping teammates' heads and slipping ice cubes swiped from a cooler down their backs. Babe and teammate Gloria Russell, a fun-loving javelin thrower, initiated late-night pillow fights. More than one pillow was torn open by the coat hooks jutting out from the berths, causing thousands of tiny feathers to swirl like snowflakes.

Riding in the next car was the team's coach, George Vreeland, a stern fireplug of a man who coached the Prudential Insurance team of Newark, New Jersey. Not a single member of Vreeland's team had qualified for the Olympics. He was disappointed by that outcome but felt certain the Americans could win at least three gold medals in their six chances in LA.

By the time the train reached the edge of the Rockies, the women had had all they could take of Babe's relentless razzing and chest-beating. Their exasperated reactions were just what Babe hoped for: she wanted to seize a mental edge over the women she'd soon need to beat to win gold medals. "She constantly wanted to be on center stage," complained Jean Shiley, Babe's hurdles rival, years later. "I have often wondered *why* she was so obnoxious. Maybe she never got the attention she needed as a child, or maybe she was trying to psych us out— although that was not a term anyone had ever heard of then."

Babe rarely spoke with her teammates; she displayed almost no curiosity about their backgrounds and hopes. Instead, she barked at them. To whoever would listen (and even to those who would rather not), Babe would declare, "I'm the greatest—no one's better than me, Babe

Didrikson." Speaking about herself in the third person was becoming a habit. The way Babe figured it, if you attached your name to the word *greatest* enough times, even the people who didn't care much for you might begin to believe it. Not surprisingly, Babe's mental games cost her any chance of winning the title of team captain. The women nominated three candidates — Babe, Shiley, and Lillian Copeland, the team's shot putter. Like Shiley, Copeland had been a member of the inaugural U.S. women's Olympic team in 1928. Before the vote, she pulled Shiley aside and quietly explained that she was going to withdraw because she was worried that "if she didn't, Babe might win in a three-way split of the votes and that we just could not have that," Shiley recalled. Babe already behaved as if she ran the team; it would be too much to bear if she had the official title bestowed on her, too. "Such a braggart," Evelyne Hall said of Babe. So Copeland withdrew her name from consideration and, sure enough, Shiley won.

The train stopped for a two-night layover in Denver, the Mile High City. It had not occurred to Babe that Denver had earned its nickname because it was built a mile above sea level. She "expected to see a city that was built a mile high in the air." The stopover gave the women a chance to work out at the University of Denver stadium, where Babe noticed that the high altitude caused her to get winded more quickly than usual.

The first night at the Brown Palace Hotel, no one wanted to share a room with Babe. This chore fell to Shiley, who figured it was one of the responsibilities of being team captain. In the hotel lobby, someone from a local radio station interviewed several of the team members, somehow overlooking Babe, though not for long: Babe played a few tunes on her harmonica loud enough to interfere with the interviews.

After Denver, the train stopped in Albuquerque, New Mexico, just for an hour or so. On the platform, Babe hopped on a Western Union bicycle and started pedaling, beating her chest, and screaming, "Did you ever hear of Babe Didrikson? If you haven't you will! You w-i-i-i-l-l-l-l!" Her teammates watched, mortified. At the station, colorfully dressed Native Americans were selling good-luck items. Evelyne Hall paid a nickel for a handmade beaded rabbit's foot — not just for luck for herself, she'd say later, but for every member of the team. That included Babe, a gesture the obnoxious Texan would have been extremely unlikely to reciprocate.

"Hail, hail, the gang's all here," the young women sang as they stepped off the train at Los Angeles's Union Pacific Station on the morning of July 23, exactly one week before the Tenth Olympiad was to begin. To the cynical reporters congregated on the platform, these young women exuded cockiness. But Shiley told the reporters that they should not confuse the ladies' excitement with overconfidence. She refused to make any predictions about gold medals, saying that she and her teammates were prepared to train hard and do their very best.

Babe, however, stepped forward and erased the spirit of Shiley's humble introduction. "I came out here to beat everybody in sight," Babe said, "and that's just what I'm going to do." At that moment, the only athletes in sight were her teammates. A reporter asked Babe how many events she planned on entering. "As many as they'll let me," she said. Turning to Vreeland, Babe asked, "How about four, coach?" Vreeland said that she would be limited to three because Olympic rules prohibited her from entering any more than that. What Vreeland didn't say was that Babe had no choice; she had qualified for just three events. If Babe could somehow compete in a fourth event, it would have to be by default — a teammate's injury opening a slot for her.

The women posed for a team photograph before riding chartered buses to the Chapman Park Hotel, where they would stay with the other 168 women athletes from 38 countries. The Chapman Park, a five-story brick-and-stucco hotel, was located on Wilshire Boulevard, a short walk from the famous Wilshire Hotel and the Brown Derby. The male athletes resided in the plush Olympic Village, a newly built neighborhood of sun-kissed bungalows and the first commune-style housing facility to be constructed for Olympic athletes. That facility, in Baldwin Hills, a neighborhood southwest of the city's downtown that overlooks the Los Angeles basin, was the crown jewel of the games. When author Damon Runyon visited the pink-and-white portable bungalows, he was smitten by the accommodations and the carefree ambience. "Naked young men are sprawled out here and there on the turf, all of them tanned the color of an old saddle," Runyon observed. "It is difficult to distinguish the Americans from the Argentines or the Japanese or the Filipinos. The California sun has painted them all alike." The perimeter of the village, ringed by a ten-foot barbed-wire fence, was patrolled by men on horseback. At one point, a woman climbed the fence and boldly strolled around seeking autographs from some of the scantily clad men. As the security force ejected her, hundreds of athletes stood by applauding her courage.

The Chapman Park Hotel was far more modest, but the American women, many of whom were poor and had had their fill of Depression-era austerity, would not dream of complaining. They were thrilled with the quality of the double and triple rooms and the buffet-style feasts served from long tables bedecked with Olympic banners and pennants. As Shiley put it, "I was just glad there was something on the table. I didn't care what it was."

Every late afternoon, tea was served in the garden. The Americans socialized with the other athletes from around the world, learning a few words of Spanish, Polish, German, or Japanese. Grace Walker, the director of women's housing at the Chapman Park, was awed by the easy and "splendid" camaraderie between the Americans and their foreign rivals. "It seems to be youth calling to youth over the barriers of language, custom and rivalry," she said.

The press was fascinated by the women athletes, who were making their Olympic debut in the United States. Most feature writers chose to ignore their training regimens and instead showcase their wardrobe choices and "beauty diets." "I eat anything I want — except greasy foods and gravy," Babe told one reporter. "I pass the gravy. That's just hot grease anyway, with some flour and water in it."

At the Chapman Park, Babe moved into a triple room with a young sprinter named Mary Carew and Ruth Osburn, whose record-smashing discus throw in Evanston had helped deny Babe an Olympic slot by pushing her into fourth place.

Carew was a shy, modest seventeen-year-old girl from Medford, Massachusetts, whose blazing speed made her a cinch for a slot on the 400-meter relay team. She and Babe could not have been more different. "It seemed to me that I was so insignificant and modest and retiring that they thought I would be good for this big bragger," Carew later said. Once they became roommates, she and Babe got along famously. Within days, Babe had become her surrogate big sister. Carew doubted that she belonged at the Olympics, but Babe bucked up her self-confidence. "Hey, kid, you're just as good as anyone else until the race is over," Babe told her. "Don't forget that."

Unlike most of her teammates, Carew found Babe's me-first attitude irresistible. "Everything she bragged about, she could do," Carew said. "And she bragged all of the time. She wasn't liked by the other girls because nobody likes a bragger, but she didn't care, evidently."

As courteously as Babe treated Carew, she went out of her way to mistreat her other roommate. "There was something there — I think it was because I defeated her—everybody seemed to think that was it, even my coach," Osburn recalled. "It was just one of those things—you see people you dislike—but you try to stay away from them." It was impossible to stay away from someone whose bed was only a few paces away. Babe would be impossible to elude on the practice field, too.

Each morning, the women practiced at the University of Southern California, the University of California at Los Angeles, or a nearby high school. Babe prepared for the three events she had qualified for. With a frown, Coach Vreeland watched Babe's form as she hurdled, with her front leg bent almost awkwardly—the way she had done it ever since she first started hopping hedges back home. Vreeland also watched Babe's javelin motion and found fault with it as well.

He wanted to tinker with Babe's mechanics, but she said no. "My own coach, Colonel McCombs, had told me I should stick to my natural style," Babe later said. "And I know today that he was right. There's no one way to do anything in athletics. You have to find the way that works best for you." Vreeland accepted Babe's stubborn explanation and even told her that he admired her loyalty to the Colonel's teaching.

Babe also practiced for a fourth event, the discus, in case one of her teammates who had qualified for it was injured. During her throws in Evanston, Osburn had strained the muscles in her arms and ribs. To avoid aggravating the injury, she decided she would do almost no throwing during the training sessions and instead only run to stay in shape. Every morning, Babe checked on her roommate's condition, walking beside her on the practice field to ask if she was still "hurting."

"You know," Babe told Osburn one morning, "I can beat any discus thrower there is." Osburn tried to ignore her, but Babe wouldn't let up, continuing to needle Osburn until "she knew she was going to make me mad," Osburn later recalled. Sure enough, she got so angry that she agreed to prove again that she could throw the discus farther than Babe. Vreeland overheard this last piece of their argument and forbade

Osburn to pick up a discus before the games began. Babe's diabolical gambit was thwarted.

At the same time, Lillian Copeland, another discus thrower, criticized the AAU for having ignored the three-event rule in Evanston. "Women stand no more chance of suffering physically from athletics than men," she told the *Los Angeles Times*. "The same things that wear out men, wear out women — poor supervision, poor preparation and over-indulgence." But there was a rule on the books, and it should have been enforced. "To set it aside, even for an athletic prodigy such as Babe Didrikson, is unwise in my mind," Copeland argued. That kind of public swipe at Babe was extremely unusual. It is not known whether Babe was aware of Copeland's comments.

Practice ended by noon each day, and the women returned to the hotel. With their afternoons free, most of them went shopping. In the evenings, they mingled with movie stars and hotshot columnists from back east. Babe and her teammates met actors Clark Gable, Janet Gaynor, Norma Shearer, Norma Talmadge, Joe E. Brown, and Will Rogers. When Babe met Rogers, she challenged him to "any kind of sport." His reply: "Not me.... I'll take someone easy."

Babe's brashness made an instant impression on the newspaper reporters and radio broadcasters. For the sporting press, her down-home personality and her unabashed confidence — along with the novelty of the women's track-and-field team — were an irresistible combination. The dean of America's sports columnists, Grantland Rice, met Babe during the week leading up to the games and was instantly smitten. "She will be one of the sensations before the Olympic curtain comes down," Rice predicted.

Another of America's leading sportswriters, Paul Gallico, set eyes on Babe for the first time in the lobby of the Chapman Park. He watched her stride right up to a woman wearing the jacket of a foreign country and tell her, "Ah'm gonna whup yo' tomorrow." Gallico, who stood

6 feet 3 inches and weighed 190 pounds, recalled that it was easy for some of his colleagues in the press to mistake that kind of declaration as unseemly cockiness. "It was just a simple declarative sentence spoken by a simple declarative person," Gallico later said.

Another time, while several reporters watched, Babe jauntily confronted Helene Madison, the American swimming star who had already smashed sixteen world swimming records. "What's your time in the 100-meter freestyle?" Babe asked. After Helene replied, Babe said with a chuckle, "Shucks, lady, I can beat that by three seconds just practicin'!" Babe surprised a talented U.S. diver named Georgia Coleman by asking her, "Say, you're a pretty good diver, aren't you?" Coleman nodded. "You haven't seen me get going yet, have you?" Babe said. "Nope, they won't let me enter the swimming events, but I can show you all."

Babe's barbs were the product of resentment—or at least that's how it appeared to her teammates and reporters. The swimming team had been dubbed the glamour girls of the U.S. women's Olympic team, particularly by Louella Parsons, the Hollywood gossip columnist whose nationally syndicated column was enormously popular. Parsons said that several of the swimmers, including Eleanor Holm and Louisa Robert, were so beautiful that they could appear someday on the silver screen. No Hollywood columnist predicted that Babe could have a career in pictures, but no woman athlete had more newspaper column inches devoted to her than Babe.

On the eve of the games, Babe made her own predictions. "What I want to do most of all in the Olympics is to win four firsts—something no girl has ever done," she wrote in a story that carried her byline in the *New York Times*. "If they will let me enter the discus throw, I think I can do it.... Much of the credit for my performances should go to Colonel M. J. McCombs of Dallas, my coach, who always has kept up my confidence by such remarks as this: 'You can win that event — now get out there and do it.' So far I guess he has not been disappointed."

A writer for the *New York Times* declared, "The Babe is no boaster and no braggart. She tells you simply what she can do, and then she does it." The reporter asked Babe if she knew how to sew, and Babe bragged about winning first prize in 1930 at the Texas State Fair for a dress she had sewn. "I've never played with dolls though," Babe said. "When I was a little girl, I'd rather play with my dad's hammer or hatchet than fool with dolls." The comment was picked up by a wire service and reprinted in newspapers across America.

The sun peeked over the mountains to the east of Los Angeles on Saturday, July 30, and the city woke up determined to interrupt the Depression with a big, Hollywood-style welcoming party for the world. Every hotel bed was filled, every arriving train was packed, and nearly every restaurant table was taken. By late morning, families enjoyed picnics on the lawn surrounding the Coliseum. Around the perimeter of the wide-bowled stadium, vendors beneath white umbrellas peddled pieces of Americana — flags, buttons, hats, and programs, almost all in red, white, and blue. By noon, the crush of spectators — a record 105,000 had each paid $2 for a seat (the last one was sold that morning) — began streaming into the Coliseum for the opening ceremonies, scheduled to begin at 2:30 p.m. sharp. The men sported white shirts, slacks, and straw hats. The women wore brightly colored dresses and wide-brimmed hats to shield them from the hot California sun. In the sky, several small airplanes flew looping laps, with banners sporting tacky advertisements streaming behind them. Inside the Coliseum, a gigantic five-ring Olympic insignia filled most of the peristyle at the east end of the stadium. Beneath it was Coubertin's Olympic motto: "The most important thing in the Olympic Games is not winning, but taking part. The essential thing is not conquering, but fighting well."

President Herbert Hoover was the first head of state to skip an opening ceremony. Vice President Charles Curtis took his place in the presidential box. The Depression had dramatically curtailed the participation of countries and athletes around the world; only slightly more than half the number of those athletes who had competed in Amsterdam had made the trip to Los Angeles.

The parade of 1,332 competitors from 39 countries began. First, as tradition dictated, was the Greek team, followed by the rest of the countries in alphabetical order. Last to enter the stadium were the host Americans. A roar greeted the 357 men and 43 women as they marched around the stadium. The women wore crisp uniforms consisting of a white skirt and blouse, a red vest and hat, and stiff, high-heeled buckskin shoes.

Once all the athletes were assembled, an artillery salute triggered the raising of the Olympic flag. "In the name of the President of the United States," declared Vice President Curtis, "I proclaim open the Olympic Games of Los Angeles celebrating the Tenth Olympiad of the modern era." U.S. Navy lieutenant George C. Calnan recited the Olympic oath, while the athletes, speaking in more than a dozen languages, repeated it quietly. As trumpets blared, more than 5,000 "doves of peace" (actually white pigeons) were released, swirling around the stadium in unison and then upward as the Olympic torch was lighted. A white-robed chorus of 1,200, accompanied by an orchestra of 250, then sang "The Star-Spangled Banner." The ceremony projected an almost holy ambience. Despite the heat, no one in the stands removed their coats or their hats, except the members of the Los Angeles City Council. "To some of us," one reporter said, "this was as sacrilegious as shedding one's raiment in church." Damon Runyon declared himself "absolutely awed by the majesty of the spectacle, the like of which we shall not see again."

On the sweltering infield, Babe stood fidgeting and sweating. Her feet and ankles itched; it was the first time in her life she had worn stockings. She rarely wore high-heeled shoes, and the stiff buckskins were too tight. She couldn't wait for the pageantry to end. "We had to stand there in a hot sun for about an hour and a quarter while a lot of speeches and things went on," Babe later said. "My feet were hurting more and more. Pretty soon I slipped my feet out of my shoes. Then another girl did. By the end I think everybody had their shoes off."

And so on the infield of the great Coliseum they stood, the seventeen members of the U.S. women's track-and-field team, making their American debut in their white stockings.

The following day, more than fifty thousand people were on hand in the Olympic stadium for the first slate of track-and-field events — the men's high jump, shot put, and 400-meter hurdles preliminaries. The Olympic debut of the women's javelin, Babe's first event, was scheduled for 5:30 p.m. In that morning's newspaper, columnist Westbrook Pegler noted that most of his colleagues in the press box thought it was inappropriate for women to participate in track-and-field events (Grantland Rice was the notable exception). They should be "prevented from cluttering up the lot with delicate parodies of the mighty feats that males perform," Pegler wrote, adding that swimming and equestrian events were better suited to them.

Babe's official Olympic uniform consisted of white shorts and a white tank top with a red, white, and blue stripe crossing the front diagonally. Some of the women, including Babe, objected to the looseness of the male-style track uniforms and tailored them to cover up, sometimes using elastic bands to cinch the baggy shorts to their upper thighs.

Babe was an underdog to her two German competitors in the

javelin, Ellen Braumuller, the Olympic record holder, and Tilly Fleischer. By the luck of the draw, Babe threw first. She paused a moment,
the javelin lifted over her right shoulder, parallel to her right ear, and
her left hand resting on her left hip. Then she took off down the sandy
runway, taking a dozen long strides before slinging her arm back and
rotating slightly to the right. As she began to throw, Babe felt her
hand slip off the handle just for a moment before she regained her grip
and heaved the spear forward. A jolt of pain shot through her right
shoulder. Her forward momentum was so strong that it forced her to
hop on her right foot half a dozen times until she regained her balance.
She peeked at the javelin's low-flying trajectory; it had almost no arc,
"like a catcher's peg from home plate to second base," Babe later said.
The javelin flew past a German flag marking the distance of the Olympic record. When it finally speared the turf, an official marked it with a
blue flag at 143 feet 4 inches. When that distance was announced —
more than 11 feet farther than Braumuller's Olympic record printed in
the official program — the crowd roared.

Babe's throw was short of the women's world record (153 feet 4½
inches), but her debut was even more impressive than she had predicted.
With her arms joined above her head, she beamed at the cheering
crowd, despite the pain still coursing through her right shoulder. Pegler
became an instant believer that Babe belonged on the field, writing that
the javelin "stuck in the grass and twitched angrily as though taunting
the other girls to throw that far."

Neither one did. Braumuller finished second, missing Babe's distance by a mere nine inches. Fleischer took the bronze. Neither of
Babe's other two throws came close to her first. Some in the crowd
thought that Babe's overconfidence about her first throw made her only
half-try, but she was hurting. "Nobody knew it," Babe admitted years
later, "but I tore a cartilage in my right shoulder when my hand slipped
making that throw."

With the American women's first gold medal hanging around her neck, Babe stood on the highest step of the podium, wearing a tight smile as the national anthem was played over the loudspeakers. She then gave a radio interview to Los Angeles–based KHJ—the first post-event radio interview given by an Olympic gold medal winner in the United States.

That evening, Babe, still clad in her blue Olympic sweat suit, bounded into the Chapman Park Hotel lobby to cheers from a crowd of fans seeking her autograph. "My hand slipped when I picked up the pole," Babe explained to reporters. "It slid along about six inches and then I got a good grip again. And then I threw and it just went." Fred Steers said that if Babe's hand had not slipped, the javelin would have traveled at least 155 feet and shattered the world record.

Babe's gold medal promptly turned women's track and field into a marquee event. Some of the most cynical sportswriters began to think that Babe might just do what she had predicted: take three gold medals home with her to Texas.

Three days later were the qualifying heats for the 80-meter hurdles. Babe and her teammate Simone Schaller broke the tape tied at 11.8 seconds, a tenth of a second faster than the record Babe had set during the semifinal in Evanston. The judges declared Babe the winner, although Schaller was sure it was a dead heat. In the second qualifying heat, Babe's teammate and principal rival, Evelyne Hall, won in 12 seconds flat.

The 80-meter hurdles final was held at 3:30 p.m. on Thursday, August 4. Six women were competing, with Hall starting in the inside lane and Babe in the lane just to the right of her. As the women dug their starting holes, Hall was surprised to see that someone had already dug holes in her lane. She quickly tried to fix them so that she felt comfortable.

The starter was a German official, who would use his native language to start the race. This made the women nervous. "Auf du Platze," said the official, then "Fertig." Babe jumped too soon; another false start and she'd be disqualified. "Auf du Platze...Fertig," he repeated, and they were off. Babe began more slowly than usual, and after the first hurdle, Hall had a lead of two lengths. Babe was last.

Babe's hedge-hopping style may have been crude, as Coach Vreeland had said, but her strength was her speed between the hurdles. She quickly cut into Hall's lead, had caught up to her by the fifth hurdle, and then passed her. Babe expanded her lead until the ninth hurdle, when Hall surged to pull even. The two women cleared the tenth and final hurdle side by side, then crossed the finish line, made of yarn, together. Hall hit the yarn neck-high, and the force drew blood across her neck. Babe appeared to hit the yarn at the same time with her left arm raised. She kept running beyond the finish line, keeping one arm raised in triumph as Hall made a quick left turn off the track, her head down.

Who had won?

"Well, I won again," Babe told Hall as several judges listened.

Hall said nothing, but a few dozen athletes in the tunnel each wagged a single finger at her to show that they believed she had finished first. "You won, you won, you won," they told her. But, oddly, Hall just shook her head and held up two fingers, as if to say, *Maybe not. Maybe second.*

"Later," Hall said, "I learned that at that very moment a couple of judges were looking at me. It's possible they made their judgment from this gesture of mine. I really don't know. Babe had so much publicity, it was impossible to rule against her."

In the press box, Arthur Daley of the *New York Times* called it "an eye-lash victory" for Babe. Damon Runyon said, "They hit the tape apparently together." Other reporters thought that Hall had won.

It is impossible to pick a winner from the film of the race or several of the more enduring photographs. One photo, taken from Babe's side of the track, where several of the judges were standing, seems to show Babe with the slightest edge. But pictures can be deceiving.

For nearly thirty minutes, the five judges huddled to determine the winner. Babe and Hall stayed away from each other. Finally, the judges announced that both had finished in 11.7 seconds, a new world record. But since the official Olympic clock did not keep hundredths of a second, they had to rely on their judgment. Babe was awarded her second gold medal.

Hall was heartbroken. For the rest of her life, she felt robbed. Despite that initial moment of uncertainty, she felt sure that she had won or, at worst, had finished in a tie with Babe. For decades, she hoped to be given a gold medal or even half a gold medal, but it never happened. "I thought for sure 1984 would be the year that they would recognize that it really was a tie and do something about it," she said in 1987, when she was seventy-six years old, about the year the Olympics returned to L.A. "I felt that it would not take anything away from the Babe because she was a well-known athlete and a good athlete. But it certainly would have helped me in many, many ways. It would have given me the satisfaction, if nothing else."

For the medal ceremony, Babe stood on the first step of the victory stand with her gold medal, Hall on the next step with her silver. They turned to the peristyle, watching the two American flags being raised, along with the flag of South Africa for the bronze medalist, the Olympic torch just behind. Babe gazed at the stands and saw a panorama of patriotic color — thousands of spectators holding small American flags, all standing and singing "The Star-Spangled Banner."

"All Olympians will tell you that the greatest thrill of all was when they stood on that victory stand," Hall said a half century later. "I can still close my eyes and remember that thrill — the pride and excitement I felt when I stood on that stand."

Once again, Babe's self-promotion as the presumed winner, combined with her triumphant reaction at the wire, might have helped persuade the judges that she had won. "If it was horse racing," she said, "you'd say I won by a nose." Brash as ever, Babe did not accept this stroke of good fortune with anything resembling gallantry. Hall hadn't caught up right before the finish line, Babe said; Babe had *let* her catch up. "Sure, I slowed up a little," she said afterward. "I just wanted to make it a good race." Later, she admitted that there was one sure way to influence the judges: "All you have to do to win if it's close is throw up your arm just before the finish."

The only thing standing in the way of Babe's unprecedented gold medal sweep was Jean Shiley. Quietly, the women of the U.S. track-and-field team were rooting for Shiley to defeat Babe in the high jump and shut the Texan's mouth once and for all. Shiley recalled that her teammates streamed into her room at the Chapman, saying, "We couldn't beat her, Jean. You've got to beat her, cut her down to size."

Evelyne Hall, of course, wanted Shiley to win the most. "We were all actually praying for Jean Shiley to win," Hall said. "We were very high-strung and we put a lot of pressure on Jean to beat this obnoxious girl."

The high jump, held on Sunday, August 7, was the last of the six women's track-and-field events. The Coliseum was nearly full of spectators wanting to see whether Babe would win a record third gold medal. Like the hurdles, the high jump would be remembered for decades as a controversial event clouded by the questionable judgment—and even ineptitude—of the five judges.

While Babe was in Los Angeles, she told reporters that she "was the only girl, as far as I know, that jumped western style, like the boys." In a western-style jump, also known as a western roll, the jumper turned away from the bar before jumping. The risk of that style was that his or her shoulders could go over the bar first, turning the jump into a dive.

This was forbidden by the rules, which explicitly stated that the jumper's feet had to cross the bar before the shoulders. Jean Shiley's coach, Lawson Robertson, had advised her not to attempt the western roll. "There is too much danger of fouling," he had told her, "because your shoulder often precedes your body across the bar." As a result, Shiley used the more popular style among women high jumpers — the scissors jump, with the feet going over the bar first, making it nearly impossible to be called for a foul.

As expected, Babe and Shiley outlasted the other four jumpers, including the favorite, Carolina Gisolf of the Netherlands, who held the world record at 5 feet 3¾ inches. When the two Americans broke Gisolf's record — and their own U.S. record, set in Evanston — they were the only ones remaining in the competition. The bar was then raised to 5 feet 5 inches. Shiley jumped first and cleared the bar. Babe knocked down the bar on her first try but cleared it on her second.

The bar was raised another inch to 5 feet 6 inches. Babe jumped first and soared so high she appeared to clear the bar by at least 4 inches. "I felt like a bird," she recalled. "I was up around five-ten, higher than I had ever been, and it was a sensation like looking down from the top of the Empire State Building." But when she fell to the sandy pit below, her left foot clipped the standard, knocking down the bar. "It was the most astonishing jump any woman ever dreamed about," Grantland Rice wrote. "But luck was against her." Shiley missed her jump, too.

The bar was lowered to 5 feet 5¼ inches. Shiley jumped first, clearing it. Then Babe jumped, kicking up her feet first and rolling over the bar to clear it.

The judges huddled for a moment, then separated, calling a foul on Babe's last jump. They said that her shoulders had gone over the bar first, making it an illegal dive. It turned out that two of the other high jumpers, Eva Dawes of Canada and Helma Notte of Germany, had told the judges that Babe was fouling on every one of her jumps. Even

George Vreeland, who was watching from the stands, sent a note to Shiley urging her to alert the judges that Babe was fouling.

But Shiley had refused. "I felt that...well, I have to go back to my training in high school," she explained years later. "You played the game out and you smiled no matter how much it hurt. No poor sportsmanship."

The foul gave Shiley the gold medal. Babe was stunned. She attributed the judges' decision to "confusion." After all, hadn't she been jumping that way all afternoon? When she protested to the officials, one told her, "If you were diving before, we didn't see it. We just saw it this time." As a consolation, the judges decided that Babe and Shiley would share the world record.

Afterward, Babe seemed to accept the defeat with humility. "I think they should have at least warned me earlier in the jumping. You don't change your form in the middle of an event. But it's okay with me. Jean Shiley is a great jumper."

Twenty years later, in her autobiography, Babe said, "Today it wouldn't matter which part of me went over first. You're allowed to get over the bar any way you possibly can, as long as you take off from the ground on one foot. But back there in 1932, the rule cost me my first-place tie."

In the press box, the reporters had been openly rooting for Babe to win a third gold medal. It was the great story they yearned to write. As they saw it, the judges had robbed Babe—and them. Rice dismissed the judges' ruling "as another of those queer rulings or decisions that have occurred far too often in these Games." Babe may have lost, but to most press observers, she had won not only for herself but for all women. "Mildred (Babe) Didrikson, 128 pounds of feminine dynamite, came through...when all competitors of the so-called stronger sex failed in their world-record attempts."

On the podium, as "The Star-Spangled Banner" was played, Shiley stood with her gold medal, weeping. Babe, standing on the second-highest step for the first time, grimaced and rolled her eyes.

Despite the heartbreaking finish, Babe was anointed the undisputed female star of the Olympics. She had won two gold medals and one silver medal and had set two world records and an Olympic record. Several newspapers declared Babe the greatest woman athlete in the world, dubbing her "Iron-Woman."

"She is an incredible human being," Rice wrote. "She is beyond all belief until you see her perform. Then you fully understand that you are looking at the most flawless section of muscle harmony, of complete mental and physical coordination the world of sport has ever known. There is only one Babe Didrikson, and there has never been another in her class—even close to her class."

Within an hour of Babe's silver medal performance, Rice told his friends in the press box there was not a sport on earth that she could not master.

"OK, what about golf?" asked Westbrook Pegler.

"All right, golf," Rice said.

He had Babe summoned to the press box, where he told her that he believed she had gotten a raw deal. Several of the other writers agreed.

"I have jumped that way all the time," Babe told them.

Rice changed the subject. "When can we play golf?" he asked Babe.

"Tomorrow?" she said.

Part II

———•———

PLAY

9

All Them Roses

G olf is like no other game," Grantland Rice wrote in his autobiography, *The Tumult and the Shouting*.

You are attacking an inert ball. Also, you are on your own. You
are the referee. Nine times out of ten you must call the penalty on
yourself—if a penalty is to be called. You can play the game by
the rules or you can cheat. You are meant to play the ball as it
lies, a fact that may help to toughen your own objective approach
to life.

Golf gives you an insight into human nature, your own as
well as your opponent's. Eighteen holes of match or medal play
will teach you more about your foe than will 18 years of dealing
with him across a desk. A man's true colors will surface quicker
in a five-dollar "Nassau" than in any other form of peacetime di-
version I can name.

Golf lends itself nicely to the 19th hole, a period of refresh-
ment, happy talk and commiseration. I've got a host of columns

from the locker room...not only about and with name golfers but about and with headliners of every sport and business. Peeled down to his shorts, a highball in one hand, an attested score card in the other, it's hard for a man to be anything but himself.

And on a golf course, it's also hard for a woman to be anything but herself—especially when she's pretending to be something she's not.

On the morning of August 8, 1932, Rice, wearing Scottish-style golf slacks, a white shirt, and a bow tie, sat behind the wheel of a borrowed Buick in front of the Chapman Park Hotel. He was waiting for Babe Didrikson to hop into the backseat so that he could put the Olympic champion to his own all-around character test at Brentwood Country Club in western Los Angeles. Rice had invited three other scribes to tag along. This trio—Westbrook Pegler of the *Chicago Tribune,* Paul Gallico of the *New York Daily News,* and Braven Dyer of the *Los Angeles Times*—had considerably less faith than Granny in Babe's ability to play embarrassment-free golf. Rice was a near-scratch golfer who almost never traveled to an out-of-town assignment without his clubs. He was easily the best of the four men, and so it was his idea to team up with Babe in a match-play format against Gallico, Pegler, and Dyer.

Babe had earned Rice's invitation by bragging during the Olympics that she once shot an 82 and could drive the ball 250 yards. This average score and, more important, that average drive was a head-swerving feat, especially when you consider Babe had claimed she had played only ten rounds during her life. Once again, she could not help herself from playing mind games with her competitors. She said nothing to the men about her stint on the Beaumont High School golf team or the thousands of swings she had taken at a Dallas driving range.

Inside the Brentwood clubhouse, while the men sipped their coffee and chatted, Babe made a big show of recruiting Olin Dutra, the club pro (who would win the PGA championship that year), to give her a few quick pointers. Dutra gave Babe advice on her grip, stance, and swing. "Look at the ball real hard—that's the important thing," the pro told her as the writers looked on and scribbled in their notebooks. Babe feigned a struggle to get the grip just right.

"I could tell she was a natural from the first swing I saw her take," Dutra recalled a half century later. "She had sort of a baseball grip, but I showed her how to set up for the ball, to keep her eye on the ball, and to follow through. She had great timing, the kind of timing you can't teach."

On the first tee, Babe, using a set of oversized clubs, was given the honor of playing first. She laid her ball flat on the ground, and Rice rushed forward to put a tee under it for her. Without bothering to take a practice swing and with her hands wrapped crudely around the club, Babe reared back and smashed the ball high and far down the middle of the fairway. It flew a good 240 yards.

"Boys, look at that," Rice roared. Gallico just rolled his eyes.

Babe's initial soaring drive would prove to be her best shot of the first five holes; her iron shots rarely went where she intended, and her putting touch was elusive. But on the 215-yard par 3 sixth hole, Babe used a gracefully swung two-iron to put the ball just ten feet from the flagstick. On the ninth, Babe smashed the ball dead straight into the wind, and it stopped rolling 250 yards from the tee—"one of the best drives I've seen at Brentwood," Dyer gushed, "and I've played there plenty."

On the front nine, Babe shot a wobbly 52, although the score didn't really matter. The four men had never seen a lady golfer exhibit such a muscular swing off the tee. But Babe's swing wasn't just powerful. It was precise.

They chalked up the front nine to practice. The real match would take place on the back nine. The stakes were a few bucks and even more valuable bragging rights. As they set off for the tenth tee, Pegler, Gallico, and Dyer had begun believing Rice's hype: perhaps Babe was a natural at this game, too.

On the twelfth hole, Babe's tee shot soared 240 yards, and she was the only one of the five players on the green in two shots. She won the hole with a par. By now, whispers about what was going on had swept Brentwood. Rimming the thirteenth tee was a group of a few dozen spectators and a handful of caddies eager to follow the fivesome. Babe crushed a 260-yard drive, her best of the day.

The men shot Babe a look. They didn't have to say anything.

"It's the audience," Babe told them. "What did I tell you?"

By the par 3 seventeenth hole, Babe and Rice had pulled even with their opponents. Both Babe and Rice drove their balls into bunkers, while Gallico landed his on the green with a shot at a birdie putt. Rice motioned for Babe to step to the edge of the tee box, away from the other three golfers. "Babe," Rice whispered, "we have to do something."

"I know," Babe whispered back.

Babe walked toward Gallico and asked, "Paul? How about I race you to the green?" Gallico immediately accepted the challenge. (He "takes no challenge from any woman and few men," Rice later said.) On Rice's say-so, Babe and Gallico took off. Babe had a disadvantage — a long dress that fell nearly to her ankles — but she outran Gallico down the short fairway, teasingly maintaining a two-foot gap between them, "like Rusty the electric rabbit at a dog track," Rice later observed. When Gallico reached the green, he collapsed in an exhausted heap. He remained on the ground for a long moment, catching his breath and wheezing a bit. Rice and the other scribes laughed.

The race worked as Babe had planned. "When it came his time to putt, Paul four-putted," Rice recalled. "We won the hole and the match."

Babe shot a 43 on the back nine, earning the respect of all the writers — except Gallico, who did not appreciate losing the race or the round, and he would soon seek revenge with his typewriter. Later that week, in his nationally syndicated column, Rice recounted the match, saying that Babe's performance "with borrowed clubs, over a strange course" was "beyond all understanding."

"She is the longest hitter women's golf has ever seen—for she has a free, lashing style backed up with championship form and terrific power in strong hands, strong wrists and forearms of steel," Rice wrote. In her physique and technique, he recognized the tools of a future champion "not in track and field, where she already had proved her gold medal rating—but in golf, a sport where a gal might compete with men on their own terms....If Miss Didrikson would take up golf seriously, there is no doubt in my mind...she would be a world beater in no time."

The way Babe read it, Granny wasn't extending an invitation. This was an order.

After the closing ceremony in Los Angeles, the "gold medal girls," as they were called, rushed back to the reality of surviving the Depression with little money and fewer prospects. First, they had to find a way home. The U.S. Olympic Committee gave Jean Shiley a train ticket home to Philadelphia. She cashed it in for a bus ticket, using the extra few dollars to buy her family some Olympic souvenirs. "I couldn't afford it unless I went home by bus," Shiley said. "I sat up all the way—it seemed like ten thousand miles. It took forever." By the time she returned to Pennsylvania, she had a gold medal around her neck and only a few pennies in her pocket.

Evelyne Hall's husband and mother had driven from Chicago to Los Angeles to watch her win the silver medal—in a car that, Hall discovered by a collect telegram received in LA, was going to be repossessed by a finance company when she returned home. She had been invited to an end-of-Olympics party at Pickfair, the estate of Mary Pickford and Douglas Fairbanks, but she was forced to skip it, as her paid stay at the Chapman Park Hotel had ended. Hall could not afford to pay for a room for herself, her husband, and her mother for even one night, so they got in their car and started the long drive back to Chicago.

Unlike her teammates—and in violation of the Olympic ideal that only amateur athletes could compete in the games—Babe had none of those worries. She was a paid representative of the deep-pocketed Employers Casualty Insurance Company, which planned to pay all the expenses for a heroine's welcome back in Dallas. Babe flew home on a chartered American Airways transport plane. In the Dallas newspapers that morning, bold headlines for the Texas "Wonder Girl" and "reigning queen" dominated the front page. A full-page ad in the *Dallas Journal* blared, "WELCOME HOME, BABE." Bold headlines promised a "Great Tribute" and a "Stupendous Welcome for Babe Didrikson."

On a warm, cloudless day, an overflow crowd of ten thousand people—including the mayor, the police chief, and the fire chief—packed the terminal at Love Field to greet Babe. She walked down the plane's steps wearing blue sailor pants, a blue-striped white blouse, and a blue gob cap. She was carrying three white javelins, which complemented the outfit.

Beneath the awning of the terminal building, Babe spotted Momma, Poppa, Ole Jr., and Lillie, who looked happy though a bit dusty and worn-out from a difficult car trip from Beaumont that had included two flat tires. Babe wrapped each of her family members in a long, tight hug. Momma cried.

Babe's parents felt self-conscious about their frayed appearance, but because their daughter paid no mind to it, they soon didn't either. "Big shots was all lookin' at us country folks, but we didn't care," Lillie said. "Babe didn't care."

Babe threw her arms around her coach, Colonel McCombs. She was embraced by each member of the Golden Cyclones, clad in matching pressed white dresses trimmed in a brilliant yellow. Homer R. Mitchell, the president of Employers Casualty, stood behind a microphone and called Babe "Dallas' most distinguished citizen."

"You are a citizen of the world," Mitchell declared. "We claim you as our favorite daughter."

Suddenly shy, Babe took her place behind the microphone. "I don't have any plans for the future," she said. "The only thought I had in Los Angeles was to win and get back home." She said that she had loved every moment of the Olympics — the winning, of course, but also meeting the Hollywood stars and starlets and having her picture taken with Clark Gable. And she said that Will Rogers had invited her to play golf on his private course. "He only caddied for me," Babe said, and the crowd laughed. A swirl of reporters and photographers shouted her name. Asked if she had anything else to tell the crowd, Babe said, "I want to say hello, that's all."

Babe then climbed into the elevated backseat of the Dallas fire chief's sparkling red limousine. Hundreds of roses were draped over the side of the car and covered the seat and floor. There were roses everywhere.

"Come on up here," Babe yelled to Lillie. "Come on."

Lillie clambered into the gleaming limo and plopped down right next to her little sister. "And there were roses all over us, all over us," Lillie recalled. "It was such a time with Babe there. I cried, we were so happy in all them roses. I don't know if I should be there, but Babe said it was okay — because I was with *her*." The Colonel and Babe's chaperone, Onie Wood, followed Lillie into the big red car and found their seats.

Thousands cheered and waved at Babe as the Dallas police band played "Hail to the Chief" and a high school band played "Hail, Hail, the Gang's All Here." Momma, Poppa, and Ole Jr. rode in a car trailing Babe's. With the Golden Cyclones marching alongside the limo, each carrying an American flag, Babe's parade wound its way through the

Dallas business district as ticker tape, confetti, and scraps of white and yellow paper showered down. Throngs of people four and five deep lined the streets, cheering and waving. The crowd's kinetic pulse could be timed with the shouts of her name — *Babe, Babe, Babe*. The sound raised "chill bumps" all over her body; those bumps remained all day. Babe wished she could grab hold of that feeling and slow down time, to hang on to this heaven.

The parade wound up at the Adolphus Hotel, the site of a luncheon honoring Babe. Hannah was stunned by the ballroom decorated with sparkling lights and the tables festooned with freshly cut flowers. She accepted hundreds of handshakes, hugs, and congratulations from many of the seven hundred attendees. Hannah kept saying thank you, telling folks she couldn't believe all the good her baby girl had just done.

The first thing Babe saw when she walked in was a mammoth 125-pound watermelon that a wealthy Texas farmer had sent. "Man, that's the biggest watermelon I ever saw," Babe said, and everyone laughed.

After lunch, dignitaries took their turn at the microphone to shower Babe with more accolades. She just sat at the head table smiling. Finally, it was her turn to speak. The young woman who always used a few dozen words when five or six would have done just fine stood up and said, "I'm tickled to be back home. Thank you." And then she sat down.

That afternoon, Hannah walked out of the Adolphus carrying a white linen napkin monogrammed with the hotel's name. She had taken it inadvertently. When she went back into the lobby to return it, a hotel manager said, "No, Mrs. Didrikson, you keep it. You keep it for a memento."

Later that day, a reporter asked Babe if she intended to become a professional athlete. "If I decide to turn professional, it will not be for sixty days or more," Babe replied. "I am definitely going to enter the National Golf Tournament for Women next month. And what's more,

I believe I'll win it. From now on, I am going to forget about track and field events and play golf daily in order to be on my game for the National."

Then it was Beaumont's turn to honor Babe. As Babe's plane approached the airport, a small plane circled several times over the city. Fire whistles alerted the citizens of Beaumont that its Olympic hero had come home.

Wearing a white piqué jumper and a dotted swiss blouse, Babe was greeted at the airport by thousands of friends, neighbors, acquaintances, and strangers. She kissed Momma and Poppa, who had driven home, and then the photographers called for a picture. "Bet you don't like that much, Babe," one of her friends yelled sarcastically.

Babe perched herself in the high backseat of the local fire chief's car, which was again decorated with hundreds of red roses. Lillie joined her. As they moved slowly up Pearl Street, the girls of the Miss Royal Purple high school basketball team marched on both sides of the car and listened to Babe describe her triumphs in Evanston and Los Angeles.

On the Edison Hotel's rooftop, the Kiwanis Club hosted a one-dollar-a-plate luncheon attended by nearly five hundred people. Babe was showered with gifts, including the key to the city, an engraved certificate of merit from the citizens of Beaumont, and a silver cup from her former Miss Royal Purple teammates, engraved with the words "We knew her when."

When Babe spotted her high school coach Lilburn Dimmitt, she yelled, "Hi, coach." Dimmitt had attended the Olympics and, when it was his turn to speak, he told the audience that Babe was by far the most popular athlete at the games, autographing five thousand Olympic programs in a single afternoon.

Tiny Scurlock, Babe's unofficial agent and the ever-hyperbolic sports columnist of the *Beaumont Journal,* stood up to say a few words. For perhaps the only time in his life, Tiny used few superlatives to describe Babe's summer of triumph. Despite all that success, Tiny said, she was the "same swell kid she used to be."

Then E. C. McDonald, the Beaumont High School principal, told the crowd that the last entry in Babe's high school transcript was "Withdrew February 14." A new entry would now have to be added, the principal said: "Left school to be world's greatest athlete."

After the luncheon, a Beaumont reporter named Merita Mills — who admitted she was one of only five local residents who didn't "know her when" — asked Babe what she planned to do next. "I am," Babe admitted, "about plooked out."

Mills suggested that Babe slow down, put the future aside, and take a well-deserved rest. "Spend a nice quiet week in the old hometown — go swimming in the Y pool, fool around at the old high school," Mills said.

Babe shook her head. "But I gotta practice my golf — no time for a vacation. You see, I'm planning on winning the women's championship."

10

That Big Money Talk

Six years before Babe was proclaimed the "world's greatest athlete," a woman from New York City named Gertrude Ederle had earned that hyperbolic title. At the age of nineteen, Ederle became the first woman to swim across the English Channel. Only five men had done it before her.

Few sports stories during the Roaring Twenties rivaled Ederle's quest to conquer the English Channel. Reporters rhapsodized over the 1924 Olympic bronze medalist's audacious bid to bridge a sports gender gap measured by the twenty-one miles separating Cape Gris-Nez, France, and Dover, England. "I felt that I would sooner be in that tug the day she starts than at the ringside of the greatest fight or at the arena of the greatest game in the world—for this, in my opinion, is to be the greatest sports story in the world," writer W. O. McGeehan gushed.

At 7:08 a.m. on August 6, 1926, Ederle plunged into the dark, icy water off Cape Gris-Nez. This was her second attempt to swim the Channel; a year earlier, she hadn't been able to finish. The simple fact that she was trying again, beating three other women swimmers determined to swim the Channel before she did, was itself an accomplishment. Making it to England, however, was something else. By late afternoon, Ederle was being buffeted by pounding swells, pelting rain, and pesky winds. From a nearby tugboat, her trainer, Thomas Burgess, yelled, "Gertie, you must come out."

"What for?" she asked.

At 9:39 p.m., Ederle reached Kingsdown on the English coast, where a British immigration official asked to see her passport. The rough weather had lengthened Ederle's swimming course to the equivalent of thirty-five miles, a distance she had covered in an astonishing 14 hours 31 minutes. Her time shattered the English Channel record by 2 hours 2 minutes.

No woman athlete in American history had ever received the rush of adulation lavished on Gertrude Ederle. When she returned home, Manhattan threw her a ticker tape parade grander than the ones that had saluted the greatest heroes of World War I. Two million people lined Broadway to catch a glimpse of the sports heroine, whom President Calvin Coolidge had dubbed "America's Best Girl." New York City mayor James J. Walker compared her feat to Moses parting the Red Sea, Caesar crossing the Rubicon, and Washington crossing the Delaware. Trudy Ederle was bombarded with movie, stage, and commercial offers totaling nearly $1 million. After she received hundreds of marriage proposals, a songwriting duo wrote, "You're such a cutie, you're just as sweet as tutti-frutti, Trudy, who'll be the lucky fellow?"

In a matter of weeks, however, nearly all the most lucrative offers had been withdrawn. With few prospects to swim for money, Ederle joined the vaudeville circuit in 1927. She earned $2,000 a week, but after a year she suffered a nervous breakdown from the strain of giving six performances a day. She was also hampered by poor advice from uncouth business managers. By the end of the decade, Ederle was nearly broke. She was forced to slink off the public stage, resurfacing momentarily in 1939 when she swam, along with three hundred show-girls, in Billy Rose's Aquacade at the New York World's Fair. She had been hearing impaired since the age of five and had lost all her hearing by the late 1930s. During World War II, she worked at LaGuardia Airport as an aircraft instrument technician.

In 1975, Ederle was a nearly anonymous sixty-eight-year-old woman living in a modest apartment in Queens. She never married. Her next-door neighbors had no idea who she was or what she had done. "Don't write any sob stories about me," she told a reporter. "I'm not a million-aire but I'm comfortable." The reporter wondered if she had any idea why the world had so quickly forgotten her astonishing feat. "I would be stupid if I hadn't realized that people couldn't stand forever on street corners playing brass bands," she said. "It doesn't really matter if they've forgotten me. I haven't forgotten them."

In those first heady days after crossing the Channel, with offers of love and money flooding in, Gertrude Ederle could have been forgiven for believing that no one had a better chance to make a life as a profes-sional sportswoman than the "world's greatest athlete."

Now, six years later, it was Babe's turn to try.

The eyes of the whole world are upon you. This was the caption on a post-Olympics cartoon in the *Amarillo Globe* depicting a gigantic, goddess-like Babe astride the earth.

Babe could feel those eyes. She could feel them when she was practi-cally forced, within a week of returning to Texas after the Olympics, to travel to Chicago—first by plane, then, thanks to a sudden storm, by train—for a track-and-field exhibition featuring a smattering of Olym-pic stars. The travel mishaps meant that she barely made it to the event on time, but she had help. Several police cars rushed her from the train station to Soldier Field, where the convoy escorted her onto the field from an entryway at one end of the stadium. "Here comes the Babe!" the announcer shouted. In a reenactment of the Olympic qualifier in Evanston, the officials delayed two events for Babe. She finished first in the high jump and second in the discus throw, although her distance would have been good enough to take the discus gold medal in the Olympics if she had qualified for it. She was by far the most popular woman on the field, and the outpouring of affection attracted the interest of the leaders of the Illinois Women's Athletic Club, who were displeased that their club was now infamous for being the forty-four-legged also-ran to Babe in Evanston.

By the time Babe returned to Dallas, a letter from the Illinois club was on her desk. The club offered Babe a monthly wage of $300, quadrupling her current salary. This was precisely the kind of letter Babe had tried to get Tiny to concoct on the sly, and now it was here, the real thing. Babe was overjoyed. Without hesitation, she showed the offer to Homer R. Mitchell, the president of Employers Casualty.

"Why, Babe," he said, "I think we can give you $300 a month to stay here."

"Well, that's fine," she said, keeping her elation in check. "Because I'd rather stay here where my friends are."

Babe's goal was to quickly cash in on her Olympic success. Quadrupling her salary at Employers Casualty was a promising first step, although the raise would not make her wealthy or even help her father pay off the mortgage on the house on Doucette Street. In the first heady days after the Olympics, Babe had fielded a series of fanciful offers, most as far-fetched and lucrative as the ones dangled before Gertrude Ederle. One was to become a bullfighter in Mexico. Another was to star in short sports films. A third offered her $65,000 a year to play professional basketball. Each offer was a preposterous mirage, however, tendered for publicity purposes and withdrawn as soon as the headline had faded. "People kept telling me how I could get rich if I turned professional," Babe said. "That big money talk sounds nice when you're just a kid whose family has never had very much."

With the hope that one offer might last long enough to grab, Babe obtained a court order from a Dallas judge giving her "the legal right to transact her own business affairs." Curiously, she had claimed to be only nineteen years old, when she was actually twenty-one.

Next, Babe met up with Grantland Rice in Dallas to make a Sportlight short called *The Wonder Girl*. In the late 1920s and early 1930s, Rice produced dozens of these short biographic films, which were exhibited in two thousand movie theaters across the country. Filmed on the campus of Southern Methodist University, the ten-minute picture is a rapid-fire demonstration of Babe playing every imaginable sport. She throws a discus, shot put, javelin, and baseball. She high-jumps, long-jumps, jumps over hurdles, sprints, swims, and dives. She dribbles and shoots a basketball. She hits golf balls, tennis balls, and baseballs. Clad in a black football uniform, she even catches and punts a football. But nothing is more impressive than Babe's throw from deep left field to home plate. She rears back, her right arm fully extended behind her, and fires the baseball toward home plate. The ball travels in a long, high arc, takes one hop, and is snared by the catcher.

But that 24-frames-per-second commercial had no payoff beyond the documentary: Babe seemed almost entirely unaware of the difficulty of what she was trying to do. So far, she'd managed to convince the men in charge to bend the rules for her but that had taken place in the amateur arena. Now she was imagining a professional sports life for herself at a time when few such opportunities—indeed few employment opportunities at all—existed for women.

By 1932, 25 percent of employable Americans were out of work, and the percentage of unemployed women was much higher. Because it was so difficult to find a job, athletic women tried to make a living through sports. Bowling champion Floretta McCutcheon toured the country, giving exhibitions and setting up leagues for women. Hazel Hotchkiss Wightman ran tennis clinics for women and organized tournaments across New England. Two female African American basketball teams barnstormed the country. One, sponsored by the *Philadelphia Tribune,* was headlined by Ora Washington, a tennis champion. It was no coincidence that the few opportunities for women in sports were as part of a team. Trying to make a living by excelling in an individual sport was far more challenging. But that wasn't going to stop Babe.

"What I really wanted to do at this point was to become a golfer," said Babe, the nudge toward the game by Grantland Rice still fresh. Each day after working at Employers Casualty, Babe rushed to the Dallas Country Club or the driving range to practice her game. On weekends, she and her brother Louis, who also worked in Dallas, would take the train to Beaumont, but those quick trips soon became tiresome. Babe needed her own wheels.

She visited a Dallas Chrysler dealership, where she drove off the lot in a fire-engine red Dodge coupe, retail value $835. Babe drove so fast that Louis, worried about his safety (there were no seat belts in those days), grabbed the dashboard and held on until his knuckles turned white. "She was always comfortably ahead of anybody behind her, and anybody ahead had better take the shoulder," Louis recalled. "She believed that little thing called an accelerator was a toy put there for one purpose — speed." When visibility was limited by heavy rain or fog, Babe kept her foot pressed to the gas pedal and stuck her head out of the window to get a better look at the traffic coming her way.

Babe had driven the car off the dealer's lot without paying a single dollar as a down payment. Later, Louis said that the car had been "loaned" to her, but Babe claimed that she had made arrangements to pay $69 a month, a high sum. News of Babe's new Dodge soon reached the AAU's southern office in New Orleans. With her constant talk about becoming a professional, AAU officials had already been on the lookout for any evidence of Babe being paid to play. Her new Dodge seemed proof that she had exchanged something of value with the dealer. And if that was true, Babe *was* a professional athlete.

Sure enough, in early December newspapers in Dallas and Chicago began publishing an advertisement for the coupe that included a photograph of Babe clearing a hurdle. The caption quoted Babe's endorsement: "Speed — unyielding strength — enduring stamina — that's the stuff that makes real champions, whether they're in the athletic arena or in the world of automobiles."

On December 5, the AAU suspended her from amateur competition. The penalty, issued before anyone bothered to inform Babe, made her ineligible to play basketball with the Golden Cyclones or to compete in AAU track-and-field meets. Daniel J. Ferris, the AAU secretary-treasurer, said in a telegram that Babe would remain suspended until she proved "beyond a doubt" that the advertisement was not due to "any act of omission or commission on her part." In other words, the AAU had found Babe guilty without giving her the opportunity to defend herself at a hearing. And now the burden was on Babe to prove her innocence beyond a reasonable doubt.

She was furious. She had been torn over whether she should become a professional athlete or remain an amateur. For weeks, she had mulled over the decision, going back and forth. And now a few strangers in the AAU had settled that question for her? She called it "a bunch of hooey."

Amateurism was a lofty, abstract ideal that the AAU had aggressively tried to defend. The organization's arcane, often unfair rules of amateurism had resulted in the punishment of dozens of top athletes, but no athlete had suffered more than Jim Thorpe. The winner of two Olympic gold medals in 1912 for the pentathlon and decathlon, Thorpe had his medals stripped from him a year later when it was revealed that he had played semipro baseball, earning $2 per game, in 1909 and 1910.

Thorpe admitted the violation but pleaded for forgiveness from the AAU. "I hope I will be partly excused by the fact that I was simply an Indian schoolboy and did not know all about such things," he said. "In fact, I did not know that I was doing wrong, because I was doing what I knew several other college men had done, except that they did not use their own names." The public was untroubled by Thorpe's semipro past, in large part because his many accomplishments seemed to eclipse his few transgressions. But AAU secretary James E. Sullivan retroactively removed Thorpe's amateur status for the Olympic Games and asked the International Olympic Committee to follow suit. It did, unanimously. It was not until 1982, nearly three decades after Thorpe's death, that the IOC restored his two gold medals to his heirs.

Avery Brundage, the national president of the AAU in 1932, was as big a stickler for the amateur rules as Sullivan had been. Summarily dismissing Thorpe's earlier challenge, Brundage declared, "Ignorance is no excuse."

It wasn't as if Babe had not seen this conflict coming. She knew that her goal of making money as a professional sportswoman was on a collision course with her need to keep her amateur standing to compete in the handful of women's golf tournaments then being played. Although she had skipped the U.S. Women's Amateur Championship because she felt she wasn't yet good enough to make her debut, her focus remained entirely on golf.

Babe saw the most beautiful set of golf clubs in the front window of the Cullum and Boren sporting goods store in downtown Dallas. "It was like a girl seeing a mink coat," she remembered. She had to have them, but she couldn't afford them.

Then Babe had an idea. She told the owner of the sporting goods store that she had an upcoming appearance at a Dallas ballpark, where she was going to receive an expensive watch. Would the store swap the golf clubs for the watch?

Babe knew that AAU rules prohibited members to accept money or gifts in exchange for athletics or promotional appearances. Nevertheless, she took the watch. The fact that Babe made such a risky trade after the AAU ban over the Dodge coupe demonstrates that she was careless about the rules. That ban carried enormous consequences. For one thing, it threatened her eligibility for the James E. Sullivan Memorial Award, presented by the AAU to the best all-around athlete of the year. Babe wanted the honor, although it became a bit less important to her after she learned that she had won the 1932 Female Athlete of the Year award from the Associated Press. Balloting for the Sullivan Award was scheduled to close on December 27, but if Babe was no longer an amateur, her name would be stricken from consideration.

More important, Babe saw the ban as a way for the sporting establishment to block her path to a career as an amateur golfer. She had perceived intimations that her blue-collar background would not be welcome in the game of golf, and she was sure that the AAU officials had suspended her "because they didn't want me to beat the rich dames."

Babe decided to fight back. "I will do everything I can to be reinstated in the A.A.U., and I don't want to turn professional," Babe told reporters. "I have played only three years of basketball and I'm not ready to quit as an amateur." In a wire to Ferris, she declared, "I positively did not give anyone authority to use my name or picture in any advertising matter."

E. Gordon Perry was the Dodge dealer who said that he had sold the car to Babe. He insisted that she had been paid no money. "Her praise of this car came from her voluntarily," Perry told the AAU. "We passed on to the home office her praise of the car, just as we did many others. Miss Didrikson, being a world figure in athletics, naturally attracted more attention than others. Her opinion of the new model car was spontaneous and enthusiastic."

In a way, Perry's statement undercut Babe's case because it was obvious to the investigators and the public that she could not have spontaneously said the words in her printed endorsement if she had been given a thousand tries. Babe just wasn't articulate enough to say those things, the investigating officials decided. The "spontaneous and enthusiastic" words attributed to Babe sounded precisely like what they were — prose written by an adman in New York.

A day later, the dealer produced evidence — a statement from Chrysler's Manhattan advertising agency — that Babe had not authorized the ad as an endorsement. But this was still not enough proof to satisfy the AAU. Officials demanded that Babe explain another telegram from the Dallas car dealer to the New York ad agency referring explicitly to Babe's endorsement. The inquiry would go on.

Babe was losing patience. She knew that the Golden Cyclones basketball team was struggling to find competition. She decided that she would let the AAU make her decision about turning pro for her. Maybe it was an omen. She wired her decision to turn pro to the AAU with her "kindest regards" just a few hours before the organization voted to lift its suspension, admitting it had suspended her by mistake. Babe didn't care; she was ready to go.

Her decision was motivated partly, but not entirely, by money. The Chrysler Corporation felt bad enough about what had happened that it invited Babe to attend an auto show in Detroit for pay. Adman George P. Emerson of the Ruthrauff & Ryan agency was enlisted to try to find Babe other commercial and professional sporting opportunities. Her first plan was to "do some film work," she told reporters, and to swim the English Channel, just as Gertrude Ederle had done. She said nothing about golf.

But her decision was also an impulsive one, triggered as much by anger as by her concern that the AAU was going to deny her appeal and she'd have to turn pro anyway. She could not resist taking a parting shot. "Not until this last weekend did I realize what a terrifying business it is to maintain one's self as a member in good standing in the A.A.U.," she told reporters in a written statement. "Being an athlete and being a member of the A.A.U. are two quite different things. I am amazed to discover that there are 350 pages of regulations and do's and don'ts." She added, "I'd rather try to smash another world's record" than memorize all those rules. These words, like Babe's endorsement of the Dodge, sounded as if someone else had written them. In fact, they had been written by Emerson and his colleagues.

Accompanied by her big sister Esther, Babe hopped a train from Dallas to Chicago courtesy of Chrysler. She arrived on Christmas Eve, managing to avoid the press. A reporter found her in a pool hall in the Chicago Loop, where Babe announced that she had hired Emerson as her agent. She discussed a number of new ventures — starring in "sporting short" films for Hollywood, swimming, maybe playing tennis. She insisted that she would not be endorsing anything.

"Just by way of keeping myself in training, I am seriously considering taking up long distance swimming in a big way," she said. "I want to swim around Manhattan Island then do both the English Channel and the Hellespont. That means I'll have to put on some extra poundage. I have already doubled my food intake. My friends say I'm sure to lose my slim figure, but if I do I'm sure to get it back again. I've done more difficult things."

Before the end of the year, Babe and Esther appeared in Detroit at the auto show, where Babe signed autographs, played her harmonica, and had her picture taken with fans. Despite her vow not to do endorsements, she promoted the same Dodge coupe that had led to her AAU suspension.

That week, Avery Brundage did not hesitate to express his disgust in regard to the controversy over Babe's amateur standing. He couldn't resist adding a few words about his impatience with her indecision.

"You know," he said, "the ancient Greeks kept women out of their athletic games. They wouldn't even let them on the sidelines. I'm not so sure but they were right." He wasn't alone in holding this opinion. At about the same time, the nation's leading sportswriters, including some of Babe's biggest fans, began wondering the same thing.

11

Miss, Mrs., Mr., or It

It had to happen. The accolades lavished on Babe after the Olympics — one paper had proclaimed her "one of those astounding marvels who happens once in history" — would not endure. The adulation had been too great. The praise had been too loud. The backlash was inevitable.

Even during the Olympics, Babe had heard the murmurs: "too boyish," they labeled her, or worse, "all-boy." She had heard the whispers: she runs like a man, acts like a man, sounds like a man, *looks* like a man. But thanks to Babe's still considerable cheering section in the press box, most of those cutting comments remained beyond the national spotlight. Shortly after the Olympics, a local newspaper assured a concerned reader that Babe "is not a freakish looking character ... [but] a normal, healthy, boyish-looking girl." Another small-town paper highlighted Babe's deep voice and passion for fisticuffs, portraying her as a hard-boiled street thug. "She has few close girlfriends," the reporter observed, "and isn't much interested in boys."

Such uncomfortable questions about Babe began in the autumn of 1932, and perhaps not surprisingly, they were first posed by the sportswriter whom Babe had outrun on the seventeenth fairway at Brentwood Country Club. When that impromptu race was over, Babe had playfully mocked Paul Gallico, who was sprawled out, more embarrassed than exhausted, on the edge of the green. Now it was Gallico's turn, and there was nothing playful about his counterpunches. In an article titled "The Texas Babe," published in the October 1932 issue of *Vanity Fair*, Gallico described Babe's golf round on the day after the Olympics in a less charitable way than Grantland Rice had. When their eighteen-hole round was over, Gallico observed, "nobody knew whether to invite the Babe into the men's locker room for a bath and a drink, or whether to say, 'Well, goodbye kid, see you later.'" Although she left the course that day with several female friends, Gallico wrote, "the strange . . . girl-boy child would have been right at home" in the men's locker room. In Gallico's reintroduction of Babe to a national audience, she was no longer the awe-inspiring Olympic champion who just happened to be a woman. She was now a sideshow freak who deserved to be gawked at and puzzled over.

Pity and anger were the twin engines of Gallico's blandly titled but ferociously sexist article. More than a dozen times, Gallico used the word *boy* to describe Babe. Most witheringly, he pinned a label on her that would plague her for most of her life — "muscle moll." Worse, despite her early success, she was a *bitter* muscle moll, Gallico added. He portrayed Babe as a pathetic, accidental athlete imprisoned by her abnormality. She chose to compete against women in athletic contests "simply because she would not or could not compete with women at their own best game — man-snatching. It was an escape, a compensation. She would beat them at everything else they tried to do." Without athletic contests, he argued, she'd have no way to catch a man's eye.

That was hardly the end of it. During the Olympics, Gallico had observed Babe being snubbed by a clique of better-looking female teammates. He said nothing about the fact that Babe was ostracized mostly because her teammates resented her gargantuan ego (and, just as important, the way she so effortlessly backed up her bragging with stellar results on the field). After being shut out by her snickering contemporaries, "the greatest woman athlete in the world stood on the outside, looking on," he wrote.

Babe, who absorbed every word of her press coverage, was crushed by the *Vanity Fair* article. "After the Olympics—it was the most stressful time for the Babe," recalled Betty Jameson, one of the original glamour girl golfers who was good friends with Babe in the 1940s and 1950s. "She didn't know what to *do* or what to *be*. And then people kept telling her what she *should* do and what she *should* be. It didn't help." In particular, Babe knew that Gallico was right about one thing, though she never publicly acknowledged what her friends had always suspected: her need to compete was in some ways an attempt to compensate for failing to snatch a man.

Although a portion of Gallico's animus toward Babe was the product of his own insecurity about his masculinity after collapsing at Brentwood, the same insinuations had been made by others. Babe had done little to deflect these suspicions. Not long after the Olympics, a male sportswriter blushed and stammered as he embarked on a difficult question: "Uh, Miss Didrikson, do you select—uh—your private— uh, apparel with any special care. I mean do you—er—find the binding garments—er—what I mean is..."

Babe replied, "Are you trying to ask me if I wear girdles, brassieres and the rest of that junk?"

"Y-y-yes," stammered the writer, relieved by Babe's bluntness.

"The answer is no," Babe shot back. "What do you think I am, a *sissy?*"

To Babe, *sissy* meant a lady loser. It's a word she used often, usually as a shield and as a way to distance herself from other women, who she thought lacked a natural toughness. Such remarks played right into the public's lurid speculation.

In the April 1933 edition of *Vanity Fair,* Gallico concocted an even harsher indictment of Babe's personal life in a short story titled "Honey." For any slow-witted readers who might have had trouble recognizing that the title character, Honey Hadwell, was a barely disguised Babe Didrikson, there was a full-page photo of Babe, with the title "Tough Babe," on the page opposite Gallico's attack.

In the story, Honey is a hurdler and javelin thrower. But she is best known for being an oddity who is more man than woman, is more sexually agnostic than heterosexual, and, in the end, allows her self-hatred to get the best of her, despite winning a gold medal. The most withering passages lament Honey's ungainly looks. Gallico describes the unsettling dichotomy between "the most beautiful body that anyone saw on a woman because it happened to be a boy's body" and Honey's face, which "is something else again."

"Her mouth was just a pale slit," he wrote, saying that Honey never used makeup because that was for "sissies." "She had a hawk's beak for a nose and a pair of cold eyes."

The story's thin plot focuses on Honey's rapidly plummeting self-esteem. She overhears women ridiculing her behind her back about every facet of her personality, real and imagined — her down-home drawl, her habit of swearing, her lack of interest in boys, the possibility that she is a lesbian (or, as Gallico put it, a "Lez"). At several dances, a handsome Polish javelin thrower named Mike Suss courts Honey, stunning the other women who have eyes for Suss. But Honey and Suss have little in common and don't dance together a single time, choosing instead to stand "on the fringe" of the dance floor. A woman high diver wonders why Suss is paying any attention to "that dried-up tough-as-nails-little-bitch." Gallico then reveals that Suss has no interest in Honey other than to glean tips from her about javelin throwing. After he smashes the world record by ten feet, he stops paying attention to her.

By the end of the story, Honey is furious with herself, sobbing at her outsider status, despite being a favorite to win the javelin competition. She "claw[s] at herself" and calls herself a "sissy" and a "cry baby." With her right fist, she begins pounding her chin and manages to hurt herself.

The next day, Honey breaks the javelin record and wins the gold medal. But that night, alone in her room, she wallows in self-pity. Then she reveals the secret of her javelin-throwing success to the reader: "Ah throwed it right through his black heart." Honey's triumph, Gallico says, was attributable to her all-consuming desire for revenge against all the men in the world.

If there was much that was reactionary about Gallico's fixation, there was something revolutionary about Babe's challenge. Indeed, in unwittingly struggling to redefine the way American society viewed women athletes, she was redefining how it viewed women in general. Babe was always vocal about her multisport talent and athletic achievements. Such brashness was a novelty in the 1930s, when most American icons were modest about their achievements and a worn-out, demoralized public wanted humility in its heroes. In the movies, the archetype was the strong, silent cowboy, a man who let his six-shooter do the talking. The era's quintessential hero, Charles Lindbergh, called his bestselling book *We,* and in it he extended nearly all the credit for his mythic transatlantic flight to his airplane.

At the Olympics, Babe's self-promotion had been highlighted by Grantland Rice and others for its novelty, especially coming from a woman. Babe viewed it this way: if she wasn't going to tell the world what she could do, who would? But after the Olympics, as Babe continued to brag about being the best, her coarseness tested the patience of most sports fans. The novelty had worn off. Babe was not behaving the way the public expected their champion lady athletes to comport themselves.

As a result, prodded by regular media questioning of her sexuality, by early 1933 Babe had become a symbol of what mothers and fathers did not want their daughters to grow up to be. Belle Mead Holm, later dean of the women's physical education department at Lamar University in Beaumont, said that when she played softball as a teenager, her devotion to the game unnerved her mother. "I remember my mother would absolutely weep over my going to those games," Holm said. "She used to say, 'Please, I don't want you to grow up like the Babe, Belle. Just don't be like the Babe, that's all I ask.'"

More than one sportswriter wondered whether Babe was actually a man masquerading as a woman and demanded that she should undergo a "gender test." Gallico mentioned Babe as the leader of a breed of "women who made possible deliciously frank and biological discussions in the newspapers as to whether this or that woman athlete should be addressed as Miss, Mrs., Mr. or It." This sentiment became widespread in the 1930s. A sign posted on the walls of many high school girls' locker rooms read: DON'T BE A MUSCLE MOLL.

Joe Williams, the sports columnist for the *New York World-Telegram,* demeaned Babe's Olympic track-and-field records, saying that many male high school athletes could have easily beaten her in Los Angeles. It was an outrageous claim, but many readers believed it. "By her championship accomplishments, she had merely demonstrated that in athletics women didn't belong," Williams wrote, "and it would be much better if she and her ilk stayed at home, got themselves prettied up and waited for the phone to ring."

Westbrook Pegler had grown so angry about Babe telling the story of making him look silly on the golf course right after the Olympics — "all this fake cheap publicity at my expense," he called it — that he threatened in print to punch Babe in the mouth. "The trouble with Didrikson is that people have spoiled her," Pegler wrote in February

1933. "She is not so tough and I am the one who can lick her if she wants to make trouble out of it."

Other sportswriters argued that women should be limited to participating in "lady-like" sports that allowed them to "look beautiful" and wear "some pretty cute costumes." Gallico's list of appropriate female sporting events was restricted to archery, figure skating, and horseback riding—activities that would not cause women to perspire. Furthermore, many sportswriters were convinced that the rigors of athletic activities weakened women for motherhood. There was no scientific evidence of this, but that didn't stop the writers from making the case.

Babe knew that she was never going to be seen as a "glamour girl," the sportswriters' highest compliment for an attractive woman athlete. She cringed when writers said that she didn't appear "much interested in boys," and she hated when they said that her mouth was "a slit" and she had an ugly "hawk's nose."

"I know I'm not pretty," Babe told one reporter, "but I do try to be graceful."

Back in Manhattan, Babe paced around her room at the Biltmore Hotel, waiting for a knock on the door or a phone call, while her mind pondered the future. In the autumn, she had been determined to play golf, but the game was not easy, and Babe began considering other options. Over breakfast, she decided she was going to start a professional basketball team in New York. Then, over lunch with her sister, Babe talked about coaching a girls' collegiate track team. By dinner, she changed her mind again, vowing to play shortstop for a semipro baseball team, possibly against men, if they'd let her. Before going to sleep, she announced that her mind was finally made up: she would become a boxer.

How about billiards? Tennis? Babe found it easy to imagine playing *everything.*

Babe intended to use the country's press capital as a launching pad for a new career as a professional "girl athlete." At the time, there was no such thing. The era's most famous women athletes — British golfer Joyce Wethered, swimmer Gertrude Ederle, Olympic skating champion Sonja Henie — were all amateurs who conquered a single sport and then discovered there were few, if any, pay-for-play opportunities waiting beyond that first blush of stardom. The small number of women who had tried to earn a little money as athletes had done it as barnstorming sideshow acts.

One morning, Arthur Daley, the legendary Pulitzer Prize–winning sports columnist of the *New York Times,* visited Babe's hotel room. Before he began asking questions, she scrunched up her eyes and said, "Say, you aren't the fellow who took pictures of my feet out in Jersey a couple of years ago?" Babe thought she recognized Daley from the AAU meet in Jersey City.

"No, not me," Daley said.

"Don't ask me whether or not I'm going to get married," Babe snapped. "That is the first question women reporters ask, and that is why I hate those darn old women reporters."

Babe's sister Esther Nancy gasped at the rudeness of this outburst. "I don't care," Babe shot back, reminding her sister that she said the same thing to female reporters.

Daley was interested in Babe's plans. He asked her which sport she played best. "I do everything best," Babe said.

When Daley asked if she'd be interested in coaching girls, Babe shook her head. "Shucks, I wouldn't want to coach girls," she said. "I would rather train boys. They develop more rapidly and are easier to handle."

Babe told Daley that on the following morning, she intended to meet

Babe Ruth for a sparring session at Artie McGovern's gymnasium, on East Forty-second Street at Madison Avenue. The two Babes would face off. "I never met the Babe, but, gee, I'd like to put on the gloves with him for a while," she said. "I hope they have a punching bag over there. Boy, how I can punch that bag."

Daley left the Biltmore without any sense of Babe's plans. He also felt more than a bit sorry for Babe, who came off as brittle, self-hating, and spoiled. He believed she was hardly a good role model for aspiring young women athletes. The next morning, Babe hopped a train from Manhattan to Brooklyn to meet Babe Ruth at McGovern's. A few reporters showed up to record the meeting, but Ruth stood her up.

"Miss Didrikson is probably the most naïve athlete ever to turn professional," Daley wrote in that morning's *New York Times*. "Just what form of professionalism she will engage in is somewhat vague....She will keep in training while waiting for some pecuniary reason for putting her manifold talents to some use."

That pecuniary challenge fell to her agent, George Emerson. Although there were few opportunities for a world-class female athlete to earn even a modest paycheck, Emerson found two chances, in the same week, in New York.

Babe played in her first women's professional basketball game with the Brooklyn Yankees against the Long Island Ducklings. It was a tryout of sorts, and by now Babe knew that a place on a professional sports team was the safest choice. The few options for women athletes were with teams, but she knew the pay was modest, at best, and any chance for stardom was remote. Before a crowd of two thousand fans in Arcadia Hall in Brooklyn, the Long Island Ducklings couldn't wait to teach Babe a lesson in humility. She was repeatedly fouled. "I never got pushed around and fouled so much in any basketball game," she said. "They were determined I wasn't going to make a single basket. They beat me all over the place."

Near the end of the first half, a player clawed at Babe's pants, splitting them partway up the side and revealing a provocative flash of skin. After halftime, Babe took the court wearing the same torn pants, determined to score. She stole the ball at half court and dribbled all the way through the defenders toward the basket. "I jumped so high and hard going in for the basket that my arm hit the backboard," Babe recalled, "and I wound up in somebody's lap about six rows back." The harsh treatment made a permanent place on a team roster even less appealing. It felt like a job.

Still, Babe scored nine points, helping the Yankees win, 19–16. After the game, the visiting team presented Babe with an authentic Long Island duckling, bedecked with a green ribbon. Babe tried, unsuccessfully, to keep the duck in the bathtub of her hotel room, but the bird escaped from the tub and waddled around the room. So Babe had the hotel manager ship the duck, air express, to her parents in Beaumont. Not long after that, Babe won a small white pig at a country dance at the hotel. She sent the pig to her parents, too. "Momma and Poppa were nearly going crazy back in Beaumont—ducks coming to the house, and pigs coming," she recalled.

A night after her professional basketball debut, Babe turned her attention to an exhibition pocket billiards game. She was pitted against Ruth McGinnis, the champion of women's professional pocket billiards, who was just twenty-two years old. McGinnis had learned to play on her father's pool table back in Honesdale, Pennsylvania.

Over a mid-January weekend, a record crowd, each paying a dollar, jammed Capitol Billiards, on the corner of Broadway and Fifty-third Street, to witness what the promoters had dubbed the "First Championship Match of Women's Pocket Billiards." Babe was a billiards sharpshooter, but she never really had a chance, getting crushed by McGinnis, 400–62. "Babe Didrikson may be a great all-round athlete," wrote the *New York Times,* "but as a pocket billiard player, well, the less said, the better."

Having exhausted her opportunities in New York, Babe returned to Chicago. In that city, she made her debut on the vaudeville stage at the Palace Theater. Her agent, Emerson, thought her appearance would be good for the theater and also promote Babe's career.

"Give me a big city," Babe once told a friend back in Beaumont. "There are more people to please, more places to go. I wouldn't be afraid, even in New York City." Now Babe left Chicago on an eastbound train, headed again for the bright lights of Manhattan, but not for its vaudeville houses.

Babe's decision to walk away from the vaudeville circuit was fraught with risk. It carried consequences not only for herself but also for her mother and father, whom she was still helping to support by sending them at least half of her weekly paycheck. At the time, Babe had $1,800 in the bank, saved from her week of shows in Chicago and a few endorsements linked to her performance in the Olympics. That seemed to her like all the money in the world. *I can live forever on this,* she thought.

On board the train, she stared out the window at the passing landscape and wondered, *What should I play?* If she could just find a game—*any* game—she knew she could win. And winning was all that really mattered, right?

Still, Babe was being offered only one paying option—vaudeville. In her room at Manhattan's Biltmore Hotel, Emerson implored Babe to change her mind about the stage. She should grab the money, he advised, because the American public was fickle. Who could say how long they would be willing to pay good money to hear her sing and play the harmonica? Perhaps, he added, the stage was where she belonged.

Babe's sister Esther—whom everyone called by her middle name, Nancy—was there, too, softly saying, "Babe, honey, you can make a lot of money on this circuit."

Babe frowned and scratched her head. "Nancy," Babe said, "I don't want the money if I have to make it this way. I want to live my life out-doors. I want to play golf."

Golf was in some ways the least obvious choice for Babe—and the most difficult. There was no such thing as a women's professional golf tour. The few annual women's golf tournaments were amateur events that paid nothing. Most of the nation's women golfers relied on backing from their wealthy families or husbands. Babe had little in common with the high-class dilettantes whose ranks she wanted to join. These were well-groomed, well-mannered ladies from the finest families and smartest finishing schools.

But the prospect of a rough-hewn woman trying to make a life in that gilded world wasn't a problem for Babe. Nor was the will to do so. Even though she would have to prove herself the best golfer in the world, Babe always had the will to be the best. Not even the fact that she had relatively little experience bothered her. Hadn't she mastered everything she had set her mind to?

No, the true challenge at hand was far more basic. To conquer the world ahead, Babe would have to do the one thing she had never before tried. She would have to take stock of herself—all the celebrated quali-ties that had brought her more fame and honor than just about any woman alive—and then she'd have to do the unthinkable. Babe would have to change.

By March, Babe was behind the wheel of her Dodge with Momma in the front passenger's seat and Lillie in the back. They set out for California, in search of a new game for Babe to master.

One evening, at a Los Angeles driving range, a young golf instruc-tor named Stan Kertes was giving an exhibition. A trim man in his mid-twenties with slick, jet-black hair, Kertes had built a reputation as the trusted golf whisperer of Hollywood celebrities. He gave lessons to

Al Jolson, George Burns and Gracie Allen, the Marx brothers, Jack Benny, Bob Hope, and Bing Crosby, shaving strokes off the scorecards of some of LA's brightest stars. Harold Lloyd, one of the great comedic actors of the silent film era, asked Kertes if he could teach him to play well enough to card an even par of 71 at Rancho Park, his home course. Kertes trained Lloyd on the five greens and nine tees of Lloyd's private golf course on his estate. Each day, Lloyd's cameraman filmed his boss taking swings. The film was developed in Lloyd's laboratory and then shown in his projection room, a rare form of "dailies." Kertes dissected the mechanics of Lloyd's swing, giving him pointers and smoothing out his worst tendencies. In just eleven months, Lloyd shot a 71 at Rancho Park. "That was it," Kertes recalled. "He never hit another golf ball in his life. Not one."

Babe and Lillie were among the crowd of two dozen golf novices who attended Kertes's early-evening exhibition. They studied his demonstrations of how to hold a club and how to swing a driver, an iron, and a putter. Kertes thought that Babe looked familiar; he assumed she was the Olympic hero he had read about in the papers.

When the lesson was over, Babe walked right up to Kertes, introduced herself, and said, "Gee, you swing nice. Can you teach me that?"

"Sure," he replied.

Kertes liked Babe right away, admiring her warmth and honesty. He watched her hit a few long, powerful drives off the tee. He corrected her baseball bat–style grip, still unchanged from her outing at Brentwood. He said that if Babe was interested, he could teach her "basic foundation stuff." It wouldn't take too long, either.

"Yeah, but it costs too much money," Babe said. Kertes was getting paid $10 for six lessons in those days.

"I'll teach you for free," he replied.

On their first full day, Kertes let Babe borrow a new set of clubs from the driving range shop. He emphasized the importance of a firm left arm while swinging. The arm must remain straight throughout the swing, he explained, although it didn't have to be dead straight. "If the left arm bends just a little, that's okay," he told her, "and everything will be fine with the right arm too." After that first day, Kertes took Babe out to dinner, paying for that, too. Babe felt guilty about how well Kertes was treating her.

After dinner, she thanked him and said, "I'll see you."

"Do you want to quit?" he asked.

"No, I'd like to hit some more. But balls cost 50 cents a bucket."

"Come on," Kertes said. From the pro shop, he grabbed three or four buckets of balls and handed them to Babe. She hit until the lights on the range were shut off, just before midnight.

Kertes told her to come back the next day for more practice. Babe asked what time. "As early as you want," he said.

The next morning, Babe woke up before daylight. By 5:00 a.m., she was standing on the deserted driving range, practicing Kertes's tips: the grip, the stance, the rhythm of the swing. When Kertes finally arrived, he was surprised to see Babe there. Immediately grasping her stubborn determination, the promise in her long drives, the earnest way she did precisely what he told her, and even the imagination she applied to her shots, he canceled his paid lessons from that day forward to work exclusively with her.

That day, and nearly every day for months, Babe hit golf balls until her hands blistered and bled and had to be taped. "Babe used to hit a thousand, fifteen hundred balls every day," Kertes said years later. "We'd work until eleven o'clock at night." After about a week of practice, Kertes took Babe out for a round. He hit a long drive, but Babe outdrove him by at least thirty yards. "Right then," Kertes recalled, "I knew she had the makings of a champion."

By the early fall, Babe's game was steadily improving, but her savings had dwindled to almost nothing. So Babe packed up the Dodge and drove back to Beaumont. Yet again, Employers Casualty allowed Babe to return to her old job at her old salary, no questions asked. "Those people were wonderful to me," she later said. "There must have been four or five times when I had to come back to them, and always there was a job for me at $300 a month."

When she returned home, Babe was stunned to find Poppa lying on his back on the porch of the house on Doucette Street. Out of work and twenty-five pounds lighter than usual, he was suffering from a severe respiratory ailment. He needed a lung operation, fast. But the Didriksen family had no money or insurance to pay for it. Babe made some calls and learned that he could get a free operation at a university teaching hospital in Galveston.

Three days after his operation, Momma and Babe were visiting Poppa in his hospital room when the doctor walked in. "Mr. Didriksen, where's your pipe?" the doctor asked.

"I thought I wasn't supposed to smoke it," Poppa said.

"Get up and go sit on the porch and smoke your pipe," the doctor said.

A few days later, Poppa returned home, but it would be months before he'd be strong enough to work. Providing for the family fell to Babe, who realized that if Poppa didn't work, a portion of the $300 salary she was getting from Employers Casualty wouldn't be nearly enough to support the family.

As a result, she accepted a $1,000-a-month offer to play barnstorming basketball for an Iowa sports promoter named Ray L. Doan, who ran "baseball schools" for would-be ballplayers in Hot Springs, Arkansas, and Jackson, Mississippi. Doan was a short man with black hair, a touch of white flashing at his temples. He was forever rumpled, his necktie reaching only halfway down his wrinkled shirt. "Sports promoter" is a polite term for Doan's hustling profession. He was a man of elaborate gimmicks, such as staging coed baseball games and putting bearded players on donkeys in order to lure a small town's residents to come out to the local baseball diamond and pay to witness the nonsense.

Doan's idea was for Babe to be the headliner of a traveling basketball team of men and women to be dubbed Babe Didrikson's All-Americans. In fact, Babe was the only legitimate all-American, but that didn't matter to Doan.

Joining Babe on the team was an attractive woman named Jackie Mitchell, who had worked for Doan as a pitcher in several baseball exhibitions. The team played its first game in Doan's hometown of Muscatine, Iowa, then traveled throughout the upper plains and Midwest before winding up in New England. The ten team members crammed into a seven-seat sedan, traveling from small town to small town, where they played evening games against all-male local teams. Thanks to Babe's appeal, large, boisterous crowds turned out in high school gymnasiums and small auditoriums to watch the exhibitions. Babe Didrikson's All-Americans played a total of ninety-one games, winning about three-fourths of them. "We weren't world beaters, but we had a pretty fair bunch of basketball players," Babe recalled.

When the team arrived in St. Louis, the local newspaper reported on the "boyish bobbed" hairstyle that both Babe and Jackie Mitchell had. The paper described Babe as "wiry and physically hard," while Mitchell was "round-faced and...essentially feminine." They had no interest in men, except as teammates and competitors, the article reported. "Neither goes for that lovey-dovey stuff," added Harry Laufer, the team's business manager.

Each month, Laufer paid Babe $1,000 cash from gate receipts, a mammoth sum during the Depression, when many women were paid

$3 for a fifty-hour workweek. Babe's teammates were stunned to discover that she would go to the bank with the $1,000 in small bills, convert it into a single thousand-dollar bill, place that in an envelope, and mail it to Momma and Poppa back in Beaumont. "After we explained that this was a careless thing to do," Laufer said, "she finally made out a money order."

When the basketball season ended in early March 1934, Doan made arrangements for Babe to go to Florida to pitch in several major-league spring training baseball games. This was another guaranteed publicity generator and cash producer for Babe, who was paid $200 for each one-inning appearance. Babe started for Connie Mack's Philadelphia Athletics in a game against the Brooklyn Dodgers. She struck out the first two batters, but their wild swings, far from Babe's pitches, suggested they were a chivalrous gestures. She walked the third batter and hit the fourth with a pitch. The next batter smacked a sharp line drive to Dib Williams, the A's second baseman, who turned a triple play — "an honest one," reported the *New York Times*.

At a game in Bradenton, Florida, where the St. Louis Cardinals were based, Babe was the starting pitcher in a game against the Athletics. Before the game, Babe was in the stands chatting with Dizzy and Paul Dean of the Cardinals and Jimmie Foxx of the Athletics. Dizzy Dean challenged Foxx: "We'll pitch Babe against you, and I'll betcha that me and Paul and Babe can beat you guys."

So Babe started for the Cardinals. The first three batters each got a base hit. With the bases loaded, the next batter smacked a line drive into a double play, and no run scored. The next hitter was Foxx, who was a big home run threat. Foxx walloped a pitch into an orange grove on the edge of the outer reaches of left field. Paul Dean was playing left field, and he disappeared into the orange grove. A moment later, Dean emerged, holding up his glove for everyone to see: a baseball and five oranges were inside it. The umpire called it the third out. Babe had pitched an inning of shutout — wink, wink — baseball.

Babe had been such a smash in Florida that Doan made arrangements for her to become the headline act of the House of David, his most profitable barnstorming baseball team. She was easy to spot despite the chaos on the field. Her Jewish teammates wore dark, shaggy beards and long, unkempt hair beneath bright white caps. The audacious barnstorming club — a few former major leaguers, the rest knockabout semipro players — had been touring for nearly a generation. The team's shtick — the players' taboo looks of long hair and ratty beards were dictated by their devout religious beliefs — had packed small parks since 1915. Sometimes they'd try to persuade stubborn gray donkeys to carry them around the diamond, chasing after the ball, while "runners" urged their own animals to carry them from home plate to first base.

Now, chuckles aside, fans paid 75 cents to watch the only player without whiskers or four legs. They came to see Babe. She knew how to play baseball, and she knew how to make the men look silly. She threw the ball hard but hit it harder, and she usually struck out at least one man whose bat never left his shoulder. This outcome was preordained — the promoter made sure the opposing team didn't score any runs against Babe — but the fix didn't really matter. Babe still razzed the sourpuss boys on the opposing team. While winking at the crowd, she'd tell her opponents it was easier to beat them than the dumb old mule she was riding. The fans laughed.

"With a crowd, Babe, she'd really put out," said her manager, former major-league pitcher Grover Cleveland Alexander, who was also one of the team's pitchers and, besides Babe, the other reliable fan favorite. "The bigger the crowd, the bigger Babe's performance."

Night after night, in American towns and villages, from the orange groves of central Florida to the potato patches of western Idaho, crowds jammed neighborhood ballparks to watch Babe Didrikson's baseball team, even if the team wasn't named after her. It wasn't so much a ball club as it was a traveling circus act, crisscrossing the country in a bus while Babe drove herself in her car. Babe always started, pitching an inning, sometimes two. Before the game's end, Babe was back in her car, getting a head start to the next town.

"I was an extra attraction to help them draw the crowds," Babe said years later. "I was the only girl — and I didn't wear a beard. I didn't travel with the team or anything. I hardly even got to know the players."

"She was not all that good a pitcher, but she could hit," added Emory Olive, a House of David teammate. "If there was no crowd, she wasn't worth a damn."

In one memorable game at Logan Park in Minneapolis, before a crowd of more than nine thousand people, Babe hit an inside-the-park home run for the game's lone run. "Famous Woman Athlete Pitches for Whisker Team," a headline announced in the *New York Evening Post*. In one backwater town, a poster dubbed Babe the "donkey woman." The House of David press materials said that Babe possessed "a physique that the average high school or college male would envy.... One forgets that he is watching a girl, for there isn't the slightest semblance of anything feminine in her actions."

Playing a slate of nearly two hundred games, coming so soon after the ninety-one basketball games, emotionally and physically drained Babe. She was lonely, too. She carried a secret crush for one of the "whisker boys," but he never found out. There were so many games that they didn't mean much to Babe, except as a fine payday. Whereas the House of David players each earned $300 to $500 a month, Babe got $1,500.

But she was worth it. She dreamed up ways to keep her teammates and the fans laughing. At a game in Beatrice, Nebraska, local Dodge executives planned to give their ex-pitchwoman a surprise welcome. But the joke was on them: Babe had traded in her Dodge (plus $1,800) for another car. One teammate recalled, "The Dodge people were all set there . . . when we got there to play and here she drives into town in a *Buick.*"

And then there was the night in Yakima, Washington, when Babe was sitting just beyond the dugout in a folding chair. (She never sat in the dugout with her teammates.) A woman fan leaned over the railing and yelled, "Hey, sweetheart, where are your whiskers?" Without hesitation, Babe turned and shouted back, "I'm sittin' on 'em, sister — just like you are."

The crowd loved it, but that kind of moment was rare. On many evenings, especially when she tried to urge a donkey to carry her from home plate to first base, Babe felt as if her life had become a sad punch line. "Sometimes in those early barnstorming days," she remembered, "I wasn't sure if people were laughing with me or at me."

12

The Best Interest of the Game

My name had meant a lot right after the Olympic Games," Babe observed, "but it had sort of been going down since then." Two years on the barnstorming circuit had eroded her all-sport reputation. In many small towns, she had become a faded parody of a once world-famous athlete, someone to be mocked and ridiculed. "Fewer sporting figures ever thudded with the ravishing rapidity that la Didrikson did," a *Chicago Sunday Times* reporter wrote. Another Chicago paper labeled her "a virtual nobody."

Babe blamed herself for failing to find a way to safeguard her Olympic fame. "I hadn't been smart enough to get into anything that would really keep me up there," she said. Those days were "a mixed-up time for me." She had earned roughly $25,000 in the two full years following the Olympic Games. Although that was an enormous amount for a young woman during the Depression, by late 1934 Babe had only about $3,700 left. Much of her earnings had gone to her parents and siblings, and even to her nieces and nephews to help them pay for school. A big chunk had been used to pay Poppa's hospital bills when he was treated for his respiratory illness. She'd also bought a new Dodge for Poppa and a new bedroom set and kitchen stove for Momma. Some months, she had faithfully deposited a sizable chunk of her $300 Employers Casualty check into an annuity. Other months, during the basketball and baseball tours, she had deposited as much as $600 into it. But when her monthly income began to dwindle in 1934, she skipped several months, and the default on those payments ended up costing her the entire sum.

"I had to find some way to build my name up again, so I could make some money," Babe said. "There had to be money — not just for me but for the family."

There had to be money. There always had to be money. After the House of David tour, Babe tried tennis, figuring "there could be money in that — it's a sport where you can sell tickets and people can sit down and watch you play." Tennis was one of the few paying options available to women athletes in the 1930s. Babe practiced the forehand and the backhand but found serving to be nearly impossible. The cartilage she had torn in her right shoulder at the Olympics had never properly healed, and she couldn't serve with any consistency or without pain. All that was left was golf, the toughest game of all.

"Most things come natural to me," Babe told a reporter in 1933, "and golf was the first that ever gave me much trouble."

Poppa had taught Babe that in many circumstances, fables are better than the truth. Babe would tell a lot of tall tales about how she returned to golf. These stories were a way to appeal to writers, to make her golf comeback seem as magical as a teenage girl's three-medal triumph at the Olympics.

And the bigger the comeback, Babe figured, the bigger the fable needed to be. She told one story about having first tried golf with borrowed clubs at El Tivoli Golf Club in Dallas. After five miserable holes, Babe declared, she quit on the spot, labeling the game "silly." She couldn't understand why people would want to invest five or six hours a day "to hit a little white ball and then chase it." Her motive was to persuade people that she was a natural at a game that had for a long time carried no appeal for her. Another favorite tale was the claim that she did not play a full eighteen holes until her famous post-Olympics match with Grantland Rice and his pals at Brentwood. Prior to that, she explained, she had dabbled in the game fewer than ten times, never playing a full round, which was a lie. She also stated that the first time she held a club in her hands was in a Dallas sporting goods store. When she felt the shaft in her hands, she said, she just knew. She had to play.

Most of all, Babe portrayed herself as an accidental golfer, picking up the game—and mastering it—in a matter of hours as a small crowd watched, awestruck. In one version, Babe said that she just stopped by the Stevens Park Golf Course in Dallas with Colonel McCombs, who hit a bucket of balls on the driving range while Babe sat in his car and watched. Babe claimed that this was just McCombs's way of luring her into trying a game that had never interested her. Intrigued enough by what she saw, she sneaked out of the car and grabbed her own bucket of balls. The first ball she hit twisted like a pretzel, and she broke the club on a post. But her second shot "sailed out sweet and true, 264 yards."

Another story Babe told was that she got hooked on golf at a Dallas driving range, watching in astonished silence as nearly every golfer struggled to hit the ball well. "I had never paid much attention to golf," Babe liked to say in the telling. Watching those people hacking away, she had an epiphany: "I could do a lot better than any of them." Babe would go on to say that she borrowed some clubs and then swung and missed on her first attempt. Soon enough, however, she "hit a couple right and they went about two hundred yards." She then described hitting the ball such a long way that "the little Scotsman who ran the driving range came running up.... He was shouting." After a quick lesson from this clubhouse pro, Lefty Stockhouse (the preposterous name is a clue that this story is bunk), Babe said that she began driving the ball at least 250 yards, relishing the "sweet feeling" as she watched those dimpled white spheres soar high and far and true.

Despite the fact that each new story contradicted at least one earlier published account, eager sportswriters ran with them, repeating every word in their columns. Babe confided to friends that reporters were easy to snow; they wanted to believe the hokum she fed them. It was as her father had taught her — the more fantastic the story, the more they lapped it up. Besides, Babe knew that the truth was too often a messy bore. "Those stories about her driving the ball two hundred and fifty yards the first time she swung a club or about shooting in the nineties her first round — they are just not true," said Beatrice Lytle, the coach of Beaumont High's golf team, which Babe played on for two years. "She could out drive me after a while, it is true, but she never did beat me on the Beaumont course."

Another one of Babe's favorite golf stories was that she fell in love with the game in 1934 as she watched the great Bobby Jones, whom Babe called "a great idol of mine." There is some truth to this story, though quite a bit of fiction, too. Only a month after her House of David tour ended, Babe returned to Dallas and her old clerical job at Employers Casualty. She had begun taking lessons from George Aulbach, the club pro at the Dallas Country Club — lessons paid for by Employers Casualty.

After Babe heard that Jones was coming to Texas to play an exhibition at the Houston Country Club, she drove from Dallas to see him. Although the exhibition was shortened by rain, Babe and an adoring throng of hundreds watched Jones play several holes. Babe was amazed by his unflappable demeanor and cool confidence, making mental notes of how he methodically addressed the ball, the precise uniformity of every approach. *This* was how the game was meant to be played.

Babe also stood in awe of Jones's immense power. "Even in the short time I got to watch him,...I was impressed by the way he stepped up there on the tee and slugged the ball," she said. "He was out to hit the ball just as hard as he could. And that's always been my kind of golf.... Seeing Jones sort of fired up my own golf ambitions." Not quite true, of course. Her golf ambitions had long been fired up. Still, what a story—Bobby Jones had shown her that golf could be a way of life.

By the autumn of 1934, Babe felt sure enough in her game that she decided it was time to figure out what kind of golfer she really was. Her first test was the Fort Worth Women's Invitational, an amateur event that attracted the best women golfers from across the southern United States to River Crest Country Club. Reporters asked Babe how she'd do in the first round of her first tournament. "I think I'll shoot a 77," she predicted, a terrific score for the challenging course. Sure enough, she shot a 77. The *Dallas News* headline announced Babe's comeback:

Wonder Girl Debuts
In Tournament Golf;
Turns In 77 Score

Although Babe's score qualified her for match play, she lost in a head-to-head match the very next day. Her fairy-tale debut ended there. Still, her 77 caught the attention of the editors of *Golf Illustrated,* a large-circulation publication with a male-dominated readership. The magazine published a full-page picture of a confident Babe swinging a club. "Soon after this brawny lass so nearly stole the show at the Olympic Games of 1932, we were informed that she had taken a few swings at a golf ball with astonishing results," the caption reads. "For example, it was claimed that her first sock yielded 245 yards.... Now comes word from Dallas that Miss Didrikson is competing over her first tournament...and in the qualifying round had taken the medal with a 77 leading by five shots.... So we claim that her 77 is remarkable and *with experience gained in time,* this girl may be a national figure in golf." The italics seemed to hint that the editors were hedging their bets.

More valuable than Babe's first experience in a tournament was meeting a well-connected, wealthy Fort Worth couple named R. L. and Bertha Bowen, who took an instant liking to her. And why not? She was something you didn't see often inside a country club—brash, outspoken, risky, and *"fun,"* Bertha Bowen said years later. R.L. was president of Community Public Service, a power company, and his striking wife—about five feet six inches tall, with shoulder-length brown hair and matching wise eyes—was an influential member of a group that organized and ran women's golf in Texas. The Bowens were one of Texas's most powerful couples, and Bertha, whom Babe later called B.B., would become one of the most important and lasting friends in Babe's life.

Babe returned to Dallas for more practice. The Women's Texas Amateur Championship was scheduled for the third week of April 1935, and Babe knew that if she had any chance of establishing herself as a golfer, she needed to win that tournament.

"I settled into as tough a siege as I've ever gone through for any sports event in my life," Babe later said. Beginning in January, nearly four months before the tournament, she began a rigorous training regimen. Sure, she had "plenty to learn," but her commitment to winning the next tournament was pathological. "I only know of one golfer who practiced more than Babe," said Gene Sarazen, one of only five men to win golf's grand slam, "and that was Ben Hogan."

Every weekday, Babe woke up before the sun rose and hit balls at a

Dallas driving range for three hours before heading to work. During lunch, she ate a sandwich and spent the rest of her lunch hour in the office of her boss at Employers Casualty. His office was the only one with a carpet, and there she practiced putting on the carpet and chipped balls into the boss's leather chair. In front of a closet-door mirror, Babe stood and worked on her grip, following the advice of Stan Kertes and George Aulbach. Babe returned to her desk and worked until 3:30 p.m. She then went to the Dallas Country Club for a one-hour lesson with Aulbach. "Then I'd drill and drill and drill on the different kinds of shots," Babe recalled. "I'd hit balls until my hands were bloody and sore. I'd have tape all over my hands, and blood all over the tape." Babe practiced until the sun set, then went home, ate dinner, and climbed into bed and read, and reread, *The Rules of Golf,* the U.S. Golf Association's official rule book. Line by line, she tried to memorize the book. She didn't want to lose because she didn't know a rule. On weekends, Babe practiced twelve to fifteen hours a day, leaving her almost no time for anything else.

For nearly four months, Babe pursued this hyperpace. She was oblivious to the possibility that she wouldn't be allowed to participate in the tournament, in much the same way she had been unaware of the debate about women's participation in the Olympics when she began hurdling hedges on Doucette Street. She simply could not imagine that anyone would refuse her the chance to play.

But someone did. Babe's application for the Texas state championship was denied. The Women's Texas Golf Association had raised questions about the legitimacy of Babe's membership at the Beaumont Country Club. (Membership in a country club was a requirement of entry.) In fact, what the tournament organizers were really trying to do was find some excuse to exclude her. Many of the organizers objected to her blue-collar background and powerful style of play. Nearly all the competitors were members of Texas high society, wealthy wives of prominent husbands who didn't think someone as crass as Babe belonged at River Oaks Country Club, the upper-crust Houston club hosting the tournament. However, Babe's Beaumont Country Club credentials checked out—she was a fees-paying member—and she was reluctantly granted permission to play.

One of the most vocal opponents to Babe's participation was one of the Lone Star State's finest amateur golfers, Peggy Chandler, a finalist in the event for three straight years. She could not have been more different from Babe. A beautiful product of Dallas's high society and considered the most fashionable lady golfer on the circuit, Chandler blanched at the idea of Babe competing at River Oaks. "We really don't need any truck drivers' daughters in our tournament," Chandler said.

Babe heard about the comment, and the words hurt. But Bertha Bowen urged Babe to ignore the cattiness at River Oaks, which Bowen described as "a pretty swish place."

When Babe enthusiastically signed up for a pretournament driving contest, several women boycotted the event to protest Babe's participation. It wasn't just her background that bothered them. The women also believed that Babe's muscular physique should have disqualified her.

In response, at Bertha Bowen's urging, Babe decided to parody the driving contest. On the tee, she took intentional "girlish" swings that dribbled the ball no more than twenty or thirty yards. Many of the women watched with horror, though a few permitted themselves a giggle. The male caddies and a few dozen male spectators laughed out loud.

When Babe had just one shot left, she stopped the girlish act and took her usual big swing, smashing the ball 250 yards, easily far enough to win. For an encore, she stayed on the tee, slamming a few dozen balls with her usual powerhouse swing. No ball traveled less than 250 yards. The spectators cheered.

Babe just smiled and accepted a few handshakes of congratulations but said nothing. She really didn't have to. Those encore drives had said it all: *I'm here, ladies. Here to stay.*

The tournament began with nearly one hundred women competing in a single qualifying round. The top thirty-two finishers would face off in match play. Babe qualified by shooting an 84, five strokes behind Peggy Chandler's 79, the best score of the qualifier. Babe won her first match, six holes up with five holes to play. She won her next match even more easily, eight up with six to go. And she won her third match, 3 and 2 (three holes ahead with two holes to play). This qualified her for the semifinals, against Mrs. R. E. Winger of Fort Worth, one of the players who had skipped the driving contest.

The morning of the semifinals was overcast and windy, with a few stray sprinkles. Babe and Winger managed to play nine holes, with Babe leading by two holes, when heavy rain interrupted play. The women waited in the clubhouse for several hours before resuming on the tenth tee. The green was so drenched that Babe decided to use her pitching wedge to try to sink her putt, but she stubbed it short. Winger used her putter to win the hole. Babe's lead was cut to a single hole.

They stayed even over the next four holes, but Winger won the fifteenth to even the match. They halved the next two holes (meaning they finished each hole with the same score) and began the eighteenth with the match still all square.

Babe's drive was long, but it disappeared into a stand of tall trees along the right edge of the fairway. Winger's tee shot was not nearly as long as Babe's, but she managed to keep her ball in the fairway. On their second shots, Winger deposited her ball in a bunker, while Babe safely played hers back onto the fairway. On their third shots, they both put the ball on the green — Babe's twenty feet from the cup, Winger's twenty-three feet away.

The rain had stopped, but the green was soaked, requiring both women to putt with more power than usual. Winger made a lovely putt, but it stopped just inches shy of the hole. Babe, forced to hit uphill, slammed her putt, water drops spraying off the ball as it made its quick journey toward the flag. It kept going...and going...and then dropped in the hole.

The men and women in the gallery whooped and hugged one another. A few women even wept. "Babe smiled, walked off the green—still America's wonder girl athlete and probably the most promising woman golf player in the United States," Bill Parker of the Associated Press wrote. For the final match, scheduled the following day, Parker declared Babe the prohibitive underdog. After all, this was only Babe's second tournament, and she had to face Peggy Chandler, who had won the qualifying medal (for having the lowest qualifying round) and would be playing in the final for the fourth consecutive year.

Babe and Chandler knew that a lot more than the tournament trophy was riding on the outcome. This was a storybook showdown: the favorite a fashionable, genteel country-club woman from Dallas and the underdog a blunt, rough-looking woman from the wrong side of Beaumont. The favorite had bad-mouthed the underdog; the underdog had refused to go home. The favorite's goal was a comeuppance; the underdog's was revenge.

The skies were overcast, and the course was still slick and wet on Saturday morning, April 27, 1935. The forecast called for occasional showers, but tourney organizers were encouraged that the fairways and greens were not as waterlogged as they had feared. The women would play eighteen holes in the morning and another eighteen in the afternoon to determine the Women's Texas Amateur Championship—a test of endurance as much as skill.

A few paces from the practice putting green, the two players posed for a revealing photograph. In the photo, Babe is wearing a striped short-sleeved shirt and a long, slightly creased white skirt with black buttons. Her socks are rolled down to the tops of her black-and-white golf shoes; her pulled-back hair is a bit unkempt. Despite her trademark sideways smile, Babe looks tentative, uncomfortable. Chandler, by contrast, is the portrait of style and grace. She is wearing a navy blue short-sleeved top and a pressed white skirt, slightly shorter than Babe's but still reaching far past the knees. Her black socks are pulled up, and not a single hair in her bobbed hairstyle is where she doesn't want it to be. Her left hand rests jauntily on her left hip while clutching a starched white straw hat. Chandler, beaming a big smile, looks pressed, confident, and beautiful. Perhaps most telling, her right hand is resting on Babe's left forearm, a gesture signaling condescension.

On the par 5 first hole, Babe, who wasn't usually a fast starter, made an eagle 3. Chandler bogeyed the hole. Babe continued to win holes, using her long drives to set up easy approach shots. Throughout the front nine, as the sun attempted to peek through the clouds, Chandler's drives stopped rolling thirty or forty yards shy of Babe's, leaving her with longer, and often trickier, iron shots. Chandler's short game also suffered. She deposited her ball into several bunkers that she struggled to escape, and she missed several putts of ten feet or less. By the thirteenth hole, Babe had built an improbable five-hole lead.

But on the final six holes of the morning round, Chandler roared back just as Babe's game became unhinged. Suddenly, Babe's long drives were flying into the trees, and she missed several putts within five feet. Babe was exceptional at scrambling to get herself out of trouble, but she was failing to find the recovery shots needed to halve the holes. Chandler won six straight holes. When the women broke for lunch, Chandler held a one-hole lead. Inside the clubhouse, members of the gallery thought that Babe would not be able to recover from her back-nine collapse.

When Babe and Chandler emerged from the clubhouse, the sun was shining. Many of the fairways had dried out, although there were still small puddles in some of the hazards. Babe had settled down, making better recovery shots when she got into trouble. Chandler continued to play terrific golf. The women traded birdies on the fourth hole, then Chandler slowly began to pull away. By the eighth hole, she had built a commanding three-hole lead. On the eighth green, Babe sank a twenty-five-foot putt for a birdie. Chandler finished with a par, and Babe won her first hole of the afternoon. Her confidence surged. She was now two holes down.

Babe won the next hole, Chandler the one after that. Trading holes didn't help Babe, but she found a way to win the next two to draw even. The match remained tied until the sixteenth hole — the thirty-fourth hole of the final, a 500-yard par 5. The longer holes had favored Babe throughout the tournament. Chandler hit a straight tee shot about 210 yards. Babe's drive flew 250 yards, but it rolled into a ditch crossing the center of the fairway. Chandler's second shot was a smoothly hit two-iron that landed about 30 yards shy of the green's edge. Babe climbed into the ditch and used a three-iron to extricate her ball, but it soared over the green. Bad luck: the ball landed 20 yards beyond the green's back edge on a dirt road ringing the golf course. Worse luck: it splashed into a puddle in a deep tire rut. Babe was in bad shape, but Chandler's ball was farther away from the hole, so she hit first. Using a pitching wedge, Chandler left her third shot just a few feet from the cup, a short putt away from an almost certain birdie four. The pressure was on Babe, who knew the tournament would likely be decided by this swing. *I can't afford to lose this hole*, Babe thought. *I can't afford to lose any holes at all if I am going to win this golf championship.* Only the top half of Babe's ball was visible in the brown water in the rut. *You can't make any more mistakes. You've got to take your time and play this one just right.* Babe grabbed a sand wedge from her bag, a club given to her that spring by Gene Sarazen. She mulled over her instructors' advice: on this kind of shot, it was important to stand with nearly all her weight on her left foot. Then Babe remembered the first rule of golf that practically everyone had taught her: *Look at the ball real good.*

Babe swung. The ball leapt out of the rut with a splash of muddy water, bounced on the green, and slowed immediately with the faintest hint of a backspin. Babe could see her ball running straight for the flagstick. Then she heard a roar. Lady luck: an eagle three! It was a phenomenal, once-in-a-lifetime shot. People in the gallery rushed up to Babe from behind to congratulate her. In the melee, someone knocked her into the muddy rut, dirtying her hands and knees. Babe chuckled as several fans lifted her to her feet.

"The gallery just screamed and hollered," recalled Bertha Bowen, who had watched Babe's eagle from the green's fringe. "It was really something, because in those days you just did not do that on a golf course. You barely even clapped politely, but here was this little gal with all the ability in the world and people just *had* to hoot and holler for her."

With two holes to go, Babe was up by one. Chandler and Babe halved the thirty-fifth hole. On the last hole, another lengthy par 5, Babe was on the green in two shots, while it took Chandler three shots to get there. Babe left her ball just shy of the hole with her third shot, but Chandler, with no chance of winning the hole, conceded Babe the birdie and the match. By a margin of two holes, Babe was the most improbable Texas women's golf champion. When she was handed the trophy, she was asked how she felt now that she had won her first golf tournament. "On top of the world," she replied.

It had taken her a few years to get there, but Babe now believed that the Texas title was a launching pad to that year's national championship. In just two weeks, she would play in the Women's Southern Amateur in Louisville, Kentucky, her second stop on the amateur tour.

Peggy Chandler graciously congratulated Babe, but back in the clubhouse, many members of the Women's Texas Golf Association—the men and especially the women—were furious. How could *that woman* have won *our* tournament?

"Staging a sensational finish," wrote the *Houston Chronicle,* "the irrepressible Babe Didrikson Saturday rudely upset the polite circles of women's golf in Texas by defeating the veteran Mrs. Dan Chandler of Dallas two up to take the State title." The national press saluted Babe, but Paul Gallico, who was friends with Dan and Peggy Chandler, spoke glowingly of Peggy.

"Maybe Mildred was wearing her hat perched on the top of her head as she sometimes does, outraging Peg's esthetic sensibilities," Gallico wrote in his nationally syndicated column the following day. "Peggy is one of the few lady golfers I know of who knows how to dress. Or maybe it was Mrs. Chandler's neat and feminine clothing that made Didrikson mad. The Texas Babe seems to be working out a lifelong vendetta on sissy girls."

Naturally, Grantland Rice was brimming with pride, feeling more than just a bit proprietary about Babe's upset victory. He offered his readers this poetic salute:

> *From the high jump of Olympic fame*
> *The hurdles and the rest*
> *The javelin that flashed its flame*
> *On by the record test—*
> *The Texas Babe now shifts the scene*
> *Where slashing drives are far*
> *Where spoon shots find the distant green*
> *To break the back of par.*

Babe could have been forgiven for thinking that her victory might just help her gain acceptance into Peggy Chandler's rarefied world, or at least win her some respect, even the grudging kind. But neither of those things would come that quickly or that easily.

She is a pro. She must go. That was the message sent to the U.S. Golf Association (USGA) by Mrs. Willard Sullivan of Ashland, Virginia, the secretary of the Women's Southern Golf Association. The formal complaint, filed just one day after Babe's first tournament win, challenged Babe's amateur golf standing, arguing that if an athlete is a professional in one sport, the athlete must be considered a professional in every sport. The complaint asked that Babe be banned permanently from golf's amateur ranks.

The consequences were enormous. There were about a dozen women's amateur golf tournaments in America in 1935, but there was only one professional tournament, the Women's Western Open. A ruling against Babe's amateur status threatened to end her golf career before it really began.

Peggy and Dan Chandler had a friend on the USGA's Executive Committee, Charlie Dexter of Dallas. The Chandlers also were friends with Joe Dey, the executive director of the USGA. At the Chandlers' behest, Dexter and Dey worked behind the scenes to get the job done. Peggy Chandler even appealed to Dey directly, saying, "Joe, you aren't going to let Babe get away with this."

A verdict was returned in just two weeks. Archie M. Reid, chairman of the USGA's Amateur Status Committee, ruled that Babe was immediately banned from all amateur golf tournaments. With shades of Jim Thorpe's Olympic ban, the committee had concluded that Babe's professional standing in other sports — baseball, basketball, and billiards — barred her from amateur status as recognized by the USGA. Reid advised the southern association to reject Babe's entry in the Women's Southern Amateur in Louisville, although the USGA did not make that public at the time. The USGA also announced that Babe was barred from competing for the 1935 national championship. The decision was made "for the best interest of the game," Reid told the press.

The committee had used a nine-year precedent to reach its decision. Mary K. Browne, a former national tennis champion, had been barred from amateur golf for three years after the committee concluded that she had played professional tennis in exhibitions around the country. The rules were explicit: if an athlete is paid for competition in her chosen sport — or any other sport — she forfeits her amateur standing.

Inside one of Fort Worth's most sumptuous homes, the telephone rang. Bertha Bowen answered it and heard a small, broken voice: "Mrs. Bowen, I've just been ruled out of amateur golf. What should I do?"

13

Diamond in the Rough

Bertha Bowen went to war. She hired a lawyer for Babe, who sent a telegram to the USGA urging it to reverse its decision. She lobbied her friends in Texas to defend Babe's right to compete as an amateur. Ben S. Woodhead, president of the Beaumont Country Club, beseeched the USGA to grant Babe a full and fair hearing. All appeals were denied; the decision would stand. Across the country, Babe's fans were outraged.

"The biggest joke of the year," Jimmy Demaret, a three-time winner of the Masters, called it.

"The dirtiest deal I've heard of in a long time," said pro golfer Jack Burke Jr., who would go on to win the Masters and PGA Championship in 1956.

"Silly—a pity," declared Betty Hicks, the U.S. Women's Amateur champion who had recently turned pro. "They're throwing away the greatest boost they've had in amateur golf in years, simply because she had to live and found a livelihood in other athletic fields.... People know she can put the shot and jump the hurdles, but can she play golf?

That uncertainty packs 'em in. And the USGA turns down a peach of a chance to make some money."

Bowen was furious that a high-society woman in Dallas had caused Babe to be expelled from amateur golf. She knew these people — and their snobbery — all too well. "I was just furious at those people who had been so cutting to her," Bowen said. "The fact that she was poor and had no clothes did not mean she had to be ruled a professional." And now that they had seen that Babe could win, generosity regarding her admission had thoroughly evaporated.

What was most confounding was that Archie Reid, the man who had issued the USGA's decision, had approved Babe to play in the Texas championship the previous February. "The mere fact that Miss Didrikson is a professional in some other sport would not in itself bar her from amateur golf," he had written in a letter to the secretary of the Women's Texas Golf Association on February 18, 1935. So why, just three months later, had Reid decided to change his mind? Bowen and Babe's other allies knew that the formal complaint, which was lodged by a Dallas socialite close to Peggy Chandler, and the USGA's reversal had nothing to do with the fact that Babe had earned a few bucks playing professional basketball in a Brooklyn gymnasium or billiards in a Manhattan pool hall. Banishing Babe was intended to protect the game as the province of the wealthy and, at the same time, boost the chances of the high-society golfers to win future tournaments.

Without telling anyone, Bowen vowed to do everything she could to help Babe regain her amateur status and rejoin the world that had excluded her. But that wasn't all she wanted for Babe. Bowen also wanted that world to accept her, to *embrace* her. This wasn't a makeover; it was a do-over. And though that kind of overhaul would not be easy, Bowen had a few ideas. You might not be able to remove all of Beaumont's rough edges from Babe, but you sure could try to camouflage a few.

*   *   *

With the help of Bowen's lawyer and friends, Babe issued a muted response to the USGA's decision. "What the USGA says goes, and there's nothing I can do about it," she said. This diplomatic reply surprised reporters, who had expected Babe to complain as loudly and bitterly as she had when the AAU had banned her nearly two years earlier. But golf's leaders were a sensitive lot with long memories and an abiding faith in the rules. There was no tolerance for tantrums or troublemakers. If Babe graciously accepted their decision and served out her sentence, she was told, the USGA would be more amenable to approving her application for reinstatement as an amateur. Babe's — and Bowen's — strategy was smart.

Initially, the USGA said that Babe would be banned from competing in amateur golf tournaments for one year, so another motive for Babe's low-key response was the hope that the ban would be lifted after a year. But a month later, the USGA extended the ban to three years. Again Babe surprised everyone by praising the organization for "sticking to its rules." This was a new, polite Babe, one who was unrecognizable to the public.

"Of course, I was disappointed when they told me I couldn't compete as an amateur, but I admire them for barring me too," she stated. "They were big enough to adhere to their rules. And as it all turned out, I'm very happy." Babe expressed confidence that "women's golf" would continue to flourish. It even had a "greater future in this country than men's golf," she said.

"Golf is a game of coordination, rhythm and grace," she proclaimed. "Women have this to a much higher degree than men, as dancing shows."

The rules permitted professionals to apply for reinstatement of their amateur status, but only if they did so within five years of their last professional event. Then they had to endure three years without accepting any further payment for playing that sport. If they could do that, they'd win reinstatement.

The Women's Western Open, the lone tournament for professionals, was scheduled to be held in June, outside Chicago. At a May press conference in Dallas, Babe reintroduced herself to the public as a "business woman golfer." Back to the old Babe, she cockily announced her intention to win the Western. "They may as well wrap up the cup and give it to me now for I'm going to take it," she declared. She also announced that she had signed a $2,500-a-year contract with P. Goldsmith Sons, a Cincinnati-based sporting goods company that would manufacture a line of women's golf club in Babe's name, "just as if I was already Bobby Jones or something," she later said.

A day before the Women's Western Open, Babe won the tournament's driving contest, averaging nearly 260 yards per drive. With a gusty wind at her back, she smacked one ball 336 yards. She shot a 78 in the qualifying round, the best score in the field. But Babe, possibly pressing hard because of her prediction, played a sloppy quarterfinal round, spraying balls all over the course and failing to control her putter. She was eliminated.

Summer was coming, but Babe didn't have much to keep her busy except practice. Then she was presented with an irresistible idea by a thirty-year-old sports promoter named Fred Corcoran, the tournament manager of the PGA Tour who had traded that job to become the business manager of golfer Sam Snead and, later, many other athletes. How about going on a ten-week exhibition tour with Gene Sarazen? Babe had met Sarazen that spring at the U.S. Open, and he had given her the pitching wedge she'd used to beat Peggy Chandler. Corcoran believed that this unlikely pair could attract sizable galleries playing together against other pairs of golfers in a barnstorming tour of New England and the Midwest. Babe would be paid $150 per round.

The money was nice, but Babe was even more excited about the opportunity to learn by observing one of the world's finest golfers. Sarazen was the first man to win all four major championships in his career—the Masters, U.S. Open, PGA Championship, and Open Championship in Britain. At thirty-three, he was at the peak of his career and the height of his popularity. He had already headlined several exhibition tours, but usually with more established golfers than Babe. He agreed to hit the road with Babe because, as he put it, he had some downtime and was "just out to make a few bucks." Sarazen's wife joined them on the tour as Babe's (and Gene's) chaperone.

Their inaugural exhibition was at Tam O'Shanter Country Club in Niles, Illinois, where Babe and Sarazen faced the pro Johnny Rogers and Helen Hicks, one of the first women golfers to turn pro. Babe dressed up for the occasion in a too-formal dress and uncomfortable patent leather shoes. The long grass of the fairways made it difficult for her to move around, and she and Sarazen lost.

Within days, Sarazen could tell that Babe was more than worth the $150 per round she was being paid. The galleries were big and boisterous, and the crowds relished watching Babe's powerful drives off the tee. Some traveled 280 yards, and more often than not she outdrove Sarazen.

"She was still a big draw because of the Olympics," Sarazen said. "People wanted to come out and see this freak from Texas who could play golf, tennis and beat everyone swimming up and down the pool. She had a great outlook on life. She was quick with the needle."

Babe knew precisely what her role was. "Gene played the golf," she said, "and I put on the show." Their duet was something no gallery had witnessed—a traveling vaudeville act from the first tee to the eighteenth green. No one was safe from Babe's improvised barbs. She poked fun at Sarazen, whom she called "Squire," at the crowd, and, most pointedly, at herself. On the first tee of each exhibition, the announcer delivered a lengthy introduction of Babe's Olympic and barnstorming résumé and Sarazen's golf victories. When the announcer finished, Babe always asked, "Well, can we *play* now?" Then, after a long drive off the tee, Babe would ask the gallery, "Don't you men wish you could hit a ball like that?" The men would laugh, and the women would laugh harder.

Sarazen especially loved it when she made him the butt of some joke. When Sarazen sliced a ball into a stand of trees, Babe would tell the gallery, "Well, there must be a bottle of Scotch over there in those bushes." Babe was always smiling and laughing, and whenever Sarazen hit a rare bad shot, she would cackle at him. "She had a gift of playing to the gallery," he said. "It just came naturally to her."

This was truly a novelty act. In the mid-1930s, golf galleries had grown accustomed to players being deadly serious and ignoring them. Rarely, if ever, did golfers talk with members of the gallery; the fans were invisible. But Babe made them part of the action. People loved hearing a wiseacre woman with only one tournament win to her credit ridicule one of golf's greatest players. Even better, Babe encouraged members of the gallery to serve her questions; she then volleyed back spontaneous, often hilarious answers. Word spread quickly around the country's clubhouses that a ticket to a Sarazen-Didrikson exhibition was guaranteed fun.

Babe didn't just make people laugh with her mouth; she also used her clubs, performing an array of trick shots. One of her favorites was sticking her foot in front of the ball and hitting the ball with her putter, making it hop over her foot and into the cup. Babe would drop three or four clubs down on the green, separated by a few feet, and putt her ball so that, bouncing along, it hopscotched over all the clubs. On the tee, she'd set up five balls and drive them, rapid-fire, so that the fifth was launched before the first had stopped rolling.

At the Myopia Hunt Club outside Boston, Babe played eighteen holes, then walked into the clubhouse and challenged the president of the club to a game of tennis. She didn't have any tennis shoes, so she played him in her bare feet. "Can you imagine playing barefoot at Myopia?" Sarazen recalled years later. "She beat him, too."

Sarazen loved the hustler in Babe, who was always scheming for an easy angle or a quick way to squeeze a few extra bucks out of someone. One evening when Babe was in a bar, after a few bottles of beer, she started shooting craps against a group of men. Sarazen assumed that the gambling could only end badly for Babe, and he would feel responsible if she lost her day's pay to a bunch of hustlers. He tried to persuade her to leave with him.

"Squire, don't worry," Babe said. "I can beat these guys. I'm from Texas." And she did.

Besides all the kidding, Babe used Sarazen to help improve her game. Between matches and during a two-week break when Babe was the guest of the Sarazens at their estate in Connecticut, he coached her. "If I was going to be the best, I wanted to learn from the best," she said. "And he was the best in championship golf at that time."

Sarazen was impressed with Babe's natural swing, especially her powerful drives. "She had the rhythm; it was just as if she was throwing the javelin," he said. "She was very intense and wanted to learn." Babe carefully watched Sarazen's moves. After an eighteen-hole exhibition, she'd go back out and practice what she had seen him do. "She learned all her golf by watching," he said. "If she couldn't do it, she'd ask me about it. She was a very heady golfer. She was too much show business to ever develop a really sweet swing. She wanted to wallop the ball because that pleased the public."

The best woman golfer of the era was Joyce Wethered, the legendary British champion who Bobby Jones had declared was the best golfer, male or female, he had ever seen. Wethered's game was the opposite of Babe's; she relied on finesse. The combination of a balletic swing and an unbreakable concentration made her practically unbeatable. Five years in a row, she won the English Ladies Championship.

By the time she toured the United States, in 1935, Wethered was thirty-four years old and had retired from British amateur golf. The Great Depression had hit the rest of the world, and Wethered, who needed money for her family, turned professional and embarked on a tour.

"From a quiet house or a secluded part of a hotel," writer Enid Wilson said of Wethered, "she would come to the first tee, smile charmingly at her opponent when they met at the commencement of their game, and then, almost as though in a trance, become a golfing machine. She never obtruded her personality, and those who played her had the impression that they, the crowd and the state of the game had ceased to exist in her mind and that her entire faculties were being focused on swinging to perfection and holing the ball in the fewest number of strokes. The match concluded, Miss Wethered would vanish and be seen no more until the starter called her name for the next round."

On the eve of an exhibition match against Wethered at a club outside Chicago, Babe was presented with a new set of Goldsmith clubs emblazoned with her name. She had no time to try out the clubs and get comfortable with them. Although she could have used her old clubs for the round, she decided to break in the new set against Wethered. After all, Goldsmith was paying her $2,500.

Uncomfortable with the new sticks, Babe shot an ugly 88 to Wethered's 78. Babe "couldn't hit the ball at all," Sarazen recalled. "Was Babe upset about losing to Joyce? Naw." Babe told Sarazen that the fat endorsement deal more than made up for the humiliating defeat. "Squire," she said, chuckling, "I got me some *do-re-mi*. Watch me from now on, boy."

Their tour ended in early September 1935. Babe had saved about $2,700, a bankroll that she knew from experience wouldn't last long. In Octo-

Ole and Hannah, Babe's parents, were first-generation Norwegian immigrants who noticed their youngest daughter, even as a baby, knew precisely what she wanted and never hesitated to tell you. "I'm afraid no crib I can build is going to hold her," Ole told Hannah. (Babe Didrikson Zaharias Collection, Lamar University)

Along Doucette Street in Beaumont, Texas, Babe, Arthur ("Bubba"), and Lillie gather for a photograph taken by their father. Babe is wearing shoes, though, like her siblings, she often scampered barefoot around Beaumont's south side. (Babe Didrikson Zaharias Collection, Lamar University)

Babe was a star Beaumont High School basketball player before becoming a two-time all-American for Employers Casualty Insurance Company of Dallas. She is guarded by Royal Purples teammate Jackie Bridgewater. (Babe Didrikson Zaharias Collection, Lamar University)

A "one-girl track team," Babe soars over the final hurdle in the lead of the 80-meter hurdles, one of five events she won on July 16, 1932, that gave Employers Casualty the national AAU championship at Dyche Stadium in Evanston, Illinois. Still considered the greatest single-day performance in women's track-and-field history, Babe's wins secured her a slot on the U.S. Olympic team. (Bettmann Archive / CORBIS)

"I felt like a bird," Babe said later of this easy jump over the high hurdle at the Olympics on August 7, 1932. In the most controversial decision of the Los Angeles games, the judges later disqualified Babe for her western roll jumping style, denying her a three-gold-medal sweep and forcing her to settle for the silver medal. (Babe Didrikson Zaharias Collection, Lamar University)

Dallas celebrates Babe's Olympic triumph by throwing her a parade on August 12, 1932. The fire chief's red limousine carries Babe and her sister Lillie—and a blanket of red roses—through the downtown streets lined with fans and well-wishers. (Bettmann Archive / CORBIS)

One of the more humbling sideshow detours taken by Babe was her stint on the barnstorming House of David baseball team, playing donkey baseball and often attracting vicious catcalls from the stands. (Babe Didrikson Zaharias Collection, Lamar University)

Golf pro Stanley Kertes demonstrates the proper grip to Babe at Riviera Country Club in Los Angeles in June 1933. Babe later credited Kertes with being her most influential golf instructor. (Bettmann Archive / CORBIS)

Near the practice green at the River Oaks Country Club in Houston, Babe and her opponent, Peggy Chandler, pose for a photograph before Babe's upset victory in the Women's Texas Amateur Championship of 1935. Days later, friends of Chandler, the three-time tournament champion, launched a successful challenge of Babe's amateur status with the USGA. (Bettmann Archive / CORBIS)

Before a raucous gallery during a November 1937 charity match at Fresh Meadow Country Club in Lake Success, New York, Babe, who was paired that day with Babe Ruth, pulverizes a tee shot, proving she can match the Bambino for power. (Bettmann Archive / CORBIS)

Flanked by Bing Crosby and Bob Hope, Babe watches Patty Berg drive off the first tee at a charity tournament at San Gabriel Country Club in Los Angeles County in January 1940. (Bettmann Archive / CORBIS)

After becoming the first American to win the British Women's Amateur, on June 12, 1947, Babe and her husband, George, dance the Highland fling for reporters aboard a press tugboat in New York Harbor. (Bettmann Archive / CORBIS)

Bill "Tiny" Scurlock, the Beaumont sports columnist and editor and longtime booster of Babe's athletic career, visits his friend at the Hotel Dieu Hospital in Beaumont in April 1953. (Babe Didrikson Zaharias Collection, Lamar University)

Betty Dodd, a young pro golfer from San Antonio, Texas, helps Babe unpack at her Tampa home in July 1953 after her first stay in the hospital. Dodd was Babe's closest friend in her later years—some, including George, suspected and whispered that they had an intimate relationship. (Bettmann Archive / CORBIS)

After winning by twelve strokes, Babe hoists the U.S. Women's Open trophy at Salem Country Club on July 3, 1954. The tournament's first three-time champion, Babe considered the win among the greatest of her life and one that she shared with everyone who had prayed for her recovery and comeback. (Bettmann Archive / CORBIS)

On June 26, 1956, Babe celebrates her forty-fifth birthday at a surprise party thrown for her by George in a lounge at John Sealy Hospital in Galveston, Texas. She would die of cancer there three months later. (Babe Didrikson Zaharias Collection, Lamar University)

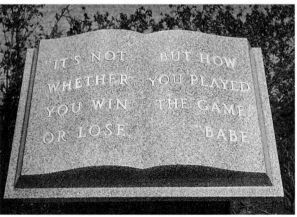

Across the street from Beaumont Country Club is Babe's final resting place at Forest Lawn Cemetery, which is marked with this memorial engraved with words Babe neither said nor believed. (Babe Didrikson Zaharias Collection, Lamar University)

ber, she had another professional tournament to play, thanks to Bertha
Bowen. Every fall, Bowen and her friends staged the Fort Worth Wom-
en's Invitational, a three-day amateur event. This year, they decided to
change it into an event open to amateurs and professionals. The tourney would be christened the Women's Texas Open, only the second
women's competition in the United States to welcome professional golfers. The change had been made to accommodate Babe.

Bertha Bowen invited Babe and another golfer, Helen Dettweiler, to
stay with her during the tournament. When the two women pulled up
in front of the Bowens' fine house in one of Texas's wealthiest neighbor-
hoods, Babe "sat out in the car for a long, long time" before she felt
comfortable enough to knock on the front door. She still wasn't sure
she belonged with these people, but Bowen immediately put her at
ease. Babe ended up staying for three weeks.

The Women's Texas Open was played at Bowen's home course,
River Crest Country Club. Prior to the tournament, Babe met A. G.
Mitchell, River Crest's professional, who admired Babe's grit and honesty and dubbed her "a diamond in the rough." Bowen liked that. "It's
true she did things that were a little bit rough," she said, "but she was
sincere. And she was grateful, too."

An unruly driver caused Babe to bow out in an early round. But more
important, during her three weeks in Fort Worth, she bonded with
Bertha and R. L. Bowen. The couple was childless, having lost an infant
son to an illness in 1930. Babe was quickly becoming something of a
surrogate daughter or younger sister to Bertha. Years later, Babe would
say that Bertha and R.L. were "like my godmother and godfather."

Babe and R.L. shared a love of competition — or, more precisely, a
love of winning. In the middle of the night, Bertha would be awakened
by the racket that R.L. and Babe made as they laughed and argued over
their cutthroat games of pool on the Bowens' billiard table.

"You go to bed," Bertha would tell them. "It's late."

"I can't quit 'til I win, B.B.," Babe would say.

Babe became a project for Bertha. Her behavior and tastes were odd and often off-putting. For lunch she ate a can of pork and beans or an onion sandwich, washed down with her favorite drink, strawberry soda. For dinner, she rarely ate a proper meal. She seemed content to get most of her nourishment from chewy banana candy.

Bertha tried to encourage Babe not to be shy around the women at the Bowens' country club, to flash her usual biting humor. But she was almost painfully bashful, intimidated by the women she was sure were judging her harshly. "If you have once been poor, you never really feel that being rich is quite, well, quite natural," Bertha said. "It's hard to break into society when they don't want you."

A far bigger hurdle was Babe's glaring lack of money. She "was so poor it was pitiful," said Bertha, who watched Babe wash her single good dress every evening. How could Babe win acceptance from the country-club set wearing the same old blue checked dress? (Indeed, in her 1955 memoir, *This Life I've Led,* Babe is wearing that dress in three photographs.) When the Bowens were invited to a formal party during the tournament, they asked Babe to join them. "She hemmed and hawed because she didn't have any clothes," Bertha said. "Well, we got her an evening dress." Babe felt it looked like a garish costume. "I'm not going to wear that naked thing," Babe yelled. Bertha finally cornered her in the kitchen and forced her to try it on.

Some of Bertha's country-club friends were furious: not only had she befriended Babe, but she had made Babe a full-time pet project. "Why are you fooling around with *that girl?*" they'd ask, refusing even to say Babe's name. Once they knew Bertha wasn't going to change her mind, they tried to persuade *"that girl"* to wear a girdle on the course. Babe refused. The one time Bertha convinced her to try it, she heard Babe's car screeching into her driveway just minutes after she had left for the club. "Goddamn, I'm choking to death," Babe hollered, rushing to her room to yank off the girdle. She never put one on again.

But Babe embraced Bertha's other fashion tips, allowing her hair to grow out and be styled in a nice wave. For hours, like a schoolgirl, Babe would sit in front of Bertha's makeup mirror, experimenting with different colors and shades. Babe "was eager to be proper," Bertha said. She began painting her fingernails red, and after much cajoling, Bertha persuaded Babe to go shopping at Neiman Marcus, where Bertha spent $700 on a new wardrobe for her. Babe was so touched she wept.

Golf was a "genteel sport," golfer Betsy Rawls said. "It was probably the most respectable sport for women there was in this country. Golfers were a very refined group. Being in that group gave Babe instant respectability in her eyes."

But Babe wanted more than respect; she wanted to belong. And the lure of money and fame was more than enough incentive for her to change her image and her behavior.

Her makeover now complete—or as complete as it would be—Babe returned to southern California, this time with her parents, Lillie, and her younger brother, Bubba. They found an unassuming two-bedroom duplex in West Los Angeles with a fold-down bed in the living room and a cramped kitchen. The rent was $27 a month. Each morning, Momma awakened Babe, served her breakfast, and told her, "Now go play your golf." Babe resumed taking lessons from Stan Kertes. Many days, she'd hit balls at a driving range from midmorning until after dark. Many nights, the owner would keep the lights on past closing time for her. Crowds came to watch Babe smash the ball.

The Goldsmith company booked Babe some exhibitions in California; Stan Kertes joined her on a few. The tour was a good way for Babe to show off her new look to sportswriters. She wanted her transformation saluted, or at the very least noted.

Paul Gallico observed the new Babe at an exhibition in Ohio. "I hardly knew Babe Didrikson when I saw her," he said. "Hair frizzed and she had a neat little wave in it, parted and prettily combed, a touch of rouge on her cheeks and red on her lips... The tomboy had suddenly grown up." Gallico sat with Babe on a golf course bench, just off the first tee, and was pleased that she spoke "shyly, with infinite femininity."

"I got 'em," Babe suddenly told Gallico, as she "lifted the edge of her tweed golf skirt to disclose the silk-and-lace undergarment beneath. Then she opened her handbag and let me peer at the usual female equipment of lipstick and compact, eye shadow and lace handkerchief. She had gone all the way and was delighted with it."

Henry McLemore, the senior sportswriter for the United Press, was stunned when he first set eyes on her at an exhibition in early 1937. "The Babe was just a sweat-shirty Texas gal then," McLemore said, describing his previous meeting with Babe in 1931. "Her hair is worn in a soft brown, curly cluster about her face. Her figure is that of a Parisian model. Her tweeds have the casual authority of New Bond Street and her ruby red nails were a creation of Charles of the Ritz."

At last, the sportswriters approved: now *this* was a woman. Never mind that Babe had obviously plotted her metamorphosis as a way to win acceptance from them, the country-club women, the USGA, and everyone else. Her goal was a golf career. Yet whispers and rumors that Babe was a lesbian persisted. A few people even wondered whether Babe had changed to catch the eye of a woman she had begun fancying. Two decades later, in her autobiography, Babe denied that she had "switched over to being feminine" as some "sudden" and cynical ploy. And she offered girl athletes this piece of advice: "I am afraid that the only real first class advice I can give is get toughened up playing the boys' games, but DON'T GET TOUGH. There's a lot of difference there." In her book, she brazenly reinvented her history, saying that she'd had a number of boyfriends as a teenager in Beaumont and several suitors in Dallas, though most of her friends later refuted this, and there is no evidence to support it. "For a while," Babe insisted, "there were two that were fighting each other." She even claimed that she'd had the opportunity to marry several men—one an unidentified professional ballplayer (not, apparently, the House of David teammate on whom she'd had a crush), whose heart she had broken. But she'd had no time for romance, Babe claimed—"too busy working on my sports career."

Now she was twenty-six years old. Most of the men in the press box said, *Maybe, just maybe, we had Babe all wrong.*

14

The Girl, the Minister, and the Wrestler

Outside the clubhouse at the Griffith Park Golf Course, Babe was limbering up for the Los Angeles Open, a PGA Tour event that was truly open. Players did not need to qualify, and there was no rule barring the participation of women. Nevertheless, no woman had tried to play with the men until a promoter had come up with the idea and decided the first should be Babe. "I knew I wasn't going to beat the top men pros," she recalled, "but I was still trying to establish myself as the greatest woman golfer."

As she took her practice swings, Babe knew something else: she wasn't the only golfer "who didn't have any business" playing in the first PGA tournament of 1938. She was assigned to a threesome with C. Pardee Erdman, a Presbyterian minister who was a professor of religion at Occidental College in Los Angeles, and George Zaharias, a big-time professional wrestler whose nickname was "the Crying Greek from Cripple Creek." It was the minister's and the wrestler's first PGA

Tour event, too. Babe described the unlikely threesome of part-time golfers as "the girl, the minister and the wrestler."

When George heard he was playing with Babe, he considered dropping out. Think of it: George Zaharias, the nastiest villain in all of wrestling, was going to have to suffer the indignity of playing golf with…a *girl?* "Well, I knew she was good, for a girl," George later said, "but I figured I would be paired for that first round with some of the big pros, [Walter] Hagen maybe, to draw a crowd. I was always crowd-conscious.…I was paired with a girl and, hell, I didn't want to go out there with a girl, no matter what girl."

George, with an 8 handicap, was a very fine player. A few of his friends had encouraged him to play in the event after he had broken 80 in December 1937. His friends talked him out of skipping the 11:00 a.m. tee time. When he arrived, he was introduced to the other two members of his threesome.

"George," sportswriter Braven Dyer said, "here's your partner today. Meet Babe Didrikson."

"Hi, Babe," said George, as he shook her hand.

"Hi, George." Babe beamed her slightly crooked grin at this husky bear of a man with the slicked-back, jet-black hair, deep-set dark eyes, and meaty hands that felt like well-worn catcher's mitts. At twenty-nine, George stood 6 feet tall and weighed 230 pounds, mostly muscle. He was in the best condition of his life.

Cameramen asked Babe and George to pose for a few pictures. A photographer suggested that George place Babe in a mock wrestling hold. He wrapped his arms around her, pretending to apply a neck hold.

"Am I holding you too close?" George asked, laughing.

"No," Babe said with a smile. She didn't mind at all.

At another photographer's urging, Babe put George in a neck hold. She liked that, too.

Both the men and the women were required to tee off from the same tee box. Babe smashed a drive about 250 yards down the center of the fairway. George's tee shot was also straight and far, rolling about 30 yards past Babe's. "Say, fella," Babe said, "you must be a player."

They marched up the fairway, stealing glances at each other. The attraction was mutual and instantaneous. George felt the electricity buzzing around them.

On the sixth or seventh hole, Babe walked up the fairway, a few paces ahead of George. She peeked coyly over her shoulder at him. "What are you looking at?" Babe asked.

"I'm looking at you.... Say, you know you're my kind of girl."

"Well, that's good enough for me — you're my kind of guy."

They were so much alike. Both were first-generation children of dirt-poor immigrants who generously helped their parents financially. Both were show people and hustlers who knew how to entertain a crowd and the press. Both carried oversized appetites for fame and money. The biggest difference was how they competed. After all of those years of donkeys and make-believe major-league strikeouts, Babe's performance was now the real thing, whereas George's was a well-honed piece of performance art. In the 1930s, his character, "the Crying Greek from Cripple Creek," was the most dastardly villain in all of American wrestling. George was a scowling thug whom the fans reviled. "The fans... pay money to see me wrestle," he often said, "probably in the hope I'll get my neck broken." Fans relished watching George get pummeled into the mat, and he always took a bad beating. Toward the end of each match, George wept in the ring, the tears rolling down his fat cheeks while he begged pitifully for mercy. His tears were real. George could cry real tears just by remembering some heartbreaking moment from his childhood. There were so many to choose from.

George was born Theodore Vetoyanis in Pueblo, Colorado, in 1908.

He was the oldest son of Gus and Dimitra Vetoyanis, immigrants from Tripoli, Greece, who had arrived in America the year before Ted was born. Gus's first job was in a Colorado steel mill, but he and his wife soon went to work for a rancher on a farm outside Pueblo. The work was more difficult and the hours longer than at the steel mill, but they earned a bit more money. The Vetoyanis family lived in a one-room adobe hut with a dirt floor. Because he was the oldest and both parents were gone for twelve to fourteen hours each day, George was put in charge at the age of nine. There wasn't much food, often just Greek bread, and never enough to satisfy the appetites of four children. "I always remember our being in a starved condition," said George's younger sister, Joan. "As young as he was, George knew that he had to keep us going day in and day out." George and his siblings softened the hard Greek bread by dipping it in black coffee, but that didn't taste good to little Tom, George's youngest brother. "One day George came up with the idea of mixing olive oil, vinegar and salt and pepper in a bowl and beating it with a fork," Joan recalled. "He then taught us to dip our bread into it, and to this day I can remember how good it tasted."

In his teens, George was a shoeshine boy before moving to Oklahoma City to work for his uncle's hat-cleaning business. At the age of sixteen, he dropped out of high school, surviving on the dollar bills he made hustling pool games. At the age of nineteen, he was in Chicago with only a dime in his pocket when he saw a sign outside a gym: WRESTLERS WANTED — 1 DOLLAR A DAY. He trained for two years using the name Ted Victory. His first match, in South Bend, Indiana, did not go well. Ted Victory was the wrong name for a wrestler who appeared wobbly and insecure in the ring and, despite his 235-pound bulk, proved as easy to frighten as he was to hurt. "After one year, I still knew nothing about wrestling," George recalled. "I hadn't earned a quarter, but I had earned this big cauliflower ear." So he traded wired wins for wired losses and changed his moniker again. This time he chose George Zaharias, borrowing the surname of his late grandfather.

George was sent to Texas to wrestle on the "gasoline circuit," so called because the matches were often separated by hundreds of miles, usually covered by car or bus. One evening in 1931, George happened to be in Beaumont for its Match of the Month. The arena was practically empty.

"How come such a lousy turnout?" George asked the promoter.

"Babe was in a basketball game tonight, George. That's always a tough break for us."

"Babe who?"

"Haven't you heard about Babe Didrikson?"

"No," George said, "tell me more."

Beginning in the 1920s and especially during the Depression, professional wrestling was big business across America. The ring proved to be an irresistible and inexpensive lure for people looking for a cheap evening of entertainment. There were two kinds of wrestling matches featuring two very different kinds of wrestlers. There were the real wrestlers — outstanding athletes known as "shooters," whose competitions were real. But the public wasn't much interested in on-the-level matches by dozens of men whose names were hard to remember. The shooters drew at best modest crowds. Then there were the wrestling showmen, who were more of a vaudeville act than anything else. The showmen were fictional characters with catchy nicknames that usually reflected fanciful backstories. Much of what went on in the ring was scripted by promoters, who determined each match's winner. The showmen earned a hundred times more than the shooters.

"George was one of the best of the showmen," said Sid Marks, a friend of George's who headed security at the Horseshoe Draw Poker Club in Los Angeles. "He was probably the best villain in the business....He was a great actor—there were no actors like him in wrestling." The *Chicago Tribune* called him "the foremost ham of the wrestling art."

By the mid-1930s, George's bad-guy act was cherished by so many fans that he was regularly headlining the cards at the Grand Olympic Auditorium, the biggest venue in Los Angeles. Seated in the first few rows were film actors such as Jack Holt, Ralph Bellamy, Edmund Lowe, and Victor McLaglen, all there to see George do his crying act.

In the ring, George used every conceivable crooked (though phony) trick against his opponents — sticking his thumb in their eyes; kicking them in the head while they were on the mat; biting them on the legs, arms, and even feet. George ridiculed members of the audience, raising his middle finger at the booing, hissing fans and mocking their taunts. Each match began with George appearing to cruise to a quick victory, but inevitably his bowed opponent would make a remarkable comeback and begin beating him to a pulp. Near the end of each match, he would turn from scoundrel to coward. He'd whine, tremble, cajole, and beg his opponent — and the crowd — for forgiveness, which was never delivered. Finally, the Crying Greek from Cripple Creek (a town about forty miles from Pueblo) would shed real tears.

George was so popular a draw that he was paid as much as $15,000 for one night of work. Despite the sham wrestling, however, he sustained real injuries. Once, the aptly named Man Mountain Dean, a towering, three-hundred-pound behemoth, broke George's arm. Six weeks later, George and Man Mountain faced off in a highly anticipated rematch. This time, Man Mountain tossed George into the arena's fourteenth row, breaking his leg.

By the time he met Babe, George was still wrestling, but he was also beginning to promote events, an occupation carrying the promise of even bigger paydays. Backstage before a match, George would tell each competitor whether he was going to win or lose. Sometimes a wrestler didn't want to do what he was told, and George would use Sid Marks as an emissary. "You want to *win,* you think? Forget it," Marks would say. "Ask yourself another question: Do you want to *work?* You do? Then do as you're told to do. *Lose.*"

Midway through their first round at Griffith Park, it was clear to George that he had no chance of qualifying for the final thirty-six holes. Perhaps the large gallery following the odd threesome distracted him. Or perhaps it was Babe.

George quietly set two goals for himself: charm Babe Didrikson, and don't let her win. He narrowly achieved the latter, carding an 83 to Babe's 84. (Pastor Erdman defeated them both with a 75.) He was also successful in his pursuit of the former. "We kept jokin' with the preacher," George said, "that maybe he'd just have to up and marry us — we were getting along so well."

On the eighteenth green, George invited Babe and the pastor to join him for a few drinks on the clubhouse patio. As Erdman and Babe sipped Cokes, George drank bottles of cold beer. George and Babe talked for a long time, but Babe finally excused herself, saying she had to go home because her mother and sister were waiting with her dinner.

"I'll be seeing you tomorrow," George said.

Their play didn't improve the following day, and they missed the cut. George asked Babe to join him for a steak dinner at his apartment, which he shared with his two younger brothers. Babe phoned home to tell Momma and Lillie she was going out on a date. They were both surprised and thrilled by this news. George and Babe left Griffith Park driving their own cars. Babe followed George, but he noticed in his mirror she made a left turn she wasn't supposed to make. He quickly turned around to chase after her. When he caught up to her, he asked, "Are you trying to run away from me?"

"Of course not," said Babe, blushing.

At George's apartment, Babe met his brothers. While George broiled steaks, the Zaharias brothers, who were also wrestlers, put a few playful holds on Babe. George watched his brothers "pretty close to see that they didn't get rough with me," Babe said. "Which they didn't, of course."

During dinner, Babe and George made plans to watch the third round of the Los Angeles Open. The next day, after a few hours on the other side of the ropes, he asked her if she'd like to go out dancing with him that night. "Sure," Babe said, "I love to dance."

That evening, George came by Babe's apartment, and he met Momma and Lillie. "Momma liked him straight off," Babe said. Before George and Babe left for the evening, Momma reached up and patted George on the cheek. "My Babe likes you," she told him.

At the Cotton Club, the LA spin-off of the famous New York City hot spot, Babe and George danced for hours, stopping only for a few drinks (Babe also liked to drink beer) and to get their pictures sketched in charcoal. It was Babe's idea to sign her portrait and give it to George. He then signed his and gave it to her. It was past one o'clock when George finally dropped her off.

"Babe, you're out late," Momma said. "I was worried about you."

"Oh, Momma, it's all right. George and I wanted to do some dancing."

"Well, that's fine. He's a nice man."

From there, Babe said, they began "going together real steady." George gave Babe a new nickname — "Romance." She liked that, too.

After suffering years of disguised loneliness, Babe was in love. Perhaps not surprising — given how long she'd waited and the couple's athleticism — in those early days their sex life was "searing," Babe's friends said. In the mid-1940s, Babe was asked by a newspaper editor in Los Angeles, "Of all the records you've broken and all the events you've won, what was the single most thrilling experience of your life?"

"The first night I slept with George," she replied, prompting a ripple of shock. (Although such a response was typical of Babe, most women of that era did not talk so openly about sex, even among their closest friends.)

In those early days, Babe and George had one problem—finding time to be together. Conflicting schedules often pulled them apart, and she hated to be away from him, even for a day. In the late winter, Babe, Momma, and Lillie drove to Phoenix to visit Babe's sister Dora. Their plan was to stay a few days, then drive to Beaumont to visit Poppa. The trip would keep Babe and George apart for a few weeks. But the farther Babe drove from California, the more she missed him. When they reached Dora's house in Phoenix, Momma knew something was wrong. "You want to go back to California, don't you?" she asked Babe.

"Yes, Momma, I do. Would you and Lillie mind taking the train the rest of the way to Beaumont?"

"Yes, we'll take the train. You go on back and see George."

When she arrived at George's Los Angeles apartment, his brothers were there but George was gone. He had left a note: "Romance, I'm in San Francisco." If that's where George was, that's where Babe wanted to be. George's brother Chris drove her to San Francisco. The 460-mile trip took all night. When they knocked on George's door at the St. Mark's Hotel, "he came out and said, 'Come here, Romance,'" Babe recalled. "He gave me a big kiss. And then I wasn't lonesome anymore."

When Babe played in an exhibition in Cincinnati early that spring, George—Babe was now calling him "Romance," too—switched his schedule to be with her, becoming, for the first time, "a galleryite." In May, George's bookings took him on the road, and they did not see each other again until June, when they got together at the Broadmoor hotel in Colorado Springs, about forty miles from George's parents' home in Pueblo. Babe was scheduled to play in the Women's Western

Open, in Colorado Springs. Before the tournament, George introduced her to his mother and father. "His mother didn't speak too much English," Babe recalled, "but she and I got along fine just the same."

The Women's Western Open was one of only two professional events that Babe was eligible to compete in that year. The stakes were high, but she was eliminated in the semifinal round. "That particular summer," she later said, "losing a golf match didn't seem to matter as much to me as it ordinarily did."

George and Babe found an apartment in St. Louis, where George was wrestling often and had begun his promoting business. On July 22, 1938, George told Babe, "I bought this diamond, you know, a two-carat ring. This will make some girl happy."

"That would make me happy," Babe replied.

George slipped it on her finger. Babe kissed George and asked, "When?"

"Five minutes from now?" Impossible: they both wanted their families by their sides.

Weeks, then months, passed. Babe and George were busy with their appearances; they were apart more than they were together. They managed to go to Beaumont, where Babe introduced George to Poppa and Tiny Scurlock. Because George had wrestled often in Beaumont, Tiny had written about him. Tiny and Ruth Scurlock had dinner with George and Babe at the home of a Greek friend. Babe drank too much ouzo and began slurring her words. "George moved right in and took care of her, so fondly and so gently for such a giant," Ruth recalled. "Babe seemed to love that, she seemed to like to play 'the little woman,' to have someone there to protect her and defend her. It was a role she had never played before."

In December, they were both in St. Louis and still had no wedding date set. "We're going to get married this week," George said, "or call the deal off."

This was not a suggestion; it was an ultimatum. Babe could take it or leave it. "It's a deal," she said. "Let's go." And the pattern that they'd follow throughout their married life was set: George made the decisions for Babe.

On December 23, 1938, they were married, without their families present, in the living room of a friend of George's, Tom Packs, the city's leading wrestling promoter. Leo Durocher, of the St. Louis Cardinals, was George's best man. Leo's former wife, Grace, was Babe's matron of honor. Grace Durocher, a dress designer, made Babe a powder blue dress and a blue hat. The ceremony lasted ten minutes. When it was over, Babe plopped herself into a big chair in the living room and let out a satisfied sigh. "Well, honey, do you feel any different now?" George asked.

She said, "Yeah," but she wasn't so sure that she did.

"Honey," said George, "I've got you at last."

"No, I've got you."

Just as important, they had each other's support. Their union was a product of opportunity. George gave Babe what Peggy Chandler and all the other women golfers had — a wealthy husband who could support her. George also helped Babe win over some cynical members of the public and press, the ones who had doubted that she was a "real" woman or wondered whether she really had eyes for men. It certainly helped that George was a macho sports star — "a Greek God," as Babe often called him. He also played up her domestic side in conversations with the press. When they settled in a rented duplex in Los Angeles, George said, "Right away she was a housewife." The perfect kind; the kind who thought "all the time" about her husband. "Honestly, she surprised me," George said. "With all of her accomplishments in sports and the vast amount of time she had spent in practice and competition,

I didn't see how she could have been so familiar with the routine of housekeeping."

Babe did, in fact, effortlessly and enthusiastically embrace the role of a housewife, whose primary job in the 1930s was keeping her husband happy. As it turned out, she was a fantastic cook, serving Norwegian meatballs and Texas fried chicken. George devoured the home cooking and began to put on weight—lots of it. Within a few years, he'd weigh more than three hundred pounds. She sewed her own drapes and refused to accept weekly help with the cleaning and washing. "She would have none of that," George explained. "She not only did her own work, but found time to paint and redecorate the house."

"I loved all the pretty things," Babe said years later, "and I still love all the pretty things."

In turn, Babe gave George, the budding sports promoter, a marquee athlete whose career he could manage. He had a lot of ideas about how Babe could reestablish herself as a world-class athlete through golf. "Golf is a racket, just like boxin' and wrasslin' are rackets," George boomed. "It's gotta be run the same way."

George envisioned Babe building a golf career as a show woman for hire, appearing in as many exhibitions and making as many other appearances as the public demanded. It wouldn't matter if the pay was modest. What mattered was the work. George believed that Babe's stardom could burn as brightly as it had in the weeks after the Olympics—but this time it would endure. All she had to do was play golf often enough that the galleries could not forget her. This relentless work ethic, after all, had been the engine of George's success. Babe just needed to pursue the golf racket his way.

And, George decided, she would begin on their honeymoon.

15

What Momma Wants

Their honeymoon began in Hawaii—a few weeks loafing on the beach in Honolulu, in a rented house steps from the surf, where Babe tried cooking some local dishes. Then they boarded a ship for Australia. The couple traveled first class, but "it was like a morgue," Babe later said, "dressing for dinner every night, and nobody having any fun. There was no action." Much more exciting was the ship's third-class section, where the passengers threw boozy parties every evening. So Babe and George traded their first-class cabin for the lesser accommodations and much more fun. The new room wasn't nearly as luxurious, but they enjoyed dancing, drinking, and singing with a group of entertainers traveling to Australia to perform.

It turned out that performing was just what George had quietly planned for Babe, too. He had made all the arrangements for Babe to play dozens of golf exhibitions in Australia and New Zealand, as well as for sixteen wrestling performances for himself. George figured their honeymoon would be time better spent if they earned some money along the way. *I mean,* he wondered, *how much time can you spend romancing your new bride, anyway?*

This would be life with George: a feverish hunt for action, almost always the paying kind. An Australian promoter named Archie Keene booked appearances for Babe at the finest golf courses in Sydney, Perth, Medlow Bath, and Melbourne, as well as at some rough, out-of-the-way tracks in a dozen other towns, a few so small they were marked by a single signpost. Keene loaned Babe and George "a little bitty English car" with the steering wheel on the right-hand side. George struggled to get his large frame in and out of the small vehicle. In one newspaper cartoon, the Zahariases' car is stuck in the mud, with George sitting behind the wheel looking over his shoulder as Babe struggles to push it out.

Babe and George loved Australia, mostly because the Australians loved them. The newlyweds met the prime minister, who watched Babe play a few holes and complimented her on her "watchability." Reporters were just as dazzled, although at first they questioned the breathless reports from America that Babe could drive the ball as far as many men. She showed them that indeed she could. "The plain fact is that Miss Didrikson is a vastly better golfer than...any other woman we have seen," Australian golf writer Jack Dillo wrote. "She can hit a ball farther than all except a very few men....She hit drives of 230, 245 and 250 yards on the first three holes....If Miss Didrikson tightens up her short game, she may get a place among the best men professionals in golf."

One day, Babe and George drove for more than two hours deep into the bush to reach a frayed nine-hole course of overgrown fairways and cracked greens. Babe was stunned by the poor condition of the club-house, which was nothing more than an old barn filled with cobwebs. Inside, Babe and George found nearly a dozen women busily cleaning up the mess. By the next day, the course and the clubhouse had been magically transformed. All the greens had been cut, and the festive clubhouse was now bedecked with billowing ribbons, ornate decorations, and long tables covered with tablecloths and set with cakes, cookies, and gleaming pots of tea. Hundreds of people from the region streamed onto the disheveled course to see the famous Babe. One family had driven a horse-drawn carriage 120 miles to be there. With George and the appreciative gallery trailing behind, Babe played eighteen holes and then shared tea with the local people in the clubhouse. Babe always looked back on that day fondly; she never forgot the backcountry's surge of affection and hospitality, as heartfelt as it was surprising.

That day was only the prelude to the honeymoon's highlight. Babe secured a permanent place in the hearts of millions of Australian golf fans the following afternoon when she played brilliantly with their national golf hero and Australian PGA champion, Charlie Conners, at the waterlogged Yarra Yarra Golf Club. Thousands of umbrella-carrying spectators turned out in their raincoats and rubber boots, getting so close to Conners and Babe that they practically got in their way. "I'd look back, and the fairway behind us would be just black with people following after us," Babe recalled. On the par 5 eighteenth hole, Babe hit the finest four-iron of her life. "The ball sailed high over a clump of trees," she said, "and went on the green right up to the pin." Her tap-in gave her an eagle and a 72 for the round, just one stroke off Conners's 71. The Australian press was amazed that Babe had nearly tied the best male player in the land.

After Australia, Babe and George sailed to New Zealand, where she played a few more exhibitions. In Auckland, when they arrived at a pristine course very early one morning, "nobody was there," George recalled. "But before we had played more than three or four holes, there must have been six or seven thousand people. They just wanted to see her." On their return to the United States, the newlyweds stopped for a few more weeks in Hawaii, where George competed in several wrestling matches while Babe worked on her game and continued to improve, shooting as low as 68.

The honeymoon afforded Babe and George the chance to test their new relationship: he commandeered the couple's decision making, an arrangement that Babe welcomed at first but quickly found confining. Babe also realized that George's gargantuan appetite wasn't limited to food. He often drank too much, usually whiskey or bourbon. George became belligerent when drunk, and his hangovers made him even more irritable and impatient.

In October, they finally returned to their rented duplex in West Los Angeles. There wasn't much for Babe to do, and she quickly became bored. "Here I'd been practicing all the time, and developed this fine golf game, and about all I could do was play exhibition matches," she recalled. The charm of her vaudeville act on the fairways and greens was quickly fading. With Gene Sarazen, Babe had relished the rounds punctuated by her jokes. That tour had given her the opportunity to collect shot-making tips from one of the game's best. But without a partner to riff off of, Babe's act had gotten old. She didn't want to spend the rest of her days being a one-woman sideshow performer.

George, too, had reached a crossroads. His weight was ballooning, and he had struggled to overcome a number of nagging injuries. Babe was sure he'd get hurt again. She urged him to retire. George agreed, deciding he'd become a full-time promoter. He obtained a license from the California athletic commissioner to stage wrestling matches at the Olympic arena in Los Angeles. But he most wanted to manage Babe. "I had a great career of my own," George recalled many years later. "I found myself dedicating myself to her and letting her do what she wanted."

George knew that Babe's happiness depended solely on getting the chance to win real golf championships, so he decided she should try to regain her amateur standing from the USGA. If she became an amateur again, she'd have more than a dozen tournaments to play—and more were being added to the schedule each year. There would be no purses to win, but that didn't matter because George was wealthy. There would be competition, which is what Babe needed to establish herself as the greatest player not just in America but in the world.

"We got up a program," George recalled. "I told her she would win every tournament." They sought advice from Pardee Erdman, the low-scoring pastor who was also a West Coast officer of the USGA, and Darsie L. Darsie, a golf writer for the *Los Angeles Herald*. The USGA rules stated that a golfer was eligible to apply for amateur reinstatement if she had not been a professional for five years. The five-year anniversary for Babe was coming up in May 1940. After applying, Babe would have to endure a three-year waiting period during which she would have to drop all professional contracts and paid appearances. She'd also have to refuse any prize money in the professional tournaments that she played.

On January 21, 1940, Babe officially applied for reinstatement, writing Joe Dey, the executive secretary of the USGA, that she wanted to forgo being a professional athlete. "The money had always come second with me," she later said. "The money had been necessary, but what I really loved was the sport itself."

This was easy to say now that she had George to pay the bills. In 1939, George earned more than $100,000, while the average family in America was subsisting on $1,500 a year. It wasn't just that George was wealthy; he was also extremely frugal—some of his friends said he was cheap and shameless about accepting freebies—and he was smart with his investments. He had the resources to support Babe and her extended family through the coming lean years, and he was willing to do it.

Babe had an idea. In 1940, she met amateur golfer Betty Hicks. "Why don't you and me start a feud," Babe told Hicks, "and then we can go on an exhibition tour, and make us both a bunch of money?" Years later, Hicks laughed at the memory. "Babe knew how to milk the publicity cow," she said, but the feud (and the tour) never happened.

To keep her game sharp, Babe played in the only two women's professional tournaments — the Women's Western Open and the Women's Texas Open. Babe won both but refused the modest prize money. These were her first golf victories since she had defeated Peggy Chandler in 1935. Because the two tournaments were the only ones Babe was eligible to play, the press dubbed the twin victories her "Little Slam." The triumphs made her three-year wait for amateur standing even more agonizing. She yearned for a distraction, some new athletic challenge that would help make the time pass just a bit faster. Babe found it in Beverly Hills.

The lingering pain in her right shoulder caused by the awkward Olympic javelin throw had vanished by the time Babe met Eleanor Tennant at the Beverly Hills Tennis Club. Eleanor "Teach" Tennant was considered the top tennis teacher in California, instructing leading women players such as Alice Marble and Little Mo Connolly. George made arrangements for Tennant to give Babe daily lessons. Not surprisingly, Babe said, "I went all out on my tennis, just the way I had in the past on basketball and track and golf." She played as many as seventeen practice sets in a single day, wearing down the soles of her white tennis shoes and wearing holes in her tennis socks. Even George, the toughest of taskmasters, felt that Babe was training too hard. Worried that it was only a matter of time before she got injured, he urged her to slow down, to rest a day or two a week.

"Rest?" Babe would say. "I've got another set to play."

The rigorous training schedule was prescribed by Tennant. "If Babe is going to be a top player," Tennant told George, "she'll have to practice all the time."

In a matter of months, Babe began beating Tennant and a handful of the top male players in Hollywood, including actors Peter Lorre, John Garfield, and Paul Lukas. Babe then started playing with Louise Brough, another Tennant protégée. Babe and Brough played doubles, once beating Pauline Betz and Margaret duPont, who would both later go on to win the national singles championship. Brough and Babe played so well together that they intended to compete as partners for the national doubles championship.

In the autumn of 1941, Babe was proclaimed tournament ready by Tennant. Babe applied for entry in the Pacific Southwest Championships, the last major tournament on the women's tennis calendar. Within a week, her application was rejected by the U.S. Lawn Tennis Association (USLTA). The president of the Southern California Tennis Association, Perry Jones, explained that because Babe had taken money to play other sports, she would never be eligible to play an amateur tennis match. The way the tennis world saw it, once a pro, always a pro. The harshness of the ruling stunned Babe and Tennant. Both had assumed she'd be permitted to play. "It was that old issue of professionalism again," she recalled. "It hadn't occurred to me that the question would come up at all in tennis, since I'd never even played the game."

If Babe couldn't try to win tennis championships, what was the point of playing? She quit the game and never touched a racket again.

Next up, bowling. The game was just beginning a blaze of immense popularity that would sweep America. George considered trying to cash in on the wave by purchasing a bowling alley in the Los Angeles area, and although in the end he decided not to, Babe became intrigued by bowling and "decided to take a whack at this game myself."

When Babe bowled with George, she claimed it was the first round of her life. This was a lie. As a teenager and through her early twenties, she had bowled at Beaumont's bowling alley on Hazel Street. George suspected as much after watching Babe effortlessly roll a booming ball down the lane, scattering pins and racking up spares and strikes. "Come on, now," he told her. "Don't give me that stuff about not knowing how to bowl. You're throwing that ball down there like a professional."

Babe quickly became obsessed with the game, playing nearly every night despite George's warning that if her right hand and arm became too muscular, it might mess with the mechanics of her golf swing. (Babe imitated the style of the best players, who hooked the ball so that it curled into the sweet spot of the pins.) Bowling presented no worries about amateur or professional standing; everyone was an amateur playing for the love of the game. Babe joined the Southern California Major League, playing for a team sponsored by King's Jewelry, and established herself as the team's "anchor woman." King's Jewelry scored a team record 2,765 points for a block of three games, with Babe rolling a 237, the highest single-game score. Spurred in large part by Babe's contribution, King's Jewelry cruised to the league championship in 1941–1942.

The California press heralded Babe's bowling prowess, proclaiming her "one of the best women bowlers in Southern California." A reporter gushed, "Tenpins' titans are hereby warned that...Babe...has begun to frequent bowling alleys," and "already she's scored a 268 and regularly hits 200."

Three or four times a week, first during those tennis workouts and then during her bowling days, Babe kept her golf game sharp by playing practice rounds, usually at Brentwood Country Club, where she shot a club record 64. No woman or man had ever shot a score that low at Brentwood. Perhaps not surprisingly, she soon tired of Brentwood and began practicing most often at Hillcrest Country Club, which had a Jewish membership. Babe played there so often that one day the president of the club approached her, shaking his head with a deep frown. "I don't know what we're going to do about you," he said. "You're out here almost every day. Guess we'll have to declare you an honorary member of our faith and have you join the club."

A highlight for Babe that summer was playing with Sam Snead, one of the leading golfers of the era, in an alternate-shot tournament, a format where players on the same side take turns hitting the same ball. The duo shot a 68, a score that Babe believed was a record for a lady-pro alternate-shot exhibition, a common tournament format in those days. She was awed by Snead's swing — "so intricate and yet so smooth."

World War II began at an oddly opportune time for Babe. Most women's golf events were canceled during the war, making her three-year abstinence easier to endure. In January 1942, George was so angry about the Japanese attack on Pearl Harbor that he tried to enlist, hoping that one of the services could find something for him to do, perhaps teaching the boys unarmed defense. If George went to war, Babe intended to take a commission in the Women's Army Corps. But every branch of the military rejected George because of his varicose veins. So, instead, George arranged charity wrestling matches in the United States to benefit the USO. Babe contributed to the war effort by playing charity golf exhibitions with celebrities, including Johnny Weissmuller, Mickey Rooney, John Montague, and Babe Ruth. Fred Corcoran, the sports promoter who had put together Babe's tour with Gene Sarazen, also arranged exhibitions for her. Babe's most popular charity events featured Bing Crosby and Bob Hope. Of the two, Crosby was the better golfer — in fact, Babe called him the finest player among all the Hollywood stars. While Crosby focused on trying to outplay Babe, Hope's job was to make the galleries laugh — and he did, from the first tee to the eighteenth green. "There's only one thing wrong about Babe and myself," Bob Hope liked to say. "I hit the ball like a girl and she hits it like a man."

At San Gabriel Country Club, Babe teamed up with Patty Berg, one of the leading amateur golfers, against Crosby and Hope. On the first tee, Babe smashed her drive 280 yards. Hope fell to his knees, pounded the ground with his fists, and pretended to cry out loud. Everyone laughed. Crosby rushed over and theatrically consoled Hope. Then Crosby teed off. When his drive stopped rolling far short of Babe's ball, it was his turn to pretend to cry, with Hope rushing over to console him. The gallery loved it.

On another hole, Babe was the beneficiary of a lucky bounce. Her ball flew into a crowd ringing the green, ricocheting with such force off a woman's hand that it loosened the diamond from her wedding ring. The ball caromed onto the green and stopped just short of the hole. When Babe tapped in the miracle birdie, Hope just rolled his eyes and asked the gallery, "Now do you see what we're up against?"

Babe's wartime schedule also featured charity rounds with the game's top male professionals, including Byron Nelson and Ben Hogan, with whom she played several times in California and once in Chicago. Teamed up with George, Babe played against Bill Nary, who four decades later still fondly recalled Babe's natural ability and love for the game. She also took lessons from Tommy Armour at Medinah Country Club, outside Chicago. Her brother Louis credited Tommy with being one of her most important golf instructors, perhaps as influential as Stan Kertes.

In 1942, Babe and George moved to a two-story home in the fashionable Lakewood section of Denver, where George had relocated his wrestling promotion business. When the press wasn't looking, Babe volunteered to help troubled children in Denver play golf and swim.

She also told them stories about the benefits of good sportsmanship, a lesson that she herself did not always remember. In January 1943, a Denver juvenile court judge appointed Babe as a recreation consultant, thinking that she would be a role model for the city's disadvantaged youths. The judge later lauded her for working "without salary" and "with great spirit."

In August of that year, Babe learned that Poppa had died of lung cancer (a diagnosis that had come long after his lung surgery). She returned to Beaumont for his funeral. Though heartbroken, she was glad that Poppa wouldn't suffer any longer. Then she noticed something strange. Everyone was crying except Momma.

"Momma, why aren't you crying?" Babe asked.

"Babe, if I cried, then you children would start fussing over me," Momma said. "I want you to cry for Poppa."

It turned out Momma had a rule: when someone is depending on you, she told Babe, "you're not allowed to be sad." Hannah's restraint was impressive, but Babe could tell that Poppa's death had devastated her. Now she would need her daughters more than ever. Babe also worried about her mother because she had diabetes and felt lethargic most days. "Stop worrying about me," Momma told Babe. "I'll be just fine." But Babe continued to worry.

Finally, Babe was reinstated as an amateur golfer on January 21, 1943, three years to the day after her application for reinstatement. A letter from the USGA made it official. Nearly all the national amateur tournaments had been canceled for the year, but there were a few local contests in southern California on the schedule. A month after the letter arrived, Babe played her first match as an amateur—a special single-day, thirty-six-hole charity event against Clara Callender, the California Women's

Amateur champion, at the Desert Golf Club in Palm Springs. In the morning round, Callender shot a 72, but Babe finished with a 70. In the afternoon session, Callender shot another 72, but this time Babe shot a 67, shattering the course record and winning the match, 4 and 2 (meaning Babe had won four more holes than Clara with two left to play).

Two weeks later, Babe competed in the Midwinter Women's Golf Championship at the Los Angeles Country Club's North Course, a long, challenging track. Babe and Callender had a rematch in the final round, which Babe won, 4 and 3. The highlight was Babe's double eagle on the par 5 tenth hole. "The hole was 405 yards, and it ran uphill," Babe recalled. "I had a tee shot of more than 250 yards. I used a six-iron on my second, and darned if that ball didn't drop on the green and trickle right into the cup."

The following spring, Babe played her first major tournament as an amateur, the Women's Western Open, the same tournament she'd won as a professional in 1940. She won that, too, defeating Dorothy Germain, 7 and 5. And the next year, in June 1945, Babe traveled to Indianapolis to defend her title at Highland Golf and Country Club. After winning her first match, she received a phone call from George, who was in Denver. That morning, Babe's mother had suffered a massive heart attack. She was in critical condition at a Los Angeles hospital and not likely to pull through. Babe told George she would come home right away.

"Your Momma wants you to finish the tournament," George said.

Babe then called her sister Esther Nancy, who was at the hospital with Momma. She told Babe the same thing. Because strict wartime travel restrictions made it impossible for Babe to get a seat on any plane or train out of Indianapolis, she played her quarterfinal match the following morning. "I sure didn't have my heart in it," she recalled, "but somehow I played well enough to win."

That night, Esther Nancy called Babe to tell her that Momma had died. "I've got to get back," Babe said.

Esther Nancy said no again. "You go ahead and win that tournament. That's the way Momma would want it."

Babe didn't listen. She tried to buy a plane or train ticket to Los Angeles, enlisting the help of tournament organizers and other "big shots" in Indianapolis to pull a few strings. But every seat on the westbound planes was taken by a soldier or a military officer. They had top wartime travel priority. Babe was stuck.

Peggy Kirk, a young golfer who was new on the amateur tour, had just met Babe a few days earlier. They had made plans to have dinner later in the week. Peggy told Babe she was sorry to hear about her mother's death.

"Thank you, Peggy," Babe said.

"What are you going to do?"

"I'm going to win this thing for my mother."

The next day, Babe played the semifinal against Marge Becker. More than once, she had to wipe the tears from her eyes before she could tee off or putt. "What kept me going was that I felt I was playing for Momma now," she recalled. After twelve holes, the match was even, but then Babe pulled away, winning, 4 and 2. That night, Babe had dinner with Kirk and her friend Marge Row. Everyone knew that Babe's mother had died, and Kirk assumed that Babe would cancel their date. But Babe, not wanting to mourn by herself, insisted that they get together in her suite at the Indianapolis YMCA. "We didn't know what to expect that night," Kirk recalled. "She takes out her harmonica — I didn't even know she played — and she starts playing all these songs, playing one thing after the other. I think it was soothing her, you know, because her mother just died. She barely spoke — she just kept playing that old harmonica."

After listening to more than an hour of mournful music, Kirk told Babe, "You've got to play tomorrow. You better get something to eat." Babe agreed, ordering steaks for everyone and thanking them for keeping her company.

Most of the golfers on the amateur circuit rooted against Babe. This was fueled, in part, by resentment of her success. Most of them also knew that Babe had more confidence than all of them combined. ("She didn't need any help in the self-esteem department," Betty Jameson noted.) But the next day, during the thirty-six-hole final, Babe had an enormous rooting section when she faced Dorothy Germain, the woman she had beaten in the same tournament in 1944.

Babe usually didn't need much more motivation than the prospect of winning. But now, she said, she had something else: "Inspiration."

"If Babe has more than one reason to win, you might as well forget it," Kirk later said. "Of course she was going to win."

Babe shot a 72 in the morning, setting a women's record for the twenty-six-year-old course and taking a comfortable lead into the afternoon session. Using a tissue at times to wipe away tears, she managed to hold off a back-nine charge by Germain. The 4 and 2 victory was Babe's second consecutive Women's Western Open title and the third of her short career.

Early the next morning, Babe had a seat on a Los Angeles–bound plane. But during a stopover for fuel in Kansas City, she lost her seat to a military officer with a higher travel priority. She took another flight that stopped over in Albuquerque, New Mexico, but then she was bumped from that flight, too. George frantically tried to charter a plane from Albuquerque to Los Angeles, but none was available. Babe hopped a flight to Phoenix, and after a layover there, she finally made it to Los Angeles. Momma had died four days earlier, but the Didriksen family had held off on burying her so that Babe could say goodbye.

George and Esther Nancy met Babe at the airport and presented her with two items — a pearl necklace and a ladies' Rolex watch. Babe had given both to her mother, who had cherished them. They drove straight to the funeral home chapel, where Momma was laid out in a casket. What was it that Momma had said about not letting people see you be sad? Babe kept her emotions in check until she was alone with her mother's body in the chapel. Then she wept.

16

Mrs. Z

Hannah Didriksen's body was flown home to Beaumont. She was buried in Forest Lawn Cemetery, in a plot marked by a simple rectangular headstone, beside Ole's grave. The funeral was held on June 26, 1945, Babe's thirty-fourth birthday. She was too heartbroken to say even a few words.

Babe had had no more devoted cheerleader than Momma. No one knew her moods and needs better; no one else knew the right thing to say every time. Momma understood that beneath Babe's hard outer shell lurked a sudden, merciless impetuousness and the only way to tame it was to tend to her ego. Momma also understood that her daughter's bragging was just a clumsy attempt to persuade the world that she was likable, even lovable — a tough sell, Momma knew, because braggarts are not so easy to like.

Momma wasn't just her youngest daughter's adviser, coach, and psychiatrist. She was also the full-time curator of Babe's athletic career, a biographer who was even more dogged and devoted to the Babe brand than Tiny Scurlock. On the wide pages of several bulging scrapbooks, she'd meticulously pasted hundreds of newspaper and magazine clippings that would become the single largest archive of Babe's wondrous athletic achievements. This was the surest way that Hannah knew to feed Babe's appetite for praise and affirmation, and wherever she went, the scrapbooks went with her. Yet now those books had been left behind. Was there a lovelier — or more loving — gift, Babe wondered, that a mother could bequeath to a daughter?

Now Babe needed George to step up. She had always leaned on him, but now that Momma was gone, she expected him to do even more, especially "the little things," like bucking her up when she was down, indulging her when she needed it, and, perhaps most important, minding the scrapbooks. But after the spring of 1945, there were only a smattering of newspaper clippings to be pasted. George believed that it was more important for him to try to help Babe *produce* clippings. He didn't really know how to help Babe the way Momma had — "all that self-esteem stuff," he called it — and he lacked both the time and the desire to learn. George knew how to sell an idea to the public, and he knew what it took to fill every seat in an arena. He assumed that if he could help Babe become the greatest woman golfer of all time, she'd be happy and they'd have a happy marriage. And so George figured that he was being a good husband if he worked as Babe's round-the-clock manager and coach, making decisions for her about everything. He even gave her golf pointers, which were usually useless.

In 1940s America, husbands rarely if ever sacrificed their own successful careers for their wives' careers. But that's what George did for Babe. Besides staging weekly wrestling matches in Denver that often drew standing-room-only crowds, George busied himself managing an array of investments in Colorado and California. He was part owner of a successful Beverly Hills custom-tailored men's clothing store frequented by Charlie Chaplin, Damon Runyon, and Bugsy Siegel, as well as a Denver cigar store frequented by a less famous but equally loyal clientele. He also owned a number of apartment buildings in the Los Angeles area. These investments produced a steady stream of income. But George had made a handful of big, cash-hemorrhaging investments. One was a ramshackle motel in Denver. (When Babe visited the place, she said, "George, the only way you're going to make a profit on these rooms is to rent them by the hour.") He lost an unknown but hefty sum propping up the San Diego Gunners (also called the Bombers), a mismanaged minor-league football team that played before sparse crowds in the struggling and soon-to-be-defunct Pacific Coast Professional Football League.

R. L. Bowen described George as "a wheeler-dealer" with "walrus hide," who never knew how to sit still and came and went as he pleased. In the middle of the night, before dawn, during dinner, or whenever the mood struck, George would climb into his shiny new Buick and just drive off, often disappearing for weeks. He never asked Babe's permission; he just left. He had business to conduct, or people to see, or he just wanted to get away. As George saw it, Babe had nothing to complain about. He was making the money that paid for her to pursue her dreams.

In a widely distributed interview with the Associated Press, Babe insisted that George never touched the money she had made over the years. "He makes me keep my earnings myself," she said. "Besides, every day he deposits a $100 defense bond in my name." This was a flat-out lie. There is no evidence that Babe invested a single dollar in defense bonds. Instead, George and Babe pooled their funds and often spent them as fast as the money rolled in.

George had complete control of the couple's checkbook. "George is the business head of the family," Babe liked to tell reporters. But unlike most American women, Babe had the ability to make a comfortable living on her own if she decided to turn professional again. Strictly speaking, she didn't need George's money. But her family did, and Babe was uncertain whether she had enough earning power to live comfortably and support her brothers, sisters, and a smattering of nephews and nieces. In exchange for his support, she allowed George the complete freedom to manage their combined earnings. He did not consult Babe on spending decisions, but she was required to consult him. In the years to come, she would increasingly bristle at this arrangement.

As tight as George could be with money, he spent it freely on everything associated with Babe's career. His generosity on her behalf awed most of Babe's friends. One night in the mid-1940s, George was in Los Angeles doing business, while Babe was back in Denver. After drinking too many cocktails, George arrived, uninvited, on the doorstep of Stan Kertes, Babe's first golf instructor in LA. George barged in, declaring he was hungry, and without an invitation, he raided Kertes's icebox, sloppily eating a whole turkey with his bare hands at the kitchen table while Kertes sat and watched. Then George demanded that Kertes go with him to see his investment adviser. "I objected since it was so late," Kertes recalled, "but George got on the phone, got the fellow out of bed and we went there. He was sitting in his bathrobe, just out of bed, bleary-eyed. George had lots of property around L.A. then, and he said to this fellow that he wanted to give me a piece of property on Santa Monica Boulevard with six motel units on it. 'Stan, I want you to have it,' he said, 'because you gave Babe those free lessons for all those years. I want to pay you back for that, Stan.' Well, George was in his cups. I finally managed to talk him out of giving it to me.... I didn't need anything from him or from Babe."

"Babe, once called a 'muscle moll' by a careless sportswriter, is anything but. Sports have taken away none of her femininity, and her husband, Gentleman George Zaharias, of the bone-bending set, says she is a perfect wife. The Zaharias home in Denver, where Gentleman George is now a successful promoter of the pretzel pastime, is a scene of domestic tranquility." Those words were coauthored by Frank Finch and Braven Dyer, the *Los Angeles Times* sportswriter who introduced Babe and George on the first tee at the Los Angeles Open, for an article published in *Sport* magazine in November 1946. The new magazine, founded just two months earlier, declared Babe the top female athlete in the United States.

It was George and Babe's idea to invite a few friendly journalists into their home in Denver to write high-profile feature stories for national magazines, including *Sport*. This was part of a carefully orchestrated campaign to be seen by the public as meeting culturally accepted behavior. But beneath the surface, major cracks had formed in their marriage. George was on the road too often, and when he was home, he often didn't pay much attention to Babe. She objected to his slovenly eating habits and three-day drinking binges. They shared a tendency to blow up at each other, arguing for hours, and their stony silences lasted for days and sometimes weeks. "This was not a perfect marriage," Babe's brother Louis said. "Later, it became rocky. Separations became frequent. Mildred was welcome everywhere, but George wasn't. He started drinking a lot. I personally thought he was overbearing and unjust with Babe. But she stood by him."

Near the end of his life, George admitted, "We started getting at each other's throats much of the time."

In front of the friendly reporters, however, Babe and George laid it on sickeningly sweet, playing the role of the blissfully happy couple with what they both swore was the perfect marriage. George gushed about Babe's domestic prowess, and Babe saluted George as the doting husband. Not surprisingly, the reporters, given unprecedented access, slurped up this fairy tale and regurgitated it for their readers.

Reintroducing Babe as the happy homemaker was an attempt to put to rest any lingering questions about her sexuality and her ability to win acceptance from America's ritziest country clubs. The stories did not resemble revealing profiles; instead, they sounded like superlative-laden press releases. "I wish those people who wanted to make a tough mug out of me could get a look at me now," Babe said, motioning toward their lovely new English Tudor home, her rose garden, and her affectionate husband.

Sometimes Babe "tried too hard" to portray herself as a happy housewife, her friends said. That included drawing attention to her painted nails, her new outfits, and even her breasts. "Sometimes she overdressed a little—she'd wear frilly blouses that didn't look right," Peggy Kirk recalled. "Goddamn these things," Babe once shouted, pointing at her breasts after missing an easy spare while bowling. "They sure do get in the way."

In its flattering profile of Babe, *Sport* included more photographs of Babe's homemaking than her golfing. In one, she happily pours coffee for George at their dining room table. In another, a beaming Babe pushes a lawn mower—in high heels. "Naturally, the Babe is posing in these pictures," the caption reads. "But the domestic angle is no fake." Readers would have to take the magazine's word for it.

In 1947, Babe and George invited Pete Martin, a writer for the *Saturday Evening Post,* to their home. His article, titled "Babe Didrikson Takes Off Her Mask," suggests that the "other Babe"—the muscle moll—had been a front shielding Babe's true domestic self. One of the featured photographs shows George washing dishes and Babe, in the background, holding up a trout she had caught in the Rockies. The caption says, "With a few assists from her amiable husband, Mrs. Zaharias does all her own housework."

Babe told Martin that she no longer wanted to be called Babe Didrikson. She preferred Mildred or, if Martin was inclined, "Marvelous Mildred." Babe attempted to use the article to make a clean break from her past, one that she rarely spoke about. Friends have said that she rarely, if ever, discussed her Olympic gold medals. She had so little interest in that stage of her life that she kept them out of sight, stuffed in a drawer or cupboard.

Despite trying to get "Mildred" to stick, Babe continued signing her name "Babe Zaharias." She also told some people to call her "Mrs. Zaharias" or "just Mrs. Z." Pete Martin's article portrayed "Mildred Zaharias" as an entirely feminine, happily married housewife who adored her husband even more than golf. "You can't tell a husband how much you love him after he's dead," Babe told Martin.

Martin contrasted the Babe Didrikson whom the nation had met during the 1932 Olympics with this new, revamped version. "She was said to have 'a door-stop jaw and piano-wire muscles,'" Martin wrote, noting that a sportswriter in the early thirties had described Babe as being "born halfway between masculine flats and angles and the rubbery curves of femininity"—code words hinting at the whispered speculation that Babe was a lesbian. Martin described himself as being bowled over by Babe's remarkable transformation. Was it really possible, he wondered, that Babe had become...*voluptuous?* He offered his readers the statistics to prove it: "The bust measurement of this ex-Texas girl...is now a Valkyrian forty inches. The bust measurement of Jane Russell, Hollywood's leading sweater-filler, is only thirty-eight and one half inches. Mildred Zaharias' waist is twenty-seven inches; her hips thirty-seven. She weighs 140. There is little resemblance to the so-called 'muscle moll' of yesteryear. Her arms are no more muscular than those of any normally healthy woman, although her legs are still impressive columns of flesh and sinew."

Martin also was impressed by how effortlessly Babe had shed her "Spartan" wardrobe: "Perfume, lipstick and fingernail polish lie on her dressing table. Style and class hang in her closets." (Bertha Bowen would have been proud.) This kind of intimate prose was rarely used to describe any athlete, male or female, during the 1940s.

If that wasn't enough peering behind the Zahariases' curtains to titillate readers, Martin described what it was like poking around Babe and George's bedroom. "Our bed wasn't big enough," Babe told Martin. "He used to lie there reading the papers with his arms all spread out. I got tired of sleeping on what was left of the bed, so I went downtown and had one made eight foot square." Martin did, however, leave it to the reader to imagine how Babe and George got along *in* that bed.

George now weighed more than three hundred pounds. Martin described how difficult it was to find clothes for such a giant of a man: "As many yards of cloth are required to fashion a sports coat for him as to make an ordinary-sized man a coat, vest and pants. His neck bulges out below his hairline in a shelf of flesh, and his shirts are made to order. The stores simply don't carry them that big."

"Everything I do, I do for George," Babe gushed. "He's the only thing I've got on my mind. I'd give up golf if he couldn't be with me."

More hokum. When Babe embarked on a yearlong tour that crisscrossed America, George almost never joined her. Indeed, with each passing year, they were growing apart.

After the war ended, the major women's amateur tournament schedule resumed, and Babe was ready. She won the Women's Texas Open in the fall of 1945. She also defeated one of golf's new glamour girls, Betty Jameson—a twenty-six-year-old former feature reporter from San Antonio—in a seventy-two-hole challenge match. Babe and Betty ran into each other in the near-empty locker room at the Los Angeles Country Club less than an hour before their match. It was their first meeting.

"My, but you're a big girl," Babe said. "So...you ready to finish second?"

On the course, they were followed by an enormous, boisterous gallery, including film star Gary Cooper. Jameson did finish second, and she never forgot Babe's supreme confidence. "I thought I was pretty confident, and I also thought I was the best there was," she recalled. "But I had nothing on the Babe."

Early one evening in November 1945, Babe picked up the phone in the living room of her Denver home and called Peggy Kirk. It was the first time the two had spoken since the evening they had spent together in Indianapolis five months earlier, after Babe's mother's death.

Babe asked if Kirk was planning on playing in an upcoming four-ball tournament in Hollywood, Florida. (Four-ball is a match between two teams with two players. Each golfer plays her own ball, but each team gets the score of the lowest-scoring team member.) "I need a part-ner for that International Four-Ball," she told Kirk, "and you might as well win a tournament."

Kirk ignored a momentary pang of resentment at Babe's catty remark and quickly accepted the invitation. This was the great Babe Didrikson recruiting her as a partner, after all. When that happened, Kirk knew, you checked your ego at the door. Two weeks later, they met in Hollywood. On the driving range prior to the first round, Babe noticed that Kirk was hitting errant shots and shaking with nerves.

"What's wrong with you?" Babe asked.

"Oh, Babe, you've won all these tournaments—every one in Flor-ida, and now I'm worried that it'll be my fault if you lose."

"Look, Peggy, I can beat any two of 'em without you. I'll let you know if I need you. So let's go."

In one round, Kirk shot an ugly 7 on the first hole. As they walked to the second tee, Babe put her arm around her and said, "Now Peggy, why don't you see if you can just par from here on in?" The remark boosted Kirk's confidence, and she ended up shooting a 74 for the round. Babe and Kirk didn't win the tournament, but it was not Kirk's fault; Babe was off her game.

When the season ended, the Associated Press voted Babe the Female Athlete of the Year, an honor she had first earned thirteen years earlier. Babe later described herself as getting "a special charge out of that 1945 award, because it had been so many years since I'd had this recognition."

Award in hand, Babe had big plans for 1946. A full postwar schedule of twenty amateur tournaments beckoned. "I want to establish the longest winning streak in the history of women's golf," Babe told a reporter for *Coronet* magazine in 1946. But a single goal, even one as ambitious as a winning streak, was never enough for Babe. She also wanted to win that year's U.S. Women's Amateur.

Babe began slowly, losing the Women's Western Amateur in the semifinals in June. But the following month, in her adopted hometown of Denver, she defeated Polly Riley, a chunky, gum-chewing twenty-year-old, for the Women's Trans-Mississippi Championship. In the thirty-six-hole final, Riley stubbed a two-foot putt, losing a pivotal back-nine hole by a stroke. "You sure shoulda snagged that one, Polly," Babe told her. Riley was all confidence, but that remark rattled her, and she lost by six holes.

Babe won her next two tournaments, the Broadmoor Ladies Invitation and the All-American Open Championship for Women at George S. May's Tam O'Shanter Country Club in Niles, Illinois. At this point, Babe and George claimed that she was taking a three-win streak into the U.S. Women's Amateur. But, in fact, Babe had lost her match in the first professional U.S. Women's Open in Spokane, Washington, on August 26. The women on the tour grumbled that Babe had conveniently forgotten about that one in order to keep her "streak" alive.

The U.S. Women's Amateur was arguably the marquee event on the women's golfing calendar. This was the first national amateur championship of Babe's career, held that year in Tulsa, Oklahoma, at

Southern Hills Country Club, an extremely long course that swallowed up players with little power off the tee. "I always liked that kind," Babe later said.

Because one of her goals was to claim the National, Babe felt the pressure. After all, she had wanted this prize "for more than thirteen years," she explained, "from the time I first took up golf seriously. It would be a terrible thing to go through an entire golf career without ever winning the National." Babe breezed through the thirty-six-hole qualifying round, finishing third, and she easily defeated her competitors— Peggy Kirk, Maureen Orcutt, and Helen Sigel— to qualify for the final against Clara Callender, who had recently married and was now known as Clara Sherman.

Babe and Sherman were even after six holes, but then Babe took over. "I was hot; she wasn't," Babe recalled. By the time they broke for lunch after eighteen holes, Babe was ahead by five holes, and she wouldn't look back. On the par 4 eighth, Babe made an eagle—her 130-yard second shot, with a nine-iron, went into the cup for a two— and by the ninth hole in the afternoon session, the U.S. Women's Amateur belonged to Babe. Her winning margin of 11 and 9 was the second widest in the history of the championship.

In some tournaments, you get lucky—the ball takes a fortunate bounce, hits a tree, and ricochets onto the fairway or even the green, and you get another break or two or even three that you don't really deserve. Babe said that she never liked "winning that way." At the U.S. Women's Amateur, she didn't. It was one of the best rounds of her life. "I'm never really satisfied unless I can feel that I'm hitting the ball just right," she said. And during the National, she was.

Babe kept winning. In October, she won the Women's Texas Open for the second time, defeating Betty Hicks, 5 and 3.

It was the last tournament of the season, and her glittering record ensured her second consecutive selection as the Associated Press Female Athlete of the Year. Babe drove home to Denver to spend some much-needed time with George. She was looking forward to recuperating, tending to her rose garden, and buying some furnishings for their home — "the first full-fledged house we'd ever owned." Babe didn't just plan on taking the holidays off; she intended on taking the winter and spring off, too, skipping the slate of tournaments in Florida and elsewhere in the South.

George was thinking about her streak. "Honey," he told her, "you've got something going here.... You want to build that streak up into a record they'll never forget. There are some women's tournaments in Florida at the start of the winter. I think you should go down there."

Babe didn't want to — she was bone-tired and needed a long break from tournament golf. But George insisted. He was her coach, trainer, and manager, after all, and he wanted her to play every tournament she could. The competition would be "soft," he said, especially in some of the smaller Florida tournaments. She should not pass up a chance to extend her winning streak. Babe reluctantly acquiesced, but on one condition: George needed to join her. He agreed but at the last minute backed out, citing a series of wrestling and boxing matches that he needed to promote in Denver. Babe and George drove to Pueblo, where they spent the night with George's mother and father. The next morning, George returned to Denver while Babe drove her car toward Florida. After 150 miles on the road, Babe turned around and went back home.

"What are you doing here?" George asked.

"The farther I got down the road, the more lonesome I got," Babe said. "I'm not going to go."

During the romantic first year of their courtship, Babe had driven from her sister's house in Arizona, back to Los Angeles, and then on to

San Francisco to be with George. He had appreciated the gesture then, but not now. This was business.

George insisted that she leave for Florida immediately. Babe was heartbroken. She liked having George on tour with her because he was good company and he helped her relax in the evenings by giving "the best rubdowns." But, following orders, she departed.

In late January, Babe began a long stretch of playing a tournament a week, all over Florida. Some of the courses were in sorry shape, so much so that the rules allowed the players to move a ball out of a bad lie on the fairway. Although galleries sometimes objected, it was accepted practice because the unwatered fairways were so chopped up. Babe's Florida tour began at the Tampa Women's Open. She moved south to the Helen Lee Doherty Women's Amateur at the Miami Country Club. The following week, she played the Florida Mixed Two-Ball Championship in Orlando, teaming up with Gerald "Gee" Walker, the big-league ballplayer. She won them all. Her legitimate winning streak was now five in a row, although Babe and George were claiming eight.

Babe called George back in Denver. "I'm tired of traveling around down here by myself," she told him. "I'm ready to come home."

"No, honey," he said. "Don't do that. You're in a hot streak. Stay with it."

Babe nearly lost her next two tournaments. In the Palm Beach Championship, Babe was trailing Jean Hopkins in the final round by two with three holes to play, but she managed to win every one of the last holes to win by a hole. In Hollywood, Florida, at the Women's International Four-Ball, Babe teamed up again with Peggy Kirk. In the final against Jean Hopkins and Louise Suggs, the match was all square after thirty-five holes. It was nearly dark, but the officials allowed the players to tee off on the final, par 4 hole, and a couple of them made their second shots. Then someone accused a fan of picking up one of the second shots from the rough and throwing it onto the green, but it was so dark that no one could be sure. Some people in the gallery shouted that the match should be suspended; others insisted that they finish. The officials finally called off the match. The next day, Babe and Kirk won the eighteen-hole playoff, 4 and 2.

That gave Babe seven straight wins. Win number eight was the South Atlantic Women's Amateur Championship in Ormond Beach, Florida; win nine was the Florida East Coast Women's Amateur Championship in St. Augustine; and win ten was the Women's Title-holders Tournament in Augusta, Georgia, the sister tourney of the Masters. In Augusta, Babe trailed Dorothy Kirby by as many as ten strokes but roared back to win by five strokes, carding a seventy-two-hole total of 304. (Unlike the other tournaments, the Titleholders penalized players who moved a ball out of a bad spot. "It's golf as golf should be played," Babe said.)

Next came the North and South Women's Amateur in Pinehurst, North Carolina. George had finally joined Babe, who played against Louise Suggs and nearly had her streak snapped. On the par 3 seventeenth hole in the final, Babe was ahead by one hole, but her tee shot landed at the base of a tree, making a swing at it impossible. Babe prepared to try a billiards-style trick shot by hitting the ball off the tree and hoping it would carom left onto the green. Reaching down quickly to brush away a clump of pine straw, she accidentally moved her ball, costing her a penalty stroke. "I wound up with a five," Babe said, "while Louise came out of a bunker to get down in four and square the match."

George watched grimly from the gallery, puffing on a cigar, as Babe called the penalty on herself. He felt certain that the penalty would cost her the tournament, ending her winning streak in the most unfortunate way imaginable. Babe and Suggs halved the first extra hole, but on the second hole, Babe sank a lengthy birdie putt to win.

Babe and George returned home to mull over her next move.

"Honey," George said, "you want to go over to Scotland and play in the British Women's Amateur in June. You need something like that to top off your streak, the way Bobby Jones went over and played those British tournaments the year he made his grand slam." An American woman had never won it, and it would be a great feat if Babe was the first.

But Babe was dubious. "I won't go unless you go with me," she said.

"Sure, honey, I'll go with you. I'll make it if I possibly can."

"I know you," Babe said. "You're giving me some more of that old con. You won't go. You'll never be able to get away for that long."

Babe sought the advice of Tommy Armour, the pro who had helped her straighten out her drives back in the early 1940s at Medinah Country Club in Illinois. Armour, a Scotsman, said, "Mildred, you go.... It doesn't matter who's in the tournament. This is the one you must win."

Armour's enthusiasm made up Babe's mind. George didn't join her, of course. She made preparations to travel on the *Queen Elizabeth* alone for the trip to Scotland, where she was determined to become the first American woman to win the fifty-four-year-old British Women's Amateur Championship. Babe was growing accustomed to traveling alone. Hadn't she traveled to the Olympics in Los Angeles by herself, without any family to buck her up and cheer her on? That had turned out OK. But back then, of course, she'd had no husband. Now Babe couldn't help but feel that aside from traveling alone, she was being abandoned.

17

The Highland Fling

B abe landed at Southampton, England, on a scorching early June day, the hottest in more than half a century. She was ill prepared for that kind of heat, and, worse, she had overpacked — several bulky pieces of luggage, two cameras, a knitting bag, even a fur coat. She lugged her belongings aboard the packed boat train bound for London. Because there were no empty seats, Babe stood in the aisle the entire way, as the sweat streamed down her back.

In London, Babe tried to hail an empty taxicab to Kings Cross Station, where she would catch the train for Edinburgh, but she had unknowingly cut off a large crowd of waiting travelers. "Lady," Babe was told, "you'll have to wait in the queue."

"Queue? What's a queue?" The locals explained that Babe needed to stand in line, along with everyone else, until her turn came. After twenty-five taxis came and went, Babe and several strangers packed themselves and their luggage into a taxi for the ride to London's central train station. At Kings Cross, as Babe was unloading her baggage, the station gates were suddenly thrown shut. "What in the world is this?" she asked a police officer. "Why are they closing the gates?"

"The King and Queen are coming," the officer said.

Workmen unpacked bouquets of flowers and unfurled a long red carpet up the steps of the train station. Babe watched as King George VI and Queen Elizabeth emerged from a black limousine. They waved quickly to their subjects before hurrying up the red carpet into the train station. Not long after they disappeared, Babe followed them, dragging her belongings up the carpet to catch her train.

"Lady, you cannot walk on that carpet," a man in a uniform told her. "You cannot go that way."

"I'm sorry," Babe said, "but I have to get my ticket. I have to catch that train to Edinburgh."

The man told Babe that she needed to use the Kings Cross annex, which was open to the public while the king and queen boarded the royal train, bound for one of their country estates up north. Clutching her first-class ticket, Babe barely made her 1:00 p.m. train. Again, all the seats in the first-class compartment were filled with passengers, many of them men in uniform. "Doesn't a first-class ticket mean that I get a seat?" Babe asked the conductor.

"No madam. First come, first served."

Once again, Babe was forced to stand in the aisle for the ten-hour journey. The train was "hotter than ever," she recalled. "The windows were open — we'd have suffocated otherwise — and soot from the engine was blowing in. There were black specks all over my face and hair. I was dripping all over. My curls had come down....I thought I was going to faint any minute." Babe wondered whether this trip would be worth it, and she silently cursed George and his relentless push for her to outdo herself. If the decision had been hers, she would have stayed home in Denver and tended to her roses.

Babe's train rolled into Edinburgh after 11:00 p.m. She was exhausted. This was hardly the beginning she had envisioned, but at least she didn't have to stand in a taxi queue here. A hired car was waiting to take her directly to her hotel in Gullane, a small town outside the Scottish capital. "From then on," she said, "things couldn't have been nicer."

Gullane is a majestic medieval village nestled on the southern shore of the Firth of Forth, in East Lothian, on Scotland's craggy east coast. The village is only eighteen miles up the road from Edinburgh, but to Babe it felt a thousand miles away from the civilized world.

When Babe checked in at the North Berwick Inn, a grand old stone hotel and pub doing business since the sixteenth century, she was greeted by a desk clerk who declared himself a big fan. The next morning, in the dining room, she was asked what she'd like for breakfast. "Well, I'd like some bacon or ham and eggs and some fried potatoes and toast and coffee," she said. "But I don't suppose I can get that here." Postwar food rationing was still in effect in the United Kingdom.

"Mrs. Zaharias," a waiter said, "we've got all that. The manager is keeping some chickens out there just for you." The manager had purchased a large supply of bacon and ham from a nearby American boat just for Babe.

"That's as nice a thing as I ever heard of," Babe said.

After an authentic American breakfast, Babe strolled out the hotel door and squinted into the faint Scottish sun, which was already high in the sky, where it would remain until past midnight. On the cobblestone streets, nearly everyone — men, women, boys, and girls — rode bicycles, with their pant legs tucked inside their socks so they didn't get tangled in the chain and spokes. Rather than renting a bike for her trip to the Gullane Golf Club, Babe decided to walk up West Links Road, bordered by brightly colored, centuries-old homes. Behind ancient stone fences, most of the Scots recognized Babe. "Hello, Mrs. Zaha-rias," they said. "Just call me Babe," she replied. She said the same to the newspaper reporters: "I wish you'd ask everybody just to call me Babe."

Perched above the coarse, jagged coast, the Gullane Golf Club is a chain of three golf courses carved into a grassed-over volcanic plug. The club's jewel is Gullane No. 1, the track that was hosting the 1947 British Women's Amateur Championship. Gullane No. 1 is a hilly links course that runs up Gullane Hill, where the seascape view is among the most spectacular in Scotland, then runs back down. Ferocious sea winds lash the course's undulating fairways and tall grasses. Joyce Wethered, the famed British golf champion, adored the first tee. "The way of approach is down the village street," she said. "One steps straight off it, as it were, on to a village green, to tee up beneath the shade of plane trees, their brown leaves dry and crackling underfoot." The famous British golf writer Bernard Darwin proclaimed the Gullane Golf Club "one of the most beautiful spots in the world."

It *was* beautiful and, in Babe's mind, also intimidating, despite the fact that this craggy patch of land could be confused with a working sheep farm. A large flock enjoyed full run of the three courses, grazing on the fairways and greens. When players got too close, the animals ducked into a bunker or waded into the deep rough. On Sunday, the courses were closed, and families used the fifty-four fairways and greens to stroll, fly kites, eat picnic lunches, and read the newspaper.

Inside the clubhouse, the men warned Babe to try to steer her ball clear of "the winds." She assumed they meant the unpredictable sea gusts, but "the winds" was the locals' phrase for the hedgelike thickets of tall grass bordering on what passed for the fairways. The men also pre-sented Babe with a hospitable perk: a gentleman clad in a well-pressed white coat and armed with a scooper. The man's assignment was to walk a few paces in front of Babe to pick up any sheep droppings on the greens.

Along the shore, Babe spotted crews of former Polish soldiers removing large cement pillars roughly five feet thick and eight feet above the ground. These pillars had been installed during the war along the coast to defend against an invasion. The workmen were rushing to finish the last few pillars before the championship began.

Babe was surprised to discover that there were no practice greens or tees at Gullane. "They just practice by playing around the course," she recalled. After dinner each evening, Babe played a round of eighteen holes. She wanted to get accustomed to the course's layout, as well as to the size of the golf balls, which were slightly smaller than those in the United States. She happily discovered that her usually long drives carried even farther at Gullane because the June sun had still not adequately softened the ground hardened by a bitterly cold winter. The fairways were heavy enough to allow Babe's big drives to roll even farther, too.

Each evening, George phoned from Denver to check in. "Hi, honey," Babe said one evening. "It's eleven o'clock at night here, and I just got in from playing a round."

"Good Lord," George said. "Now take it easy, will you?" Like Colonel McCombs before him, George thought that Babe overtrained in the days leading up to her most challenging matches, burning valuable energy required for the real thing.

On just her second night of practice, Babe lashed awkwardly at a ball buried in the tall, wet grass, pummeling the ground with her club and chipping a bone in her left thumb. The following morning, she visited a town doctor, who prescribed a painkiller and wrapped her thumb in an elastic bandage. Babe said nothing to the press or anyone else about her injury. "I didn't want anybody to think I was trying to build up an advance alibi for myself," she explained years later, "so I just wore a glove over it, and nobody noticed that there was anything the matter with my thumb." She was surprised to learn that her injury actually improved her accuracy. Her sore thumb made it impossible to swing as hard as usual, which kept her ball from veering off into the winds.

Babe was then confronted with a trickier dilemma — her wardrobe. She had packed for summer weather, putting only a few light sweaters in her suitcases, including an orange cashmere sweater with angora in it. Despite the steamy start to her trip, the weather in Scotland had turned cold and damp. When the British newspapers revealed Babe's problem, Gullane residents dropped off care packages containing heavy clothing. Then, in the morning post, dozens more packages arrived from all over the British Isles. Dubbed by the press "Bundles for Babe," the packages were piled nearly as high as the ceiling in the inn's lobby. Babe opened a dozen packages and selected a smart-looking "siren suit" — the type of outfit worn by British air-raid workers — and a pair of slightly faded, slate blue corduroy slacks that kept her legs warm. Golf fans across Britain dubbed those corduroys "Babe's slocks." After she started winning, they called them her "lucky slocks."

On the first day of the tournament, Babe strolled from her inn to the first tee of Gullane No. 1, which is just off the main road that connects Edinburgh and North Berwick. The tee was surrounded by a fence of white posts with a top rail, which spectators leaned on to watch the players begin their rounds. Babe hurdled over the rail, a spectacle that amused the very small group of early-morning spectators.

"I thought Scotland was golf country," Babe said to the club secretary. "Where are all the people?"

"They'll be here."

Fourteen years earlier, in 1933, Helen Hicks, a twenty-two-year-old amateur golfing sensation, was asked this question by a reporter: "What chance has an American girl of winning the British title, and how soon?"

"I think in a very few years," said Hicks, fresh off winning the U.S. Women's Amateur Championship in Buffalo. "It amuses me—all this hooey about a championship abroad. We all go over there with an alibi, ready-made. The weather! You'd think we never had wind or rain here."

Hicks was also asked this question: "Could Babe Didrikson, in your opinion, ever become a champion golfer at her age?"

"I don't think so," Hicks said. "Golf is different from anything she ever tackled, a fact which she'll learn if she ever attempts to play in a championship. In track competition, it's all over in a jiffy. Golf takes six days—long days, with nights in between, and a 36-hole final."

Fourteen years later, despite Hicks's optimism, an American had still not won the British Amateur Golf Championship—the premier women's golf championship in all of Europe—which had begun in 1893. In 1929, one of the greatest American golfers, Glenna Collett Vare, had come closest to winning but lost in heartbreaking fashion to Joyce Wethered. Ahead by five holes with just seven to play, Vare's collapse was so complete that the loss ranked as the most devastating of her career. She made the final the following year but lost again.

Babe knew that her legacy as one of the game's greats was likely on the line at Gullane. Bobby Jones had won the Open Championship three times and the Amateur Championship once. And all of the era's finest American men players—Walter Hagen, Sam Snead, and Gene Sarazen, all players Babe admired and had played with—had won the biggest championship on British soil.

Babe was one of ninety-nine amateurs entered in the championship and one of only three Americans. The event attracted the finest women golfers from the United Kingdom and Ireland. A dozen were members of the Curtis Cup team. A biannual match started in 1932, the Curtis Cup pitted a team of amateur golfers from the United States against a team from Great Britain and Ireland. (The match had been postponed during World War II but would resume in 1948 at the Royal Birkdale

Golf Club in Southport, England.) Each day of the Women's Amateur Golf Championship consisted of two matches — an eighteen-hole round in the morning and another eighteen-hole round, against a new opponent, after lunch. There was no qualifying round, and the name of your first opponent was pulled from a hat. Babe's first opponent was a woman named Helen Nimmo, a member of the Gullane Golf Club.

Sure enough, the people arrived just in time to see Babe and Nimmo tee off, and the large gallery followed them avidly around the course. This was the quietest, most well-behaved gallery that Babe had ever seen. They didn't yell or holler or cheer or even applaud. "Well played," a few would say. Or, "Fine shot." Their manners were unnerving. Babe didn't hear any applause until she clinched the first round on the twelfth hole. Then the gallery clapped as if the tournament were a piano recital.

Babe depended on the crowd's enthusiasm. She fed off it and felt deprived of fuel without it. During the lunch break, Babe pulled aside the tournament marshal, Helen Holm, a former British Women's Amateur champion. "I wish these people would just holler and enjoy themselves the way the crowds do back home," Babe told her. Holm described the long-standing Scottish tradition of restrained appreciation for good play. Gallery members tried not to distract the players with unnecessary noise. That way, every player had an equal chance to concentrate on making her shots.

Babe had another problem. Gullane Golf Club had assigned her an eighty-year-old caddie, who insisted on advising her on every shot — club selection, wind speed, everything. On one hole, Babe wanted to use a wedge, but the caddie handed her a three-iron. "Would you please leave the clubs in the bag and let me pick them out?" Babe asked.

"Madam," the caddie said, "the wind is against you. You should take this three-iron and run the ball up there."

"I don't play two and three-iron pitches on little short shots," Babe said. "I'm used to hitting the ball up in the air." She used the wedge. (A story in the British press claimed that Babe had insisted on a new, younger caddie, and the eighty-year-old was replaced with a seventy-five-year-old.)

On the sixteenth hole that first afternoon, Babe won her match against Janet Sheppard, a Midlands amateur with a strong tournament record. Babe's long drives astonished the crowd. "It seems cruel to send our girls out against a game like that," one Scot said.

As she sometimes did in the United States, Babe decided to play the bye holes—the remaining two holes. They didn't count, but Babe saw it as a chance to entertain the large gallery, a kind of encore on the greens. If this stunt didn't loosen up the crowd, nothing would. On the seventeenth tee, Babe quietly put a kitchen match behind her ball. When she hit the ball, the match crackled "like a small cannon." The crowd laughed and cheered. With her ball stuck in a deep sand trap, Babe balanced a second ball on top of the first, swinging an iron gently into both. The club motion made one ball pop in front of Babe. She caught it in her shirt pocket while the second ball hit the green and rolled into the hole. The crowd roared. They had never seen such a crazy trick. Then on the eighteenth green, Babe bent over and putted the ball backward, between her legs. It went into the hole. She remained on the fringe of the eighteenth green for an hour, signing autographs and shaking hands.

The next day, a sign was posted on the clubhouse wall: PLEASE DO NOT PLAY THE BYE HOLES. The event's administrators did not appreciate their storied championship being turned into an impromptu circus. In fact, several elderly Gullane Golf Club members complained to Helen Holm about Babe's antics, saying her uncouth style had deeply embarrassed them and the club.

Holm just shook her head. "You are speaking of the finest woman golfer that has ever been seen here," she told them.

The Scottish fans agreed with that assessment. The next day, Babe's gallery had grown in size and sound.

That morning, an older woman with a thick Scottish accent approached Babe with an urgent message: "Did you know that there is a jinx against American women in this tournament? Why, your greatest players have come here, women like Glenna Collett and Virginia Van Wie, and they've never been able to win." Babe was taken aback, but the woman went on: "Aren't you worried about the jinx?"

"I didn't come over here to lose," Babe replied and walked away. She had no idea who the woman was, but Babe assumed she might have been a former player.

The woman likely credited the jinx with knocking out the other two American women — Helen Sigel and Ruth Woodward — in the early rounds of the championship. Their early exits meant that Babe was the only player left with a chance to become the first American to win the British Women's Amateur.

Babe defeated her next three opponents — Mrs. Val Reddan, a former Irish champion; Mrs. Cosmo Falconer, a Scottish champion; and Frances Stephens, a slender teenager from Lancashire, who kept pace with Babe for twelve holes before losing, 3 and 2.

Several times in the clubhouse and on the fairway, the odd Scottish woman warned Babe, "Don't forget about the jinx."

In the semifinals, Babe faced the Scottish champion Jean Donald, the daughter of a beloved local doctor. This was a highly anticipated, all-champion eighteen-hole match that attracted more than eight thousand people to Gullane, a larger crowd than had attended the men's Amateur Championship at Carnoustie in late May.

Donald three-putted on the first hole, then Babe strung together three straight birdies. The match was never close. When Babe walked off the twelfth green — up by six with just six holes to play — she reapplied her lipstick. A writer later said that Babe was so sure she'd win the match on the next hole that she put on the lipstick to freshen up for the photographers. Babe did win on the next hole, and with a platoon of photographers crowding around, she and Donald danced the Highland fling, one of the oldest Highland dances, performed by soldiers to celebrate victory in battle. Babe called her opponent "a real good sport."

In the final thirty-six-hole match, Babe would face Jacqueline Gordon, a Middlesex woman whose consistent play all week had vindicated her selection for the 1948 Curtis Cup team. The night before the final, Babe struggled to fall sleep. She kept worrying and wondering about the jinx. Her room was uncomfortably cold, and the heater wasn't really helping. She had pulled down the blackout shades to blot out the late-evening sunlight. Finally, she got out of bed and ordered a pot of tea.

When the desk clerk brought it, Babe admitted to him that she was having trouble sleeping because she kept worrying about the local woman's warnings about the American jinx. "Mrs. Zaharias, don't take any notice of her," the clerk said. "Everybody here wants you to win."

Several hours later, Babe woke up in a much better mood. It was a beautiful, warm morning, the nicest of her stay in Scotland. She dug out some of her warm-weather clothes: pink-and-white-checked Bermuda shorts and a light sweater. She wore white golf shoes, a matching white visor, and a white glove to hide the bandage wrapped on her left hand. "Oh, I was a doll that morning," she later said.

The first tee was surrounded by an enormous crowd that had come to witness the first drives by Babe and Gordon. When Babe spotted a Union Jack flag, she stood at attention and saluted it. The crowd applauded. She then searched for an American flag. Someone pointed to one stretched on the roof of the clubhouse. Babe turned toward the Stars and Stripes, got down on her knees, and bowed three times. The crowd loved it.

The press had proclaimed Babe "the prohibitive favorite," and most wagers at the bookies were placed on Babe. But if Gordon was intimidated by the press or the oddsmakers, she did not show it during the morning round. After eleven holes, Gordon led Babe by two, and by the end of the morning session, they were tied. Each had shot a 75. This was shaping up to be Babe's toughest challenge. She tried not to think about the jinx.

"Babe, go git your slocks on," the Scottish fans told Babe as she walked off the eighteenth green. "Go git your slocks on." The way the fans saw it, Babe needed her "lucky slocks" if she had any chance of defeating her pesky challenger.

By lunchtime, the weather had suddenly turned cold, and Babe walked quickly back to her hotel. Her white golf shoes had also given her some trouble — the soles were cracked in a few places and needed to be repaired. After lunch and a brief nap, she changed back into her siren suit and slate blue corduroy slacks. (She later said it wasn't because of any superstition. "I was just cold!" she insisted.) Back at the club, Babe carried her cracked golf shoes to the shoemaker's shop. A sign in the window said: "Sorry. Closed. Gone To See The Babe." When someone informed the lady shoemaker that Babe required her immediate attention, she returned quickly and fixed Babe's shoes in time for the afternoon round.

On the first hole, Babe broke the deadlock by making a par to Gordon's bogey. On the par 5 second hole, Babe made an eagle three. That's all it took. She knew she was in charge.

On another hole, Babe hit a monstrous 260-yard drive, leaving herself a short wedge shot to the green. As she walked up the fairway, she fell in step behind two elderly men wearing kilts. "I've watched Walter Hagen and Bobby Jones and Gene Sarazen and all those Americans who've played here," one told the other, "and none of them could hit the ball better than this girl can."

Babe smiled. She caught up with the men, draping her arms across their shoulders. "How would you boys like to see me knock this little wedge shot right into the cup?" she asked.

"Ah," they said, laughing. "That would be fine."

And Babe almost did it. Her ball stopped on the lip of the cup. The two old Scotsmen watched, speechless.

Babe won the match by five holes with four left to play. The crowd stood and applauded her for what seemed to be fifteen minutes.

"The pants did it," she said on the fourteenth green, laughing.

Then she dramatically removed the glove from her left hand, showing the reporters her bandaged thumb. "It caused something of a sensation," she recalled.

Babe danced another Highland fling and hurdled over a brown brick wall near the clubhouse. When she was presented with the amateur trophy — "the big cup," Babe called it — she sang a Highland song. The fans loved it. A reporter asked Babe to reveal the secret of her success. "I just loosen my girdle and let the ball have it," she said.

This line was published in all the newspapers in Britain and beamed all over the world. Some commentators in the United Kingdom thought the quip, one of Babe's most famous, was unbecoming for the British Women's Amateur champion. Babe later insisted that she had not uttered those words in Scotland, but had first said them at the Celebrities Championship in Washington, DC, the previous month.

Despite that one false note, she had become the darling of the British press. "Surely no woman golfer has accomplished in a championship what Mrs. Zaharias has achieved in this one," said the *Manchester Guardian*. "She is a crushing and heartbreaking opponent."

A London newspaper declared, "We have not seen a fairway phantom like her — not in 47 years. What a babe!"

At the ceremony for the presentation of the handsome silver trophy, Babe wore a blue gabardine dress and white-and-blue shoes. She said she looked forward to returning "back home to George. This is the first time in nine years that I have been separated from him for so long."

Before going home, however, Babe indulged in a two-week victory lap around a few of Scotland's finest golf courses. First she played the Old Course at St. Andrews. Spectators were forbidden to follow her, to allow her privacy. But when Babe spotted more than a thousand people penned in a long distance away, she waved them over and yelled, "Come on!" The crowd followed her for all eighteen holes. On the eighteenth green, Babe told the gallery how much it meant for her to play the storied course, even though she said later, "The course gave me an awful letdown." This was golf's birthplace, and Babe ruminated over all the legends of the game who had blazed the path across the Old Course. "And I thought of all the great matches that had been decided on that course," she recalled, "and the hearts that had been broken there."

On a foggy day at Muirfield, Babe shot a 71, her best score in Scotland. Afterward, she was invited for tea inside the all-male clubhouse. She also played Gleneagles, at Tommy Armour's club, Lothianburn, in front of a raucous throng of three thousand fans. In Edinburgh, she spent her final evening in Scotland as the guest of the Ladies' Golf Union. At the train station, fans serenaded Babe on the platform, singing "Auld Lang Syne."

"I'd already been away from George longer than I ever had been since we got married," Babe recalled. "I wanted to get back home."

On the London-bound train, she had a private compartment filled with flowers. Her return trip to Southampton on the boat train was also quite different from her first trip. Babe didn't have to wait in any line, and a porter tended to her luggage. She even had a seat.

As the *Queen Elizabeth* approached New York, a tugboat carrying seventy-one reporters, photographers, and newsreel cameramen met the big ship. As Babe was standing on the rail, she spotted "a big guy with a white shirt" aboard the tug. "That's George," she said, then shoved two fingers into her mouth and whistled. At the same moment, the *Queen Elizabeth* blasted its horn.

"Hey, George, here I am!" she hollered.

George yelled, "Honey, I could hear your whistle above the *Queen Elizabeth*'s."

Babe gave it right back to him. When a rope ladder was dropped to allow the members of the press to climb aboard the *Queen Elizabeth*, George was the first to climb up. When the big ship listed at the same time, Babe said, "Hey, honey, watch out. You're going to turn the *Queen Elizabeth* over."

Aboard the ship, Babe, true to form, answered more than two hours' worth of questions. She plopped a blue Glengarry hat atop George's head and taught him the Highland fling. Then she showed the reporters the trophy bearing the inscription "Ladies' Amateur Golf Club Challenge Cup, Subscribed for by the Ladies' Golf Union, 1893." It bore the names of all the winners since 1893, and for the first time, it would spend a year in the United States.

"Seeing George again," Babe said, "gave me a greater thrill than I got when I won the championship." George vowed never to be apart from Babe for that long again. "You can't imagine how I felt while the Babe was over there playing those matches," he told reporters. "I kept the transatlantic wires busy enough to pay my fare twice across and back."

In Manhattan, Babe was suddenly in the highest demand of her career. She fielded a flood of offers. George and Babe met with Fred Corcoran, the now legendary promotional director of the PGA, who offered to represent Babe if she decided to turn pro. Corcoran represented the top stars of golf and baseball, including Sam Snead and Ted Williams.

Corcoran met George for the first time that day. He asked him what type of contract he wanted Babe to sign, if she decided to turn professional. "You and Babe work everything out," George replied.

Babe and George found time to see their old friend Grantland Rice. Although he was suffering from pneumonia, Rice insisted that he visit them in their hotel room for an interview for his column. "I spent a short half hour at their hotel quietly celebrating with Babe and George Zaharias—two wonderful kids, who I feel constitute an unusually warm and wonderful American love story," Rice wrote.

At last, it was time to return home to Denver, where fifty thousand people attended the city's parade honoring Babe. Each sport Babe had played was represented by a float. She stood on the last one, waving and smiling, surrounded by a carpet of red roses. At City Hall, Mayor Quigg Newton presented her with an oversized golden key to the city. It was 16 feet tall and weighed 250 pounds. Asked how she planned to transport the key home, Babe said, "George will carry it."

Part III

AGAIN

18

A Piece of Work

Before the lunchtime rush on August 14, 1947, a few dozen New York reporters congregated inside Toots Shor's restaurant on Fifty-first Street to hear Babe announce that she was abandoning the amateur sporting life again. As George saw it, his wife was seizing the opportunity to go out on top. Wasn't Babe riding a double-digit amateur tournament winning streak? After she won the Broadmoor Ladies Invitation in Colorado Springs after returning from Scotland, the press was reporting her winning streak as seventeen in a row, not counting her Spokane defeat. But even at fourteen consecutive victories, Babe's streak was unmatched by any male or female golfer in American history. The closest anyone had come was Byron Nelson, who won eleven straight PGA Tour events in 1945. A fellow Texan, Nelson said, "In Texas we call someone like Babe Zaharias 'a piece of work,' but brash as she could be at times, she sure could back it up."

There was precedent for joining the professional ranks, too. Patty Berg had turned pro in 1940, at the age of twenty-two, and had a contract with Wilson Sporting Goods. Betty Jameson and a handful of others also had made deals with corporate sponsors and played exclusively in each year's half dozen professional tournaments. Without those endorsements, some of the women could not have survived simply by playing golf.

But Babe wasn't sure that turning pro now was the wisest choice. At the start of the decade, she had struggled to recapture her amateur status, and the memory of that three-year USGA-imposed penance was still fresh. How much more money did George and Babe need, especially considering she no longer had parents she needed to support? How many T-bone steaks could they eat? But George and Fred Corcoran said that she really didn't have a choice. There was too much cash to be made.

The most tantalizing offer Babe received was from a Hollywood filmmaker, who told George by phone that he was willing to pay Babe $300,000 for a series of ten movie shorts about sports. There was talk of a book and a new golf exhibition tour. Several of America's finest country clubs in New York, Chicago, and Los Angeles clamored to sign Babe as their resident club pro. Sporting goods companies, women's clothing manufacturers, and watchmakers jostled for the privilege to use Babe's name to sell their products.

Babe made her decision official in a telegram to Charles W. Littlefield, president of the USGA: "I wish to advise that after considerable deliberation, I have decided to accept a motion-picture offer. Therefore, I will be unable to defend my title in Detroit in September. I wish to express at this time my sincerest thanks to you and the officials of the United States Golf Association for the many courtesies and considerations extended to me."

But things weren't that simple. At Toots Shor's, a reporter asked Babe the obvious question: where are you going to play golf? Wasn't the point of becoming an amateur having two dozen tournaments to play every year?

"Well, I'm going to enter the U.S. Open Championship—for men," she replied. Her impromptu response stunned George and Corcoran, who had no idea that she was contemplating playing in America's men's open championship. The reporters dashed out of the restaurant to hustle the story onto the wires. In a matter of days, the USGA passed a rule specifically prohibiting women—or, more precisely, Babe—from competing for its top prize. "As the championship has always been intended to be for men, the eligibility rules have been rephrased to confirm that condition," the USGA said in a statement. "Thus, the USGA has declined an informal entry submitted on behalf of Mrs. George Zaharias." (That rule has since been changed, and women are now allowed to play in all USGA championships.) No matter—Babe's reentry as a professional had captured all the headlines. Besides, she said later, "I don't suppose I'd have finished around the top if they had let me in there. But I don't think I'd have been at the bottom either. I wouldn't have disgraced myself."

Babe tried to justify her decision to abandon the amateur ranks by framing it as a desire to give back to the game that had made her a worldwide star. Within days, however, the proposed $300,000 movie deal fell through—at least that's what Babe and George told reporters. Pete Martin, the *Saturday Evening Post* writer, was convinced that no such offer had ever existed. He asked Babe to identify the film studio, but she refused, so Martin asked Corcoran, who said that George had been in discussions with Spyros Skouras, the president of 20th Century Fox. But Skouras told Martin that "negotiations were still in a highly tentative status—so tentative that no figure for the Babe's services had been set." Martin was withering in his assessment of Babe's hype, writing that the $300,000 offer, which had been widely reported, "may turn out to be more fabulous than any of the fables that have ever sprung up about the Babe." He went on to declare that no athlete had "ever claimed to have been offered such a colossal sum to turn professional."

The deceit did minimal damage to Babe and George's credibility. After she ended up making three sports-related movie shorts for Columbia Pictures for far more modest pay, many fans assumed she had been paid the preposterous sum that had been reported.

Corcoran had assumed a big chunk of George's management of his wife's activities. Yet could he, one of the nation's leading sports agents, and George, who owned one of the sports world's biggest egos, comanage Babe? Was there enough of Babe to go around? Nothing about this shared management arrangement was going to be easy or simple.

In the beginning, Corcoran attempted to be extremely deferential to George, checking in with him for advice before doing anything. At the same time, George continued to book events for Babe. But Corcoran quickly realized that George would accept almost any sum in exchange for Babe's appearances, a habit that ran counter to Corcoran's own booking strategy. Corcoran explained to George that it was not in Babe's best interest if some clients discovered there were varying rates being paid for her appearances. George didn't like the comeuppance and sulked, feeling as if he was being edged out of the aspect of being Babe's husband that he enjoyed the most.

The first thing Corcoran did was book Babe for several nongolfing exhibitions. Babe was paid $500 for pregame baseball performances in parks all over the country, including Yankee Stadium, Wrigley Field, and spring training venues in Florida. She was on the field no more than thirty minutes, taking a few cuts during batting practice and hitting golf balls with her pitching wedge from home plate into the outfield. She wanted to try to smash the ball out of the park, but the owners refused, worried that she might hurt a fan.

One night at Detroit's Briggs Stadium, Tigers general manager Billy Evans tried to slash Babe's fee from $500 to $450. He told Corcoran that the stadium was already sold out because the Tigers were playing the

Red Sox and the fans wanted to see Ted Williams, not Babe Didrikson. When Corcoran refused to lower the fee, Evans finally agreed to pay it. That night, a steady rain delayed the start of the game. When Babe emerged from the dugout to do her act on the parts of the field not covered by the tarp, the crowd gave her a standing ovation. The game ended up being postponed, but Babe was on the rain-slicked field for an hour. She "had given the fans their money's worth," Corcoran said.

At Yankee Stadium, a big pregame crowd watched Babe take the mound and throw a few pitches of batting practice. She beckoned Joe DiMaggio to the plate, but he refused and disappeared into the dugout. So Babe walked over and said, "Come on, Joe." He still refused, until Babe went into the dugout and grabbed his arm and a bat. Babe hit DiMaggio in the ribs with a pitch, though he wasn't hurt. DiMaggio smashed a few of her pitches, then finally took a big, pantomime swing and missed. Without a word, he sat back down. Although many writers have reported that Babe struck out DiMaggio, his third strike was a gift to Babe and the fans.

At a Sarasota, Florida, ballpark during spring training, Babe and Ted Williams faced off in a golf-driving contest. Williams outdrove Babe, but not by the distance some fans had expected. When Williams dribbled one ball off the tee, Babe shouted, "Better run those grounders out, Ted. There may be an overthrow."

Corcoran also signed Babe to endorse an array of products, from cigarettes and clothes to watches and car batteries. She was in such high demand that companies that produced similar products hired her, an odd arrangement that is almost never seen today. For example, Babe signed an $8,000-a-year lifetime contract with Wilson Sporting Goods, which began manufacturing Babe Zaharias golf clubs. She simultaneously re-signed with P. Goldsmith Sons, another sporting goods company, which promised its dealers in a sales brochure, "'Babe' Didrikson

Coordinated Golf Equipment...Will Establish a New Record in Sales for You." Goldsmith also promised, "THE NAME 'BABE' DIDRIKSON ON A GOLF BALL AND A GOLF CLUB WILL GUARANTEE ITS SALABILITY!!"

Babe gave advice to Serbin, a dress manufacturer, on the design of a golf dress and a blouse with buttons on the sleeves that accommodated a wider swing—"sensible sports shirts for gals who want comfort with grooming," Babe called it. At the same time, for $10,000 a year Babe agreed to wear Weathervane sports clothes. Like the sporting goods companies, the two rival clothing manufacturers did not mind sharing Babe.

Suddenly, she was that ubiquitous. In a widely published print advertisement for Timex watches, Babe was pictured methodically driving a golf ball in one picture and happily washing dishes in another. "Housekeeping and golf—I love them both," she said. She endorsed cigarettes (Babe was a pack-a-day smoker, although this endorsement was the public's first hint of that fact) and even leased her name to the maker of the Prest-O-Lite Hi-Level Battery.

Corcoran brokered a book deal with A. S. Barnes, a New York publisher. In the 125-page illustrated book titled *Championship Golf,* Babe (identified on the cover as Mildred Didrikson Zaharias) offers advice on every aspect of the game, from tips on grips and putting techniques to advice on practice and concentration. In the close-up photographs shot at Leewood Golf Club in Eastchester, New York, Babe demonstrates her golfing techniques while appearing to be dressed for a formal dinner: she is wearing a dress with buttoned sleeves and a chunky bracelet, and her fingernails are painted red. She dedicated the book to George, Stanley Kertes, Tommy Armour, the USGA, the PGA, and "the sports writers and the many other friends I have made as a golfer." In the introduction, she recounts her record-setting track-and-field career, her time playing "big-time basketball," and "a fling at many other sports, but when that golf bug hit me it was fatal. I've never recovered and hope I never will. I expect to play golf until I am 90—even longer if anybody figures out a way to swing a club from a rocking chair." The how-to portion of the book is dry:

Q Why do you and most other leading players grip your putter differently from your other clubs?

A No two grips seem to be quite alike in putting. Each player has one that is all his own. The important point in putting is to be comfortable and relaxed. Any grip that you find by experience to be effective and that leaves you comfortable and relaxed is a sound grip.

Despite receiving mixed reviews, *Championship Golf* sold moderately well. Fresh off that success, Babe signed a contract to write a nationally syndicated newspaper column for the McNaught Syndicate. Titled "The Babe Says—" the column would consist of golf tips to be ghostwritten by Betty Hicks, a published writer. George hated the first three drafts, however, saying that Hicks's writing didn't "sound like Babe." The column was killed before even one was published.

Soon Corcoran was booking so many baseball and golf exhibitions for Babe that in a single month, she took seventeen plane rides. George always bragged that no amount of physical exertion could slow down Babe. But now she was feeling exhausted, irritable, and resentful. She was out crisscrossing the country while George was home in Denver and Corcoran was in his office in New York. The two men were competing against each other to fill her calendar and, not incidentally, also to outdo each other. The result: Babe was living out of a suitcase.

"Mildred wouldn't turn anybody down," her brother Louis said. "She was on the move. We kept telling her and her husband, too, that she was overdoing it, and that no human could hold up under that much stress and strain."

It was inevitable that the hyperkinetic pace would catch up with

Babe on the golf course. At the Women's Texas Open in Fort Worth that October, she lost in the quarterfinals to a little-known amateur named Betty Mims White. The stunning upset ended Babe's winning streak. Babe pinned all the blame on the frenzied pace prescribed by her handlers. "I honestly believe that if I had squeaked through, I'd have gone on and stretched my winning streak to twenty-five or thirty tournaments," she later said. "For a while after that loss a little of my incentive was gone. I didn't have quite so much to work for, now that my string was broken." Babe's audaciousness was, of course, typical. It was hard enough to win fourteen tournaments in a row, but twenty-five or thirty?

Even as she lost "a little...incentive," Babe wasn't going to lose her determination to get back on the winning track. In her next tournament, the Hardscrabble Women's Invitational in Fort Smith, Arkansas, Babe demolished the field, shooting a seventy-two-hole score of 293, a record low score for women in tournament stroke play.

At the end of 1947, Babe was selected the Associated Press Female Athlete of the Year for the third consecutive year.

By 1948, Babe felt as if she were right back where she had started a decade earlier—running around the country doing exhibitions with golfers such as Sam Snead and Ben Hogan. The only difference was the paycheck. For each appearance, she was now being paid $100 more than her male counterparts. There were more professional tournaments for women than there had been ten years earlier, but the schedule was still overrun with amateur tournaments. In 1948, she won just $3,400 from her tournament play, although her endorsements and exhibitions brought in more than $100,000, a sum that exceeded Ted Williams's salary. That seemed to make the trade-off worthwhile—at least on most days.

The highlight of her hectic schedule was her first U.S. Women's Open victory in August at the Atlantic City Country Club. Babe never lost her early lead, winning the $1,200 first-prize check by eight strokes.

Before and during the event, there was a lot of focus on a $1,000 bonus offered to anyone who could break 300. In fact, a club member had offered the bonus after Babe had threatened not to play because the purse wasn't high enough. On the final green, Babe needed to sink a five-foot putt to finish with a 299 and win the bonus. But she stubbed the ball, leaving it six inches short of the money. "Oh well," Babe said with a shrug. "Couldn't get a putt down. It doesn't make any difference to me, because I'd only have to give the $1,000 to the government. I'm in that kind of income bracket."

Even with all the travel, Babe craved more competition. There were now seven tournaments on the professional calendar, but that wasn't nearly enough for Babe. "Once again George came up with the answer," she said. "He got the idea that there should be a professional tournament circuit for women, just as there was for men."

The idea for a new professional tour actually came from L. B. Icely, the president of Wilson Sporting Goods. Men had the PGA Tour, Icely said. Why shouldn't women have the same thing?

Women had already founded a professional tour, but it was a failing experiment and the tour was on its way out. In 1944, a woman named Hope Seignious chartered the Women's Professional Golf Association (WPGA). Betty Hicks, the 1941 U.S. Women's Amateur champion, was a WPGA charter member and its president. But the WPGA never caught on with the public. For one thing, the postwar era was not the proper environment in which to begin a women's professional tournament circuit. The postwar baby boom had just begun, and the gender discrimination absent by necessity during the war had resurfaced as government and private industry focused on providing jobs for millions of male veterans. The only other organized opportunity for women athletes was the All-American Girls Professional Baseball League, founded in 1943 by Philip K. Wrigley. Still relatively popular in the late 1940s, the league owed a big chunk of its gate receipts to the fact that the women played in pastel shorts that showed off their legs. Golf promised no comparable incentives.

The golf world did nothing to smooth the WPGA's attempts to win public support. An organization of golf equipment manufacturers refused to sponsor the new tour. Women's amateur associations perceived the tour as a threat, and its leaders aggressively pressured a number of prestigious country clubs to refuse to host professional tournaments. For years, women's amateur golf leaders had complained bitterly that the USGA failed to help them or recognize them. Now these same leaders were giving a cold shoulder to the upstart WPGA. The men's professional golf organization, the PGA, also viewed the new WPGA as a rival.

As a result of the pressure, the earliest professional tournaments had to be played on tattered public courses. In fact, the WPGA's first tournament, the newly christened U.S. Women's Open, wasn't even held until August 1946, in Spokane, Washington. (That was the tournament that Babe lost but refused to acknowledge.) The purse was an unheard-of $19,700 from the slot-machine proceeds of the Spokane Athletic Round Table. In 1946 and 1947, the WPGA also sponsored an exhibition tour headlined by Betty Hicks.

Aside from a shortage of events on the women's pro schedule, there weren't all that many competitors. When Babe joined the professional ranks, she was only the eighth female professional golfer, joining Hicks, Patty Berg, Helen Dettweiler, Mary Mozel Wagner, Kathryn Hemphill, Betty Jameson, and Helen Hicks. And unlike the men, the women not only were expected to play but also were expected to organize the tournaments, sharing the responsibilities for travel arrangements, rule making, and public relations. When the association met in

March 1947 to choose a new president, chaos erupted; none of the members wanted one of their own in charge. It was a recipe for failure. "It didn't collapse financially," Betty Hicks said of the WPGA. "It just sort of faded away."

When Icely offered to fill the void, he didn't just envision a women's professional golf tour; he pledged to put up his own corporate money to get it going. Fred Corcoran agreed to organize the new tour. There was early talk about merging with the moribund WPGA, as a polite gesture to Hope Seignious, but she stubbornly refused.

"Well, okay, we thought, in England they call them 'ladies' and in a way it sounded classier than women,'" Corcoran recalled. "We decided to call our tour the 'Ladies Professional Golf Association.'" But to a few of the charter members, the name might as well have been the *Lady's* Professional Golf Tour. Because the lady that the tour was created to showcase was Babe.

19

The Lady's Tour

On a cool day in Miami in January 1949, inside the Venetian Hotel on North Bayshore Drive, Fred Corcoran presided over the first official meeting with the purpose of creating the Ladies Professional Golf Association (LPGA). Among the attendees were Babe, George, and Patty Berg. Their first order of business was to try to buy the charter belonging to the now defunct WPGA. This was a goodwill gesture to salute the pioneering work of Hope Seignious. Corcoran called Seignious to ask whether she'd sell; she refused. It was just as well, he decided. Perhaps it was better to start from scratch. The WPGA had failed despite being owned by a handful of professional players whose noble goal was to promote women's golf. The way Corcoran and L. B. Icely envisioned it, the LPGA would be owned by deep-pocketed corporate sponsors. Their goal was to have a tour that promoted its players and its sponsors' products—not necessarily in that order.

Four of the original charter members—Patty Berg, Helen Dettweiler, Betty Jameson, and Babe—each had at least one sponsor that sold golf clothes, golf shoes, and golf clubs. Corcoran targeted these manufacturers. In exchange for a promise that the women would wear and use their products, would they provide the purse money needed to get the fledgling tour going? "Potential sponsors were polite when I called them," Corcoran recalled, "but you could hear them stifling a yawn over the phone."

That first year, only Icely's Wilson Sporting Goods agreed to provide any cash — $15,000, which became the sum total of the LPGA's prize money in 1949. Babe won the biggest slice of that pie, $4,300.

Corcoran, whose salary as the director of the LPGA was paid by Wilson Sporting Goods, understood that the players needed money from endorsements and exhibitions. There wasn't enough prize money to help them defray their considerable travel and living expenses. So if the LPGA had any chance of survival, it needed more than one sponsor. In 1950, Alvin Handmacher, chairman of the Weathervane Sports Clothes Company, which had previously sponsored Babe, pledged $15,000 for the Weathervane Cross-Country Golf Tournament, a series of four matches in as many cities with a $5,000 first prize going to the low aggregate scorer. The infusion of money encouraged a number of amateur golfers to turn pro and chase the money. "There were a lot of women golfers who couldn't afford to go on playing amateur golf forever, but couldn't risk the uncertainty of a professional career without any prospect or hope of making it pay out," Corcoran recalled. "Handmacher's prize money and the additional tournaments at way stations gave them the courage to take the first step."

The Weathervane series quickly became one of the premier women's events. "Let's make no mistake about it," Corcoran said. "Alvin put the Ladies PGA in business."

And Babe made sure the LPGA stayed in business. "She was the color, the gate attraction," Corcoran said. "She was, without a doubt, the greatest woman athlete the world has ever seen — and probably the greatest woman golfer of all time." No one had to tell Babe what she needed to do. She did what she had always done — the same shtick that she had performed onstage at the Palace Theater and atop a donkey riding around a baseball diamond. She gave the people a show.

In February 1950, Babe's legend grew — and with it the chances of the LPGA's success — when the Associated Press announced the winner of its award for the best female athlete of the first half of the twentieth century. The voting wasn't even close: Babe won with an astonishing 319 first-place votes and a total of 1,030 points; the second-place finisher, tennis star Helen Wills Moody, finished a distant second with 394 points. "My gosh, I don't know if I deserve it," Babe said, the false modesty causing many of her fellow players to roll their eyes, "but I guess they know what they're doing. I'm thrilled to death." Corcoran recognized that Babe's triumph would attract further interest in the LPGA.

During that year's U.S. Women's Open, the players met in the lounge at Rolling Hills Country Club in Wichita, Kansas, to officially begin the new tour. It was September 28, 1950, and the original six charter members were joined by seven former WPGA members to form the LPGA. Today these thirteen women are revered as the founding mothers of what became the most successful women's sports association in the world. Patty Berg was elected its first president, and the LPGA was incorporated in New York with a lengthy list of bylaws and rules.

Perhaps not coincidentally, Babe scorched the field at the Open, crushing Betsy Rawls in the final round by making seven birdies and winning by nine strokes. Her tournament score of 291 tied a course record. "A big thrill," Rawls said of playing with Babe. "I loved watching Babe. She was just spectacular to watch.... She was a big star then and I didn't expect anything of myself."

"Babe was an entertainer," said Marilynn Smith, a Kansas pro and one of the LPGA's founding members, who'd win twenty-one LPGA tournaments in her career. "She knew you're not just out there hitting a golf ball. I don't think we realized it; maybe she was one step ahead of us. She was always entertaining—and that's what got the people out to see us. Once they came out, they could see we were pretty good golfers, too."

At the early board meetings, George Zaharias was a bombastic, and eventually unwelcome, presence. By now, George weighed almost 350 pounds. Some of the women believed that he showed up at meetings "feeling good," if not outright drunk. None of the women, including Babe, appreciated hearing George growl, "Women's golf belongs to me."

In addition, George wasn't accustomed to being told to follow the rules. "I don't give a shit about them by-laws," he told the LPGA board. For her part, Babe found George's behavior embarrassing. His disheveled appearance and stark demands for control bothered her most of all. She asked him to stay away; he refused.

Early board meetings were chaotic affairs, marked by shouting, tears, and arguments over everything from public relations strategy to scheduling. Disagreements often centered on the distribution of the work. Some of the women felt that others weren't pulling their weight. Betty Hicks called the arguments "mild pyrotechnics," although one screaming match caused a hired stenographer to hurl her pad and pencil and quit. Inevitably, the new tour's behind-the-scenes anarchy spilled over onto the fairways. More than once, players argued bitterly in front of galleries, which seemed to relish the bursts of drama.

The LPGA's hardscrabble beginnings made the tour even more accessible to the fans. For one thing, some of the public courses hosting those early tournaments were in shambles. The wheat-colored fairways on one Oklahoma course were cracked and parched by a stubborn drought; the ball carried farther but lent the tournament a bush-league feel. The women stayed in ramshackle motels, driving themselves from event to event in cars often sidelined by blown tires and overheated engines. Frayed nerves sometimes led to hurt feelings and lengthy spats. "We get along real well," Betsy Rawls once said. "Some of the girls I won't have dinner with for a whole year." But even with hurt feelings, Rawls later said, "we all had to play every tournament because you couldn't skip one. If one or two people dropped out of a 30-player field, it could be disastrous." For each woman, playing the tour was "a labor of love," Marilynn Smith said. "God knows there wasn't much money." In 1953, for instance, Betty Hicks collected $3,750 in prize money, but she "spent $3,335 of it on hotels, meals, tips, airplane tickets, automobile tires, caddies and cab fares" and put forty thousand miles on her car's odometer.

Despite the setbacks and disputes, the players worked hard to raise money and grow the tour. Prior to each tournament, they would hit golf balls at a local ballpark, then take the microphone and ask people to come out to watch them play that weekend. They threw "swing parades," where each player lined up to swing using a different club. Most attended Kiwanis Club luncheons, talking up the tour. Although some skipped these organization-run social events and fund-raisers, Babe always insisted on attending, knowing that her presence added some much-needed star power.

At the midpoint of the twentieth century, the American sports fan preferred baseball, boxing, and horse racing, in that order. Football was still a decade away from beginning its stranglehold on the American sports psyche. And golf—particularly women's golf—was far down the list. Although sports fans had seemed indifferent to a women's golf tour in the year or two following the war, by 1950 the nation's mood had changed. The baby boom was in full swing, and Americans were looking for new ways to enjoy the first blush of postwar economic prosperity. Despite its halting start, the LPGA came along at the right moment. Big-name sponsors quickly followed Weathervane, including MacGregor, Spalding, and Golfcraft. In 1951, the LPGA's first full calendar year of events, $50,000 in prize money was divvied up at fourteen tournaments. Babe was the tour's leading money winner, taking home

$13,550. By 1955, the total amount had increased to $160,000 for thirty scheduled tournaments.

"Women's golf owes everything to Babe," Peggy Kirk later said. And naturally, Babe knew it. One day in 1950, as Babe was walking down the first fairway at an LPGA tournament, she draped her arm across Marilynn Smith's shoulders and said, "You know, kid, it's always nice to play with you because you have such a nice gallery." Smith laughed. She was a rookie on the tour, but the point was clear: the gallery belonged to Babe.

On the tour, every woman played in Babe's imposing shadow, but no one resented it more than Louise Suggs. Born in 1923 in Atlanta, Suggs was an attractive brunette whose deadly touch on the greens was matched by a deadly serious demeanor. She was arguably the second-best player on the tour, but her humorless, often bland style ensured that she'd never win even half the press praise or the fan affection lavished on Babe.

From 1950 to 1955, Babe won twenty-nine professional tournaments and Suggs won twenty-five. But if you read the newspaper coverage of women's golf across those years, you'd have no idea that Suggs was winning nearly as often as Babe. Whereas banner headlines proclaimed Babe's victories, news of Suggs's wins was relegated to the inside pages, nestled next to the American Legion ball scores. When Suggs beat Babe in a final-round match—something she did six times—"the headline usually said Babe lost, not Louise won," Betty Jameson recalled. "Oh, and that annoyed Louise Suggs.... You know, she didn't deserve that." The most glaring example of the lopsided press coverage occurred after Suggs, still an amateur, won the British Women's Amateur in 1948, the year after Babe had won it. Because she was the second American woman to win and had a more muted personality than Babe, the coverage was understated, something Suggs resented for years. "I knew her as well as anybody would know her, I guess," Suggs said of Babe. "Very charismatic. A bully."

The rivalry between Babe and Suggs was, for both women, all-consuming, distracting, and ultimately exhausting. "Louise was the frankest and most outspoken player on the tour," Betsy Rawls recalled. "I think Babe felt threatened by Suggs. Louise played with dignity and by the rules." In Suggs's opinion, "Babe had to win and she didn't give a damn how."

Suggs believed that Babe routinely violated the game's rules and flouted its dignity with her tough-talking, crude demeanor. Rawls agreed. "Babe tried to intimidate people, to tell you the truth," Rawls said.

In March 1952, at the New Orleans Women's Open, Suggs was lining up a short shot on the edge of the eighteenth green. When Babe noticed, she grabbed her harmonica and loudly blew a tune, while fellow golfer Betty Dodd, a close friend of Babe's, strummed her guitar. The incident bothered Suggs for years.

Despite her fame and dominance, Babe was as blunt, boastful, and hard-edged as ever, seizing any mental edge within reach. "Hey girls, Babe's here!" she'd announce as she breezed into the clubhouse before a tournament. "Now who's gonna finish second?" Or, "Why are you girls botherin' practicing?" Before one tournament, Babe loaned an eleven-iron to Peggy Kirk, who began using it with dazzling results. After watching Kirk for a few holes, Babe confiscated her club. "I'm sure as hell not going to help anyone beat me," she said.

Many years later, in 1995, Suggs recalled Babe's treatment of her fellow players this way: "According to her, the rest of us were spear carriers."

Babe often exaggerated her scores for reporters. After she shot an 80 during a practice round before a tournament in Denver, reporters asked her for her score. "Oh, about a 70," she told them. Kirk, who had played with Babe, was astonished by this fib. Later, she asked Babe why she'd felt compelled to shave ten strokes off her score. "Well, I could have had a 70 if I had tried," Babe told her. "Besides, you gotta tell 'em what they want to hear. Nobody wants to hear I shot an 80."

This was just Babe being Babe, recalled Kirk, who forgave her for most of these indiscretions. But Babe's antics and her fresh mouth deeply offended Louise Suggs, who believed that players should never do anything to dishonor the game. Suggs was especially offended when she once caught Babe cheating during the final round of a tournament.

It was August 1951, and Babe and Suggs were playing in the All-American Open Championship for Women at Tam O'Shanter Country Club in Niles, Illinois. One version has it that, with Suggs watching on a back-nine hole, Babe retrieved her ball from a stand of trees and illegally took a drop—in the middle of the fairway, at least fifty feet from where her ball had landed. Suggs was so upset by the illegal drop that she lost her concentration, and Babe went on to win the tournament. After the match, Suggs refused to sign Babe's scorecard, according to Betsy Rawls and several other players. "Suggs lost all respect for Babe after that," Rawls said.

"There were times that you'd sit down and try to talk to [Babe], saying, 'Now look, don't do these things,'" Suggs recalled. "The reply might be, 'You mind your business, and I'll mind mine.' I mean that was the gist of the conversation, and that's the way it wound up." She added, "It affected everyone, and in the Rule Book, the USGA Rule Book, if you see a person that takes advantage of the Rules, and if you don't call them on it, you're just as guilty as that person. And that was the whole thing—in speaking up, you're protecting the rest of the field."

Although Marilynn Smith heard the "cheating stories," she refused to believe them. "Babe was too proud—she wanted to win, fair and square," Smith recently said. "Would she try to get a mental edge over us? Sure, all the time. But that's not cheating." Several other players have also said that they never saw Babe cheat.

But Suggs insisted, "Everybody knew what was going on but nobody could do anything about it. So it just got to the point where it was a laughing stock type situation and you just kept your mouth shut and went on about your business as best you could."

At a tournament in Tampa, Babe's ball became lodged next to a concrete statue of a lion. According to the rules, this was an obstruction that could not be moved. But George, who was watching from the gallery, didn't see it that way. "As far as George Zaharias was concerned," Betty Hicks later said, the statue "simply became a loose impediment. George picked it up and moved it. It was not fixed or growing, and this huge concrete statue became a loose impediment...only because George was strong enough to move it."

Babe did other things to annoy her fellow players. If she was struggling through a bad few holes and it started to rain, she'd use influence with the tournament organizers to call off the round. She would make prank phone calls to players on the eve of a tournament, usually late at night, disguising her voice to sound like a German woman or a small girl.

And she was not always a gracious loser. "She really hated to lose," Betsy Rawls said. "I don't think I've ever seen anybody that took losing less gracefully than Babe did. She would get angry at everybody around her. She would—oh, she would sulk." One player recalled that she snapped a putter in two over her knee like a toothpick, after missing a key putt during a $1 "Nassau" (a Nassau is a three-part wager, with the golfer with the lowest score on the front nine, back nine, and full card winning separate bets). She often played gin rummy, usually for a few dollars, with club members in the evenings and would sink into a deep funk if she lost.

On the second hole at the 1951 Women's Western Open in Philadelphia, Babe was distracted by a platoon of photographers who insisted on snapping pictures as she hit her second shot out of the rough. When her shot failed to reach the green, she turned to one of the photographers and said, "Okay, now I suppose you want another picture." As the gallery murmured its disapproval, she said bitterly, "These cameramen must take their pictures, I suppose." When she reached her ball lying on the edge of green, Babe picked it up with an angry flourish. "You can have this one, Patty," she said. "I can't do anything with all this clicking." Babe had a chance to halve the hole, but she conceded instead. That might have cost her the tournament. She lost the match by just one hole to Patty Berg.

The other players on the tour gossiped about the outburst, sure that it would hurt the LPGA. Babe overheard these remarks but didn't care. Those other women were there to be beaten, not befriended.

Betsy Rawls recalled that Babe often made comments on the golf course "that were designed to upset her opponent. She'd move when somebody was lining up a shot. Her whole manner would be intimidating. She would ignore the person, never say, 'Good shot,' never be gracious....She always thought that she should win a tournament. Never thought that she should lose. She would use every device she knew of to win a golf tournament. And that's what she lived for. That was her life. Her self-worth was based on winning, on beating people at something—if not golf, anything." Earlier, journalist Lawrence Lader had observed that Babe possessed the same take-no-prisoners approach to golf that heavyweight champion Joe Louis had in the boxing ring—"a cold indifference to what people think or say about her."

As she had done at the 1932 Olympics, Babe made friends with younger players, such as Marilynn Smith, whom she did not perceive as a threat. "Babe could be a very friendly type," Betty Hicks said, "as long as you weren't simultaneously after the same objective." She also liked having a young protégée. "She put me at ease immediately," Smith recalled. "She looked out for me." Another young amateur, Shirley Spork, was having breakfast one morning with Babe, George, and Smith. Babe was trying to persuade Spork to join the LPGA. Spork, only nineteen years old, said meekly that she was only an amateur. Babe stood up and theatrically tapped her on the head. "There," she said. "You're a pro."

But of all the young golfers, Babe became fastest friends with Betty Dodd, whom she met on the tour in San Antonio, Dodd's hometown, during a Red Cross charity exhibition Babe played against Betty Jameson in 1947. Dodd, who began playing golf at age thirteen, was a high school junior at the time. Three years later, Dodd, now nineteen, was playing the amateur circuit when she ran into Babe again in Miami. Babe was then thirty-nine years old.

Dodd was as thin as a whippet, with piercing brown eyes and a mop of auburn hair that looked as if it had not seen a brush for at least a fortnight. When Dodd first joined the LPGA Tour in 1951, Bertha Bowen, who knew the Dodd family from San Antonio, asked Babe to look after the young woman, maybe give her a few pointers. "I wrote Babe about her and I guess when they met they liked one another right away," Bowen recalled. But Bowen was always astonished at how slovenly Dodd looked. "Her shirt was hanging out and her hair was hanging in her eyes," she recalled. "Betty was from a good family and she had many advantages Babe didn't have. But she would go around looking just awful."

One spring, Babe and Dodd visited Bowen at her home in Fort Worth. Bowen came home one day to find Babe giving Dodd a permanent. "Sit still!" Babe yelled as she fussed with Dodd's hair. "Bertha made a lady out of me and I'm gonna do the same thing to you."

Soon, however, Babe would discover that she needed Dodd more than Dodd needed her.

*   *   *

"Babe Zaharias was openly, hostilely, aggressively, bitterly, laughingly, jokingly, viciously and even sometimes lovingly competitive," Betty Hicks observed. More than a few of the LPGA players would have challenged the idea that Babe's competitive zeal was *ever* demonstrated in a way approaching "lovingly."

Indeed, Babe acted as if she owned the tour. And in those early years, she did. She won seven of her twelve tournaments in 1951, including the All-American Open Championship for Women, the World Championship, and the Women's Texas Open. She was the leading money winner for the year, with $15,087. Yet Babe could make that sum by performing in a month's worth of exhibitions.

Because the tournament purses were small, Babe insisted that she be paid secret appearance money, usually $1,000, just for showing up. George May, the tournament director of the All-American series at the Tam O'Shanter, was one of several organizers who acquiesced to Babe's demands. If she broke 80, May would pay Babe a bonus of $1,000. (Because she always broke 80, May's threshold didn't amount to much of a test.) This was a Babe-only bonus. The other players, particularly Louise Suggs, were outraged, but Babe kept accepting the money. She felt that she deserved it, and she probably did. Her presence ensured the sale of hundreds of tickets that would have gone unsold if she didn't play. Her husband, George, had planted this idea in her mind, but it was a rule that Babe, George, and Fred Corcoran ferociously enforced.

The money rolled in. By 1951, Babe was making far more than George, a fact that gnawed at him. That year, *Time* magazine dubbed her "Big Business Babe." During a three-year stretch, Babe played 656 exhibitions, earning $500 a round and $600 on Sundays. She declined to divulge her annual salary to reporters, though they asked often. She confided to friends that by her own rough estimate, she was quickly approaching the $1 million career mark. Corcoran confirmed her bankability: "She has become the first woman athlete to bring her annual income up to six figures."

"I'm making it fast'n Ah can spend it," she liked to say. "Where I go, the galleries go. Let the rest starve." To Babe's colleagues, it was as if she were cramming her amazing success down their throats.

"We weren't out there for the money, that's for sure," Shirley Spork later said. "It wasn't easy making ends meet, either. In 1950, it was the year they started Holiday Inn. And we traveled — we went from Holiday Inn to Holiday Inn. They were cheap. If we could, we stayed in members' homes, and we were thankful for that. We drove everywhere; we didn't fly anywhere. Babe was the only one getting rich."

In 1953, the players demanded that Babe, who had just been elected president of the LPGA, call an emergency meeting to discuss her under-the-table income. Several of the women complained bitterly not only that Babe was receiving bonuses but also that she steadfastly refused to reveal details about them. To some, the secrecy was even more offensive than the money. Babe listened in quiet fury.

"If it wasn't for us pigeons, you wouldn't have a tour," Spork, one of the LPGA's thirteen founding members, told her.

Babe just laughed. "You're right, kid." Then she let them have it: "Let me tell you girls something — you know when there's a star, like in show business, the star has her name in lights on the marquee. Right? And the star gets the money because the people come to see the star, right? Well, *I'm* the star and all of you are in the chorus. *I* get the money. And if it weren't for me, half of our tournaments wouldn't be."

The other top players there — Louise Suggs, Peggy Kirk Bell (Peggy had gotten married in 1953), and Betty Jameson — listened in stunned silence. Even by Babe's standards, this burst of ego was something to behold. There really wasn't anything they could say. Babe was never going to back down, and she certainly wasn't going to share the money. Later, Bell acknowledged, "Well, Babe was right. . . . She was the star." Afterward, Bell quietly told her friend, "Babe, you shouldn't have said it. I would have said it for you."

Marilynn Smith was also there and just shrugged. "She kind of always got what she wanted," Smith later recalled. "And nobody was going to stop her, either."

On the tour, Babe's dominant play was obvious, especially on the tee. Babe's drives lacked the fluidity of Joyce Wethered's, but she demonstrated pure power. "She came along with that great power game and it led to lower scores and more excitement," Patty Berg said. "She even changed the swing. It used to be built on the Scottish method and we hit waist high, more flat. Babe would swing high and hard."

Bell once asked Babe how she managed to produce monster drives. Babe reached over her left shoulder with her right hand and patted her back just above her shoulder blade. "I take it away with this muscle on the backswing, then hit it," she told her friend. Bell later explained, "That muscle in the upper left side of your back is a key one. If you can stretch it out like a spring going back, you'll get incredible speed coming down, and a lot more distance."

"She was the swashbuckling type," Smith said. "Babe had a different swing from everybody. She would swing the club on a power shot, and the force of it made her fall backward on her right foot. Babe hit more of a low driving ball with a lot of roll. The roll gave her the distance."

Babe's low driving shots often veered into the trees or crashed into bunkers, but she'd shrug it off; she was easily the best scrambler on the tour. "She was smart enough to create a way to get out of trouble," Betty Jameson said.

Babe also possessed a nearly flawless short game, a rare thing for a big hitter. Gene Sarazen had shown her how to escape like a cool cat from a bunker. Babe cherished the sand wedge that he'd invented and given her back in the 1930s. It was one of the most trusted clubs in her bag. And on the greens, her smooth putting rarely let her down. Within five feet, Babe was automatic. "She was strongest on the greens," Betsy Rawls said. "She had that very soft touch."

It wasn't enough for the women of the LPGA to prove their ability to American galleries. Fred Corcoran wanted them to prove they were the best women golfers in the world. So he put together a transatlantic, coed golf tournament: the six top-finishing American women in the 1951 Weathervane Cross-Country Golf Tournament would go to Great Britain to play the top six British men.

Leonard Crawley, a British golf writer and former captain of the British Walker Cup team, accepted Corcoran's challenge and didn't even try to camouflage his glee. He told Corcoran that he wanted to play "that Babe person." In the British press, Crawley mercilessly mocked the American women's chances to defeat him and the other men—or British women, for that matter. Hadn't the British Isles invented golf?

When Babe heard about Crawley's challenge, she told Corcoran, "Save him for me." She'd go to the United Kingdom under one condition—"only if I can have Crawley." So in July 1951, Babe, Betty Jameson, Peggy Kirk Bell, Patty Berg, Betsy Rawls, and Betty Bush flew to London for a first-of-its-kind eighteen-day tour of Britain. The British press loved it; this would be Babe's first return visit since her 1947 amateur victory. Memories of her Highland fling were still fresh in the Brits' minds.

First, the American women played the British men at Wentworth. "Now, Mildred, you go up there and hit," Crawley said, pointing to the forward women's tee.

"Hell, no," Babe said, "I'm goin' to stay back here and hit with you, son." (All six women hit from the men's tees.) But Babe wasn't finished. "Leonard, I'd like to make you a bet. If I beat you, I want you to shave off that big ol' mustache. Is it a deal?"

During the morning session, on Wentworth's East Course, the men and women played to a draw. At lunch, the men drank heavily in the pub. After lunch, the players resumed play on the West Course. Babe shot a 74, crushing Crawley, who walked off the eighteenth green without uttering a word to waiting reporters. He got into his car and drove away. "It was their own fault for treating the women too lightly," writer Enid Wilson said, "and over-lubricating themselves at lunch." For days, the British press skewered Crawley for refusing to shave off his handlebar mustache.

At Sunningdale, the American women crushed British and Irish male candidates for the Walker Cup team, sweeping all six matches. In a best-ball match at Wentworth, Babe and Patty Berg went up against a pair of Walker Cup team nominees. On the seventeenth hole, the women trailed by one hole.

Babe drove her ball into the tall grass, but she remained supremely confident. "Don't worry, Patty," she told Berg. "We're going to pull this out. We'll tie this hole and eagle the next one. All you have to do is get on this green."

"Fine, fine, Babe," Berg said, "but I've got to *find* the ball first."

Not only did Berg find the ball, but she hit it onto the green. Now Babe knew just how to achieve the mental edge they'd need to win: she would putt first, assuming that if she made it, the men would tighten up, even crack under the pressure. But the men's ball was farther away, and they had the honor of putting first.

"Babe is beside herself over this," Berg later explained. "It is counter to her strategy." One of the men "is lining up the putt and he is standing over it all ready for his backswing and all of a sudden Babe shrieks, 'Time out!' We all look at her. *Time out?* It is the first and last time I'd ever heard this expression on a golf course, but Babe was determined to stop him. Everyone was horrified. A distinguished gentleman comes out on the green and talks very quietly to Babe. She gestures like mad and tries to convince him that she should putt first. He stares at her and then he says, very stiffly, no."

The male golfer sank his putt, Babe made hers, and the women went to the eighteenth hole still trailing by one hole. On eighteen, Babe "hits the longest drive I have ever seen," Berg said. "We get an eagle, we take the hole and we tie them for the match. She picked me up and carried me right off the green."

The women also played six British men at Ganton, where a British pro named Charlie Ward defeated Patty Berg by a single hole (and won the first prize of £150). The gallery at Ganton was astonished by the women's long drives off the tee, especially Babe's. At the post-round ceremony on the clubhouse steps, Babe stole the show, cracking jokes and wrapping her big arms around the mayor of Scarborough.

When the women made their triumphant return home, Corcoran was elated. "Wonderful, wonderful," he told the Associated Press. The women were on top of the world. Corcoran could now promote the LPGA Tour as the place where Americans could watch and celebrate women golfers so talented that they made the British *men* look silly on their home turf.

In the spring of 1952, Babe was spending most of her spare time on the tour with Betty Dodd. In many ways, Dodd, then twenty-one, resembled a young Babe — rough around the edges, athletically gifted, a bit of a tomboy, and Texas blunt. Dodd idolized Babe and was flattered by the attention and praise lavished on her by the supremely confident star.

Dodd quickly became Babe's best friend, even closer to her than Peggy Kirk Bell. The pair often had dinner together, and they entertained the other players on many evenings with their music. While Babe played her harmonica, Dodd played her guitar. They even cut a phonograph record together at a recording studio, on the Mercury label: "Detour," featuring a harmonica solo by Babe on the A side, and Dodd singing "I Felt a Little Teardrop" on the flip side.

Perhaps inevitably — particularly after all the questions about Babe's sexuality twenty years earlier — a few women began saying that Babe and Dodd were having a lesbian relationship. Bell, in particular, laughed at that kind of talk. "Gay? Babe wasn't gay!" she told a friend. "We had a lot of trouble keeping her away from the men!"

George did not like Dodd. It seemed to him as if a third person had suddenly barged into his marriage. "He blamed me if she didn't want to go home" from the tour, Dodd later said.

Babe made a cameo appearance in *Pat and Mike,* a 1952 film starring Katharine Hepburn and Spencer Tracy. The script, cowritten by Ruth Gordon and Garson Kanin, was a thinly veiled portrait of the Didrikson-Zaharias marriage. In the movie, Hepburn plays Patricia "Pat" Pemberton, a multisport, cocksure athlete who is considered the best in the world. Tracy plays Mike Conovan, a savvy and sleazy sports promoter who makes his living fixing sporting events. After meeting the wisecracking, independent Pat, Mike is prepared to give up his life of crime. He wants to help make her a star — legitimately. They fall in love, but their relationship, like Babe and George's, is complicated by the role reversal.

Directed by George Cukor, *Pat and Mike* began shooting in January 1952 at several locations in Los Angeles. Most of the tournament scenes were filmed at Riviera Country Club. Several women golfers were invited to make cameo appearances, including Babe, Helen Dettweiler, Beverly Hanson, and Betty Hicks. But Babe was given the feature role, facing off against Hepburn's character in the final at the Women's National Match Play Championship. A public-address announcer excitedly introduces Babe as "Mrs. Babe Zaharias" and "the Mighty Babe." (The film offers the most accessible chance to see Babe's powerful swing off the tee, her soft touch on the green, and her inimitable brand of self-confidence.)

While filming, Babe and Hepburn, both accustomed to being the top stars, did not get along. Actor Jim Backus later observed that Hepburn appeared perplexed and increasingly frustrated that Babe didn't gush like a schoolgirl at her. "Hepburn did everything to get her attention," Backus said. But Babe was unimpressed by her, telling friends that Hepburn was "double-parked with herself." As they filmed at Riviera one morning, a stretch limousine drove across the fairway. A back door swung open, and out stepped Humphrey Bogart.

"Look who's here!" Hepburn shouted. "It's Bogie! Bogie! Bogie!"

Babe said with a shrug, "Lady, never say that word on a golf course."

The film also depicts the continuing speculation about Babe's sexuality. When Pat easily wrestles two gamblers, Mike looks on aghast, as if his worldview has been turned upside down.

"What have I done?" Pat asks him.

"Too much," he says. "I built you up into some kind of Frankenstein monster.... I like everything to be five-O, five-O. I like a he to be a *he* and a she to be a *she*."

The original script called for Pat to defeat Babe in the final, but Babe refused to lose. When she threatened to pull out of the production, the script was hastily changed. In the new version, Babe sinks the winning putt, retrieves her ball, and, while kneeling on the last green, kisses the ball before lifting it toward the heavens. Pat congratulates Babe, who then jogs jauntily off the green, where she is engulfed by the celebrating gallery. For Babe, this scene was not negotiable: art had to imitate life.

20

The Unspeakable

When Pete Martin of the *Saturday Evening Post* gazed at the mammoth, 350-pound hulk that George Zaharias had become, he shook his head and told Babe, only half-kiddingly, "He's not much of a glamour boy."

"He's a glamour boy to me, mister," Babe snapped.

Although deep strains undermined their more-apart-than-not marriage, Babe and George defended each other whenever attacked. "George did what he wanted," Betty Jameson recalled, "but he also allowed Babe to do her thing. It was a trade-off."

Whenever George was on the road, which was often, he craved some assurance from Babe by phone that he was still in control. He worried compulsively that she would decide—or discover—she no longer needed him. So whenever George joined Babe on the tour, he went overboard trying to prove his value by putting her needs first, usually in ways that everyone could see. "Some nights he'd pound on my door," Peggy Kirk Bell recalled, "and say, 'Peg, you go over there and sleep in the room with Babe. I want her to win this tournament tomorrow and

I snore.' And then he'd take my room." Bell added, "All he wanted to do [was to] make her more famous than she was."

But by 1951, Babe found it hard to defend her husband in public anymore. "When I married George, he was a Greek God," Babe liked to tell the women on the tour. "Now he's nothing but a goddamn Greek."

George hadn't just let himself go; he had become an embarrassment to Babe, whose golfing talent and star power had combined to win over the cloistered golf world that had snubbed her for so many years. Now his slovenly behavior and uncouth manners threatened her seat at the game's head table. George's prodigious appetite for food, drink, action, and control had become legendary on the tour. At dinner in some of the most posh clubhouses in America, the lady golfers and country-club leaders watched, horrified, as he attempted to satisfy a hunger that seemed capable of consuming the world. People quietly ticked off the bottles of beers he consumed over the course of an evening (one golfer remembers counting to twenty-two), and yet still, somehow, he did not appear to be "in his cups" (the women's polite phrase for falling-down drunk). When he traveled, visitors saw hams, turkeys, and cases of beer piled high in his hotel room. He drank olive oil out of a tall glass. He peeled the wrapping from quarter-pound sticks of butter before eating them like bananas.

At a club in Orlando, Florida, George and Babe were hosting a dinner at a large round table with a dozen friends. George suddenly grabbed a full loaf of bread from the bread basket and began dunking one end into a tall glass of milk.

"George," Babe said, her eyes blazing, "don't you know that ain't polite?"

"What ain't polite?" he snapped.

"It ain't polite to eat with your elbows on the table," she snapped back, making sure everyone could hear her disapproval.

After the LPGA began and Fred Corcoran took over a big part of George's management portfolio, George became "needier," friends of Babe said. According to Betty Jameson, she had already become a far bigger star than he ever was, and he yearned to "bask in her glory."

"When Babe was at her zenith, George used to beg her to come stand with him on street corners," said R. L. Bowen. "Poor George — he just wanted to be seen with her." Babe, however, did not always want to be seen with him.

"He was fat," Peggy Kirk Bell said. "That bothered Babe."

In 1950, Babe and George moved from their Tudor house in Denver to Sky Crest Country Club (now Twin Orchard Country Club), located just outside Chicago. In October, Babe had been invited to become the club professional at Sky Crest, a Jewish-only club. She would be paid $20,000 a year. It was quite an honor, and Babe claimed that she was the first woman in America to become a full-time club pro. She was wrong; a woman named Bessie Fenn had actually been hired as a full-time pro by the Breakers in Palm Beach, Florida, in 1926. Even so, it was a step up for Babe, who had previously worked part time as a pro at Grossinger Country Club in New York. When Babe wasn't playing tournaments or staging exhibitions, she was at Sky Crest giving lessons to club members. "It was hard work," she later said, "but I loved it."

The Zahariases lived in a rented house on the golf course. "We were really living high off the hog," Babe recalled. One evening, George told Babe, "Come on and get dressed. I'm taking you out to dinner tonight." Babe put on one of her finest new dresses "and got all dolled up for dining and dancing and whatever else George had in mind." She figured they'd go to some swank Chicago steak house. Instead, George drove to an unassuming diner on the city's outskirts. They found two stools at the counter, where George ordered them each a hamburger, a bowl of chili, and a glass of buttermilk. Babe smiled — this had been her usual "on the road" meal after they met in Los Angeles.

"Say, what is all this?" Babe asked.

"I just didn't want you to get out of the habit," he said. Babe understood that the burgers and buttermilk were George's way of reminding them both not to forget where they had come from, no matter what happened.

Despite this touching moment, Babe and George argued sloppily and furiously and more frequently in public. Their spats almost always occurred when George drank too much. In a Houston country-club lounge after a tournament, he insisted that Babe play another tournament the following week. Babe was bone-tired and wanted to take a break. As usual, George said no. "George started drinking," recalled Thelma Didriksen, the wife of Babe's brother Louis. "And he drank so much and so fast, until the waiters didn't even pick the glasses up. There was a row of glasses, one row after the other." Babe did as he demanded and went on to play the next week's tournament.

Marilynn Smith recalled watching a drunken and fuming George shove Babe forcefully to the dance floor in Tampa. "We were all eating dinner, and they left the table — he was angry at her about something," Smith said. "He just sort of flung her to the ground, and she fell hard. She picked herself up and walked away." Betty Dodd told several friends that George beat Babe. Other friends said that they saw bruises on Babe's legs and forearms, though not on her face.

"Mildred would come see us when she and Zaharias had trouble," Louis said. "Sometimes she had bruises from their clashes." Babe would ask Louis to "beat George up." Louis was an ex-fighter, a welterweight, and he had to explain to Babe that George "weighed nearly three hundred, and that was a bit too much for a welterweight. I couldn't have put a dent in the big bruiser . . . and Babe was fragile within his physical power." By the summer of 1952, their separations and silences had become lengthier, punctuated by more frequent fights. At times, George thought that Babe "believed her own publicity" and was too full of herself. "Goddammit, Babe, I was a celebrity, too—and don't you forget it!" he said. Maybe, Babe once said, George had become so big that there wasn't room enough for the two of them.

More than once, Babe raised the possibility of divorce, but George just laughed it off. He cornered Betty Dodd one night and told her, "Me and Babe have been together and nobody's gonna break us up."

Years later, George acknowledged that they "both had tempers." Their marriage, he said, "finally became like cats and dogs, but love still existed."

Perhaps their marriage would have been different if they'd had a child. When Babe was twenty-one, she looked forward to the day she would become a mother. "Every normal woman looks forward to having children, and I don't think I'm much different from most women," she told a journalist after her Olympic triumph in 1932. "At least I know I like children, and expect to have some of my own."

During the war, Babe had at least one miscarriage. She told Peggy Kirk Bell that her babies were "swimmers," her odd euphemism for miscarriages. "I'd give up every trophy I ever won if I could have a baby," Babe told her friend.

Babe and George explored adopting a child, but it was out of the question. The agencies would never place a baby with a couple who lived on the road and were rarely together.

Since their first duplex apartment in Los Angeles, Babe and George had lived mostly in rentals, each place nicer than the previous one. But the temporary feel of them only seemed to encourage and even justify George's rootlessness. Babe longed for a "dream house" of her own. If they owned their own home, one they could build from scratch, Babe thought, perhaps that could be the anchor for their chaotic marriage.

But George stubbornly resisted, ridiculing Babe's "obsession" as a troubling symbol of her fixation on material things. Babe's friends suspected that George didn't want a permanent home because not having one made it easier for him to keep Babe on the road playing competitive golf and conducting exhibitions—and maintaining a lifestyle that was producing the couple's biggest, steadiest income. "He wanted her going," Betty Dodd said. "He wanted to push her as hard as he could. To the next tournament, the next exhibition, the next this, the next that. He didn't want her to be happy in one place where she might not want to go do those things."

In the summer of 1951, after only half a year at Sky Crest Country Club, Babe wrote a letter to the Bowens complaining about her job. She said that she and George wanted to break her contract because the long hours of lessons had become unbearable and demeaning. "There is no rest for him or me," she wrote. "As long as I am here, they all want me for lessons....Even if you charge them $50 per hour, it doesn't make any difference. They pay and love it, but I'm not as hungry as I used to be."

That was the problem: Babe's hunger had subsided. She was becoming burned out. In the fall of 1951, Sky Crest dismissed Babe after several members complained that she had tried to hustle them out of more money for lessons. It's unknown whether that was the real problem or they had become disenchanted with Babe's sudden change in attitude. Either way, a new home was now a necessity.

George had heard that Forest Hills Country Club in Tampa, Florida, was for sale. After he and Babe flew to Tampa to inspect it, they bought the club, which included a hotel, for the bargain-basement price of $40,000. It seemed a good investment. George was happy because he was sure that after they made renovations and attached Babe's name to it, the club would double or maybe triple in value. He decided they'd rename it the Tampa Golf and Country Club. Babe was happy because the course was the perfect site for their new home—a sprawling pink stucco caddie house, just a few paces from the putting green and a bit farther from a pond guarded by a lovely stand of palm trees. She planned on designing and overseeing its renovation from top to bottom.

When they first toured the property alone, they went for a walk along the western edge of the course. The rain was falling over Tampa Bay, and they spotted two palm trees on a vista, with a big double rainbow between them.

"Honey, this is it," George said.

"Yeah," Babe said, "Rainbow Manor."

Rainbow Manor. It sounded like a quiet place just to sit and do nothing, maybe watch the sun set and reminisce about the moments, not so long ago, when you felt you could fly. A converted caddie house certainly did not qualify as Babe's dream home, but it would do for now. Someday, perhaps, George would let her have the real thing.

With Sky Crest behind her, it was time for Babe to get back out on the road. Pouring her energy back into the tour, she had already won the Titleholders Championship and the first two legs of the Weathervane series by April 1952. George accompanied her on a trip to the West Coast for half a dozen tournaments.

At the Richmond Women's Open in Richmond, California, Babe shot a disappointing 77 in the final round, fading to a fifth-place finish. That evening, she was exhausted and felt pain shooting through her left hip—the same pain she'd felt there, off and on, for the past four years. Sometimes the pain shot upward; other times it went south. Whenever it hit, George urged her to soak in a hot saltwater bath. Sometimes that helped. He'd also give her a massage. This time the pain was so intense it brought tears to Babe's eyes.

She kept playing, at tournaments in Bakersfield and Fresno, before traveling up to Seattle for the third leg of the Weathervane at Broadmoor Country Club. "Well, those 36 holes were just agony for me," she recalled. Her eleventh-place finish was the worst of her career in a stroke-play tournament.

Afterward, Babe hoped that a few days of rest in Seattle would ease the pain, but its grip only tightened. Now she could barely stand.

"I think I'd better go to a hospital," she told George.

"I think so, too," he replied.

George had business to do in California. Betty Dodd and Babe drove to Salt Lake City, but the pain became too excruciating to continue on to Texas. They flew back to Beaumont, where Babe insisted that she visit her longtime family doctor, W. E. Tatum, who was then eighty years old. Tatum had been the Didriksen family doctor since Babe was in grade school, and she was most comfortable with him. She'd never liked doctors, however, and admittedly had seen Tatum only a handful of times during her adult life. Babe's confidence in him came from the sure-handed way he had always treated Poppa and Momma and her siblings.

From the airport, Babe was driven directly to Hotel Dieu Hospital, a Catholic hospital in Beaumont. Dr. Tatum discovered that she had a strangulated femoral hernia, or a protrusion at the top of her left thigh bone that stopped the circulation of blood. If she had waited another week to see him, she "might have been a goner," Babe said later. The doctor also diagnosed Babe as anemic, a condition brought on by extreme exhaustion. An operation was postponed for several days to allow her to regain some strength. After the successful hernia surgery, Babe flew home to Tampa to recover.

Facing the longest doctor-ordered layoff of her adult life, Babe felt trapped. She kept her wrists limber with her irons and chipped and putted a few balls. After just one month, she was convinced that she was ready to rejoin the tour. "I'm feeling fine now," she wrote to Tiny Scurlock, "but still won't do anything for a couple months and I got a warning just today from The Doctor. Take it easy, he says—I'm not ready."

In June, Babe was strong enough to fly to Philadelphia to serve as the honorary starter for the U.S. Women's Open at the Bala Golf Club. But that wasn't enough for Babe: she insisted on hitting the ceremonial first ball. Grabbing a three-iron on the first tee, she drove the ball 180 or 190 yards—a distance, she later pointed out, that few of the players had exceeded that first day.

Babe returned to Tampa. Each week, she phoned Dr. Tatum to ask if she could return to the action. She had pinned her hopes on playing both the All-American and World Championship tournaments at Tam O'Shanter in August. On the first day of the All-American, Tatum called Babe to give her the green light. "Why didn't you tell me last week," Babe said, "so I could have gone up there and played in both the All-American and the World?"

"Because I didn't want you to play in both of them," he said.

Babe flew up to Chicago to play in the World Championship. Because she had won the World all four times it had been played, the women on the tour had dubbed it "the Babe Zaharias benefit." But Babe may have come back too soon; she "ran out of gas again," finishing third behind Betty Jameson and Patty Berg.

Babe returned to Tampa even more determined to win that fall's Women's Texas Open at River Crest Country Club, site of the 1947 defeat that had halted her record-setting winning streak. She didn't need to beat the players; she needed to exact some revenge from that narrow, tough course. Babe won the final round, 7 and 6, defeating Polly Riley, a five-foot two-inch Texan who was as competitive as Babe.

Afterward, Babe and Riley exchanged a few angry words when Riley accused Babe of rubbing her nose in the lopsided defeat.

The victory tacked an exclamation mark on Babe's most dismal year in golf. She won only four of her twenty tournaments in 1952. For the first time, she was not at the top of the LPGA money list, instead finishing fifth, with only $7,503.25 in winnings.

Back home in Tampa for the holidays, Babe never felt well enough to play eighteen holes. Her lethargy extended to everything else. Babe, George, and Betty Dodd went down to Key Largo to fish with her brother Ole, but even that wasn't its usual fun. Babe could not understand why she was feeling more tired and out of sorts than before. Wasn't the hernia surgery supposed to end the pain and fatigue? No amount of rest or sleep seemed to restore her strength and energy. (Even George's massages weren't helping.)

In early 1953, Babe skipped the Florida winter circuit, except for the Jacksonville Open, where she finished second to Patty Berg. She finished far back at the Betsy Rawls Open in Spartanburg, South Carolina. After leading early at the New Orleans Women's Open, she faded to second.

Her tee shots lacked their usual pop. After golf each day, she barely had enough strength to eat dinner in her hotel room, often with Dodd, and then went to sleep early. She confided to Dodd that she worried the fatigue was something more serious than a hernia. "Maybe I have cancer," she told Dodd in a half-joking manner. Dodd didn't find it funny. More than once, she told Babe to go back to Beaumont and see her doctor. But Babe kept procrastinating.

George knew about Babe's health worries, too, several friends said. He reassured her, telling her she'd "be okay with a little rest."

Next on the calendar was the inaugural Babe Zaharias Open in Beaumont, the $3,500 tournament created to honor Beaumont's most famous citizen. Twenty-three women, including eleven members of the LPGA, were scheduled to compete in the fifty-four-hole tournament. Before the tournament began, Babe ran into Dr. Tatum at the Beaumont Country Club. She told the doctor she needed a checkup as soon as possible. He suggested an appointment several days after the tournament, but Babe said no. "I can't wait that long," she told him. "I have to go on from here to the next tournament in Phoenix." So she made an appointment for the morning after the final round.

Babe forced herself to play, taking some comfort in the fact that it was a three-day, rather than the usual four-day, event. After the first two days, Babe had a one-stroke lead over Louise Suggs, with a score of 142, two strokes under par. "The last day it was more of an effort to play than ever," Babe said. Dodd told Babe that she would need two pars on the final two holes to win. She three-putted the seventeenth for a bogey.

On the par 4 eighteenth hole, she needed a par to tie for first place or a birdie to win. Babe now felt, she said later, as if she were "crawling on [her] hands and knees."

Off the tee, Babe hooked the ball behind a tree. "One more bad shot," she recalled, "and I was going to blow this tournament." Babe's ability to scramble had saved her so often in the past. Countless times, when her ball was up against a fence or a tree or deep in a trap, she used her power to scoop it out of trouble, onto the green, and close to the pin. Now Babe did so again, using an eight-iron to put her ball on the green, thirty feet from the flagstick. She now needed to sink the long putt for the win.

Standing over her ball, Babe turned to the quiet gallery and asked, "You don't think for one minute I'm going to miss this, do you?" Sure enough, she sank the improbable thirty-foot birdie putt to win the first Babe Zaharias Open. Dodd, Patty Berg, and several other women rushed onto the green, grabbed Babe, lifted her into the air, and carried her toward the clubhouse, in front of television cameras and a film crew. She was elated and exhausted.

Babe was staying at her sister Lillie's house. That night, Dodd and her parents came by to take Babe out for a celebration dinner. Babe was lying on the guest room bed, clad in her golf clothes, looking pale. Dodd's father said, "Babe, we'll send something for you to eat. You must go to bed."

For years, Babe had feared that she might have cancer. Along with her near-chronic fatigue, she had also found blood in her stool over the past several months. She didn't share any of this with George. She also didn't tell her doctor. "She was too modest, that was the problem," Bertha Bowen said. "She didn't like examinations, so she put off going to the doctor."

The next day, April 6, 1953, Babe was sitting in Dr. Tatum's office. He first checked on how well she had healed from the hernia operation. "Well," he said, "everything seems to be all right."

Tatum kept checking Babe. Then she saw his face turn white.

"I've got cancer, haven't I?"

"Now, Babe, we don't know that."

Babe first thought about George: how he'd react to this news, how she wished he were with her. He had stayed behind at Lillie's house to run a few errands and pack their car for the drive to Phoenix for that weekend's tournament. Babe wished that Dodd, who had gone to San Antonio to visit her family, were there, too. George and Babe had intended to drive from Beaumont to San Antonio to spend one night with the Dodds. Then they were all going to caravan to Arizona for the start of the Phoenix Weathervane on Thursday morning.

"Here's what I want you to do," Tatum said. "I want you to go to Fort Worth and see a specialist there, a proctologist, and have him make some tests."

"Can't I see him when I come back this way to play in the Texas Women's Open in October?" she asked.

"No, you'll have to go there today. I'll phone ahead and make the arrangements."

Babe drove back to Lillie's, where she told George that they had to go to Fort Worth. They arrived at the Fort Worth office of Dr. William C. Tatum (no relation to Dr. W. E. Tatum in Beaumont) just after the dinner hour. He took a biopsy and told them to return to his office for the laboratory results on Wednesday.

At 11:00 that morning, Babe and George sat holding hands in the doctor's reception room. The doctor's wife, who worked as his secretary, escorted them in to see her husband.

As soon as Babe and George sat down in side-by-side chairs, Tatum said, "Babe, you've got cancer."

George reached out and took Babe's hand. The doctor kept talking: Babe had cancer in the rectum and needed surgery as soon as possible. The doctor talked about the particulars of the operation, using charts and photographs to show them how it would be done. Her rectum and part of her colon would be surgically removed, and she would have a colostomy. The doctor talked about the usual recovery time after such an operation — probably a few months, maybe longer. He explained the painstaking maintenance of the colostomy bag. Then he mentioned golf. Babe might be able to play again, but probably not tournament golf. Tatum talked for nearly two hours. Babe and George would have trouble remembering some of what he said.

Babe wept in the elevator. George was shaking; he had never seen Babe cry. They returned to the Bowens' home, where R.L. and Bertha had waited out the previous two harrowing days with them. Together, they entered the Bowens' living room and walked in separate directions — George to the patio out back, where he cried alone, and Babe to the guest room, where she tossed her brown bag on a chair, closed the door, and lay down on the double bed.

Bertha tapped gently on the door. Babe let her in. "B.B., I've got it—the worst kind, grade four," she said, smoking a Pall Mall cigarette. "I'm not worried about myself. I'm worried about George." Bertha wept and hugged Babe, then went out to the kitchen to phone her husband. "R.L., come home quick!" she said. "The worst has happened!"

Alone in the guest room, Babe prayed, asking God a few questions: *Why did I have to have this? Why does anybody have to have it?* Babe was not the most faithful churchgoing Christian in southeast Texas, not by a long shot. But she still remembered the prayers taught to her thirty-five years earlier at the Lutheran church in Beaumont. "When you get sick," she'd say, "God is the one you go to. He gives you the spiritual muscle that you need."

Now Babe was asking herself: *Haven't I always tried to do the right thing? Played benefit golf matches for the American Cancer Society? Pitched in for Damon Runyon's Cancer Fund?* Then she went back to God with another question: *What in the world have I done wrong in my life to deserve this?*

That morning, Betty Dodd had pointed her brand-new Ford toward Fort Worth. Along the way, a gravel truck rammed into the car's rear end. She wasn't hurt, but the Ford was demolished. It had to be towed to a service station, where Dodd used a pay phone to call the Bowens' home.

When Babe picked up the phone, she was crying. "I've got to be operated on," Babe said. "I've got to have a col...col..."

"Colostomy?" Dodd asked.

"That's right."

George called Dr. W. E. Tatum in Beaumont, who asked them to return at once. The operation would take place within the next ten days. Babe and George decided to stop overnight in Newton, Texas, where Babe's older brother Louis lived.

As George carried a suitcase to their Cadillac in the Bowens' driveway, Babe spotted her golf clubs in the trunk. She scooped up the clubs and shoved them into R.L.'s arms. "Here. I want you to have these, because I won't be needing them anymore."

21

The Muscle Is Spiritual

Inside Room 201 at Beaumont's Hotel Dieu Hospital, Babe asked Betty Dodd, "Do you think they'll *really* have to do it?" The *it* was a colostomy. Dodd seemed to think that Babe feared the colostomy more than the cancer.

The surgery would remove a malignant tumor from Babe's lower rectum. Then doctors would suture her anus and reroute her intestinal tract to allow solid waste to pass through an incision in the left side of her abdomen. Every day, for the rest of her life, Babe would have to change the colostomy bag or irrigate it. In 1954, the bag was held in place by a nylon belt wrapped around the abdomen, with the incision protected by absorbent paper. The most common worry about having a colostomy bag was that an accident might occur in public. Fear of such an embarrassment caused some people to retreat from life, forgoing the activities that they loved. For someone swinging her golf clubs as hard as Babe did, having an accident was a real risk.

The bad news about Babe's "malignancy"—the era's favorite euphemism for cancer—flashed across the country. During the 1950s, many

Americans were still ignorant about the ferocious disease. It certainly didn't help matters that the American media reported little or nothing about it, often because famous patients such as Senator Robert Taft of Ohio and writers Gertrude Stein and Damon Runyon insisted on maintaining their privacy. The horrors of cancer were communicated in whispers. For instance, when Babe Ruth had an operation on his neck in January 1947, newspaper articles said nothing about cancer. Indeed, his slow recovery was attributed to "bad weather." The most popular euphemism used for Ruth's throat cancer was "pulmonary complications." Keeping the cancer a secret was a choice made by Ruth and his family. It wasn't until his death, on August 16, 1948, that the newspapers finally acknowledged that the baseball legend had suffered from cancer for eighteen months. Ruth's obituary in the *New York Times* described his cancer as "one of the best kept secrets in modern times" and praised the slugger's courage in quietly fighting "the scourge that kills more than 170,000 Americans every year and is responsible for one out of every eight deaths."

Heart disease killed at least twice as many Americans as cancer, but it was cancer that Americans dreaded most. Consequently, millions of Americans postponed doctor visits, even when they suspected a problem. Many preferred not knowing they had the disease.

At first, few newspapers and magazines described where Babe's "malignancy" was located. Tiny Scurlock, writing in the *Beaumont Journal,* was one of the few journalists to say it was located in the rectum. A few other papers dropped a big clue, reporting that Babe had visited a proctologist. But most reporters and their editors chose to avoid the grisly details, saying just that Babe was "seriously ill" and suffered from a "malady."

No news organization, however, shied away from making pronouncements about Babe's prognosis: her career was over.

"The fabulous athletic career of Mrs. Mildred (Babe) Didrikson

Zaharias, spanning more than two decades and including virtually every competitive sport, apparently was at an end today," wrote the Associated Press in a dispatch published on April 10, 1953, in newspapers across the country. The story said that Babe was "suffering from a malady reportedly of a malignant nature."

"I don't know yet if surgery will cure her," Dr. William C. Tatum of Fort Worth told reporters, "but I will say that she never again will play golf of championship caliber." Bertha Bowen flatly told reporters that "Babe will never be able to play golf again. She took the report that she is a very sick girl standing up."

"This is a terrible thing," George Zaharias said on the steps of Hotel Dieu Hospital on the day his wife checked in. Someone asked him if Babe would play tournament golf again. He refused to say and walked back into the hospital, crying.

From the beginning, not only was Babe willing to talk openly about her cancer, but she was willing to proclaim that she'd play championship golf again. "I am definitely not out of sports," she said one day after Tatum's bleak pronouncement and four days after she tried to give away her golf clubs to R. L. Bowen (a gift that he had adamantly refused). "We want to get a little rest, and then I'll be back in sports." She was even willing to predict that she'd be at the top of the leaderboard again. "I feel confident that with God's help, I will be back soon to play and win."

Leaning in a corner of Room 201 of the Hotel Dieu Hospital were Babe's golf clubs. Betty Dodd had put them there.

Telegrams, letters, and flowers poured into the hospital. Some envelopes had no address, just said "The Babe" or had Babe's photo, cut out of a newspaper, pasted on them. First the letters came in by the handful. Then a basket was used. Finally, each day's mail was delivered to

Babe's bedside stuffed in a big wicker clothes hamper. "BEST OF LUCK AND LOVE FROM YOUR SWEETHEARTS IN THE PRESS STY," read one telegram signed by forty-one reporters covering the Masters in Augusta, Georgia. By phone and telegram, Babe received get-well wishes from Bobby Jones, Ed Sullivan, Bob Hope, Grantland Rice, Mickey Rooney, and Walter Winchell.

Babe also heard from dozens of people who insisted they had the cure for her disease. Some of the purported remedies arrived in packages, including herbs from South Africa and holy water from various springs. Other people offered themselves. A Native American man showed up one night wanting to heal Babe with his hands. Another woman confronted Babe in the hallway, saying that God had sent her to save Babe. "She was very sincere about it," Babe later said.

George was losing patience with the barrage. He suspected that these charlatans just wanted cash. George knew there was only one thing Babe needed. "Get Babe the finest surgeon," he told Dr. W. E. Tatum. "I don't care what it costs."

Once she came to terms with it, Babe was matter-of-fact about the impending surgery. "Let the pros do it," Babe told Peggy Kirk Bell. Fortunately, one of the finest surgeons available just happened to be working down the road in Galveston, at John Sealy Hospital at the University of Texas Medical Branch. His name was Dr. Robert Moore.

"I certainly hate to meet you under these circumstances," Dr. Moore told Babe. He was a devoted golfer and a longtime fan.

"Doctor Moore, under these circumstances I'm tickled pink to meet you," she said. "I know I've got the best."

Across the hallway from Babe's room, a nun named Sister Tarsisis had been diagnosed with rectal cancer eighteen months earlier. She'd refused to have surgery and had "wasted away to almost nothing." Doctors asked Babe to speak with the sister. After their discussion, Sister Tarsisis assured Babe that she'd reconsider her decision.

George had to go to Denver for a few days to finalize the sale of his motel, but Babe would have company: Betty Dodd had moved into Babe's room, sleeping on a cot at the foot of her bed. Dodd knew her way around a hospital bed. In her late teens, she had worked as a nurse's assistant at a hospital in San Antonio.

In the days before her surgery, Babe clung to the slightest chance that the doctors would decide, during the operation, to perform a temporary colostomy, meaning that they would be able to reconnect the intestine later. "I still didn't like the idea of a colostomy," Babe said. "I didn't want my body changed permanently like that."

And despite her public optimism, she thought about "all the people I know and like and love, and who know and like me — would they ever see me alive again? The girls I've helped be better golfers, the girls I've beaten, the girls who've beaten me. And me, dead. Maybe alive, but bedridden, helpless, maybe I'd never play golf again!"

But as the operation drew close, she stopped thinking about that possibility. It was time to go to God again — not with a question this time, but with a request. *Please, God, let me play again.*

The surgery was scheduled for Friday, April 17, 1953, at 2:00 p.m. By late morning, all the preparations were complete, the final round of X-rays had been taken, and the pints of blood donated by Ole and Louis, who had the same blood type as Babe, were ready.

Babe had asked to see an old friend that day. At noon, Tiny Scurlock walked into Room 201 wearing his usual big smile. It was a social call, but Tiny also had his notebook out. He had a story to write.

"I'd rather play 18 holes of golf tomorrow than keep this engagement, but let's go," Babe said. Tiny asked if she had a message for his readers. "Tiny, tell everybody to pray double hard for me, and I'll be back. And tell people to give their money to the Cancer Fund instead of sending flowers." It had been Babe's decision to speak openly about her disease, both as a cautionary tale for others and as a way to steel herself for the struggle that lay ahead.

Inside Room 201, Tiny carefully jotted down Babe's words. Then Babe had a favor to ask: "Say, for goodness sakes, Tiny, I'm tired of being on the sports page. Put me on page one."

Before Babe was wheeled into surgery, George, who was back from Denver, leaned down and gave her a kiss on the cheek. "Remember," he said, "you're the champion, at everything you've set your mind to. You're the best there is."

She was wheeled into the operating room. In came Dr. Moore, who enjoyed chatting with Babe in golf metaphors. "It's going to be a tough round today," he said.

"Yeah," Babe said, "but maybe we'll make a few putts."

Babe was on the operating table for nearly four hours. Within the first hour, Dr. Moore knew that a temporary colostomy was impossible. After the procedure, the doctors looked to see if the cancer had spread. It had.

Babe remembered only one thing: waking up to elevator doors opening, then seeing George's big face.

"Colostomy, honey?" Babe asked.

"Yes. It's all right."

Then she fell asleep.

When the surgery was over, Dr. Moore escorted George and Betty Dodd to an office. He shut the door and told them he was sorry to say he had found more cancer in Babe's lymph nodes. George began crying. The colostomy had been a success, but the cancer would likely give Babe more trouble within a year. Then he suggested that it might be best if this bit of news was kept from Babe. She would need all her strength to cope with what had just been done. George and Dodd agreed to say nothing.

The next day, the headlines reported that Babe had come through the operation "okay." An unnamed doctor was quoted as saying, "If things go as well as it looks, she could possibly take part in athletics again. But how soon is something else, it's a little too early to say."

Within a week, the feeding tube was removed from Babe's nose, and she began eating solid food again. Dr. Moore cauterized where she had had the colostomy. She wasn't sleeping well, but she needed to get used to the idea that the colostomy was permanent. It would be a whole new way of life. It wouldn't go away. It's not like putting a Band-Aid on something that is going to heal. She would have this bag on her side, collecting small dabs of excrement, for the rest of her life. Babe stared at her golf clubs propped up in the corner of her room.

One morning, after her bath, Babe stood up and had an accident. "With this type of operation you have no control," Betty Dodd recalled years later, "you never know when something is going to happen.... Everything let go. Instinctively I just put out my hands. It was not that big a thing but from then on she wouldn't let anyone take care of her but me." Even while Babe was still in the hospital, Betty irrigated Babe's colostomy bag at least every other day. This involved putting on rubber gloves and putting her fingers inside Babe's incision. George never did this, nor did Babe want him to. Betty was the only one she trusted to do it.

Nearly two weeks after her surgery, Babe got out of bed one day and went to the children's ward. She also visited some elderly ladies on another floor. She cracked jokes, enjoying the company.

Then Betty had a sudden hernia attack and had the same operation Babe had had the year before. For nearly a week, Babe and Betty were recuperating in the same room. "Two invalids," Babe joked.

Babe's spirits also were raised by visits from Patty Berg and Bertha Bowen. Thelma Didriksen, Babe's sister-in-law, helped Betty tend to her most intimate needs. George was rarely there. Although he stayed in Galveston for a while, Babe's friends and relatives were surprised at how infrequently they saw him during the month after her operation.

But George made sure he was there the afternoon Babe invited film crews and photographers to her room. Flanked by George and Betty, Babe smiled for the cameras, holding up a fistful of get-well letters. She equated her response to her cancer with her reaction to the USGA's decision to strip her of her amateur status in 1935. "I didn't do any sounding off myself," she told reporters. "When you get a big setback like that, there's no use crying about it.... You just have to face your problem and figure out what to do next." Babe had chosen to view her cancer as just another athletic hurdle. Doing so made the cancer less formidable — or at least so it would seem in the newspapers.

After one month and one day in the hospital, Babe was discharged. George carried her golf clubs, in the Wilson bag emblazoned with her name, down to the Cadillac. Babe, George, and Betty spent some time with her brother Louis and his wife, Thelma, at their home in Newton, Texas. Louis and Thelma gave Babe a painting kit, and she took up painting. "I am feeling wonderful," she wrote to the Bowens on June 5, "and the col...y is working okay." (She still couldn't write the word.) She told the Bowens that she looked forward to returning to Tampa. "You always want to go home, don't you?"

By mid-June, Babe, George, and Betty were back in Tampa. Babe's doctors allowed her to start practicing golf. A television crew from NBC filmed her pitching a few balls.

The next day, Babe played one hole at the Tampa Golf and Country Club, using a four-iron instead of a driver. She moved around in an electric cart. The next day, she played a hole and a half. The day after that, two holes. The act of swinging a club felt fine; she didn't swing as hard as usual, but she felt good. She started slowly because she tired easily.

George was back in Denver when he picked up the newspaper and saw the headline BABE ZAHARIAS PLAYS NINE HOLES. He was worried that Babe was going too fast, but she took it in stride. "Yeah, I went nine holes," she later said. "And it felt pretty good. I shot a 37."

During the last week of June, Babe played in the Babe Didrikson Zaharias Golf Tournament at the Beaumont Country Club. She won, although this was only a hometown event. Babe had become a leading spokesperson for cancer fund-raising and education. Across the country, two thousand golf courses donated proceeds to the Damon Runyon Cancer Memorial Fund, created by Walter Winchell. As a token of his appreciation, Winchell gave Babe a putter with a tiny diamond embedded in its face.

Babe wanted to return to the tour. She looked at the LPGA calendar and circled a few dates in late July—the All-American at Tam O'Shanter in Niles, Illinois. She asked the tourney organizers if she could be paired with Betty Dodd. "She was familiar with my condition," Babe later explained, "and could step in and help if I had any trouble." They agreed.

Fourteen weeks after her surgery, Babe's gallery, nearly five thousand strong, gathered around Tam O'Shanter's first tee, waiting.

"To me, shooting tournament golf doesn't just mean getting a respectable score and finishing up among the leaders," she explained in her autobiography. "It means being able to win. That's the standard the public has come to judge me by. It's the standard I set for myself. I wouldn't want it to be any other way." Her comeback wouldn't be complete without a win.

The hardest thing for Babe about coming back wasn't making golf shots. It was the worry about a sudden embarrassment: what if there was some glitch with her colostomy bag? She needed the two most important people in her life by her side: Betty, who later said, "Everywhere that Babe went after her surgery, I went.... She needed someone to be with her. It made her feel comfortable." And George, puffing his cigar.

Her will amazed her competitors. "What grit," recalled Betty Jameson, shaking her head at the memory of it half a century later. *"All grit."*

"It's not easy playing in front of 3,000 people, standing just a few feet away, with that colostomy," said Marilynn Smith. "Takes a lot of courage.... Well, we know Babe had that."

The first swing was the hardest. Babe teed off, hitting the ball with less power than usual, but everything remained in place. So far, so good.

Despite being buoyed by the fans' gush of support, Babe trailed from the beginning. She tired on the back nine each day. Betty didn't play well either, but she was more focused on Babe's well-being than her own shot-making.

On the third day, Babe was three-putting holes, something she rarely did. On the fifth hole, Babe three-putted from four feet. She walked off the green, sat down on a bench, buried her head in her hands, and wept.

Betty put her arm around her and said, "Quit, Babe. No one will care. They'll understand."

Babe looked at Betty, the tears still rolling down her face. "No, no, I don't want to quit," she said. "I'm not a quitter."

On the sixth tee, it began to rain. George held an enormous golf umbrella over Babe and put his arm around her. She cried until it was her turn to tee off.

She hit a good drive but three-putted again on the green. Her second putt stopped a few inches shy of the cup. The miss, Babe later explained, left her "shattered. I stretched out my hands, still gripping the club, and buried my face in my arms and cried." She called it the "blackest of moments." Babe hadn't just let herself down; she had let down "thousands of [cancer patients]" — they would all "be on the losing side" with her.

As she stood there with her head down, feeling defeated, she sensed George and Betty approaching. "I felt their comforting hands on my shoulder — and, in a wonderful way, the hands of many others." *Please, God, you've helped me this far. Give me the strength to go on ... please.*

Babe ended up finishing fifteenth out of thirty. The power in her tee shots was gone, and she was distracted, thinking about what might happen. "You go out there thinking you're going to hit it hard," Babe said afterward, "and then you feel like you're going to pull everything loose and you ease up on it."

A few days later, Babe played in the World Championship at Tam O'Shanter. She played better and was at the top of the leaderboard after three and a half rounds. But on the final nine, she tired, shooting a 43 and giving Patty Berg the opening to win.

A third-place finish hardly lived up to Babe's own standards. In fact, years later George equated third place with last place. But the media couldn't have cared less. They loved Babe's remarkable comeback story.

"The Babe Is Back," *Time* magazine declared. Atop a photo of Babe confidently swinging a club, the caption read, "Golfer Zaharias: The muscle is spiritual." (Babe was fond of using the phrase "spiritual muscle" to describe the engine that had powered her comeback.) The *Time* story reported that Babe's doctors marveled at her "recuperative power." She accepted news of her cancer "as calmly as she takes one of her rare setbacks on a golf course. 'I'll beat it,' she said."

In a lengthy, first-person story titled "I'm Not Out of the Rough — Yet!" Babe recounted her cancer diagnosis and identified her new mission as making people "cancer-conscious." She beseeched readers to go to the doctor and "take warning at the very first danger signal," advice that she herself had not heeded. She went on:

In my case it was just luck, and a good doctor, God bless him, that my cancer was discovered early. Another week, another month, who knows...? But don't think I'm kidding myself now that I'm out of the rough. Every six months I have to go back for an examination, never knowing what that examination will show, whether cancer will return.

But until I get the bad news, I'm living life right up to the hilt. Funny thing, how you have to be close to death to appreciate life. I heard the sentence of doom, and I had my reprieve. Now I'm going to fight cancer with all I've got, so others can get that reprieve, too. And then, like me, they'll find out that life is really worth livin', brother, really worth livin'.

Babe was preparing for the Florida winter circuit in January 1954 when she wrote a letter to the Bowens: "I am feeling fine, but still tire easily, but thought I would go and start the tour anyway. I might get lucky and come through — as I am striking the ball pretty good — I have to eventually go back to the hospital and have another job done on the colostomy as I am told that the tube leading to the opening is too large and I have a hernia in it." She postponed any procedure until the summer, at the earliest.

Babe still couldn't win, finishing seventh at the Tampa Women's Open and losing a sudden-death play-off at the St. Petersburg Open. These two defeats stung more than usual because both were Babe's local tournaments. "At this point, ten months had gone by since my operation," Babe said. "People were beginning to ask each other whether I'd ever be capable of winning tournaments again. And I was asking myself the same thing."

She mailed off another letter to the Bowens: "I'm starting to feel myself on the golf course and think I will be back winning with ease once again. I just miss the silly easy shots. I still get sorta tired on the back nine, but notice it's getting less than before.... Not bad for a weak old lady."

Next was the Serbin Open at Bayshore Golf Course in Miami Beach, Florida. Serbin was Babe's longtime and loyal sponsor. When she was at Hotel Dieu Hospital, Lew Serbin, the president of the clothing company, had visited her, the only one of her sponsors to do so. And Babe noticed. "Of the thousands of communications I received, a couple were conspicuous by their absence, too," she said. "Namely, some of the people whose products I endorse. They didn't seem to feel my endorsement would mean much again."

At the Serbin Open, Babe and Patty Berg were tied for first, two strokes under par, after the first three rounds. They remained tied after the first nine on the final day. On the back nine, Babe's body was again wearing down, but she managed to stay even with Berg with one hole to play.

The eighteenth at Bayshore is a 430-yard par 4. Babe hit a long drive into a stand of palm trees. Palm fronds were hanging down in front of her on her next shot, and a wide-mouthed bunker lay beyond them. Babe needed to slam the ball through the fronds to carry the bunker and get on the fairway. She grabbed a four-iron and swung, hitting the ball so hard that it punched a hole in a palm frond and carried to within one hundred yards of the green. It landed on a sandy patch of fairway, and Babe used a nine-iron to put the ball on the green. Babe sank her par putt to win her first tournament since the cancer operation. It was February 20, 1954.

"I guess I'll have to call this the biggest thrill of my life," said Babe, as she walked slowly off the last green. "I didn't think I would ever win another one."

That spring, the Golf Writers of America voted Babe the winner of the 1953 Ben Hogan Comeback Player of the Year Award. She barely edged out Ted Williams, who had returned to baseball after a tour of duty with the Marines in the Korean War. Also that spring, President and Mrs. Eisenhower invited Babe to the White House to attend a ceremony and luncheon kicking off the annual Cancer Crusade. Prior to the event, Babe met the first lady in the East Room. "Mrs. Eisenhower," she said, "I've fixed up my bangs so I can be right in unison with you."

"Oh, but your bangs look so nicely curled," the first lady said, "and mine never do."

The President entered the room as a band played "Hail to the Chief." Babe shook hands with him and said, "How do you do, Mr. President?"

"How do you do, Mrs. Zaharias?" he replied. Eisenhower was a passionate golfer who would play eight hundred rounds of golf during his two terms in office, causing his critics, including John F. Kennedy, to call him the "duffer-in-chief." Ike dropped his head low and, in a mock whisper, said, "I'll see you later, Babe. I want to talk to you about this game of golf."

After he was done with the photo line, Eisenhower used radioactive cobalt (cobalt 60) in the White House to light a seventy-foot red Sword of Hope, the symbol of the American Cancer Society, in Times Square. Then Babe presented the President with a miniature Sword of Hope. "Mr. President," she said, "on behalf of the hundreds of thousands of volunteers of the American Cancer Society and of the thousands like myself who have had cancer, who have known its terrible threat, and have been able to get back to our normal life, I present you with this sword of hope."

Afterward, Babe and Ike talked golf. This was as big a treat for the President as it was for Babe. She gave him pointers on his swing, with the President gripping the Sword of Hope as if it were a trusty nine-iron.

As Babe was preparing to leave the White House after the luncheon, someone slipped her a note. Peggy Kirk Bell had just had her first child, a baby girl. Babe hopped on a plane for North Carolina. Bell lived on the Pine Needles golf course in Southern Pines.

The next morning, Babe burst into Bell's hospital room. "Where's that baby?" she shouted. She cooed over the one-day-old child. Then Babe began barking stage directions. "Get the photographer in here," she said. "Where is the press conference?"

Bell was still recovering, but Babe wanted to make news.

"Name her after me," she told Bell.

"Mildred?"

"No — Babe. Babe Bell wins the Open. It'll look great in print."

While Babe was fussing over the baby, a panic-stricken nurse ran into the room, telling Babe, "President Eisenhower is on the phone — he wants to talk to you."

"Tell him to call me back, or I'll call him back," Babe said. "I'm busy right now."

A few days later, Babe took another call while visiting Bell's house. This one was from Betty Jameson, who asked if Babe had applied for entry into the U.S. Women's Open, coming up in early July. Babe had not. "And it was past the deadline," Jameson recalled. But Joe Dey, the USGA executive director, gave Babe special permission to play. "Again, [he] let the rules go by; when he wanted to he would do it," Jameson said.

Bell had wanted her firstborn to be a boy, but Babe was so happy it was a girl. "All boys are good athletes," Babe told her friend. "But there aren't many girls who are. Girls can become great athletes easily."

Bell decided that Bonnie would be a better name for her new daughter. Bonnie Bell — close enough.

The next stop for Babe was *The Ed Sullivan Show*. It was Sullivan's idea to have Babe on the program to discuss her cancer diagnosis. "I want all people to see how you've licked this thing," he told her.

On the show, Sullivan introduced Babe and told his viewers, "The whole nation was shocked to hear she had cancer." Then Babe and

Betty Dodd strolled out. After chatting with Sullivan for a moment, Babe and Betty played "Begin the Beguine," one of the songs Babe had sung twenty-one years earlier at the Palace Theater. Babe played her aluminum and wood harmonica (M. Hohner's Old Standby harmonica, in the key of C) to Betty's guitar accompaniment. Babe was paid $1,500 for her appearance, and she got Sullivan's producers to cough up $350 for Betty.

The honors kept rolling in. In recognition of her "outstanding contributions to golf within the past year," Babe won the William D. Richardson Award, presented in memory of the *New York Times* golf writer, edging out President Eisenhower by thirteen points. She was the first recipient of the Serbin Trophy, a beautiful diamond-studded gold trophy that would become highly coveted by the women on the tour. And in September, at the Ardmore Open in Oklahoma, where she finished seventh, Babe received a live gift: a palomino horse, whose nickname was Superman. Babe climbed onto the horse and did a few mini-laps around the eighteenth green. A public-address announcer said, "Here comes Superman, ridden by Superwoman!"

The fans responded with their own accolades. Letters and cards by the crateful arrived at Babe's home in Tampa. Many were from cancer patients saying that Babe had helped them fight on. "Those letters sort of built up my determination to continue in golf," Babe later said. "It meant a lot to know that so many people were rooting for me in my comeback."

Babe's hernia and cancer operations had forced her to miss two years of the U.S. Women's Open. In 1954, it was being held at Salem Country Club in Peabody, Massachusetts, a 6,393-yard course that plays to a men's par of 72—a long course. "A real golf course," Babe called it. Five days before the tournament began, Babe and George arrived in Peabody. Babe wanted the chance to play a few practice rounds.

The tournament had eighteen-hole rounds scheduled on Thursday and Friday and a final thirty-six-hole round on Saturday, July 3. Babe worried about whether she'd be able to endure the final day. She roared to a big lead with a first-round 72, followed by a second-round 71. She shot a 73 on Saturday morning, taking a seemingly insurmountable twelve-stroke lead into the final eighteen holes. Following the morning round, Betty Dodd helped Babe irrigate her colostomy bag in the locker room, then Babe lay down for a much-needed rest.

"In the afternoon, fatigue finally began to set in," Babe recalled. But it really didn't matter. On the eighteenth green, Babe holed a final putt for a fourth-round score of 75 and a seventy-two-hole score of 291. Babe's four-day scorecard of 72-71-73-75 was as impressive as the scorecards of the best male professionals of the day.

On the final green, the gallery roared, applauding for nearly five minutes. This was a different Babe. Unlike the celebrations following other victories, when Babe pulled antics such as jumping into George's arms or dancing a quick jig, she was subdued. She swept off her straw golf hat and made a deep bow to the applauding spectators, then slowly raised her right arm in a dignified salute.

Barely fifteen months after undergoing major cancer surgery, Babe had won by an astonishing twelve strokes over Betty Hicks. Louise Suggs finished third, sixteen strokes behind. This was Babe's third U.S. Women's Open title, and heroically, she had played thirty-six holes on the final day.

In front of the majestic Salem Country Club clubhouse, Isaac Grainger, president of the USGA, presented Babe with the gleaming silver cup and the first-place check for $3,000. He pronounced Babe "the greatest woman athlete in the world." He praised her "wonderful mental attitude in fighting against what many would consider an insurmountable handicap."

Handicap. In the 1950s, that word was applied often to cancer. But on the golf course, the only handicap is measured by something as trivial as strokes.

The champion rose to speak. She had changed from her golf clothes into a lovely tailored dress and stood behind two bulky silver microphones, the silver cup sitting on a linen-covered table in front of her. "I don't like to keep bringing up this hospital deal," Babe said, "but when there were reports going out that I'd never play championship or tournament golf again, I said, 'Please, God, let me play again.' He answered my prayer, and I want to thank God for letting me win again."

Afterward, reporters asked Babe what her third Women's Open title meant. "Now I'm happy because I can tell people not to be afraid of cancer," she said. "I've had over 15,000 letters from people and this victory today is an answer to them — it will show a lot of people that they need not be afraid of an operation and can go on and live a normal life. I really wanted to win this one and I'm glad I could hold my concentration. Winning my first tournament, the Serbin Open, after my operation and this big one today makes me feel wonderful. That's right — now I don't expect to retire for twenty years. I promised to God that if He made me well," she said, "I'd do everything in my power when I got out to help the fight against cancer."

The victory ensured Babe's selection for the sixth time as the Associated Press Female Athlete of the Year. No other athlete, male or female, has won the award six times. Nearly a quarter of a century later, Jim Murray, the legendary sports columnist for the *Los Angeles Times,* called Babe's triumph at the 1954 U.S. Women's Open "probably the most incredible athletic feat of all time, given her condition. People all over the country who had been resisting the operation, preferring terminal cancer to it, began changing their minds — and saving their lives."

Inside the Salem Country Club clubhouse, the press conference was over. George had already drained a few bottles of beer. Babe had gotten herself cleaned up. Before leaving, she placed phone calls to Dr. W. E.

Tatum and Dr. Robert Moore. She wanted to say thanks and to tell them that her win was their win, too.

"You did it yourself, Babe," Moore said. "It was your faith, Babe... that and your courage."

Babe said no. "Actually, *we* won it," she told her doctor. "We and the thousands of people whose faith helped make me strong."

All her life, Babe had never liked giving credit to anyone for anything she did. That's what made the high hurdles and the javelin and the golf course irresistible to her. You depended on yourself to win. If you set a record, your name went into the record books. *Just one name. Yours. Alone.*

Now Babe shared the glory of the biggest title in women's golf with thousands of strangers. At forty-three years old, Babe had finally grown up.

22

Rainbow Manor

America's all-sport trailblazer was now America's all-star crusader against cancer. She and George founded the Babe Didrikson Zaharias Fund in September 1955 to raise money for cancer research. She made television and radio ads for the American Cancer Society and the Damon Runyon Cancer Research Foundation. She opened the Babe Didrikson Zaharias Chapter of the American Cancer Society in Seattle. And in every city, Babe would clear enough time on her schedule to visit a children's cancer ward. She'd glide into the room—smiling, wisecracking, laying on the thick East Texas drawl—and belt out a few tunes on her mouth organ. She'd tell the children that the disease wasn't so tough. She'd urge them to keep fighting, believing, praying. She'd tell the story about winning the Serbin Open by a single stroke ten months after her cancer surgery. She'd talk about how she won the U.S. Women's Open by a dozen strokes. The children would listen, laugh, touch the sleeve of her long dress. Their expressions were electric with hope.

From the beginning, Babe reached for warrior metaphors used in the sports arena to characterize her cancer. Reporters, columnists, and newsreel announcers followed. And not coincidentally, that's how millions of people today describe the disease: Cancer is a foe. Cancer is a battle. Cancer is beatable.

She found it hard to say no. She began compiling lists of commitments and promises so she wouldn't forget. Keeping busy made it easier for Babe to ignore the occasional warning signs transmitted by her body — the hip pain, the lower back pain, the pain shooting down her right leg, the bone-numbing fatigue, all felt simultaneously some mornings as she climbed out of bed. On other days, she woke up feeling fine. Her resiliency was proof of a remarkable comeback that transcended sports. And everywhere she went, she was inspired by the courage of other cancer patients. Their hope fed hers. She visited Sister Tarsisis, the nun who had been in the Hotel Dieu Hospital room across the hall. Sister Tarsisis did indeed have the colostomy that Babe had recommended and was doing well, with her weight nearly back to normal. Babe was thrilled.

"She gave people hope," Patty Berg said. And Babe's advice never changed: "In the name of Heaven and your own most precious possession, your life, never hesitate about the inconvenience or even the cost of a regular physical checkup. Today, if possible. Tomorrow is too late."

Suddenly, winning wasn't as important to her. When she surveyed the crowded 1955 LPGA Tournament Schedule with thirty events and $160,000 up for grabs, she didn't mentally carve up the spoils. How many times can you play the Tampa Women's Open? All her life, finding a place to play was the thing that mattered most. But now...

Maybe George was right. Perhaps she was mellowing and should just quit. Maybe she no longer needed the surge of adrenaline and affirmation that comes from victories won before adoring crowds. "At times, I feel I'd rather just ride around the course in my electric cart," she said, "or sit on the clubhouse porch, and let the rest of the girls fight it out."

The cancer wasn't gone, even if it sometimes seemed that way. Babe started feeling more run-down during the late summer of 1954, forcing her to cancel a number of public appearances in the early autumn. She didn't think the setback would last long.

George and Babe sold the Tampa Golf and Country Club for $200,000, banking a 500 percent profit in just under five years. They remained in the converted caddie house, however.

One evening, George reached across the dinner table, took Babe's hand, and told her it was time to make one overdue dream come true. They found a patch of land on the edge of the Tampa Golf and Country Club overlooking a man-made lake—a lovely spot where they could listen to the Tampa Bay breezes tickle the palm fronds. She knew exactly what she wanted: a rambling, one-story, cedar ranch-style home—"big and roomy, for George's comfort." Babe scoured home-decorating books, using a pencil and ruler on a yellow pad to sketch out design ideas, inside and out. Then she gave the sketches to the architects, who used them to draw up the blueprints.

Babe concocted an eclectic interior design—Early American bedrooms, a living room evoking a country squire's drawing room, a kitchen that was a cross between "California ranch" and "Arizona ranch." On a plane ride to Atlanta for the Titleholders Championship, she designed the kitchen, including a wrought-iron dinette set. She designed the master bath, with his-and-her washstands, and the master bedroom, featuring louvered doors and two big beds. When the workmen were building the house, Babe rolled up her sleeves and drove nails into plywood and put mortar between bricks. In one photograph in her autobiography, a smiling Babe, in a long dress and pearls, with her hands in work gloves, kneels in front of the half-built wall ringing the patio as she lays the red bricks. "It may not be 'pure' architecture," Babe says in the caption, "but for George and me it's the ultimate in comfortable living."

Rainbow Manor would be ready by June 1955. Babe couldn't wait to move in.

If it had been entirely up to her (or George), she would have quit the game. "You've proved everything," George told her. "You don't have to prove anything more." But the letters and cards—more than forty thousand from all over the world—made retirement impossible. "Every time I get out and play well in a golf tournament," she said, "it seems to buck up people with the same cancer trouble I had." She was now playing as much for others as herself.

She had another reason for staying: the continued success of the LPGA, now five years old and still experiencing growing pains. "At first there were just six or seven of us," Babe said. "Now we've got about twenty-five or thirty girls who are very fine golfers. I know the tournaments draw better when all of us are in there than when some of us aren't."

The final reason, though, trumped all the others. Whenever there was a struggle on the course, Babe kept hearing the whispers. "She's through," they said. So Babe kept playing.

But Babe couldn't finish the Sarasota Open, held the last weekend in February 1955 at the Bobby Jones Golf Club. After shooting a 79 on the first day, she walked off the course and quit. Reporters crowded around George, asking if Babe was sick again. No, George said, she was just tuckered out.

In mid-March, at the Titleholders, a young player named Barbara Romack spoke with Babe. They'd played together a few times—once in Sacramento, Romack's hometown—and Romack had marveled at "a lively sparkle" in Babe's hazel eyes. That had been five years earlier. At Augusta, as Babe was stepping into a car with her black French poodle, Bebe, Romack said hello. "That wonderful lively look in her eyes—the light had gone," she recalled. "I knew then she didn't have much time left." Romack would never forget Babe's words: "Honey, keep going with your golf. Just keep going."

Babe decided to go for a checkup before her two-year cancer anniversary appointment scheduled for that April. The doctors found that she was anemic. They ordered her to take a long vacation. In late March, Babe, Betty Dodd, and Betty's sister Peggy rented a cabin in Port Aransas, Texas, on the Gulf Coast. After fishing off a pier late one evening, they returned to Betty's Lincoln, only to discover that the car was stuck in the wet sand. The three women pushed long wharf planks under the back tires to get it unstuck, struggling while two men stood watching, amused but not helping. They finally got the car going and returned to their cabin, but Babe was racked with unbearable back pain that night. She couldn't sleep. Early the next morning, Betty called Dr. Robert Moore, who ordered Babe to go to a clinic on the island, where she was given a shot of Demerol, a potent painkiller.

"Now that I look back," Betty said, "this was the beginning of the end. The cancer had returned, but it took months to find it."

Babe felt well enough to travel to Spartanburg, South Carolina, for the Peach Blossom Open in late April. Marilynn Smith held a single-stroke lead over Babe with nine holes to go. Then Babe, whose game had been so erratic on the front nine, shifted into high gear. She buckled down, grim-faced, and started smashing those long drives off the tee. At the same time, Smith's game came undone. "It seemed like every second shot I hit would go into a bunker," she recalled. "And I was missing putts. Babe came back."

Babe won the tournament by four strokes. "It was just meant for her to win," Smith said.

It would be Babe's last tournament. "Isn't it kind of fitting," Betsy Rawls said, "that Babe would win the last tournament she ever played?"

*   *   *

Doctors at Hotel Dieu Hospital in Beaumont hunted fruitlessly for the origin of Babe's back pain. She left the hospital still feeling run-down but tried to ignore it. At last, she and George were moving into Rainbow Manor.

George loved seeing how happy the new home made Babe, who puttered about trailed by Bebe. "We would walk through it," he said, "and I would ask her if there was anything she would change, and she would say there wasn't a thing she would change."

Babe planted red, pink, and yellow roses in the garden out back. If there were two TV programs on that she liked—Jackie Gleason and Perry Como, for instance—she watched them both at the same time, one TV stacked on top of the other.

They were in their new home only one week before Babe and George flew back to Texas, this time to a hospital in Galveston for more tests. Betty had gone to Pennsylvania and New York to compete in a couple of tournaments, but Babe begged her to come to Galveston while the doctors kept searching. When Betty walked into Babe's hospital room, she was surprised to discover Babe was in traction, and she started to cry when she saw Betty's face. And Betty's cot was already set up next to Babe's bed.

The doctors thought the trouble might be a herniated disc and they'd need to operate. Then they floated another, mind-boggling theory: Babe had become addicted to painkillers.

Babe, George, and Betty were stunned. George had to restrain himself; Betty thought Babe might punch one of the doctors in the mouth. "Here she was in this tremendous pain and he tells her it's in her head, that she's psychologically addicted to drugs," Betty said. "She was just livid."

A hospital psychiatrist informed the doctors they were wrong. They relented, giving Betty and George a metal lockbox containing seven different painkillers for Babe. The search went on. The sciatic nerve running down Babe's left leg throbbed. On June 22, she was operated on for a herniated disc at John Sealy Hospital in Galveston. Because doctors at this point had found no evidence that the cancer had spread, they hoped the operation would relieve Babe's intense back pain. Babe's sister-in-law Thelma believed that the surgery was unnecessary. "She didn't have anything wrong with her back," she said years later.

At the suggestion of Fred Corcoran, Babe and George made arrangements for Babe to write an autobiography. "Babe's ready to tell her story now," Corcoran told his friend and client sportswriter Harry Paxton, who was hired to ghostwrite the book. Babe signed a contract with A. S. Barnes, the same New York firm that had published *Championship Golf* in 1948. From late spring to midsummer, in the hospital in Galveston and then at Rainbow Manor, Babe told a carefully crafted story of her life to Paxton, who tape-recorded her reminiscences.

Paxton began his preface buoyantly: "You might suppose offhand that Babe Didrikson Zaharias is too well known to require any introduction. Actually this isn't the case. To be sure, even people who never look at the sports pages can identify her as a superwoman athlete. And everybody is sympathetically aware of her valiant struggle against cancer. But only a comparative few have been in a position to know that she is also something out of the ordinary as a person."

But he ended it ruefully:

There was one unhappy new note just as this book was being completed in the summer of 1955. The Babe had met and licked cancer once. Now the doctors found that she was in for a return match. Their X-rays showed a fresh trace of cancer.

This news did not demoralize her, any more than other tough challenges have. The Babe always has been the happy-warrior type—determined but not bitter. She is a realistic competitor who never underrates an opponent—and never doubts that she has what it takes to come out on top. It was in this spirit that she faced up to the latest big battle of her demanding life.

At the end of July, Babe and George had received the news of the "fresh trace of cancer," as the doctors had called it, found on the right side of Babe's sacrum, toward the back of the pelvis. Babe seemed "relieved" by the news, Betty said. "It was almost like well, thank God, now they know I'm not nuts, you know."

George grimly announced the discovery to reporters in the hospital lobby. But, he told them, Babe "took the bad news like the mighty champion she's always been."

Upstairs, Babe was sitting up in bed as she spoke into Paxton's tape recorder: "As far as I was concerned, there was no doubt about my coming back again. With the love and support of the many friends I have made, how could I miss? They have helped me hurdle one obstacle after another, and any success I have had is due to a great extent to their devotion and consideration. Right now I want to thank them one and all, as well as the many unknown people who have befriended me and helped me on my way. Winning has always meant much to me, but winning friends has meant the most."

Babe's book was nearly complete, but in her last paragraph, she refused to accept the idea that there wouldn't be more championships to recount. "In the future," she said, "maybe I'll have to limit myself to just a few of the most important tournaments each year. But I expect to be shooting for championships for a good many years to come. My autobiography isn't finished yet."

When they heard those words, George and Betty smiled. Babe had so much hope, but it was impossible for them to be as optimistic. They knew things about Babe's cancer that Babe didn't know, couldn't know. Two years was a long time to keep a secret.

*   *   *

R. L. and Bertha Bowen visited Rainbow Manor in October. Spending a few days with old friends revitalized Babe. So did Betty's golf. From the passenger's seat in an electric cart, Babe spent an hour or two watching Betty play. She told the Bowens that she hoped Betty could "really get going next year and make herself good money." On some mornings, Babe woke up and thought, *Today's the day I'm going to play nine holes with Betty.* But the pain made it impossible.

A few weeks after the Bowens left, Peggy Kirk Bell came to town. Babe forced herself to play nine holes with Bell. She couldn't put on golf shoes because her swollen feet were so painful. "So she played in loafers," Bell recalled. They went around the course in the electric cart.

Babe had almost no punch left. Her distance off the tee was between 150 and 170 yards, the ball usually rolling just about as far as Bell's drives. "Peggy, you've got to be one of the greatest golfers in the world," Babe said. "How do you break a hundred driving this far?" Midway through their round, George showed up with a beaming used-car salesman who had always wanted to hit a few balls with Babe. George urged the salesman to join Babe and Bell.

"Sometimes," Babe said later to Bell, "George doesn't use good sense."

The pain became so bad by December that Babe returned to the hospital in Galveston. Her wedding anniversary was coming up, on December 23, then Christmas. The Bowens invited Babe and George to spend the holidays with them in Fort Worth.

R.L. sent his small plane to pick up Babe and George. A home movie was made of the plane's arrival at the Fort Worth airport: George, first off the plane, helps Babe down the steps. Looking exhausted and drawn, wearing tailored pajamas and a cotton robe (with a rhinestone Christmas tree pinned to her lapel), she walks slowly toward Bertha, who opens her arms, forces a big smile, and all but catches Babe in an embrace. Sadness, resignation, and relief cross Babe's face, somehow all at once. As the two women hug, Bertha closes her eyes, but she never stops smiling.

The day after Christmas, Babe asked Bertha to drive her to Colonial Country Club. On a narrow dirt road rambling past the slightly elevated second green, Babe told her to stop the car. Then, wearing her pajamas and robe, Babe, with Bertha's help, got out of the car and walked to the edge of the green. She knelt down and rubbed the open palm of her hand over the grass.

"I just wanted to see a golf course one more time," she told her friend.

Babe left John Sealy Hospital in late January 1956 and went home to Tampa. At the end of February, Betty was at the top of the leaderboard in the Sarasota Open, the same tournament that Babe had quit after a single round the previous year. George drove Babe down to the Bobby Jones Golf Club. With the gallery at the eighteenth green, Babe stood and watched Betty lose by a stroke to Betsy Rawls. Betty won a second-place check for $1,000. "I was dying to win it because Babe was there," Betty said, "but I just didn't."

A few days earlier, on the morning of February 20, the doorbell rang at Rainbow Manor at the appointed hour. George opened the door and greeted Joan Flynn Dreyspool, one of America's most esteemed sports-writers, on assignment for *Sports Illustrated.* "Shhhh," George said to Dreyspool. "Babe is sleeping."

After pouring Dreyspool a cup of coffee, George asked, "Would you like to see the house?"

In the bright kitchen, a lazy Susan table nestled in a bay window overlooking the patio and a lawn that ran down to the lake. There were copper pots, a modern stove, electric appliances, and knotty pine. George waved his hand and said, "Babe designed this whole works here."

In the big living room, Dreyspool looked at the trophies and cups on the shelves and a portrait of Babe, painted in 1934, above the fireplace mantel. In the den, a messy desk was stacked with letters that Babe needed to answer. Dreyspool noticed a check made out to the Babe Didrikson Zaharias Fund that George needed to deposit. George opened a cupboard door and took out a frayed cardboard golf-ball box. "Look," he said. "More medals." Inside were Babe's Olympic gold medals and her AAU championship medals, "tarnished and piled in a jumble."

They returned to the kitchen, where there was a black intercom box that was attached to a similar box in the master bedroom. George looked at the silent box and told Dreyspool, "She didn't get to sleep until 4:00 this morning. She had a bad night." It was nearly noon.

George told the story about how he and Babe had met on the first tee at Brentwood — what was it now, eighteen years ago? He described how they were married at Tom Packs's house in St. Louis less than a year after meeting. Finally, the box buzzed. George pressed a button. "How you doin', honey?"

"Pretty good," said a woman's voice, weak and far away.

Babe requested a fried-egg sandwich and some bacon. "She must feel better if she's hungry," George said as he carefully placed slabs of bacon in a hot frying pan. Next to him, a young female aide named Eddie fried the eggs. The box buzzed again. "Honey, send Joan in," Babe said.

George, carrying the sandwich on a tray, and Dreyspool walked into the roomy master bedroom, finding Babe lying on the double bed farthest from the door.

Dreyspool introduced herself. Babe, wearing red satin pajamas and propped up on pillows, apologized for oversleeping. She looked thin and drawn, though her hazel eyes sparkled. Bebe yapped until Babe made room for the dog on the bed.

Babe talked about a recent tournament in St. Petersburg, which she had attended for five days. Her legs weren't hurting, but they did "ache," she said.

"Remember, honey, how many times we'd come from a tournament and I'd rub your legs?" George asked.

"Yup, we'd head right for the hotel and the bathtub."

Babe smiled at George. "He's quite a guy, isn't he?" Babe asked Joan with that half grin. "Look at his eyes real good. There's a lot of sincerity and sweetness in his eyes. I don't know what I would have done without him."

"Oh, honey," George said, "what would have I done without you?" Today, at least, the troubles of their marriage seemed behind them.

Babe asked George to bring her a framed photograph of Momma and Poppa, which she showed to Dreyspool. "I guess I've got my father's mouth and chin," she said. "Mother used to play baseball with us, run with us and do everything. We had a good time. My Dad was a sailor — that's why I've always liked sea stories. He carved a boat and put it in a bottle. I have it in the other room."

George added, "He went around the world 19 times."

"Seventeen times," Babe said.

"That's the promoter in me," George confessed.

Babe lit a cigarette, sipped her coffee, and talked about starting the LPGA down in Miami in 1949, with George, Patty Berg, and Fred Corcoran. A women's tour was a good idea because it was *necessary*. "I had this golf game, but nothing to play in...," she explained. "I was working most of the time, playing exhibitions, but we wanted this tour. We had to have players. We felt if we could get out and help some young players, we'd get them to play good so we could have competition. George would give them lessons. Then they got good. 'Forget the lessons, George,' I told him, 'they're getting tough.'" Everyone laughed.

George said "a big thrill" for Babe was watching the LPGA grow. That was why, just the day before, Babe had insisted on keeping her commitment at Sunset Golf and Country Club, where she had presented the St. Petersburg Open winner's cup and a $900 first-place check to Kathy Cornelius. By 1956, the LPGA's tournament money had grown to nearly $200,000, and there were now thirty-five regulars on the tour. "While she was playing it," George said, "the most she could win was $1,000, and she could have made four times that much in exhibitions in four days. But money has never moved Babe much. She likes to play in tournaments. She likes the crowds, the competition."

"I just like being on stage," Babe said with a shrug. "I get such a kick out of playing for people."

She then paused a moment as pain rocketed through her chest. "I get so mad," she said of the pain. "The thing I don't understand is I've taken such good care of my body all my life. You go through it and you fight and you fight and you hope and you pray, then something worse hits you like this last one, cancer of the sacrum. It's going to make it tough for me to come back." This was the first time Babe had admitted, publicly, that her promised comeback might be impossible.

George told a story about the time Babe accepted the Ben Hogan Comeback Player of the Year Award at a banquet at the Plaza Hotel in New York. Hogan told everyone that the reason "we have Babe with us today" was that "she has prepared her body and taken such good care of it."

Babe nodded, saying that she admired Hogan as much as any golfer, male or female. "He plays to win," she said, "but to be able to play like he wanted to play, he had to lose a lot of friends."

"Now, honey, don't say that," George said.

"It's true," Babe said, "but he's won his friends back again since then. I don't say Ben's the greatest golfer in the world or the greatest swinger of a golf club, but nobody ever worked like him."

"Except you," George said.

Babe said, "They say golf came easy to me because I was a good athlete, but there's not any girl on the tour who worked near as hard as I did in golf. It was the toughest game I ever tackled."

She then reminisced about how she had done it, practicing all those long hours, first in Dallas while still at Employers Casualty and then in California. Getting good enough to win a championship is one thing. Then you have to defend it, which is harder, Babe said, because everyone is trying to knock you off the pedestal. There was a lull in the conversation. Dreyspool asked Babe about the cancer.

"I have confidence that I am going to get well," she said. "And I don't feel as though it's only for myself. I feel as though it's for those people who are interested enough to write me and encourage me. When I went back and played and worked so hard after my cancer operation in '53, I hoped I would encourage other cancer patients that they weren't through or physically handicapped, and I still hope I'll be able to prove it; that if you have the wish or sufficient desire, you'll be able to come out of it."

Babe's voice was weakening, and George brought her a pill. "I'll turn the television set on for you," he told Babe, "until you fall asleep."

Babe smiled. As the TV flickered to life, she had one final thing to tell Joan Dreyspool: "You know, I read these stories that tell why champions retire, but I've got my own ideas about it. They don't retire because they're through. They retire because they're just tired of it. They get tired of putting on their shoes. I did, too, when I got to feeling bad. . . . I don't feel that way now. I'd just love to get my shoes on once again."

23

Greatness and Goodness

A month after the visit with the writer from *Sports Illustrated,* Babe woke up after a bad night and told George to bring her back to Galveston. "That was it," Betty said. "She never left the hospital."

Betty was playing the best golf of her life, so Babe asked her sister Lillie to move into her room at John Sealy Hospital. Lillie slept on a cot. "Babe, she knew she was going to die," Lillie said. "She held my hand all the time, but she was always thinkin' of others, that girl was."

When she felt up to it, Babe went to visit the children in the cancer ward. She brought them candy, played with them, made them laugh, tried to keep herself from crying. "Don't go see 'em, Lillie," she warned her sister. "My cancer doesn't show — it's on the inside. But the children, some of them, oh, Lillie, they are such pitiful things."

Babe's brother Louis recalled, "She suspected that she was on the way out. The rest of us knew it. Babe's aching was constant. They gave her pain-killers and took regular X-rays."

Babe and George spoke often about God. Her decision to embrace God was surprising, considering she rarely went to church and her faith was absent during much of her life. "When George and I talk of God now, we feel we know Him," Babe told an interviewer that spring. "We see Him all around us, taking many forms. We see Him in the doctors and nurses, and in the sweet, unselfish, and wonderfully good-natured nuns. We see Him in the many people who showed such real concern over whether I'd be able to play golf again."

And Babe hoped that God would help her survive so that she could make cancer warnings the mission of her life. "I want to live because my life is fuller than it was before," she said. "I want to live more than for the thrill of busting a 260-yarder down the middle. I want to help crush cancer into the earth...shout from the housetops a warning against the disease."

A surprise party was thrown for Babe on her forty-fifth birthday in a hospital lounge. Fifty friends and hospital staff members sang "Happy Birthday," and Babe blew out pink, yellow, green, and white candles on a five-layer cake with white frosting. "What a nice surprise," she said. The lounge was filled with flowers and gifts, including robes, pajamas, a television set, candy, and a music box. Dozens of people had sent telegrams. Babe expressed one disappointment — not getting more money for her cancer research fund. "Perhaps they'll start coming in faster," she said of the checks. The smallest birthday gift was hand-delivered by Monsignor Daniel P. O'Connell of St. Mary Cathedral: rosary beads. "God bless you and love you, Mildred, for all that you have done for the youth of the world," the accompanying note said.

Afterward, Babe told reporters that the party was "the finest I've ever had or hope to have."

Across the ocean, at Wentworth in England, Ben Hogan and Sam Snead stopped play for a moment during the Canada Cup and International Golf Championship to say a prayer for Babe. Players from thirty countries joined them in silence.

The wire services spread news of Babe's surprise party across the country. George fed nearly daily health updates to the squad of reporters camped in the hospital lobby. At these press conferences, sometimes done right outside Babe's hospital room, George often wept uncontrollably in front of the cameras. Some in the press rolled their eyes, whispering that "the Crying Greek from Cripple Creek" had not lost his talent for weeping on cue. Even in those final days, George often quoted Babe's alleged words to the media—exhortations for people to continue writing checks for cancer research: "Business as usual. Don't stop. We've got to keep fighting and working." Several of Babe's friends objected to the attention George paid to the media; they whispered that he was turning Babe's final days into a cheap three-ring circus. It wasn't that the emotion wasn't real, but it was hard to see George cry without recalling his talent for turning on the taps.

During that last summer, the doctors made every effort to keep Babe going. She was famous, she represented hope for millions of cancer patients, and that seemed reason enough to keep her alive as long as possible. But Betty Dodd and Peggy Kirk Bell felt that the doctors went too far when they performed a cordotomy, the severing of her spinal cord. The procedure eased her pain but made her, Bell asserted, practically, though not technically, "a vegetable." Babe was wasting away. "If she had been anybody else," a nurse told Bell, "they wouldn't have kept her alive."

A personal letter from President Eisenhower arrived in Babe's hospital room on September 10, 1956. She couldn't read it herself, so George read it to her. "This is just a note to say the whole country unites with me in admiring your courage in the hospital, even more than we admired your courage on the playing field," the President wrote. "For years you have been an exemplar of greatness and goodness in things of the mind and heart—an inspiration to all your fellow Americans.

"I am sure that in these days our esteem and admiration of you is greater than ever. Mrs. Eisenhower joins me in sending our warmest greetings."

The United Press report about the President's letter said nothing about the end being near. In fact, it said, "Mrs. Zaharias is in excellent spirits and free of fever again." Neither was true.

Betty returned to the hospital on September 16. She didn't recognize her friend. "She was flat on her back and she had tubes everywhere," Betty recalled. "She recognized me, but not really, I guess. I was like someone way, way back—back in time."

Betty left the hospital heartbroken. She told herself she'd do what Babe would have wanted her to do—play more golf.

"George, I ain't gonna die," Babe told her husband just after midnight on September 27, 1956. But as the sun was rising over the Gulf of Mexico at 6:42 a.m., Babe Didrikson Zaharias passed away. George was by her side.

The day before, George had sobbed for reporters as he stood just four doors down from Babe's hospital room. "Babe never really asked God for too much," he said. "When she prayed, she asked Him to ease the pain of everyone, not just her own. She never asked Him to win any tournaments for her. She just prayed to Him to let her get well and she would do the rest. She never wanted anything but life."

George cried again as he announced Babe's death to the reporters congregated in the hospital lobby. "It's been a long battle and Babe fought it the way she knows how to fight—giving ground reluctantly, an inch at a time," he said. "She just floated away."

He needed to keep talking. "She's had enough agony, sadness and pain," he said. "God's will be done. I know she will live forever in the hearts of millions."

The big tears just kept falling. "Good God," he wailed, "I didn't know until right now how great she is..."

A more subdued tribute occurred later that morning in the Executive Office Building, across the street from the White House. At 10:33 a.m., President Eisenhower walked into a large room and took his place behind a stand of microphones to begin the ninety-sixth press conference of his Presidency.

"Ladies and gentlemen," the President told the 210 reporters assembled, "I should like to take one minute to pay a tribute to Mrs. Zaharias, Babe Didrikson. She was a woman who, in her athletic career, certainly won the admiration of every person in the United States, all sports people all over the world, and in her gallant fight against cancer, she put up one of the kind of fights that inspired us all.

"I think that every one of us feels sad that finally she had to lose this last one of all her battles."

Those words, more than any others, were cherished by Babe's family. But there were many more to come.

The flash across the country from the Associated Press read, "Babe Didrikson Zaharias, the greatest woman athlete the world has known, died today after a stubborn battle with the one competitor she couldn't beat—cancer."

At last, Babe made it onto the front page of the nation's most prestigious newspaper, the *New York Times*. Inside, an editorial offered this salute:

Babe Didrikson has finally lost the big one. It was after the greatest and most gallant struggle of her great and gallant career. This one was the hardest to lose, but she knew that "you can't win them all" and that there is one antagonist against which even the stoutest heart is not quite enough.... She didn't know the meaning of the word quit, and she refused to define it, right to the end. Her tragic death must spur us to renewed efforts to fight the foe that cut her down. But her own terrific fight against that foe can also be an inspiration to all those who must face and overcome handicaps. It is not only the annals of sport that her life has enriched. It is the whole story of human beings who somehow have to keep on trying.

Betty Dodd was in San Francisco when she heard the news. She didn't cry; she was relieved. At last, Babe was free of pain.

There was no LPGA tournament that weekend. Babe's fellow golfers were scattered across the country when the news broke out of Galveston. "She wasn't ready to go," Peggy Kirk Bell said years later. But, of course, from that moment of dancing in the hurricane onward, she never had been.

Condolences poured ·in from around the world — Ben Hogan; Rocky Marciano; Avery Brundage; hundreds of sports figures, celebrities, and politicians. "I was terribly fond of Babe," Bobby Jones said, "and I couldn't be more distressed. She took her final illness just as she played her games — giving her best."

The funeral service was held at Bethlehem Lutheran Church, 777 Fourth Street in Beaumont, at 4:00 p.m. on Friday, September 28. A crowd of three hundred or so attended, but not every seat in every pew was filled. Some Beaumont residents said that they didn't attend because they assumed there wouldn't be a seat. Inside a redwood casket lined with blue silk and white crepe, Babe's body was laid out in a powder blue gown. A corsage of baby orchids was pinned on her left shoulder. George slipped a red rosebud into her hands.

Fred Corcoran, who flew in from New York, was surprised that more of Babe's fellow golfers had not come to the funeral. Patty Berg and Peggy Kirk Bell were there, and that was about it.

Babe's brothers and Lillie sat together in the front pew, with George alone at one end. Lillie couldn't stop crying. George wept throughout. Tiny Scurlock, R. L. Bowen, and Raymond Alford, Babe's high school friend, were among the pallbearers.

"She was always just Babe," the Reverend C. A. Woytek told the congregation. "She never lost the common touch." Pastor Woytek quoted from 1 Corinthians 9:24–25: "Know ye not that they which run in a race run all, but one receiveth the prize? So run, that ye may obtain. And every man that striveth for the mastery is temperate in all things. Now they do it to obtain a corruptible crown, but we are incorruptible."

The pastor also read a poem by the late Grantland Rice, that old friend of Babe's who'd been the first national sportswriter to recognize and salute her immense talent:

> *The loafer has no comeback and the quitter no reply,*
> *When the Anvil Chorus echoes, as it will, against the sky;*
> *But there's one quick answer ready that will wrap them in a hood:*
> *Make good.*

Babe's body was cremated, her ashes lowered into the ground at Forest Lawn Cemetery, just across the road from the Beaumont Country Club. A Texas Historical Commission marker was eventually erected on the site, engraved with falsehoods. For one thing, it states that Babe was born in 1914, a lie that Babe peddled successfully most of her life and that was reflected in some of her obituaries. She was actually born in 1911. The marker also says that Babe was eighteen years old when she won her Olympic medals; she was, in fact, twenty-one. And the marker incorrectly reports that Babe was named after Babe Ruth.

Marking Babe's grave is a three-foot-high marble statue, with an open book engraved with this line: "It's not whether you win or lose, but how you played the game." Beneath it is a single word: "BABE."

Yet Babe never said those words; Grantland Rice made a variation of them famous. And for most of her life, Babe would have taken issue with the declaration that will forever mark her grave. After all, she often said, "I don't see any point in playing the game if you don't win. Do you?"

One of Babe's first memories was sitting on Poppa's knee listening to his seafaring yarns. At an early age, she learned a lesson that served her well throughout her life: the taller the tale, the better. Babe knew that if you tell a story right, no matter how improbable, people will savor every word.

But sometimes, a true story is better than a fable. At Babe's burial, George talked about the need to build a "shrine" for Babe's medals, trophies, and golf clubs. George, Betty, Lillie, and Tiny left Forest Lawn Cemetery certain they had to do everything possible to keep Babe's memory alive. But a shrine wouldn't be enough. They needed to tell the true story about Babe's life, no embellishment necessary. Tell it well enough and often enough, they were sure, and no one would ever forget it.

Epilogue
Museum for One

Even when you are looking for it, driving east on Interstate 10, the tidy brick building is easy to miss, especially in the rain. Modest and oval-shaped, it has a hard time competing with the neon conveniences of the Conoco gas station on one flank and the green expanse of soccer fields on the other.

So when you walk into this little museum, maybe it's no surprise to find that admission is free. It may be only a bit more surprising to find that you are the only visitor.

This is a museum for one: Babe. And also, now, for you.

Through the smudged glass of the display cases, you can gaze at much of the treasure collected by Babe Didrikson during her sporting life — the trophies, medals, silver cups, keys to cities, and scrapbooks, as well as some of the telegrams, fan letters, and get-well cards sent by Presidents and prime ministers, housewives and schoolchildren, now tarnished, yellowed, and fading.

For a long time, these things sat way in the back of Finger's Furniture store, behind sofas and chairs and dining room sets in a showroom not far from here. "It was there for years," Helen Caspar, who works in the small museum, tells you. "That always bothered me."

Then a group of Beaumont business and civic leaders decided that Babe deserved better. So they worked for seven years to raise $100,000 (George Zaharias wrote a check for $10,000) and got it done. The museum opened on November 27, 1976, two decades and two months (to the day) after Babe's death. On that day, Babe's family, friends, and fans gathered at the museum to swap stories.

Now here you are, inside, a fingertip away from Babe's two Olympic gold medals and the silver medal, grudgingly accepted after the officials' disqualification in the high jump. Her achievements are listed over there. In the nearly eighty years since her one-woman field day at Northwestern, no athlete—male or female—has equaled Babe's performance during a single-day track-and-field meet. She also remains the only woman athlete in Olympic history to win individual medals in throwing, running, and jumping events.

The snapshots are everywhere: Babe on a green, putter raised skyward in her right hand, lifting her left foot, as if her body's tilt could coax the ball into the hole.

Babe scraping shoulders with the other Babe—Babe Ruth. They're leaning on clubs, standing on the first tee down in Sarasota, or Palm Beach, or some other Florida winter playground.

Babe wearing boxing gloves and a mock sneer.

You can't miss the sixteen-foot-high golden key to the city of Denver, presented to Babe after she returned home from Scotland, where she became the first American to win Great Britain's women's amateur golf championship.

Look closely at the phonograph record just behind the glass, and you can make out these words on the A side: "Detour"—"Harmonica Solo by Babe Zaharias." On the flip side, you see "I Felt a Little Teardrop"—"Vocals by Betty Dodd, Harmonica Solo by Babe Zaharias."

Helen Caspar points you to a TV showing a short video about Babe's life. "It leaves out some things," says Caspar, a seventy-four-year-old lifelong Beaumont resident who works at the museum four days a week. "And it gets some things wrong. The video says Babe was born in 1914, but it was 1911. It's too bad."

Like all museums, this place is meant to preserve the past. But the mementos help you connect the dots to the future. You see the path Babe forged for other barrier-breaking women athletes: tennis champion Billie Jean King, track star Jackie Joyner-Kersee, and golfers Annika Sorenstam and Michelle Wie, who cracked the PGA Tour. In 2000, *Sports Illustrated* named its 100 top athletes of the twentieth century, male and female. Babe is the only woman listed in the top 10, along with Michael Jordan, Babe Ruth, Muhammad Ali, Jim Brown, Wayne Gretzky, Jesse Owens, Jim Thorpe, Willie Mays, and Jack Nicklaus.

"We had three people yesterday," Caspar says. "Some days, zero." But that's OK, she says, because the people who do come always seem "fascinated" by everything they see. "They leave happy," she says. "Happy and amazed."

It's getting late.

You thank Helen Caspar before leaving. Outside, the sky has cleared. You go for a walk in the big park behind the museum and sit on a bench. Two teams of young girls chase a soccer ball. They can't be more than eight or nine years old, doing that thing all little-girl soccer teams do—crowd the ball in a tightly moving knot of joyous chaos.

You wonder how many of those girls know that just over there is a tribute to the greatest all-around athlete of all time: a Beaumont girl who hurdled over society's view of who she could be. It would be lovely if a few of those girls did know Babe's name or that, once upon a time, she could do everything but fly. It wasn't that long ago, really.

Acknowledgments

The eBay listing described it as "A Diamond-Faced Putter Used by Golfing Great Babe Didrikson." When I yanked it out of the Express Mail box, the club certainly looked authentic: it had a worn green handle that was chipped near the bottom, and, sure enough, inlaid in the exact center of its worn brass face was a pebble-sized diamond. But how could I be sure this club had belonged to Babe? There was no certificate of authenticity. All I had was the word of the seller, who had assured me it was the real thing.

That was enough. Already three years into the research for this book, I leaned the old putter against my home office desk and didn't think much about its provenance. While writing, I would reach for the putter to limber up my wrists or, when the words became stuck, use it to push a few carpet putts. Then, in the spring of 2009, I spoke by phone with author Rhonda Glenn, a women's golf historian at the United States Golf Association. Several decades earlier, Glenn had befriended Bertha Bowen, a high-society Fort Worth woman who had become a second mother to Babe during the last two decades of her life. Rhonda Glenn had visited Bertha Bowen at her Fort Worth home in the late 1970s and recalls seeing an old putter of Babe's propped up against a desk in the study.

By phone, Glenn told me that she remembered Babe's putter had a tiny diamond inlaid in its brass face. My jaw dropped. "I think I own that putter," I told her.

"What?"

"It's right here. I'm looking at it."

I contacted the eBay seller and, to try to find out the identity of its previous owner, persuaded him to track down the consignment shop where he had bought the putter. After some sleuthing, the seller discovered the putter had been owned by a woman from Arkansas—Bertha Bowen's niece, who had inherited it after Mrs. Bowen died. I later discovered that Babe's old diamond-studded putter—now my putter—had been a gift to Babe from Walter

Winchell to commemorate all she had done during her courageous crusade against cancer.

Luck like that can help make a book, and I had plenty of it in the writing of *Wonder Girl*. In fact, the good fortune began even before I embarked on the seven-year odyssey to get this book published.

The idea for a Babe biography was pitched by Rand Jerris, an author and historian at the United States Golf Association. In 2004, I was living in London and had just published my first book, *First Off the Tee*. I thought I'd like to write another golf book, maybe something about St. Andrews ("Been done thirty times," Rand said) or perhaps Bobby Jones ("You'd be late to that party, too," he said).

"Why don't you write about Babe Didrikson?" he asked.

I had vaguely recalled hearing about Babe from my father, who had admired her talent and guts. But I remained undecided until I spoke with W.L. Pate Jr., the president of the Babe Didrikson Zaharias Foundation in Babe's hometown of Beaumont, Texas. W.L.'s father helped Beaumont build the Babe Didrikson Zaharias Museum, and W.L. Jr.'s affection for Babe and her monumental sporting legacy are contagious. Thank you, Rand and W.L., for encouraging me to write about Babe.

My most fortunate stroke of luck was having *Wonder Girl* embraced by the remarkable people at Little, Brown and Company, who feel like members of my extended family (I have begun research on a third book to be published by them, this one about American pro football). Editor in chief Geoff Shandler not only believed in this project from the very start but had faith in me more than a decade ago. I have spent the past ten years being dazzled by Geoff's vision, smarts, fairness, integrity, and wondrous writing and editing skills. Thank you to publisher Michael Pietsch, Junie Dahn, who gave the manuscript its first careful read, and Liese Mayer, whose tireless work on the book's behalf wowed me. Karen Landry, Peggy Freudenthal, Pamela Marshall, Amanda Brown, Heather Fain, and Liz Garriga were all wonderfully supportive. I want to extend a special thanks to Barbara Jatkola, whose brilliant copyediting and fact-checking skills put a lovely polish on the manuscript.

Many others helped with research and support: at the USGA, besides Rand Jerris's invaluable assistance, Doug Starck, Nancy Stulack, Nicole Ciaramella, and Ellie Kaiser; at Lamar University in Beaumont, Texas, where many of Babe's letters, papers, and photographs are kept in its Special Collections Department, Penny Clark and Charlotte Holliman; at the Babe Didrikson Zaharias Museum in Beaumont, Helen Caspar; at the World Golf Hall of Fame, Mark Cubbedge; and at the Dwight D. Eisenhower Presidential Library and Museum in Abilene, Kansas, Kathy Struss. Thanks also to the leaders of the LPGA for their support. My sincere apologies to anyone I might have omitted.

Every biographer is indebted to the ones who blazed a path, especially when the subject is as difficult and complicated as Babe Didrikson. My sincere admiration and thanks to them all, especially Susan E. Cayleff, Thad S. Johnson, Nancy P. Williamson, William "Oscar" Johnson, Joan Flynn Dreyspool, and Bill "Tiny" Scurlock.

My friend John Files conducted several important initial interviews and helped with the first run of research. I am grateful to the gallant pioneers of the LPGA who gave John and me so much of their time, particularly Peggy Kirk Bell, Marilynn Smith, Shirley Spork, Barbara Romack, and, most of all, Betty Jameson. I regret that Ms. Jameson died in 2009, at the age of eighty-nine, before I could finish *Wonder Girl* (she greatly approved of the book's title). I hope Ms. Jameson's indomitable spirit, undiminished on a lovely Delray Beach, Florida, afternoon in November 2004 as she regaled me with dozens of stories about Babe, infuses the pages of this book. She also generously provided me with a cache of original documents—minutes of some of the first LPGA meetings, newspaper and magazine clippings, and her own handwritten notes about Babe. When I met Betty Jameson, one of the original glamour girls of golf, she was struggling. "It's made me a little humbler, but you learn through a little suffering," she told the *Palm Beach Post* in 1999. "Just like in golf, you always learn more when you lose than when you win."

Along the way, many friends and loved ones provided invaluable advice and genuine encouragement: Jeff Gerth, Frank Bruni, Fran Brennan, Kate Jaenicke, Mariana Alvarez, Pete Cross, Christine Evans, Joe Sexton, Maureen Dowd, Jo Becker, James Bennet, Matthew Purdy, Sarah Lyall, Rick Berke, Warren St. John, Lucy and Andrew Segal, Catherine Shandler, Mark Kriegel, Chad Millman, Neil Sagebiel, Mina Peck, Damien Cave, Walt Bogdanich, Chris Drew, Elaine Sciolino, Sam Walker, Jim Glanz, Bobby Ojeda, Stewart Wood, Lenore and Ernie Alexander, Andrea Simon, Bruce Schoenfeld, Richard Deitsch, Andrew Blauner, and Bill Keller.

I am grateful for the suggestions and enthusiasm of this book's first readers: Frank and Teri Alvarez, Jill Abramson, Christine Kay, Jeff Jaenicke, Dan Barry, Richard Sandomir, and especially my mother, Liette Van Natta. Mom, you are the best and I love you.

A very special thanks to Rhonda Glenn—her editing and fact-checking were first-class and generous; her love of Babe's story inspired me.

Thank you to my fantastic agent and friend, Christy Fletcher, who once again proved she is always looking out for me. My brothers, Steve and Dean Van Natta, and Dean's wife, Jenny, lavished me with love and support.

This book also benefited enormously from the sharp editing pens and smart advice of my two favorite writers: Scott Price and Lizette Alvarez. The immense talents of both of you amaze me. Lisi, I could not have done it without you; thank you for everything.

Finally, my thanks and love go to my two favorite readers: Isabel and Sofia Van Natta, whose joy of life and love of adventure fill me with wonder.

Notes

Prologue: Matinee at the Palace

3 Fifi D'Orsay: Fifi D'Orsay was chagrined to learn not only that Babe had bumped her from headliner status for their weeklong run at the Palace but also that the promoters had given Babe the plushest dressing room. "Somebody told me that Fifi D'Orsay didn't like that," Babe recalled. "I went to her and said, 'Miss D'Orsay, I'd like for you to have my dressing room.' She said, 'How sweet of you! But I wouldn't dream of it.' And she didn't change dressing rooms with me, but we became good friends after that." Didrikson Zaharias, *This Life I've Led,* 70.

3 Bob Murphy and the California Collegians: Photograph of the marquee, Babe Didrikson Zaharias Collection, Mary and John Gray Library, Lamar University, Beaumont, TX (hereafter cited as BDZ).

3 a single gigantic word — BABE: Photograph of the outside of Chicago's Palace Theater during Babe's weeklong run in late January 1933, BDZ, doc. 11.2.22.36; "Vaudeville Acts," *Chicago Daily Tribune,* January 29, 1933, WC6.

5 The owners of the Palace: "Vaudeville Acts," *Chicago Daily Tribune;* Didrikson Zaharias, *This Life I've Led,* 70; Johnson and Williamson, *Whatta-Gal,* 118–19. A short but colorful history of the Palace Theater can be found at http://www.broadwayinchicago.com/theatreinfo_tours.php.

6 "My Lord, I can't go": "Now Appearing at the Palace Theater: Babe Didrikson, Famous Olympic Champion," advertisement, *Chicago Tribune,* February 1, 1933, 23. When Babe arrived for her debut performance that morning, she was surprised and frightened to see "a crowd of people lined up down the block." Her stage fright continued backstage. Didrikson Zaharias, *This Life I've Led,* 70.

7 "Fit as a fiddle": Didrikson Zaharias, *This Life I've Led,* 70; Johnson and Williamson, *Whatta-Gal,* 118.

8 "boop-boop-a-dee-dee": Johnson and Williamson, *Whatta-Gal,* 118.

8 She peeled off: Ibid.

8 "Oh, I'm just looking": Didrikson Zaharias, *This Life I've Led,* 72.

8 "Friday afternoon": "Vaudeville Acts," *Chicago Daily Tribune.*

9 Babe was earning: Mildred (Babe) Didrikson, "The Story of My Life," *Los Angeles Times,* January 15, 1933, E3. In this article, one in a series of ten that carried Babe's byline and was published in January 1933 by the North American Newspaper Alliance, Babe claimed that her initial salary at Employers Casualty Insurance Company was $90 a month, then raised to $125 a month after the Olympics. Her letters and other evidence, however, show that her initial salary was $75 a month. Throughout her life, Babe often lied to reporters, as she did in her own autobiography. This has long been a difficult challenge to her biographers, including this one.

9 "beginning to get in my blood": Didrikson Zaharias, *This Life I've Led,* 73.

9 "that grease paint": Ibid.

Chapter 1: Poppa's Fables

14 "What a bang": Didrikson Zaharias, *This Life I've Led,* 8.

14 Most of his stories: Ibid.

14 two-story wood-and-cement-block house: Ted Deford, "Only Memory Remains of House in Which Babe Didriksen [*sic*] Was Born," *Beaumont Enterprise,* April 12, 1970, BDZ, doc. 11.1.13.24. The Port Arthur house where Babe and Bubba were born was demolished in April 1970. Tiny Scurlock, "Babe Family History," BDZ, doc. 11.1.1.3.

14 a hurricane: Ibid.

14 "We was so scared": Johnson and Williamson, *Whatta-Gal,* 39.

15 Wind gusts exceeded 120 miles per hour: Brian Pearson, "Southeast Texas Hurricane History," *Beaumont Enterprise,* http://www.texashurricanenews.com/html/history.htm.

15 "Everything was gone": Johnson and Williamson, *Whatta-Gal,* 39.

19 "I'm a Norwegian": Deford, "Only Memory Remains."

19 "My Momma": Johnson and Williamson, *Whatta-Gal,* 38.

19 "When I was grown up": Didrikson Zaharias, *This Life I've Led,* 9.

20 on June 26, 1911: Throughout her life, Babe lied about her age. At the entrance to her grave in Beaumont, the official Texas Historical Commission marker says that she was born in 1914, the same year she claims in *This Live I've Led.* But her gravestone, a few paces from the marker, reads "1911–1956." Babe's sister Lillie made sure the gravestone was accurate: "I don't know what Babe said, but I went to a lot of trouble to get it right on the gravestone. I figured that's goin' to be there till the hereafter and I wasn't goin' to have it wrong." Johnson and Williamson, *Whatta-Gal,* 35. On Babe's 1932 application for the Olympics, she claimed that she was born in 1913, the year she used most often during her twenties and thirties. After she reached the age of forty, she began saying, at times, that she was born in 1914. On a visa application late in her life, she used the year 1919. There is no birth certificate for Babe listed at the Jefferson County Courthouse in Beaumont. But in Babe's own scrapbooks, kept by the Babe Didrikson Zaharias Foundation in Beaumont, I found the best evidence of her birth, a certificate of baptism

that lists her birthday as June 26, 1911, and her date of baptism as March 24, 1912, at Trinity Lutheran Church in Port Arthur. Also in Babe's scrapbooks is a copy of what I believe was her Jefferson County birth register, listing Babe's birthday as June 26, 1911. See also Cayleff, *Babe,* 27.

Despite fooling everyone about her age, Babe inadvertently dropped a clue in *This Life I've Led.* She wrote, "We picked up and moved seventeen miles from Port Arthur to Beaumont when I was about three and a half." According to several family members, the Didriksens moved within several weeks of the hurricane in August 1915. If Babe had been born in 1914, as she claimed, she would have been fourteen months old when her family moved to Beaumont. According to family members and friends quoted in various contemporaneous accounts, she was four years old at the time of the move.

Confusion about Babe's birth year has continued in recent years. In a widely read article published in 1996, Charles McGrath, then the book review editor of the *New York Times* and a colleague of mine, reported that Babe was born in 1912, an error that has been frequently repeated. "Most Valuable Player," *New York Times Magazine,* http://www.nytimes.com/specials/magazine4/articles/zaharias .html. Babe's birthday is listed as June 26, 1914, on the website of the Babe Didrikson Zaharias Collection at the Mary and John Gray Library, Lamar University, in Beaumont, Texas. The BDZ Collection, which includes letters, interviews, photos, and hundreds of newspaper and magazine clippings, was another invaluable resource in my research for this book. See http://biblos.lamar.edu/archive/ BabeDidriksonZaharias.html.

20 "How is it with this girl": Johnson, *The Incredible Babe,* 81. This privately published book by award-winning Texas sportswriter and editor Thad S. Johnson, a true labor of love, proved to be an amazingly useful resource. It includes detailed interviews with George Zaharias and Babe's immediate family and friends, as well as scores of details about Babe's life and times. I salute Johnson for his formidable feat of research.

20 "When Babe was born": Letter from Bill "Tiny" Scurlock to Harris Shevelson, editor of *Coronet* magazine, August 18, 1947, BDZ, doc. 11.1.1.22; Scurlock, "Babe Family History." Scurlock was an invaluable resource for me, having meticulously conducted dozens of interviews with Babe's neighbors, friends, and acquaintances, undoubtedly for his own biography of Babe or even a screenplay (there are outlines for both in his typewritten notes). But Scurlock was also Babe's biggest booster, sometimes succumbing to her habit of shading the truth about her background and accomplishments. Scurlock, for instance, loved saying that Babe was named after Babe Ruth, a "fact" that was repeated by several early biographers and dozens of newspaper accounts—including several at the time of her death—but one that was denied by several of Didrikson's siblings and closest friends. For that reason, I tried, when possible, to rely on Scurlock's observations and assertions only when I could confirm them with other reliable sources.

Chapter 2: The Only Girl

21 When she was no more than ten: Didrikson Zaharias, *This Life I've Led,* 14.

22 "One day I heard": Carol Schleuter, "Her Friends Remember Babe Was Always Athlete," *Beaumont Journal,* October 10, 1975, BDZ, doc. 11.1.12.13.

22 "Sometimes we got skinned up": Johnson and Williamson, *Whatta-Gal,* 45.

22 A ride cost 6 cents: Johnson, *The Incredible Babe,* 121.

23 One Halloween evening: Didrikson Zaharias, *This Life I've Led,* 23–24.

23 "Babe was known": Ibid., 14.

24 "If we got into trouble": Schleuter, "Her Friends Remember Babe."

24 Doucette was a straight ribbon: Cayleff, *Babe,* 31.

25 In the Didriksens' house: Ibid.; Tiny Scurlock, "Babe Family History," BDZ, doc. 11.1.1.3.

25 "real fresh-air sleeping": Didrikson Zaharias, *This Life I've Led,* 14.

25 "Don't let that dirt": Ibid., 21.

26 She wanted to *be* a boy: Ibid., 25–26.

26 "Don't tackle the girls": Ibid., 8.

27 "We never heard": Ibid.

27 "She could out-do": "Her Friends Remember Babe."

27 "He put it there for the boys": Didrikson Zaharias, *This Life I've Led,* 7. See also Scurlock, "Babe Family History."

27 "I'll build good bodies": Didrikson Zaharias, *This Life I've Led,* 7.

27 "All the boys": Johnson and Williamson, *Whatta-Gal,* 53.

28 "Poor Momma": Didrikson Zaharias, *This Life I've Led,* 20–21.

Chapter 3: The Big Blue Sugar Bowl

30 "My Gosh": Didrikson Zaharias, *This Life I've Led,* 21.

31 "I guess they didn't": Ibid., 26.

32 "Momma...I don't want": Ibid., 27.

32 "You go buy": Ibid.

33 "I wore mine": Ibid., 20. See also interview with Raymond Alford in Johnson, *The Incredible Babe,* 158. Alford recalled that Babe often practiced baseball and basketball in her bare feet.

33 "We went barefoot": Cayleff, *Babe,* 48.

33 She brought a big roast: Didrikson Zaharias, *This Life I've Led,* 18.

33 "It was a sociable": Ibid., 24.

33 "Don't you ever dare": Ibid.

34 "I can remember": Author interview with Betty Jameson. See also Cayleff, *Babe,* 47.

34 "As far back as I can remember": Mildred Babe Didrikson, no title, North American Newspaper Alliance, January 11, 1933, BDZ. See also Cayleff, *Babe,* 39–40.

34 "She was too good": Theresa M. Wells, "Greatness for Mildred Didriksen [*sic*] Indicated in 1923 Clippings Kept by Theresa Wells," *Beaumont Sunday Enterprise,* April 27, 1969, 18, BDZ, doc. 11.1.12.2.

35 "I didn't want people": Tiny Scurlock, "Babe Family History," BDZ, doc. 11.1.1.13.

35 "If we didn't do as she wanted": John Lockhart interview by Tiny Scurlock, 1511 Avenue A, Beaumont, August 18, 1947, BDZ, doc. 11.1.1.22.

35 "Oh, some niggers": Johnson and Williamson, *Whatta-Gal,* 52.

35 "She really did hate": Ibid., 53.

36 "I knew that winning": Ibid., 54–55.

Chapter 4: The Highest Hedge

37 "Before I was even into my teens": Didrikson Zaharias, *This Life I've Led,* 27.

38 a national flagpole-sitting craze: "1930s & Earlier, Shipwreck Kelly Flagpole Sitter," YouRememberThat.com, posted by Lava1964, http://www.yourememberthat.com/media/2286/Shipwreck_Kelly_Flagpole_Sitter/.

38 "Outlined against a blue-gray": Fountain, *Sportswriter,* 25–28.

39 "For when the great": Eventually, Rice would become one of the first scribes to chronicle the corrosive power of money in sports:

> *Money to the left of them and money to the right,*
> *Money everywhere they turn from morning through the night;*
> *Only two things count at all from mountain to the sea,*
> *Part of it's percentage, and the rest is guarantee.*

Inabinett, *Grantland Rice and His Heroes,* 4. See also Harper, *How You Played the Game,* 426.

39 "We are here to represent": "1928 Olympics Amsterdam," Infoplease, http://www.infoplease.com/ipsa/A0114477.html.

40 Amid the hubbub: "Sports: Track & Field — The 1928 Olympics," Herstory: An Exhibition, http://library2.usask.ca/herstory/field.html.

40 "Next year": Didrikson Zaharias, *This Life I've Led,* 28.

40 "I never was too good": Ibid.

41 "I'd go flying": Ibid.

41 "I worked and worked": Ibid., 29.

42 Aunt Minnie regaled: Johnson, *The Incredible Babe,* 123.

42 "She really did hang": Johnson and Williamson, *Whatta-Gal,* 44.

42 "Naturally, the girls": Johnson, *The Incredible Babe,* 124.

42 "an awfully hard child": Ibid.

42 "talked my Momma": Johnson and Williamson, *Whatta-Gal,* 44–45.

43 "I loved being": Ibid., 45. See also "Interview with Babe's Sister, Lillie (Mrs. O. B. Grimes)," BDZ, doc. 11.1.16.8.

43 She even stood on her head: Johnson, *The Incredible Babe,* 124.

43 "It sounded to me": Ibid.

43 They held her back: Ibid.

44 "She had great confidence": Mrs. Clyde D. Jones interview by Tiny Scurlock, BDZ, doc. 11.1.1.18.

44 All she wanted to do: "Babe Zaharias: Great Athlete and a Beautiful Lady," *Beaumont Sunday Enterprise and Journal,* November 9, 1980, BDZ, doc. 11.1.13.34.

44 "sissy-girls": Johnson and Williamson, *Whatta-Gal,* 55.

44 "She should have been a boy": Cayleff, *Babe,* 43.

44 "I can beat": Johnson and Williamson, *Whatta-Gal,* 54.

45 "Babe is her nickname": Johnson, *The Incredible Babe,* 170.

45 "She was sports": Johnson and Williamson, *Whatta-Gal,* 60. For copies of several of Babe's high school transcripts, see Johnson, *The Incredible Babe,* 163–64.

46 "Babe *had* to succeed": Johnson and Williamson, *Whatta-Gal,* 60.

Chapter 5: Letters to Tiny

47 "the Colonel": Johnson, *The Incredible Babe,* 183.

47 A 1904 graduate of Texas A&M: M. J. McCombs interview by Tiny Scurlock, BDZ, doc. 11.1.13.12. No date is given, but I believe the interview was conducted after the Olympics, most likely in late 1932 or possibly early 1933. Several other sources describe the Colonel as a graduate of the University of Missouri, but I believe Scurlock got it right.

48 Teams such as the Cyclones: Ibid.

48 McCombs had coached: Pieroth, *Their Day in the Sun,* 27; George White, "The Sport Broadcast," *Dallas Morning News,* July 8, 1932.

48 This designation was a technicality: Ikard, *Just for Fun,* 16–19. Hazel Walker, a star player of the era, described it this way: "There is a fine line in amateur ranks and being a professional. You would draw a salary for working on a real job with the company, but you might be out of the office playing basketball on the road three weeks out of a month. It was all advertising for the companies, and you might be handed money under the table." Ibid., 18.

49 a player's willingness: Johnson, *The Incredible Babe,* 178–80. See also Costa and Guthrie, *Women in Sport,* 114.

50 The publicity bonanza: Costa and Guthrie, *Women in Sport,* 114–21; Bill Cunningham, "The Colonel's Ladies," *Collier's,* May 23, 1936, 60–62. See also Johnson, *The Incredible Babe,* 183–84.

50 "How'd you like to play": Didrikson Zaharias, *This Life I've Led,* 35.

50 "She was too busy": Johnson and Williamson, *Whatta-Gal,* 63.

51 losing by one point: Johnson, *The Incredible Babe,* 194.

51 four Cyclones: Ibid., 186–87; Johnson and Williamson, *Whatta-Gal,* 66.

51 "Min Babe": Didrikson Zaharias, *This Life I've Led,* 35.

52 "Here I was": Ibid., 3.

52 "an entire fortune": Ibid., 3–4.

52 "Look at that": Ibid.

52 "Practically all the basketball players": Ibid., 36.

53 "They started hitting me": Ibid., 37. Babe claimed that she "got four or five points more than the whole Sun Oilers team did," but this is one of many boastful, untruthful claims she made in her autobiography.

53 The Colonel pushed the girls: Johnson, *The Incredible Babe,* 186.

54 "in the center": Didrikson Zaharias, *This Life I've Led,* 39.

54 Hannah carefully pasted: Babe's scrapbooks are in the possession of the Babe Didrikson Zaharias Foundation in Beaumont. I made copies of every page of the scrapbooks and relied on many of the clippings as research tools. In many cases, the publication and date of a clipping are impossible to determine. Equally frustrating was the fact that the origin of the scrapbooks is difficult to determine. Babe said— and several family members agreed—that her mother painstakingly put together her early scrapbooks, and I believe that is true. However, Babe also routinely sent many of her early clippings from the Dallas newspapers to Tiny Scurlock, either to pass on to her mother or for Scurlock to piece together his own record of Babe's athletic feats. In an interview published in *Whatta-Gal,* a good friend of George Zaharias, Sid Marks, claimed that he cobbled together Babe's scrapbooks from her time living in the Los Angeles area during the 1940s. I have no way to verify that claim, except to observe that the handwriting on the clips in her scrapbooks from the 1940s differs from the handwriting in her scrapbooks from the 1930s.

54 *Dear Tiny: Played my first game:* Letter from Babe Didrikson to Tiny Scurlock, February 19, 1930, BDZ, doc. 11.1.14.1.

55 *Dear "Tiny" — The games are coming:* Letter from Babe Didrikson to Tiny Scurlock, February 21, 1930, BDZ, doc. 11.1.14.2.

55 *Dear "Tiny" — Boy I am still:* Letter from Babe Didrikson to Tiny Scurlock, March 6, 1930, doc. 11.1.14.3. The letter has two newspaper box scores attached. Babe scored a team-leading 36 points in one game and a team-leading 18 points in the other.

56 "they are all going": Ibid. See also Johnson and Williamson, *Whatta-Gal,* 66.

56 "We had some pretty good": Albertson and Pekara, "Golden Cyclones, 1931 National Basketball Champions."

56 Agnes Iori-Robertson: Johnson, *The Incredible Babe,* 186.

56 "She was out for Babe": Ware, *Letter to the World,* 174.

57 Babe was joined by her sister: Johnson and Williamson, *Whatta-Gal,* 67.

57 "It turned out": Didrikson Zaharias, *This Life I've Led,* 38.

58 "If you have had no experience": Letter from R. C. Martin to Babe Didrikson, November 9, 1930, BDZ. See also Johnson and Williamson, *Whatta-Gal,* 68.

58 "Withdrew, Feb. 14, 1930": Johnson, *The Incredible Babe,* 162–63. See also Johnson and Williamson, *Whatta-Gal,* 110.

58 Hannah saw the broken promise: Johnson, *The Incredible Babe,* 180.

58 Babe also bought: Betsy Rawls interview, 76.

59 "What's that?": Didrikson Zaharias, *This Life I've Led,* 40.

59 She poked herself: Ibid.

59 "Colonel, how many": Ibid., 41.

60 *What gall:* Interviews with several of Babe's teammates, available at the Amateur Athletic Foundation Library, Los Angeles, http://www.aafla.org/6oic/OralHistory/. I relied on interviews conducted in 1984, timed to the return of the Olympics to Los Angeles that year, for contemporaneous recollections of Babe and the 1932 Olympic team. This book benefited enormously from these outstanding and perceptive interviews. In particular, I'm grateful to George A. Hodak, who conducted most of the interviews with an insatiable inquisitiveness.

60 The Colonel pushed the girls: Cayleff, *Babe,* 56.

60 "Practice makes perfect": Johnson and Williamson, *Whatta-Gal,* 70.

60 Babe stepped on a large piece: Letter from Babe Didrikson to Tiny Scurlock, June 23, 1930, BDZ, doc. 11.1.14.8. See also Johnson and Williamson, *Whatta-Gal,* 70.

61 Babe ran all-out: Didrickson [*sic*] High Point Scorer When Cyclones Capture A.A.U. Crown," BDZ, doc. 11.1.13.4. See also Johnson, *The Incredible Babe,* 216.

61 "Her only fault": M. J. McCombs interview by Tiny Scurlock, BDZ, doc. 11.1.13.12.

61 She set a U.S. record: "Babe Dedrickson [*sic*] Breaks Four Records; Betts Is Also Star of A.A.U.," BDZ, doc. 11.1.13.7.

61 "Babe Didrikson and Her": Johnson, *The Incredible Babe,* 216.

62 *Dear Tiny. Had the Texas A.A.U.:* Letter from Babe Didrikson to Tiny Scurlock, June 8, 1930, BDZ, doc. 11.1.14.7.

62 On the Fourth of July: Tricard, *American Women's Track and Field,* 161–62.

62 Babe broke three world records: Ibid.; Johnson, *The Incredible Babe,* 219.

62 "I have broken 6 American records": Letter from Babe Didrikson to Tiny Scurlock, July 7, 1930, BDZ, doc. 11.1.14.9.

Chapter 6: Where She Did Not Belong

64 The founding father: Findling and Pelle, *Encyclopedia of the Modern Olympics,* 453–61; Smith, *Nike Is a Goddess,* 6.

64 "The Olympic Games": Simri, *Women at the Olympic Games,* 14–16.

64 "violated the laws": Ibid., 12. See also Hargreaves, *Sporting Females,* 209.

65 "A thirty-year-old Greek named Stamata Revithi": Athanasios Tarasouleas, "Stamata Revithi, 'Alias Melpomeni,'" *Olympic Review* 26, no. 17 (October–November 1997): 53–55, available at http://www.la84foundation.org/OlympicInformationCenter/OlympicReview/1997/oreXXVI17/oreXXVI17zg.pdf; Simri, *Women at the Olympic Games,* 14–15. See also Sean Rooney, "Stamata Revithi: The First Woman to Run the Olympic Marathon," http://www.associatedcontent.com/article/479745/stamata_revithi_the_first_woman_to.html?cat=37; http://maillists.uci.edu/mailman/public/mgsa-l/2004-February/002963.html; Karl Lennartz, "Two Women Ran the Marathon in 1896," http://www.la84foundation.org/Sports

Library/JOH/JOHv2n1/JOHv2n1h.pdf. Some historical accounts say that Revithi was named Melpomeni or that a second woman named Melpomeni ran the marathon in four and a half hours, though other historical accounts say that Melpomeni ran the marathon three weeks earlier as a trial run. More likely than not, the name Melpomeni, the Greek god of tragedy, was given to Revithi by athletes who could not remember her name. Several Greek newspapers at the time confirmed that Revithi ran the marathon course the day after the official event. According to the newspaper *Acropolis,* "The Olympic Committee deserves to be reprimanded because it was discourteous in refusing a lady's nomination. We can assure those concerned that none of the participants would have had any objections." Foldes, *Women at the Olympics,* 112–14, and Lucas, "A History of the Marathon Race," 120–38.

65 "Women have probably proved": Coubertin, "L'éducation des jeunes enfants et des jeunes filles," 61.

66 "ladylike activities": Ibid.

66 We feel that the Olympic Games: Leigh, "The Evolution of Women's Participation in the Summer Olympic Games," 75–76, translated from Pierre de Coubertin, "Les femmes aux Jeux Olympiques," *Revue Olympique,* July 1912, 109–11. Leigh's work is a remarkable piece of scholarship that helped me understand women's struggle to compete in the early years of the Olympic Games.

68 "As to the admission of women": Pierre de Coubertin, "To the Athletes and All Taking Part at Amsterdam in the IXth Olympiad Games," Official Bulletin of the International Olympic Committee, 14. See http://www.aafla.org/OlympicInforma tionCenter/OlympicReview/1928/BODE11/BODE11d.pdf.

68 women were allowed only five: Pieroth, *Their Day in the Sun,* 5.

68 On a humid early August day: Leigh, "The Evolution of Women's Participation in the Summer Olympic Games," 332.

68 The world press: "The Olympic Games," *Times* (London), August 3, 1928, 6; "Americans Beaten in Four Olympic Tests," *New York Times,* August 3, 1928. See also Leigh, "The Evolution of Women's Participation in the Summer Olympic Games," 332–33, and Paula D. Welch, "The Emergence of American Women at the Summer Olympic Games, 1900–1972" (Ann Arbor, MI: Xerox University Microfilms, 1975), 57–58.

68 "There was nothing wrong": Messerli, "Women's Participation in the Modern Olympic Games," 10–11.

68–69 Many sportswriters demanded: Leigh, "The Evolution of Women's Participation in the Summer Olympic Games," 184–85.

69 "the Olympic Games except": *Bulletin du C.I.O.,* September 1929, 17; Leigh, "The Evolution of Women's Participation in the Summer Olympic Games," 185.

70 *Dearest "Tiny" Why hello old top:* Letter from Babe Didrikson to Tiny Scurlock, December 28, 1931, BDZ, doc. 11.1.14.14. See also Johnson and Williamson, *Whatta-Gal,* 72–73.

72 Jersey City, New Jersey: Didrikson Zaharias, *This Life I've Led,* 44.

72 Of the 235 women: Arthur Daley, "World's Mark Set by Miss Didrikson," *New York Times,* July 26, 1931, S1. See also Johnson, *The Incredible Babe,* 220.

73 "Bedlam": Johnson and Williamson, *Whatta-Gal,* 80.

73 First up was the 80-meter: Tricard, *American Women's Track and Field,* 171.

73 two feet four inches: Ibid.

73 Next was the broad jump: Johnson, *The Incredible Babe,* 221.

73 Babe hurled the baseball: Ibid., 220–21.

74 Babe's three wins: Tricard, *American Women's Track and Field,* 173.

74 "a modest, likeable girl": Johnson and Williamson, *Whatta-Gal,* 80.

74 "We didn't have any money": Ibid.

75 "It was my medal hunting": Didrikson Zaharias, *This Life I've Led,* photo section.

75 "this remarkably versatile girl": Daley, "World's Mark Set by Miss Didrikson," S1. See also Pieroth, *Their Day in the Sun,* 28.

75 "She has been hailed": "Name Your Weapon! Dallas Girl, Noted All-Round Athlete, Is Proficient in All Sports," *Dallas Morning News,* August 2, 1931, BDZ, doc. 11.1.13.2. Notably, this clip was also prominently displayed in Babe's scrapbook.

75 Babe wanted at least $50 more: Didrikson Zaharias, *This Life I've Led,* 44.

76 "unless it was a team manager": Letter from Babe Didrikson to Tiny Scurlock, November 6, 1931, BDZ, doc. 11.1.14.13.

76 "I got to make something": Letter from Babe Didrikson to Tiny Scurlock, December 28, 1931, BDZ, doc. 11.1.14.14.

76 "I don't care": Ibid.

77 "go to school and be a gym teacher": Ibid.

77 *Dearest Tiny, Heck I'm tired:* Letter from Babe Didrikson to Tiny Scurlock, October 5, 1931, BDZ, doc. 11.1.14.12.

78 Babe asked the Colonel: Johnson, *The Incredible Babe,* 200, 201.

79 "Is it necessary to say": Tricard, *American Women's Track and Field,* 174.

79 "No woman shall be allowed": Official Athletic Rules of the Amateur Athletic Union of the United States, 1930. See image.aausports.org/codebook/bylaws.pdf.

80 As the chief of one of the South's: Pieroth, *Their Day in the Sun,* 45. See also George White, "Sport Broadcast," *Dallas Morning News,* July 31, 1932. Pieroth first advanced this idea of Colonel McCombs winning Babe a reprieve from the AAU rule as the most likely reason she was able to compete in eight events. Based on my own careful reading of the Texas press in June and July 1932, I feel certain the rule was suspended. In advance of the AAU championship in Evanston, the Dallas newspapers reported that Babe was going to enter multiple events, attributing her plans to McCombs and other unnamed AAU officials. After the meet, when questions were raised about why Babe — and no one else — had not been held to the three-event rule, *Dallas Morning News* columnist George White reported

that McCombs had played hardball with AAU officials for a waiver. White also reported that senior AAU officials had to be dispatched to Dallas "to pacify the rebellious local leaders." A number of other articles had reported flatly that "competition will be thrown wide open, contestants being allowed to enter as many events as they desire." McCombs was often named as the source of this information, but it was also attributed to unnamed local AAU officials. The clear implication was that the AAU had, at the very least, given tacit approval for Babe to participate in more than three events. See also *Dallas Morning News,* July 3, 1932.

81 "Colonel, will I get to go up": Didrikson Zaharias, *This Life I've Led,* 44, 45.

Chapter 7: The Cyclone

82 "Anybody traveling to Chicago": United Press, "Mildred to CHI," July 8, 1932, BDZ, doc. 11.1.4.3.

83 "I have been coaching": M. J. McCombs interview by Tiny Scurlock, BDZ, doc. 11.1.13.12.

84 At the Southern Methodist stadium: Johnson, *The Incredible Babe,* 223.

84 The Dallas newspapers: United Press, "Mildred to CHI." See also "Olympics Bound!" *Dallas Morning News,* July 9, 1932, BDZ, doc. 11.1.4.5.

84 "one-girl track team": This phrase crops up in numerous letters that Babe sent to Scurlock, as well as in her autobiography (Didrikson Zaharias, *This Life I've Led,* 47).

84 On the platform: Letter from Babe Didrikson to Tiny Scurlock, BDZ, doc. 11.1.14.15. The letter indicates that Babe was scheduled to leave for Chicago on the 5:40 p.m. train departing from Dallas on Monday, July 10, 1932.

84 "radiated confidence": Pieroth, *Their Day in the Sun,* 29; *Dallas Morning News,* July 12, 1932.

84 As she settled into her seat: Author interview with Betty Jameson, who said that Babe told her that she had never been so nervous as when she was leaving Dallas for Chicago.

86 "Miss Mildred Didrikson": "Miss Didrikson Heads Field in Olympic Track Tests Today," *New York Times,* July 16, 1932.

86 "Ah'm gonna lick you": Lawrence Lader, "The Unbeatable Babe," *Coronet,* January 1948, 156, BDZ, doc. 11.1.17.1.

87 "just bounce up and down": Didrikson Zaharias, *This Life I've Led,* 47.

87 "When we woke up": Ibid.

87 "There was only one way": Ibid., 48.

88 "Representing the Employers Casualty": Ibid., 48–49. See also Red Gibson, "Babe Didrikson—Now THERE Was an Olympic Champion," August 27, 1972, BDZ, doc. 11.1.13.32. In an interview near the end of her life, Babe said that just thinking about the moment she ran onto the Dyche Stadium field gave her "goose bumps."

88 "Some of the events": Didrikson Zaharias, *This Life I've Led,* 49.

88 "For two and a half hours": Letter from Babe Didrikson to Col. McCombs, BDZ. See also Pieroth, *Their Day in the Sun,* 91.

88 "I'm going to win everything": Kim Q. Berkshire, "A Look Back: Evelyn Hall Adams, Now Seventy-eight, Remembers Controversial Loss to Didriksen [*sic*] in '32 Olympics," *Los Angeles Times,* 1988, 1–2. See also Cayleff, *Babe,* 65.

89 The first event: Tricard, *American Women's Track and Field,* 203; Evelyne Hall Adams interview, 12.

89 "They took first place away": Johnson and Williamson, *Whatta-Gal,* 82; Adams interview, 12–13.

89 "but my time": Didrikson Zaharias, *This Life I've Led,* 50.

89–90 Babe, Hall, and the third-place: Pieroth, *Their Day in the Sun,* 40; Associated Press, "Five First Places to Miss Didrikson," *New York Times,* July 17, 1932.

90 "But that was the only thing": Didrikson Zaharias, *This Life I've Led,* 49.

90 she stunned everyone: Ibid.

90 "It was one of those days": Ibid., 48.

91 "I really never went out": Jean Shiley Newhouse interview, 21.

91 In the final of the event: Associated Press, "Five First Places to Miss Didrikson." See also Johnson, *The Incredible Babe,* 188.

91 "You did it!": Didrikson Zaharias, *This Life I've Led,* 50.

92 With the crowd standing: Associated Press, "First Five Places to Miss Didrikson"; Didrikson Zaharias, *This Life I've Led,* 50–51.

92 "The most amazing series": George Kirksey, "Didrikson, Unaided, Wins National Track Championship," *Dallas Morning News,* July 17, 1932. See also Didrikson Zaharias, *This Life I've Led,* 50.

92 "Didrikson, Unaided": Kirksey, "Didrikson, Unaided."

92 "Implausible is the adjective": Arthur Daley, "Sports of the Times: A Remarkable Woman," *New York Times,* September 30, 1956, BDZ, doc. 11.1.10.4.

92 "Gangway!": "What a Girl!" *Chicago Tribune,* 1932, BDZ, doc. 11.1.1.21.

92 "I cannot think of any male athlete": Paul Gallico, "Farewell to the Babe," *Sports Illustrated,* October 8, 1956, available at http://vault.sportsillustrated.cnn .com/vault/article/magazine/MAG1131617/index.htm.

93 "Miss Mildred Didrikson": Associated Press, "Didrikson Wins National Track Championship," July 17, 1932. This report mistakenly said that Babe would be joined by fifteen young ladies. In fact, there were seventeen members of the 1932 U.S. women's Olympic track-and-field team. I have corrected the AP mistake here to make it consistent with the rest of the book.

Chapter 8: "Iron-Woman"

94 Sixteen of the American team's: One U.S. Olympic team member, Simone Schaller, was driven by car from Chicago to Los Angeles.

94 "But a trip to Chicago": Didrikson Zaharias, *This Life I've Led,* 52.

95   "She constantly wanted": Johnson and Williamson, *Whatta-Gal,* 84.

96   "if she didn't, Babe might win": Ibid., 85.

96   "Such a braggart": Ibid.

96   "expected to see a city": Didrikson Zaharias, *This Life I've Led,* 52.

97   "Did you ever hear": Johnson and Williamson, *Whatta-Gal,* 84.

97   At the station: Johnson, *The Incredible Babe,* 245.

97   "Hail, hail, the gang's all here": Pieroth, *Their Day in the Sun,* 47.

97   "I came out here to beat": Johnson and Williamson, *Whatta-Gal,* 99.

97   "How about four, coach?": Pieroth, *Their Day in the Sun,* 48.

98   "Naked young men": Johnson and Williamson, *Whatta-Gal,* 98.

98   "I was just glad": Pieroth, *Their Day in the Sun,* 86.

98   The Americans socialized: Jean Shiley Newhouse interview, 18.

99   "It seems to be youth": Pieroth, *Their Day in the Sun,* 89–90.

99   "I eat anything I want": Wakeman, *Babe Didrikson Zaharias,* 42.

99   "It seemed to me": Pieroth, *Their Day in the Sun,* 90.

99   "Everything she bragged about": Tricard, *American Women's Track and Field,* 189.

100   "There was something there": Pieroth, *Their Day in the Sun,* 91.

100   "My own coach": Didrikson Zaharias, *This Life I've Led,* 53.

100   "You know . . . I can beat": Pieroth, *Their Day in the Sun,* 92.

100   "she knew she was going": Ibid.

101   "Women stand no more chance": Ibid., 96–97.

101   "To set it aside": Ibid., 97.

101   "any kind of sport": Didrikson Zaharias, *This Life I've Led,* 53; Pieroth, *Their Day in the Sun,* 95.

102   "It was just a simple declarative sentence": Paul Gallico, "Farewell to the Babe," *Sports Illustrated,* October 8, 1956, available at http://vault.sportsillus trated.cnn.com/vault/article/magazine/MAG1131617/index.htm.

102   "What's your time": Johnson and Williamson, *Whatta-Gal,* 100; Pieroth, *Their Day in the Sun,* 90.

102   "Say, you're a pretty good": Pieroth, *Their Day in the Sun,* 90–91.

102   Babe's barbs: Ibid., 94.

102   "What I want to do most of all": Johnson and Williamson, *Whatta-Gal,* 99–100.

103   "The Babe is no boaster": Ibid.

103–104   "The most important thing": Photos of the 1932 Olympic Games in Los Angeles, Southern California Committee for the Olympic Games, http://www.sccog.org/webapp/1932-olympic-games?start=1.

104   "In the name of the President": Video of IOC film of the opening ceremonies, http://www.olympic.org/MultimediaGallery/Default.aspx?Language=uk& itemID=A3BE0902-D11A-4B73-8116-0C418869FDF5.

104   "To some of us": Johnson and Williamson, *Whatta-Gal,* 103.

104   "absolutely awed": Pieroth, *Their Day in the Sun,* 100.

105 "We had to stand": Didrikson Zaharias, *This Life I've Led,* 54.

105 "prevented from cluttering": Pieroth, *Their Day in the Sun,* 101.

106 She paused a moment: Video of IOC film of Babe's initial throw, http://www.olympic.org/MultimediaGallery/Default.aspx?Language=uk&itemID=A3BE0902-D11A-4B73-8116-0C418869FDF5.

106 "like a catcher's peg": Didrikson Zaharias, *This Life I've Led,* 55.

106 "stuck in the grass": Pieroth, *Their Day in the Sun,* 101.

106 "Nobody knew it": Jack Blythe, " 'Could Have Thrown It Farther if My Hand Hadn't Slipped,' Says Babe after Breaking the World's Javelin Record," *Dallas Journal,* August 1, 1932. See also Didrikson Zaharias, *This Life I've Led,* 56.

107 She then gave a radio interview: Pieroth, *Their Day in the Sun,* 102.

107 "My hand slipped": "Didrikson Breaks Record," International News Service, August 1, 1932. See also Pieroth, *Their Day in the Sun,* 101.

107 Fred Steers said: Pieroth, *Their Day in the Sun,* 101.

108 "Auf du Platze": Evelyne Hall Adams interview, 16–18; video of IOC film of the race, http://www.olympic.org/MultimediaGallery/Default.aspx?Language=uk&itemID=A3BE0902-D11A-4B73-8116-0C418869FDF5.

108 "Well, I won again": Cayleff, *Babe,* 69.

108 "Later…I learned": Johnson and Williamson, *Whatta-Gal,* 105.

108 "eye-lash" and "they hit": Pieroth, *Their Day in the Sun,* 108.

108 It is impossible to pick: I carefully watched the video of the IOC film of the race dozens of times, stopping it at the precise moment of victory. At every viewing, it appeared to me to be a dead heat. The same is true in every photograph.

108 One photo: The iconic photo is available at the IOC website, http://www.olympic.org/MultimediaGallery/Default.aspx?Language=uk&itemID=A3BE0902-D11A-4B73-8116-0C418869FDF5.

109 "I thought for sure": Adams interview, 18. Hall claimed that Babe had purposely impeded her by hitting her as they cleared several hurdles. Watching several films of the race, I could not see a single instance where Babe struck Hall.

109 "All Olympians will tell you": Ibid., 18–19.

110 "If it was horse racing": Didrikson Zaharias, *This Life I've Led,* 54.

110 "All you have to do": Cayleff, *Babe,* 70.

110 "We couldn't beat her": Johnson and Williamson, *Whatta-Gal,* 106.

110 "We were all actually praying": Ibid.

110 "was the only girl": Pieroth, *Their Day in the Sun,* 108.

111 "There is too much danger": Newhouse interview, 20.

111 "I felt like a bird": Didrikson Zaharias, *This Life I've Led,* 56.

111 "It was the most astonishing jump": Ibid.

111 The bar was lowered: Film of event; Pieroth, *Their Day in the Sun,* 112–13; Johnson and Williamson, *Whatta-Gal,* 106.

112 "I felt that": Newhouse interview, 22.

112 "I think they should have": Shav Glick, "Babe in the Woods," *Los Angeles Times,* December 29, 1999, available at http://articles.latimes.com/1999/dec/29/news/ss-48654.

112 "Today it wouldn't matter": Didrikson Zaharias, *This Life I've Led,* 57.

112 "as another of those queer rulings": Hudson, *Women in Golf,* 32.

112 "Mildred (Babe) Didrikson": Ibid.

112 On the podium: Newhouse interview, 25.

113 "Iron-Woman": Woolum, *Outstanding Women Athletes,* 44.

113 "She is an incredible": Abernathy, *Legendary Ladies of Texas,* 179.

113 "OK, what about golf?": William Oscar Johnson and Nancy Williamson, "Babe: Part 2," *Sports Illustrated,* October 13, 1975, available at http://vault.sports illustrated.cnn.com/vault/article/magazine/MAG1090345/index.htm. See also Johnson, *The Incredible Babe,* 284.

Chapter 9: All Them Roses

117 You are attacking an inert ball: Rice, *The Tumult and the Shouting,* 53. A "Nassau" is the most popular wager on a golf course, probably because it's not just one bet but three bets in one. The front nine holes are the first wager, the back nine the second, and the eighteen-hole total is the third. The dollar amount for each bet is generally equal for all three wagers and is set on the first tee. For example, a $10 Nassau is $10 to the winner of the front nine, $10 to the winner of the back nine, and $10 to the winner of the overall match.

118 On the morning of August 8, 1932: Harper, *How You Played the Game,* 462.

118 Babe had claimed: Ibid.

119 "Look at the ball": Didrikson Zaharias, *This Life I've Led,* 60.

119 "I could tell she was a natural": Shav Glick, "1932 Belonged to Babe," *Dallas Times Herald,* July 29, 1984, 20C.

119 "Boys, look at that": Harper, *How You Played the Game,* 463.

119 "one of the best drives": Tiny Scurlock, "Babe: Golf at Brentwood," BDZ, doc. 11.1.1.8.

120 "Babe...we have to do something": Didrikson Zaharias, *This Life I've Led,* 60–61. Most of this account is based on Babe's own recollections, which were confirmed by accounts written by Paul Gallico and Grantland Rice.

120 "like Rusty the electric rabbit": Ibid.

120 "We won the hole": Rice, *The Tumult and the Shouting,* 240.

121 "with borrowed clubs": Grantland Rice, "'Babe' Athletic Marvel: Miss Didrikson's Feats Hard to Believe Until You See Her in Action," North American Newspaper Alliance, 1932, BDZ, doc. 11.1.4.17.

121 "I couldn't afford it": Johnson and Williamson, *Whatta-Gal,* 108.

122 Babe flew home: "Welcome Home, Babe," *Dallas Dispatch,* August 11, 1932; "Dallas Welcomes Babe Didrikson Home," *Dallas Dispatch,* August 11, 1932.

122 "WELCOME HOME, BABE": "Babe Comes Home," *Dallas Journal*, August 11, 1932. See also Cayleff, *Babe*, 74.

122 "Big shots": Johnson and Williamson, *Whatta-Gal*, 109.

123 "Dallas' most distinguished": United Press, "World-Famous Babe Is Given Tumultuous Dallas Welcome amid Ticker Tape Showers," *Dallas Journal*, August 11, 1932, BDZ, doc. 11.1.4.15.

123 "I don't have any plans": Ibid.

123 "He only caddied": Ibid.

123 Babe then climbed: Johnson, *The Incredible Babe*, 291. Babe said, "Flowers were all over the place. I never again would see that many beautiful flowers...and it was a happy time."

123 "Come on up here": Johnson and Williamson, *Whatta-Gal*, 108–9.

124 Throngs of people: United Press, "World-Famous Babe Is Given Tumultuous Dallas Welcome amid Ticker Tape Showers."

124 "chill bumps": Didrikson Zaharias, *This Life I've Led*, 63.

124 Babe wished: Johnson, *The Incredible Babe*, 292.

124 "Man, that's the biggest": Didrikson Zaharias, *This Life I've Led*, 63.

124 "I'm tickled to be back": Johnson and Williamson, *Whatta-Gal*, 109–10.

124 "No, Mrs. Didrikson": Ibid.

124 "If I decide": United Press, "World-Famous Babe Is Given Tumultuous Dallas Welcome amid Ticker Tape Showers."

125 Then it was Beaumont's turn: "Tuesday to Be Didrikson Day in Beaumont as City Turns Out to Honor Athlete," *Beaumont Enterprise*, August 13, 1932, BDZ, doc. 11.1.4.16; "Beaumont's Babe to Get Tumultuous Welcome on Arrival Here Tomorrow," *Beaumont Enterprise*, August 15, 1932, BDZ, doc. 11.1.4.17.

125 "We knew her when": "Babe Didrikson Is Honored Guest at Luncheon," *Beaumont Enterprise*, August 17, 1932, BDZ, doc. 11.1.4.21.

126 "same swell kid": "Crowds Cheer Babe in Welcome Parade," *Beaumont Enterprise*, August 16, 1932, BDZ, doc. 11.1.4.19.

126 "Left school": Johnson, *The Incredible Babe*, 164. I also have a copy of Babe's high school transcript, Beaumont High School, Beaumont, TX.

126 "I am...about plooked out": "Beaumont Places Her Laurel Wreath on Brow of 'Babe,' Returning Heroine," *Beaumont Enterprise*, August 17, 1932, BDZ, doc. 11.1.4.20.

Chapter 10: That Big Money Talk

127 "I felt that I would sooner": W. O. McGeehan, "Down the Line," *New York Tribune*, June 28, 1926. See also Dahlberg, *America's Girl* (I found this book to be the finest among the three published in 2009 about Gertrude Ederle's life); Kelli Anderson, "The Young Woman and the Sea," *Sports Illustrated*, August 6, 1999, available at http://sportsillustrated.cnn.com/vault/article/magazine/MAG1017808/index.htm; and Richard Deitsch's very fine summary of Ederle's feat in *Sports*

Illustrated for Women's Top 100 athletes, "Gertrude Ederle, Swimming" (Ederle was ranked number 42), http://sportsillustrated.cnn.com/siforwomen/top_100/42/.

128 Moses parting the Red Sea: Deitsch, "Gertrude Ederle, Swimming."

129 "I'm not a millionaire": Johnson and Williamson, *Whatta-Gal,* 113–14.

129 *The eyes of the whole world:* Cartoon, *Amarillo Globe,* August 15, 1932, 1. See also Cayleff, *Babe,* 77.

130 "Here comes the Babe!": Didrikson Zaharias, *This Life I've Led,* 64.

130 "Why, Babe . . . I think": Ibid., 68.

130 Babe had fielded: Mildred (Babe) Didrikson, "The Story of My Life," *Los Angeles Times,* January 15, 1933, E3. See also Johnson and Williamson, *Whatta-Gal,* 114.

130 "People kept telling me": Didrikson Zaharias, *This Life I've Led,* 68.

131 "the legal right": "Girl Star's Plea Heeded: Court Gives Miss Didrikson Right to Handle Own Business Affairs," *New York Times,* August 30, 1932, 15.

131 a Sport-light short called *The Wonder Girl:* Fountain, *Sportswriter,* 283.

131 The ball travels: "Sport: Wonder Girl," *Time,* December 19, 1932, available at http://www.time.com/time/magazine/article/0,9171,753512,00.html. In 2004, historians at the U.S. Golf Association (USGA) located a copy of this rare film and showed it continuously for nearly a year at a Babe Didrikson exhibit at the USGA library and museum in Far Hills, New Jersey. I watched the film, which included Babe's powerful baseball throw. The description of Babe's baseball throw was provided by noted women's golf historian Rhonda Glenn, who said, "In all the films I've seen of Babe as a golfer, nothing impressed me as much as the sheer athleticism and power of this throw."

131 athletic women tried: Woolum, *Outstanding Women Athletes,* 13–14.

132 "What I really wanted": Didrikson Zaharias, *This Life I've Led,* 68.

132 "She was always comfortably": Johnson, *The Incredible Babe,* 297.

133 "Speed—unyielding strength": Johnson and Williamson, *Whatta-Gal,* 115; Cayleff, *Babe,* 95.

133 On December 5: Johnson, *The Incredible Babe,* 299.

133 "a bunch of hooey": Cayleff, *Babe,* 100.

134 "I hope I will be": Joseph D'O'Brian, "The Greatest Athlete in the World," *American Heritage,* July/August 1992, available at http://www.americanheritage .com/articles/magazine/ah/1992/4/1992_4_93.shtml.

134 "Ignorance is no excuse": Ibid. It's worth noting that Thorpe defeated Brundage in the 1912 Olympics, and perhaps Brundage was carrying a grudge.

134 "It was like a girl": Didrikson Zaharias, *This Life I've Led,* 68.

135 Babe knew that AAU rules: Ibid.

135 "because they didn't want me to beat": Lawrence Lader, "The Unbeatable Babe," *Coronet,* January 1948, 156, BDZ, doc. 11.1.17.1. See also Cayleff, *Babe,* 100.

135 "I have played only three years": "Will Seek Reinstatement: Firm Employing Miss Didrikson to Act on Her Behalf," *New York Times,* December 6, 1932, 29;

"Will Back Olympic Star: Miss Didrikson's Employers Confident She Will Be Cleared," *New York Times,* December 7, 1932, 30.

135 "Her praise of this car": Johnson and Williamson, *Whatta-Gal,* 115–16.

135 "spontaneous and enthusiastic": "Will Back Olympic Star," *New York Times.*

137 "Not until this last weekend": Johnson and Williamson, *Whatta-Gal,* 116.

137 "I'd rather try to smash": "Camera-Shy but Carefree, Miss Didrikson Moves On toward Career as a Pro," *New York Times,* December 24, 1932, 19. See also Cayleff, *Babe,* 102.

137 Accompanied by her big sister: Johnson and Williamson, *Whatta-Gal,* 116.

137 "Just by way of keeping": Ibid., 117.

138 "You know...the ancient Greeks": "Greeks Were Right, Brundage Believes," *New York Times,* December 25, 1932, sec. 3, pp. 1–2.

Chapter 11: Miss, Mrs., Mr., or It

139 "one of those astounding marvels": Cayleff, *Babe,* 77.

139 "is not a freakish looking": Ibid., 43.

140 "Well, goodbye kid": Paul Gallico, "The Texas Babe," *Vanity Fair,* October 1932, 36, 71. See also Congdon, *The Thirties,* 73–78, and Cayleff, *Babe,* 92–93.

140 "simply because she would not": Gallico, "The Texas Babe," 36.

141 "the greatest woman athlete": Ibid., 71.

141 "After the Olympics": Author interview with Betty Jameson.

141 her need to compete: Author interviews with Jameson and Peggy Kirk Bell.

141 "Uh, Miss Didrikson, do you select": Cayleff, *Babe,* 89.

142 "Honey Hadwell": Paul Gallico, "Honey," *Vanity Fair,* April 1933.

142 "the most beautiful body": Ibid.

142 "Her mouth was": Ibid. See also Cayleff, *Babe,* 92–94.

142 "that dried-up": Gallico, "Honey."

143 "Ah throwed it": Ibid.

143 *We,* and in it: Johnson and Williamson, *Whatta-Gal,* 48.

144 "I remember my mother": Ibid., 133.

144 "gender test": Ibid., 20.

144 "By her championship": Marlow, *The Great Women,* 355.

144 "all this fake cheap": Westbrook Pegler, "That Didrikson Babe Is a Sissy," United Press Syndicate, February 6, 1933, 9.

145 "I know I'm not": Johnson and Williamson, *Whatta-Gal,* 74.

146 "Say, you aren't the fellow": Arthur J. Daley, "Babe Didrikson, Visiting Here, Hopes to Box Babe Ruth in Gym," *New York Times,* January 5, 1933, 25.

147 "They were determined": Didrikson Zaharias, *This Life I've Led,* 76.

148 "I jumped so high": Ibid.

148 "Momma and Poppa": Ibid., 77.

148 "First Championship": Kevin Edwards, "Honesdale's Ruth McGinnis Remembered: Maple City Billiards Star Was Women's Sports Pioneer," http:// archiver.rootsweb.ancestry.com/th/read/MCGINNIS/2003-10/1067529165.

148 "but as a pocket billiard player": Ibid.

149 "Give me a big city": Cayleff, *Babe,* 108.

149 *What should I play?*: Didrikson Zaharias, *This Life I've Led,* 69–71.

149 "Babe, honey": Ibid., 73.

151 "That was it": "Didrickson [sic] Girl Turns to New Love, Golf," *Los Angeles Times,* Babe's scrapbook. See also Johnson and Williamson, *Whatta-Gal,* 139.

151 "Gee, you swing nice": Johnson and Williamson, *Whatta-Gal,* 138.

151 "Yeah, but it costs": Didrikson Zaharias, *This Life I've Led,* 78.

151 Kertes was getting: Johnson and Williamson, *Whatta-Gal,* 138.

151 "I'll teach you": Didrikson Zaharias, *This Life I've Led,* 78.

152 "As early as you want": Ibid.

152 he canceled his paid lessons: Johnson and Williamson, *Whatta-Gal,* 140.

152 "We'd work until eleven": Ibid.

152 "Right then...I knew": Lawrence Lader, "The Unbeatable Babe," *Coronet,* January 1948, 160, BDZ, doc. 11.1.17.1.

153 "Those people were wonderful": Didrikson Zaharias, *This Life I've Led,* 79.

153 "Get up and go sit": Ibid., 81.

154 Babe Didrikson's All-Americans: Johnson and Williamson, *Whatta-Gal,* 126–27.

154 "We weren't world beaters": Didrikson Zaharias, *This Life I've Led,* 81.

154 "Neither goes for that lovey-dovey": Johnson and Williamson, *Whatta-Gal,* 127.

155 "After we explained": Ibid.

155 "an honest one" and "We'll pitch Babe": Ibid., 128; Roscoe McGowan, "Dodgers Conquer Athletics, 4–2; Miss Didrikson Pitches First Inning for Losers, Holding Rivals Scoreless; Triple Play Saves Her," *New York Times,* March 21, 1934, 29.

155 Dean emerged: Didrikson Zaharias, *This Life I've Led,* 82–83.

156 "With a crowd": Johnson and Williamson, *Whatta-Gal,* 129.

157 "I was an extra attraction": Didrikson Zaharias, *This Life I've Led,* 82.

157 "She was not all that good": Johnson and Williamson, *Whatta-Gal,* 129.

157 In one memorable game: Didrikson Zaharias, *This Life I've Led,* 82; Johnson and Williamson, *Whatta-Gal,* 129.

157 "Famous Woman Athlete": Cayleff, *Babe,* 107.

157 "a physique that the average high school": "Yoicks! The Babe Rides to Hounds," BDZ; George A. Barton, "Sportographs," BDZ.

157 She was lonely: Johnson and Williamson, *Whatta-Gal,* 129.

158 "The Dodge people": Ibid.

158 "I'm sittin' on 'em": Ibid., 130.

158 "Sometimes in those early": Didrikson Zaharias, *This Life I've Led,* photo section. Caption written by Babe.

Chapter 12: The Best Interest of the Game

159 "My name had meant": Didrikson Zaharias, *This Life I've Led,* 85.

159 "a mixed-up time": Ibid.

160 She'd also bought a new Dodge: Author interview with Betty Jameson.

160 "I had to find some way": Didrikson Zaharias, *This Life I've Led,* 85.

160 "Most things come natural to me": Cayleff, *Babe,* 118.

161 "to hit a little white ball": Babe Didrikson, "How I Got Started at Golf," North American Newspaper Alliance, 1933, BDZ; Didrikson Zaharias, *This Life I've Led,* 58. See also Cayleff, *Babe,* 118.

161 "sailed out sweet and true": Pete Martin, "Babe Didrikson Takes Off Her Mask," *Saturday Evening Post,* September 20, 1947, 26. Babe's brother Louis repeated the broad outlines of this story, saying that it happened at a driving range on South Main Street in Dallas and that he was there to witness it. Johnson, *The Incredible Babe,* 316.

161 "I had never paid much attention": Cayleff, *Babe,* 118–19.

162 The more fantastic the story: Author interviews with Jameson and Peggy Kirk Bell. Both women said that Babe bragged about pulling the wool over sports reporters' eyes and that she liked to say journalists wanted to be told fanciful tales because it made it easier for them to write good, memorable stories.

162 "She could out drive me": Johnson and Williamson, *Whatta-Gal,* 59.

162 "a great idol of mine": Didrikson Zaharias, *This Life I've Led,* 86.

163 "Even in the short time": Ibid.

163 "Soon after this brawny": "How We Regard a Truly Astonishing Young Lady," *Golf Illustrated,* December 1934, 15.

164 *"fun"*: Glenn, *The Illustrated History of Women's Golf,* 136. Rhonda Glenn was an enormous help to me during the research, fact checking, and editing of this book. Many of my observations about Bertha Bowen and, in particular, Bowen's fascinating relationship with Babe were culled from the marvelous memory of Glenn, who knew Bowen and many of her country-club friends in Fort Worth.

164 "I settled into": Didrikson Zaharias, *This Life I've Led,* 87.

164 "I only know of one golfer": Johnson and Williamson, *Whatta-Gal,* 141.

165 "Then I'd drill and drill": Didrikson Zaharias, *This Life I've Led,* 89.

166 "We really don't": Author interview with Rhonda Glenn. See also "Miss Didrikson Barred by U.S.G.A. from National Title Golf Tourney," *New York Times,* May 15, 1935, 29.

166 "a pretty swish place": Rhonda Glenn, "A Friend Remembers Babe Zaharias," *Golf Journal,* July 1984, 30.

167 *"I'm here, ladies"*: Author interview with Glenn, who heard this story from Bertha Bowen.

168 "Babe smiled": Didrikson Zaharias, *This Life I've Led,* 120.

168 The skies were overcast: "Two Up Margin of Win," International News Service, April 28, 1935; "Former Olympic Games Star Defeats Mrs. Dan Chandler of Dallas," 1935, BDZ; "'Best at Everything' Babe Garners Another Trophy," *Newsweek,* May 4, 1935, 18.

168 the two players posed: Didrikson Zaharias, *This Life I've Led,* photo section. The caption that Babe wrote about Peggy Chandler is polite and respectful.

169 On the par 5 first hole: Ibid., 94.

170 *I can't afford:* Ibid., 95. All the italics in this paragraph are Babe's thoughts at the time, as recounted in her autobiography.

171 "The gallery just": Johnson and Williamson, *Whatta-Gal,* 146.

171 By a margin: Bill Walker, Associated Press, April 27, 1935. See also Didrikson Zaharias, *This Life I've Led,* 93.

171 "On top of the world": Didrikson Zaharias, *This Life I've Led,* 96.

172 "Staging a sensational finish": Cayleff, *Babe,* 125.

172 Paul Gallico: Author interview with Glenn.

172 "Maybe Mildred": Crawford and Ragsdale, *Women in Texas,* 300.

172 *From the high jump:* Ibid., 300–301.

173 Peggy and Dan Chandler: Author interview with Glenn, who spoke with Dan Chandler late in his life. "Of course she was a pro," Dan Chandler said of Babe. See also Betty Jameson interview, USGA Oral History Project, 3–4.

173 "Joe, you aren't going": Author interview with Jameson. See also Jameson interview, USGA Oral History Project, 4.

174 "for the best interest":"Miss Didrikson Barred," *New York Times.* See also Cayleff, *Babe,* 125. Newsreel footage of the decision, without audio, is available at http://www.texasarchive.org/library/index.php/Bars_'Babe'_From_Golf_Test.

174 Mary K. Browne: Cayleff, *Babe,* 125.

174 "Mrs. Bowen, I've just been ruled": Johnson and Williamson, *Whatta-Gal,* 146.

Chapter 13: Diamond in the Rough

175 "The biggest joke": Didrikson Zaharias, *This Life I've Led,* 98.

175 "the dirtiest deal": Ibid.

175 "Silly—a pity": Associated Press, May 15, 1935; Johnson, *The Incredible Babe,* 319.

176 "I was just furious": Johnson and Williamson, *Whatta-Gal,* 147.

176 "The mere fact": Johnson, *The Incredible Babe,* 318.

176 Bowen also wanted that world: Author interview with Rhonda Glenn.

177 "What the USGA says": "Uncertain on Next Step," *New York Times,* May 14, 1935. See also Cayleff, *Babe,* 126.

177 If Babe graciously accepted: "Uncertain on Next Step," *New York Times.*

177 "Of course, I was disappointed": "Golf Pros Joined by Miss Didrikson,"

New York Times, June 2, 1935, sec. 5, p. 1. See also Johnson and Williamson, *Whatta-Gal,* 147.

177 "Golf is a game": "Golf Pros Joined by Miss Didrikson," *New York Times.*

178 "business woman golfer": "Babe Says She Will Take Western Open," BDZ.

178 "just as if I was already Bobby Jones": Didrikson Zaharias, *This Life I've Led,* 98.

178 a thirty-year-old sports promoter: Corcoran and Harvey, *Unplayable Lies,* 180.

179 Their inaugural exhibition: Didrikson Zaharias, *This Life I've Led,* 98.

179 "She was still a big draw": Johnson and Williamson, *Whatta-Gal,* 148. See also Corcoran and Harvey, *Unplayable Lies,* 180–81.

179 "Gene played the golf": Johnson and Williamson, *Whatta-Gal,* 148.

180 "Well, can we *play* now?": Ibid.

180 "She had a gift": Ibid., 148–49.

181 "Can you imagine": Ibid.

181 "If I was going to be the best": Didrikson Zaharias, *This Life I've Led,* 101.

181 "She had the rhythm": Johnson and Williamson, *Whatta-Gal,* 149.

182 "From a quiet house": Herbert Warren Wind, "Golf and the Women," *Sports Illustrated,* July 23, 1956, 29; Wilson, *The Babe in Retrospect.*

182 "couldn't hit the ball": Johnson and Williamson, *Whatta-Gal,* 150–51.

183 The tourney would be christened: Author interview with Glenn, who said that Bertha Bowen, the tournament's cofounder, told her the proper name was "Women's Texas Open."

183 "sat out in the car": Ibid.

183 "a diamond in the rough": Rhonda Glenn, "A Friend Remembers Babe Zaharias," *Golf Journal,* June 1984, 30.

183 "like my godmother": Didrikson Zaharias, *This Life I've Led,* 90.

184 "You go to bed": Sampson, *Texas Golf Legends,* 151.

184 "If you have once been poor": Ibid.

184 "so poor it was pitiful": Author interview with Glenn. See also Cayleff, *Babe,* 129.

184 "Why are you fooling": Author interview with Glenn.

185 "Goddamn, I'm choking": Ibid.

185 "genteel sport": Lipsyte and Levine, *Idols of the Game,* 129.

186 "I hardly knew Babe": Johnson and Williamson, *Whatta-Gal,* 153.

186 "I got 'em": Ibid.

186 The Babe was just: Henry McLemore, "Babe Didrikson Gives Herr Henry Golf Lesson on Florida Links," United Press, January 27, 1937.

186 "I am afraid": Cayleff, *Babe,* 132.

187 most of her friends: Author interviews with Betty Jameson and Peggy Kirk Bell.

187 "too busy working": Didrikson Zaharias, *This Life I've Led,* 106.

Chapter 14: The Girl, the Minister, and the Wrestler

188 "I knew I wasn't:" Didrikson Zaharias, *This Life I've Led,* 104.

188 "who didn't have any business": Ibid., 105.

189 "The girl, the minister and the wrestler": Ibid.

189 "Well, I knew she was good": George Zaharias, "The Babe and I," *Look,* November 1957, 88. See also Joan Flynn Dreyspool, "Subject: Babe and George Zaharias," *Sports Illustrated,* May 14, 1956, available at http://sportsillustrated.cnn .com/vault/article/magazine/MAG1069639/index.htm. Dreyspool was a marvel of sportswriting, and her intimate portrait was one of the best I found on the dynamics of Babe and George's relationship. This article played a critical role in informing many sections of this book, including the story of Babe and George's meeting in January 1938.

189 "George...here's your partner": In *This Life I've Led,* Babe wrote that journalist Mel Gallagher introduced her to George Zaharias, but George insisted in several interviews that it was Braven Dyer of the *Los Angeles Times.* The discrepancy may simply be attributable to the fact that both men were present when Babe and George met.

189 Babe beamed her slightly crooked grin: A photo of the moment the two met appears in *This Life I've Led.* George is wearing a wide smile as he shakes Babe's hand; Babe is smiling back at him.

189 "Am I holding you": Didrikson Zaharias, *This Life I've Led,* 105.

190 "Say, fella": George Zaharias, "My Life with the Babe," *Sport,* October 1947, 52; Dreyspool, "Subject: Babe and George Zaharias."

190 "What are you looking at?": Zaharias, "My Life with the Babe," 52.

190 "The fans": Cayleff, *Babe,* 136.

191 "As young as he was": Johnson and Williamson, *Whatta-Gal,* 158.

191 "One day George": Ibid.

191 "After one year": Oliver and Johnson, *The Pro Wrestling Hall of Fame,* 160.

192 "How come such a lousy": Zaharias, "My Life with the Babe," 50. See also Dreyspool, "Subject: Babe and George Zaharias."

192 "George was one of the best": Johnson and Williamson, *Whatta-Gal,* 160.

193 "the foremost ham": Oliver and Johnson, *The Pro Wrestling Hall of Fame,* 159–60.

193 Seated in the first few rows: Ibid.

193 George was so popular: Johnson and Williamson, *Whatta-Gal,* 161.

194 "You want to *win*": Ibid., 160.

194 "We kept jokin'": Zaharias, "The Babe and I," 88. See also Zaharias, "My Life with the Babe," 52.

194 "I'll be seeing you": Didrikson Zaharias, *This Life I've Led,* 106.

194 "Are you trying to run": Ibid., 107.

195 "pretty close to see": Ibid.

195 "Sure": Ibid.

195 "Momma liked him": Ibid., 109.

195 "going together real steady": Ibid.

195 "searing": Author interviews with Peggy Kirk Bell and Betty Jameson.

196 "The first night": Johnson and Williamson, *Whatta-Gal,* 163.

196 "You want to go back": Didrikson Zaharias, *This Life I've Led,* 110.

196 "he came out": Ibid.

196 "a galleryite": Zaharias, "My Life with the Babe," 52.

197 "His mother didn't speak": Ibid.

197 "That particular summer": Didrikson Zaharias, *This Life I've Led,* 111.

197 "I bought this diamond": Oliver and Johnson, *The Pro Wrestling Hall of Fame,* 159.

197 "Five minutes from now?": Johnson, *The Incredible Babe,* 388.

197 "George moved right in": Johnson and Williamson, *Whatta-Gal,* 162–63.

198 she wasn't so sure: Author interview with Jameson, who recalled Babe telling her that on her wedding day, and in the weeks and months afterward, "she wasn't sure she did the right thing. She had doubts."

198 "Right away she was": Zaharias, "My Life with the Babe," 52.

199 "She would have none": Ibid.

199 "I loved all the pretty": Didrikson Zaharias, *This Life I've Led,* 104.

199 "Golf is a racket": Sheehan and Hicks, *Patty Sheehan on Golf,* 83.

Chapter 15: What Momma Wants

200 "it was like a morgue":Didrikson Zaharias, *This Life I've Led,* 114.

201 "a little bitty English car": Ibid., 115.

201 "The plain fact": Ibid., 115–16.

202 Babe always looked back: Ibid.

202 "I'd look back": Ibid., 117.

202 The Australian press: Cayleff, *Babe,* 143.

202 "nobody was there": George Zaharias, "The Babe and I," *Look,* November 1957, 88.

203 "Here I'd been practicing": Didrikson Zaharias, *This Life I've Led,* 119.

203 "I had a great career": Karon Stonger, "George Goes On Without Babe," *Beaumont Enterprise and Journal,* January 17, 1973, BDZ, doc. 11.2.21.2.

204 "We got up a program": "Whatta Woman," *Time,* March 10, 1947. See also Cayleff, *Babe,* 148–49.

204 "The money had always": Didrikson Zaharias, *This Life I've Led,* 120.

204 "George earned": Oliver and Johnson, *The Pro Wrestling Hall of Fame,* 160.

205 "Why don't you and me": Betty Hicks interview, USGA Oral History Project, 27.

205 "Little Slam": Didrikson Zaharias, *This Life I've Led,* 122; Johnson and Williamson, *Whatta-Gal,* 170.

205 "I went all out": Didrikson Zaharias, *This Life I've Led,* 124.

206 Brough and Babe: Ibid.

206 The way the tennis world: Johnson and Williamson, *Whatta-Gal*, 169.

206 "It was that old issue": Didrikson Zaharias, *This Life I've Led*, 125.

206 "decided to take a whack": Ibid.

207 As a teenager: Tiny Scurlock, "Babe's Early History," BDZ, doc. 11.1.1.4.

207 "Come on, now": Didrikson Zaharias, *This Life I've Led*, 126.

207 King's Jewelry scored: Ibid.

207 "One of the best": Cayleff, *Babe*, 146.

208 "I don't know": Didrikson Zaharias, *This Life I've Led*, 133–34.

208 "so intricate": Ibid., 128–29.

208 easier to endure: Author interview with Betty Jameson.

208 Babe contributed: Cayleff, *Babe*, 148.

209 "There's only one": Didrikson Zaharias, *This Life I've Led*, 129.

209 At San Gabriel: Ibid.

209 "Now do you see": Ibid., 130.

209 Babe's wartime: Ibid.

209 teamed up with: Cayleff, *Babe*, 148.

209 Her brother Louis: Johnson, *The Incredible Babe*, 33–35.

210 "without salary": Cayleff, *Babe*, 148. Babe says nothing about this volunteer work in her autobiography, but she was awarded the key to the city of Denver in 1947 in part for it. A photo of the award ceremony appears in *This Life I've Led*. The key is now on display at the Babe Didrikson Zaharias Museum in Beaumont, Texas.

210 "Momma, why aren't": Didrikson Zaharias, *This Life I've Led*, 138.

210 "Babe, if I cried": Author interview with Peggy Kirk Bell. Bell recalled Babe refusing to show any hint of emotion about her family's troubles because "Momma insisted."

210 "Stop worrying": Ibid.

211 "The hole was": Didrikson Zaharias, *This Life I've Led*, 133.

211 "Your Momma wants": Ibid., 136.

211 "I sure didn't have": Ibid.

212 "I'm going to win": Author interview with Bell.

212 "What kept me": Didrikson Zaharias, *This Life I've Led*, 137.

212 "We didn't know": Author interview with Bell.

213 "You've got to play": Ibid.

213 "She didn't need any help": Author interviews with Jameson and Bell.

213 "Inspiration": Author interview with Bell.

213 "If Babe has more": Ibid.

214 "George and Esther Nancy met": Author interview with Jameson.

214 Then she wept: Didrikson Zaharias, *This Life I've Led*, 138.

Chapter 16: Mrs. Z

216 Was there a lovelier: Author interview with Betty Jameson.

216 "all that self-esteem stuff": Author interview with Peggy Kirk Bell.

217 "George, the only way": Johnson and Williamson, *Whatta-Gal,* 166.

217 He lost an unknown: Ibid.

217 "a wheeler-dealer": Ibid., 164.

217 "He makes me keep": Will Grimsley, "Babe and George Happy Twosome," Associated Press, April 16, 1953, BDZ, doc. 11.1.6.8. See also Cayleff, *Babe,* 149.

217 "George is the business head": Cayleff, *Babe,* 149.

218 he spent it freely: Author interviews with Bell and Betty Hicks.

218 "I objected": Johnson and Williamson, *Whatta-Gal,* 166–67.

218 "Babe, once called": Braven Dyer and Frank Finch, "Top Lady Athlete," *Sport,* November 1946, 42–48.

219 "This was not a perfect": Johnson, *The Incredible Babe,* 389.

219 "We started getting": Ibid.

220 "I wish those people": Dyer and Finch, "Top Lady Athlete," 42–48.

220 "Sometimes she overdressed": Cayleff, *Babe,* 155.

220 "Goddamn these things": Ibid., 155–56.

220 "Naturally, the Babe": Dyer and Finch, "Top Lady Athlete," 42–48.

220 "With a few assists": Pete Martin, "Babe Didrikson Takes Off Her Mask," *Saturday Evening Post,* September 20, 1947, 26.

221 stuffed in a drawer: Author interviews with Bell and Jameson. Several profiles of Babe also noted that her medals were usually kept out of sight.

221 "just Mrs. Z": Author interviews with Bell and Hicks.

221 "You can't tell a husband": Martin, "Babe Didrikson Takes Off Her Mask," 26. See also Cayleff, *Babe,* 154.

221 "She was said to have": Martin, "Babe Didrikson Takes Off Her Mask," 26.

221 "The bust measurement": Ibid.

222 "Our bed wasn't big enough": Ibid. See also Cayleff, *Babe,* 154.

222 "My, but you're a big girl": Author interview with Jameson.

223 "I thought": Ibid. Jameson told me that she tried to emulate Babe's self-confidence and, at times, it worked. Years later, Jameson said, "In golf—and in life—the more you can kid yourself that you're going to succeed, the more likely you will."

223 "I need a partner": Author interview with Bell.

223 "What's wrong with you?": Ibid.

223 "Now Peggy, why don't you see?": Johnson and Williamson, *Whatta-Gal,* 175.

224 "a special charge": Didrikson Zaharias, *This Life I've Led,* 139.

224 "I want to establish": Lawrence Lader, "The Unbeatable Babe," *Coronet,* January 1948, 156, BDZ, doc. 11.1.17.1. Lader was quoting her 1946 interview.

224 Babe began slowly: Didrikson Zaharias, *This Life I've Led,* 140.

224 "You sure shoulda": Associated Press, July 3, 1946; Johnson, *The Incredible Babe,* 335–36.

225 "I always liked": Didrikson Zaharias, *This Life I've Led,* 140.

225 "I was hot": Ibid., 142.

226 "Honey...you've got": Ibid.

226 "what are you doing": Ibid., 142–43.

227 "the best rubdowns": Martin, "Babe Didrikson Takes Off Her Mask."

227 "I'm tired": Didrikson Zaharias, *This Life I've Led*, 144.

228 "It's golf as golf": Ibid., 145.

228 "I wound up": Ibid., 146.

228 "Honey...you want": Ibid.

229 "Mildred, you go": Johnson, *The Incredible Babe*, 33–35. See also Didrikson Zaharias, *This Life I've Led*, 150.

Chapter 17: The Highland Fling

230 "Lady...you'll have": Didrikson Zaharias, *This Life I've Led*, 151.

231 "Doesn't a first-class": Ibid., 152.

231 she silently cursed: Author interview with Betty Jameson, who recalled that Babe complained bitterly that George "forced" her to go to Scotland.

232 "From then on": Didrikson Zaharias, *This Life I've Led*, 152.

232 "Well, I'd like some bacon": Ibid., 153.

233 "Just call me Babe": Cayleff, *Babe*, 170. See also Didrikson Zaharias, *This Life I've Led*, 154.

233 "I wish you'd ask": Cayleff, *Babe*, 170.

233 "The way of approach": Wethered, *Golfing Memories and Methods*, 228.

233 "one of the most": Darwin, *Every Idle Dream*, 22. See Darwin quote at "Welcome to Gullane Golf Club," http://www.gullanegolfclub.com/.

233 "the winds": Didrikson Zaharias, *This Life I've Led*, 154.

234 "They just practice": Ibid., 155.

234 "The fairways": Wilson, *The Babe in Retrospect*, 60.

234 "Good Lord": Didrikson Zaharias, *This Life I've Led*, 156.

234 "I didn't want": Ibid.

235 "I thought Scotland": Ibid., 160.

235 "What chance": Nan O'Reilly, "The View of Miss Hicks," *Golf Illustrated*, August 1933, 25.

236 "I don't think so": Ibid., 38.

236 Vare's collapse: "World Golf Hall of Fame Profile: Glenna Collett Vare," http://www.wgv.com/hof/member.php?member=1119.

237 "I wish these people": Didrikson Zaharias, *This Life I've Led*, 162.

237 "Would you please": Ibid., 165.

238 "It seems cruel": Associated Press, "Buying Clubs Instead of a Dress Sent Mrs. Zaharias to Golf Fame," *New York Times*, June 13, 1947, 18; "What a Babe!" *Life*, June 1947, 87.

238 "Like a small cannon": Didrikson Zaharias, *This Life I've Led*, 163.

238 "You are speaking": Ibid., 164.

239 "Don't forget": Ibid., 168.

240 "a real good sport": Ibid., 167–68.

240 "Mrs. Zaharias, don't take": Ibid., 169.

240 "Oh, I was a doll": Ibid., 170.

241 "Babe, go git": Ibid., 171.

241 "I was just cold!": Ibid.

241 "I've watched Walter Hagen": Ibid., 172.

242 "Ah.... That would be fine": Ibid., 174.

242 "The pants did it": Associated Press, "Mrs. Zaharias Is First American to Win Women's British Golf Title," *New York Times,* June 12, 1947, 1, 18.

242 "the big cup": Ibid. Babe also refers to this trophy as "the big cup" in the caption of an iconic photograph published in *This Life I've Led.*

242 "Surely no woman golfer": Glenn, *The Illustrated History of Women's Golf,* 140.

242 "We have not seen": "What a Babe!" *Life,* 87.

242 "back home": Associated Press, "Mrs. Zaharias Is First American to Win," 18.

243 "The course gave me": Didrikson Zaharias, *This Life I've Led,* 176.

243 "I'd already been away": Ibid., 177.

244 "That's George": Ibid., 178.

244 "Seeing George again": William D. Richardson, "Champion Praises British Links Fans," *New York Times,* July 1, 1947, 33.

245 "You and Babe": Johnson and Williamson, *Whatta-Gal,* 183.

245 "I spent a short half hour": Rice, *The Tumult and the Shouting,* 368.

245 "George will carry it": Didrikson Zaharias, *This Life I've Led,* 179.

Chapter 18: A Piece of Work

249 Babe's streak was unmatched: Jim Gorant, "Byron Nelson's Streak: A Record That May Never Be Broken," Golf.com, September 9, 2008, http://www.golf.com/golf/tours_news/article/0,28136,1839204,00.html. Babe never admitted this, but she likely got the idea to set her own record after Nelson won eleven tournaments in a row over a six-month period in 1945, a streak that inspired the golf world's awe and captured the American imagination. Unfortunately, Babe's winning streak, which was longer than Nelson's, has been reported in various inaccurate ways through time. When Babe died, Shirley Povich, the legendary *Washington Post* sportswriter, reported that she had won an astonishing twenty-one tournaments in a row. Shirley Povich, *All Those Mornings...at the Post* (New York: Public-Affairs, 2005), 177. The outstanding, groundbreaking Didrikson biographer Susan E. Cayleff claimed in her 1995 book, *Babe: The Life and Legend of Babe Didrikson Zaharias,* that Babe and George had fibbed about her record-setting seventeen-win streak and in fact Babe had won thirteen in a row. Cayleff reported that Babe lost in the first round of the National Open on August 26, 1946, in Spokane, Washington. Adding further to the confusion about the streak is the fact that Babe disqualified herself, after three victories in a row, in the Women's Spring Lake Open, but Cayleff (and Babe and George) did not count this against the streak, though an

argument could be made that they should have. The tournament in Spokane was run under the auspices of the new Women's Professional Golf Association (WPGA), chartered in 1944. The accusation that Babe had intentionally misrepresented the length of her winning streak was first made by Betty Hicks, who told Cayleff that Babe had "buried her fourteenth tournament, which she lost, to keep the string alive." Cayleff wrote, "According to Hicks, 'an amateur named Grace Lenczyk of Connecticut knocked Babe out of the National Open's first round at the Spokane Country Club, 1946. Babe sorta repressed that match as she counted to 17.' In fact research reveals that Babe did lose at Spokane in the tournament, played August 26–September 1, 1946." Cayleff, *Babe,* 168. Cayleff was correct: Babe's streak was not seventeen. But Cayleff (and Hicks) actually miscounted Babe's consecutive victories. Babe had fourteen straight wins, not thirteen, as Cayleff erroneously reported in her book and as has been repeated frequently in golf publications.

In counting her seventeen-win streak, Babe began with three wins in 1946: Women's Trans-Mississippi Championship, Denver, beat Polly Riley in the finals, 6 and 5; Broadmoor Ladies Invitation, Colorado Springs, beat Dorothy Kielty, 6 and 4; All-American Open Championship for Women, Tam O'Shanter Country Club, Niles, Illinois, 310 (medal play). It was after the All-American that Babe lost in the first round to Grace Lenczyk in Spokane on August 26. She did not count this loss in tallying her streak. Interestingly, she disqualified herself from the Women's Spring Lake Open during this time, which she also ignored in her tally. (See Johnson, *The Incredible Babe,* 336.)

Babe's record-setting streak of fourteen wins in a row actually began in Tulsa, Oklahoma, at the U.S. Women's Amateur:

1. U.S. Women's Amateur, Tulsa, beat Clara Callender Sherman, 11 and 9, for the biggest margin in tournament history.

2. Women's Texas Open, Fort Worth, beat Betty Hicks, 5 and 3.

3. Tampa Women's Open, 306 (medal play).

4. Helen Lee Doherty Women's Amateur, Miami, beat Margaret Gunther, 12 and 10.

5. Florida Mixed Two-Ball Championship, Orlando, partnered with major-league baseball player Gerald Walker, won on thirty-first hole.

6. Palm Beach Women's Amateur, beat Jean Hopkins, one up.

7. Women's International Four-Ball, Hollywood, Florida, partnered with Peggy Kirk, beat Louise Suggs and Jean Hopkins in eighteen-hole playoff, 4 and 2.

8. South Atlantic Women's Championship, Ormond Beach, Florida, beat Peggy Kirk, 5 and 4.

9. Florida East Coast Women's Championship, St. Augustine, beat Mary Agnes Wall, 2 and 1.

10. Women's Titleholders Tournament, Augusta, Georgia, overcame ten-stroke lead by Dorothy Kirby to win by five strokes, at 304.

11. North and South Women's Amateur, Pinehurst, North Carolina, beat Louise Suggs on first playoff hole.

12. Celebrities Championship, Washington, DC, won thirty-six-hole tournament with a 148.

13. British Women's Amateur Championship, Gullane, Scotland.

14. Broadmoor Ladies Invitation, Colorado Springs, beat Dorothy Kielty, 10 and 9.

W. R. "Bill" Schroeder and Thad S. Johnson, from *WHO in Sports,* at http://www.babedidriksonzaharias.org/page_three.cfm?.

See also "Star Relinquishes National Laurels," *New York Times,* August 15, 1947, 21: "Her last reverse by a woman golfer took place at Spokane, Wash. August 28, 1946—almost a year ago—in the first national women's open, when she bowed to Miss Grace Lenczyk of Newington, Conn. Mrs. Zaharias won the national women's amateur championship at Tulsa in September of last year." The date given here is incorrect. Babe's defeat was on August 26, 1946. See also "Babe Zaharias' Record," appendix, in Didrikson Zaharias, *This Life I've Led;* Gibson, *The Encyclopedia of Golf,* 80, 82; LPGA official records; and W. R. "Bill" Schroeder and Thad S. Johnson, "Career of Babe Didrikson Zaharias," from *WHO in Sports,* included in Babe's scrapbook.

249 "In Texas we call": Nelson, *How I Played the Game,* 44.

250 some of the women: Author interview with Marilynn Smith.

250 the memory: Author interview with Betty Jameson.

250 "I wish to advise": "Star Relinquishes National Laurels," *New York Times.*

251 "Well, I'm going to enter": Didrikson Zaharias, *This Life I've Led,* 184.

251 "I don't suppose": Ibid.

251 "may turn out to be more fabulous": Pete Martin, "Babe Didrikson Takes Off Her Mask," *Saturday Evening Post,* September 20, 1947, 26. See also Cayleff, *Babe,* 180.

252 many fans assumed: Cayleff, *Babe,* 180.

252 Corcoran attempted to be: Crosset, *Outsiders in the Clubhouse,* 43.

252 The first thing Corcoran did: Didrikson Zaharias, *This Life I've Led,* 181.

253 "had given the fans": Johnson and Williamson, *Whatta-Gal,* 184.

253 "Come on, Joe": Ibid.

253 "Better run those grounders": Cayleff, *Babe,* 181.

254 "THE NAME 'BABE'": P. Goldsmith Sons commercial brochure with Babe's endorsement, BDZ, doc. 11.1.16.5.

254 "sensible sports shirts": Didrikson Zaharias, *This Life I've Led,* photo section. Caption written by Babe.

254 "Housekeeping and golf": Cayleff, *Babe,* 182.

255 "the sports writers": Didrikson Zaharias, *Championship Golf,* 5, 16.

255 *Q* Why do you: Ibid., 16.

255 "sound like Babe": Cayleff, *Babe,* 185.

255 "Mildred wouldn't turn": Johnson, *The Incredible Babe,* 347–48.

256 Babe pinned all the blame: Author interviews with Jameson and Peggy Kirk Bell.

256 "I honestly believe": Didrikson Zaharias, *This Life I've Led,* 183.

257 Babe never lost: Associated Press, "Open Golf Title to Mrs. Zaharias," *New York Times,* August 16, 1948, 16. See also Didrikson Zaharias, *This Life I've Led,* 184.

257 "Couldn't get a putt": Associated Press, "Open Golf Title to Mrs. Zaharias."

257 "He got the idea": Didrikson Zaharias, *This Life I've Led,* 185.

258 the WPGA's first: Crosset, *Outsiders in the Clubhouse,* 42–44.

258 She was only the eighth: Ibid., 44.

259 "It didn't collapse": "A History of the LPGA Tour," *LPGA 1996 Player Guide,* available at http://www.worldgolf.com/wglibrary/history/lpgahist.html. See also Johnson, *The Incredible Babe,* 349.

259 "Well, okay, we": Johnson and Williamson, *Whatta-Gal,* 185.

Chapter 19: The Lady's Tour

261 "Potential sponsors": Glenn, *The Illustrated History of Women's Golf,* 160.

261 "There were a lot": Cayleff, *Babe,* 188.

261 "Let's make no": Williams, *Playing from the Rough,* 57.

261 "She was the color": Hudson, *Women in Golf,* 48. See also Cayleff, *Babe,* 189.

262 "My gosh, I don't": Hudson, *Women in Golf,* 35–36.

262 the original six: Original typewritten copy of "LPGA List of Founding Members," provided by Betty Jameson. The founding members of the LPGA are Alice Bauer, Patty Berg, Bettye Mims Danoff, Helen Dettweiler, Marlene Bauer Hagge, Helen Hicks, Opal Hill, Betty Jameson, Sally Sessions, Marilynn Smith, Shirley Spork, Louise Suggs, and Babe Didrikson Zaharias.

262 "A big thrill": Betsy Rawls interview, 7, 14.

262 "Babe was an entertainer": Author interview with Marilynn Smith.

263 "feeling good": Author interviews with Betty Jameson and Patty Berg.

263 "Women's golf": Cayleff, *Babe,* 188.

263 "I don't give a shit": Ibid., 186.

263 She asked him: Author interviews with Smith and Jameson.

263 The LPGA's hardscrabble": Ibid.

263 "We get along": Rhonda Glenn, "Betty Jameson, 1919–2009: USGA Champion and LPGA Co-founder," USGA, http://www.usga.org/news/2009/February/Three-Time-USGA-Champion-LPGA-Founder-Jameson-Dies/.

264 "we all had to play": Rawls interview, 21.

264 "God knows": Author interview with Smith.

264 "spent $3,335": Cayleff, *Babe,* 188.

264 Babe was the tour's: Didrikson Zaharias, *This Life I've Led,* 190.

265 The total amount: Original copy of the minutes of the annual meeting of the Ladies' Professional Golf Association, Evanston, IL, August 2, 1954. Document provided to the author by Betty Jameson.

265 "Women's golf": Author interview with Peggy Kirk Bell.

265 "You know, kid": Author interview with Smith.

265 Suggs was an attractive: Hudson, *Women in Golf,* 42. See also *Baseball Digest,* February 1959, 20.

265 "The headline usually": Author interview with Jameson.

266 something Suggs resented: Author interviews with Bell, Jameson, and Smith.

266 "I knew her as well": Louise Suggs interview, 32.

266 "Louise was the frankest": Johnson and Williamson, *Whatta-Gal,* 188–89.

266 "Babe had to win": Ibid.

266 The incident bothered: Suggs interview, 32.

266 "Hey girls, Babe's here!": These widely told anecdotes are included in many published sources, but not, interestingly, in Babe's own book. They were recounted in author interviews with Jameson, Smith, and Bell.

266 "I'm sure as hell": Author interviews with Bell and Jameson.

266 "According to her": Hudson, *Women in Golf,* 34.

266 "Oh, about a 70": Author interview with Bell. See also Johnson and Williamson, *Whatta-Gal,* 192.

267 "Suggs lost all respect": Johnson and Williamson, *Whatta-Gal,* 188; author interviews with Jameson, Bell, and Smith. Louise Suggs declined several invitations to speak with the author.

267 "There were times": Suggs interview, 69, 70.

267 "Babe was too proud": Author interview with Smith.

268 "Everybody knew": Suggs interview, 69, 70.

268 "As far as George": Betty Hicks interview, USGA Oral History Project, 58.

268 "She really hated to lose": Rawls interview, 27.

269 "Okay, now I suppose": Associated Press, "Zaharias Loses Temper, Match," June 20, 1951. For a list of LPGA tournament winners, see "Tournament Chronology," LPGA, http://www.lpga.com/content/Chronology50-59.pdf.

269 The other players: Author interview with Jameson.

269 "She'd move when somebody": Rawls interview, 27–29.

269 "a cold indifference": Lawrence Lader, "The Unbeatable Babe," *Coronet,* January 1948, 157, BDZ, doc. 11.1.17.1.

269 "Babe could be a very friendly": Hicks interview, USGA Oral History Project, 28.

269 "She put me at ease": Author interview with Smith.

270 "There.... You're a pro": Author interviews with Smith and Shirley Spork.

270 Babe became fastest friends: Author interview with Jameson. See also Johnson and Williamson, *Whatta-Gal,* 201.

270 "I wrote Babe about her": Johnson and Williamson, *Whatta-Gal,* 202.

270 "Sit still!": Ibid.

271 Babe insisted that she be paid: Author interviews with Jameson and Smith.

271 *Time* magazine dubbed: "Big Business Babe," *Time,* June 11, 1951, 66–68.

271 Babe played 656 exhibitions: Cayleff, *Babe,* 193.

272 "She has become the first woman": Ibid.

272 "I'm making it fast'n": Ibid., 194.

272 "We weren't out there": Author interview with Spork.

272 "If it wasn't for us pigeons": Ibid.

272 "Let me tell you girls": Author interviews with Jameson and Bell. See also Johnson and Williamson, *Whatta-Gal,* 190.

273 "Well, Babe was right": Author interview with Bell.

273 "She kind of always": Author interview with Smith.

273 "She came along": Johnson and Williamson, *Whatta-Gal,* 190.

273 "I take it away": Guy Yocom, "My Shot: Peggy Kirk Bell," *Golf Digest,* July 2007, available at http://www.golfdigest.com/magazine/2007-07/myshot_gd0 707?currentPage=2#ixzz0qKdd3rQx.

273 "She was the swashbuckling type": Author interview with Smith.

273 "She was smart enough": Author interview with Jameson.

274 "She was strongest": Johnson and Williamson, *Whatta-Gal,* 191–92.

274 "Save him for me": Betty Jameson interview, USGA Oral History Project, 13–14.

275 "Leonard, I'd like to make": Author interview with Jameson. See also Jameson interview, USGA Oral History Project, 13–14.

275 "It was their own fault": Enid Wilson interview, 18.

275 "Babe is beside herself": Berg interview. Patty Berg recalled in this interview that the women concluded the match in a tie. However, in a filmed interview in 1994 to commemorate the anniversary of the USGA, Berg recalled that the women had lost the match by one strike despite the eagle.

276 Babe stole the show: *Through the Green,* September 2006.

276 "Wonderful, wonderful": Martin Whitney, "Sports Trail," Associated Press, July 27, 1951. A copy of the original wire report was provided by Betty Jameson.

277 "Gay? Babe wasn't gay!": Author interviews with Jameson, Bell, Smith, and Rhonda Glenn. Indeed, late in her life, Betty Dodd suggested to one of Babe's most prominent and meticulous biographers, Susan E. Cayleff, that she and Babe were, in fact, lovers. Dodd did not reveal this during an interview in the mid-1970s with two of Babe's other highly regarded biographers, William Oscar Johnson and Nancy P. Williamson. Dodd died in July 1993, before Cayleff's biography was published. The women on the tour who were closest to Babe remain to this day convinced that she was not a lesbian, mainly because of her constant chatter about men, even in the years leading up to her death. Perhaps Babe was a good actress on this point and managed to conceal her affair with Dodd. Several of Babe's closest friends on the tour — including Jameson, Bell, and Smith — told me that they were sure Dodd had made up the story. Certainly, Dodd was a constant companion of Babe's during her final years, and George Zaharias deeply resented Dodd's

presence in Babe's life. I don't pretend to know what happened inside Babe's bedroom and have not found conclusive evidence either way.

277 "He blamed me": Cayleff, *Babe,* 203.

278 *"Pat and Mike* began shooting": Nash and Ross, *The Motion Picture Guide, N–R,* 2354. *Pat and Mike* is broadcast two or three times a year. I first watched it in 2004, shortly after embarking on the research for this book.

278 "Hepburn did everything": Cayleff, *Babe,* 211.

278 "Look who's here!": Ibid., 212.

278 "What have I done?": Baker, *Contesting Identities,* 162.

278 "the script was hastily changed": Cayleff, *Babe,* 211–12.

Chapter 20: The Unspeakable

280 "He's not much of a glamour": Pete Martin, "Babe Didrikson Takes Off Her Mask," *Saturday Evening Post,* September 20, 1947, 26.

280 "George did what he wanted": Author interview with Betty Jameson.

280 "Some nights he'd pound": Cayleff, *Babe,* 200.

281 "When I married George": Author interviews with Jameson, Peggy Kirk Bell, and Marilynn Smith.

281 "in his cups": Author interview with Jameson. See also Johnson and Williamson, *Whatta-Gal,* 161.

281 "George...don't you know?": Cayleff, *Babe,* 199.

282 "bask in her glory": Author interview with Jameson.

282 "Poor George": Johnson and Williamson, *Whatta-Gal,* 162.

282 a woman named Bessie Fenn: Author interview with Shirley Spork. See also "Woman Golfer Rules as Palm Beach Pro," *New York Times,* January 2, 1926, available at http://select.nytimes.com/gst/abstract.html?res=F20D13FE3D5F1773 8DDDAB0894D9405B868EF1D3.

282 "It was hard work": Didrikson Zaharias, *This Life I've Led,* 188.

282 "We were really living": Ibid.

283 "Say, what is all this?": Ibid., 189.

283 "George started drinking": Cayleff, *Babe,* 199.

283 "He just sort of flung her": Author interview with Smith.

283 "Mildred would come": Johnson, *The Incredible Babe,* 398.

284 "Goddamnit, Babe": Johnson and Williamson, *Whatta-Gal,* 165–66.

284 "Me and Babe": Cayleff, *Babe,* 213.

284 "both had tempers": Ibid.

284 "I'd give up every trophy": Author interview with Bell.

285 "He wanted her going": Cayleff, *Babe,* 198.

285 "There is no rest": Johnson and Williamson, *Whatta-Gal,* 197–98.

285 George was happy: Author interview with Jameson.

286 "Honey, this is it": Joan Flynn Dreyspool, "Subject: Babe and George Zaharias," *Sports Illustrated,* May 14, 1956, available at http://sportsillustrated.cnn

.com/vault/article/magazine/MAG1069639/index.htm. See also Anderson, *The Human Tradition in America Since 1945,* 145.

286 That evening: Author interview with Smith.

287 "Well, those 36 holes": Cayleff, *Babe,* 204.

288 "I'm feeling fine now": Ibid.

288 Babe was strong enough: Didrikson Zaharias, *This Life I've Led,* 192.

288 "Why didn't you tell me": Ibid., 193.

289 Babe and Riley exchanged: Author interview with Rhonda Glenn.

289 only $7,503.25: Original copy of "LPGA Top Money List," provided by Betty Jameson.

289 "maybe I have cancer": Author interview with Jameson, who told me she heard this from Betty Dodd.

289 George knew about: Author interviews with Jameson and Smith.

290 Twenty-three women: Paul Martin, "Zaharias Open Draws Top Flight Entries; Pro Shows Wares at BCC," *Beaumont Journal,* April 1, 1953, 20; Paul Martin, "Journal Clinic Today; Zaharias Open to Start Tomorrow," *Beaumont Journal,* April 2, 1953, 30.

290 "I can't wait": Didrikson Zaharias, *This Life I've Led,* 195.

290 Babe forced herself: "23 in Zaharias Golf Tee Off Today," *Beaumont Enterprise,* April 3, 1953, BDZ, doc. 11.1.5.7; Bill Scurlock, "Fabulous Babe Descends on Beaumont," Tiny Talks, *Beaumont Journal,* April 2, 1953, BDZ, doc. 11.1.5.4.

290 "The last day": Scurlock, "Fabulous Babe."

290 "crawling on": Didrikson Zaharias, *This Life I've Led,* 196.

290 "One more bad shot": Ibid.

290 "You don't think": Hudson, *Women in Golf,* 36.

290 she sank the improbable: "Babe Captures Zaharias Open," *Beaumont Enterprise,* April 6, 1953, BDZ, doc. 11.1.5.12. See also "Initial Babe Zaharias Open Unanimously Judged Success," *Beaumont Journal,* April 6, 1953, BDZ, doc. 11.1.5.13.

291 "Babe, we'll send": Johnson and Williamson, *Whatta-Gal,* 205.

291 "She was too modest": Author interview with Glenn.

291 "I've got cancer": Didrikson Zaharias, *This Life I've Led,* 198.

291 "Here's what I want": Notes about Babe's condition on Dr. W. E. Tatum's letterhead, BDZ, doc. 11.1.6.24; Didrikson Zaharias, *This Life I've Led, 199.*

292 "Can't I see him": Didrikson Zaharias, *This Life I've Led,* 199.

292 "Babe, you've got cancer": Ibid., 199–200.

293 "I'm not worried": Author interview with Glenn, who was told this story by Bertha Bowen; Johnson and Williamson, *Whatta-Gal,* 203.

293 "R.L., come home": Johnson and Williamson, *Whatta-Gal,* 203.

293 "When you get sick" and *"Haven't I always"*: Didrikson Zaharias, *This Life I've Led,* 201. All the italics in this paragraph are Babe's thoughts at the time, as recounted in her autobiography.

293 "I've got to be": Johnson and Williamson, *Whatta-Gal,* 179.

294 "Here. I want you": Didrikson Zaharias, *This Life I've Led,* 202.

Chapter 21: The Muscle Is Spiritual

295 "Do you think": Cayleff, *Babe,* 237.

295 The surgery would remove: Brief statement that physicians and technicians agree that Babe's condition is malignant and that surgery is necessary, BDZ, doc. 11.1.6.23. See also News Bulletin, Beaumont, issuing statement that Babe had a malignancy, BDZ, doc. 11.1.6.22.

295 "malignancy": "Seriously Ill Babe May Have Begun and Ended Career Here," April 10, 1953, BDZ, doc. 11.1.6.1. See also "Major Surgery Indicated as Babe Zaharias' Condition Is Diagnosed as Malignancy," April 11, 1953, BDZ, doc. 11.1.6.2.

296 Americans were still ignorant: Patterson, *The Dread Disease,* 151, 152.

296 "one of the best kept secrets": Ibid., 152.

296 "seriously ill": "Babe Zaharias Goes Under Knife at Hotel Dieu Today," *Beaumont Journal,* April 17, 1953, 1.

296 "The fabulous athletic career": Associated Press, "Mrs. Zaharias Is Ill at Beaumont; Athletic Career Appears at End," *New York Times,* April 10, 1953, 26.

297 "but I will say": Ibid.

297 "Babe will never": Ibid.

297 "I am definitely not out of sports": Associated Press, "Messages Pour In to Mrs. Zaharias," *New York Times,* April 11, 1953, 10.

297 "I feel confident": "Babe Zaharias Goes under Knife," *Beaumont Journal.*

297 Betty Dodd had put them there: Didrikson Zaharias, *This Life I've Led,* 210. Babe writes, "One of the last things I did before the operation was to tell George, 'Honey, I want you to go downstairs and get my golf clubs and put them right in the corner of my room, because I'm going to use them again. I want to look at them and I want to feel that they're there when I come out of the operating room.' So he did, and those clubs stayed in that corner as long as I was in the hospital." But Betty Dodd told biographer Susan E. Cayleff that it was her idea to put Babe's clubs in her room and that she did so, a fact corroborated by others. Cayleff, *Babe,* 223. See also Crawford and Ragsdale, *Women in Texas,* 304.

298 "BEST OF LUCK": Didrikson Zaharias, *This Life I've Led,* 205–6.

298 "Get Babe": Ibid.

298 "Let the pros": Author interview with Rhonda Glenn.

298 one of the finest surgeons: "Surgeon of World Renown Will Operate on Babe Zaharias at Hotel Dieu Friday," April 13, 1953, BDZ, doc. 11.1.6.4.

298 "I certainly hate to meet you": Didrikson Zaharias, *This Life I've Led,* 205.

299 Betty Dodd had moved: Bill Scurlock, "Prayers Follow Babe Zaharias Today," Tiny Talks, *Beaumont Journal,* April 17, 1953, BDZ, doc. 11.1.6.14.

299 "I still didn't like": Didrikson Zaharias, *This Life I've Led,* 208.

299 "all the people I know": Cayleff, *Babe,* 233.

299 "I'd rather play": Ibid., 233–34; Patterson, *The Dread Disease,* 222.

300 "Remember … you're the champion": Patterson, 223.

300 "It's going to be a tough": Didrikson Zaharias, *This Life I've Led,* 211.

300 "Colostomy, honey?": Ibid.

301 "okay": "Babe Comes Through Operation 'Okay,'" *Beaumont Journal,* April 18, 1953, BDZ, doc. 11.1.6.15.

301 "If things go as well": "Doctors Indicate Babe May Golf Again," April 18, 1953, BDZ, doc. 11.1.6.16. See also "Babe Rests Well, in Fine Spirits," April 29, 1953, BDZ, doc. 11.1.6.17.

301 "With this type of operation": Cayleff, *Babe,* 214.

301 Betty was the only one: Author interviews with Glenn and Betty Jameson.

301 "Two invalids": Cayleff, *Babe,* 221.

302 Babe's friends and relatives: Ibid.

302 "I didn't do any sounding off": Ibid., 224.

302 Babe had chosen: "Babe Maps a Campaign to Help Fight Cancer," BDZ, doc. 11.1.6.21.

302 "I am feeling wonderful": Johnson and Williamson, *Whatta-Gal,* 208.

303 "Yeah, I went nine holes": Didrikson Zaharias, *This Life I've Led,* 216.

303 "She was familiar": Ibid., 217.

303 "To me, shooting tournament golf": "To me, shooting tournament golf": Ibid.

303–304 "Everywhere that Babe went": Cayleff, *Babe,* 225.

304 "What grit": Author interview with Jameson.

304 "It's not easy": Author interview with Marilynn Smith.

304 "Quit, Babe": Johnson and Williamson, *Whatta-Gal,* 209.

305 "The Babe is Back": Cayleff, *Babe,* 224.

305 "In my case it was just luck": Babe Didrikson Zaharias, as told to Booton Herndon, "I'm Not Out of the Rough—Yet!" *Cosmopolitan,* October 1953, 79–80.

306 "I am feeling fine": Johnson and Williamson, *Whatta-Gal,* 210–11.

306 "At this point, ten months": Ibid., 211.

307 "Of the thousands": Didrikson Zaharias, "I'm Not Out of the Rough—Yet!" 83.

307 At the Serbin Open: Associated Press, "Card of 74 for 294 Beats Miss Berg," *New York Times,* February 22, 1954.

307 "I guess I'll have to call this": Ibid.

307 Golf Writers of America: Hudson, *Women in Golf,* 36.

308 "How do you do": Cayleff, *Babe,* 226; Schedule of Dwight D. Eisenhower, Eisenhower Presidential Papers, Dwight D. Eisenhower Presidential Library.

308 "Mr. President … on behalf": Cayleff, *Babe,* 226.

309 "Where's that baby?": Author interview with Peggy Kirk Bell.

309 "No—Babe": Bell, *The Gift of Golf,* 59.

309 "Tell him to call me": Kathy Whitworth interview, 2.

309 "And it was past": Betty Jameson interview, USGA Oral History Project, 17.

309 "All boys are good athletes": Author interview with Bell.

310 M. Hohner's Old Standby: Author interview with Mike Cubbage. One of Babe's harmonicas is now at the World Golf Hall of Fame museum in St. Augustine, Florida.

310 Babe was paid $1,500: I watched a video of Babe and Betty's appearance on *The Ed Sullivan Show,* provided by the USGA. See also Cayleff, *Babe,* 210.

310 "Here comes Superman": Cayleff, *Babe,* 228.

310 "Those letters": Didrikson Zaharias, *This Life I've Led,* 218.

310 "Babe's hernia": Author interview with Bell.

310 "A real golf course": Didrikson Zaharias, *This Life I've Led,* 222.

311 "In the afternoon": Ibid., 223.

312 "I don't like to keep": Wakeman, *Babe Didrikson Zaharias,* 99.

312 "probably the most incredible": Jim Murray, "The Other Babe," *Los Angeles Times,* 1, 17, BDZ, doc. 11.1.12.18. Murray also declared that Babe did more for women "than the Equal Rights Amendment" and that "she was the greatest athlete this country has produced."

313 "You did it yourself, Babe": Cayleff, *Babe,* 227.

Chapter 22: Rainbow Manor

314 America's all-sport: Beyond the press coverage portraying Babe as a leading anticancer spokesperson, there are many pieces of evidence that have not been made public to support this sentence, including a form letter to sports editors under letterhead "The Babe Didrikson Zaharias Fund, Inc.," BDZ, doc. 11.1.7.3, and the Babe Didrikson Zaharias Fund, information, BDZ, doc. 11.1.7.1.

314 She and George founded: "Fund for Detection of Cancer Established by Babe Zaharias," *Beaumont Enterprise,* September 12, 1955, BDZ, doc. 11.1.7.2.

315 She visited Sister Tarsisis: Didrikson Zaharias, *This Life I've Led,* 214.

315 "She gave people hope": Author interview with Patty Berg.

315 "In the name of Heaven": Kalick, *Cancer Etiquette,* 85.

315 thirty events and $160,000: Original copy of "LPGA 1955 Tournament Schedule," provided by Betty Jameson.

315 "At times I feel": Didrikson Zaharias, *This Life I've Led,* 228.

316 She didn't think the setback: Quentin Reynolds, "Girl Who Lived Again, Babe Didrikson Zaharias," *Reader's Digest,* October 1954, 50–55.

316 "big and roomy": Cayleff, *Babe,* 220.

316 "It may not be 'pure'": Didrikson Zaharias, *This Life I've Led,* photo section. Caption written by Babe.

317 "Every time I get out": Ibid., 228.

317 "At first there were just six": Ibid., 229.

318 "That wonderful lively look": Author interview with Barbara Romack.

318 "Honey, keep going": Ibid.

318 "Now that I look back": Johnson and Williamson, *Whatta-Gal,* 211.

318 "It seemed like every second shot": Author interview with Marilynn Smith.

318 It would be Babe's: "LPGA 1955 Tournament Schedule."

318 "Isn't it kind of fitting": Betsy Rawls interview, 75.

319 She left the hospital: "Babe Zaharias Gets Treatment for New Cancer," August 5, 1955, BDZ, doc. 11.1.8.1; "Babe Rests in 2nd Bout with Cancer," August 7, 1955, BDZ, doc. 11.1.8.2.

319 We would walk through it": Cayleff, *Babe,* 230.

319 Babe had become addicted: Ibid.

319 "Here she was": Johnson and Williamson, *Whatta-Gal,* 208.

320 "She didn't have anything wrong": Cayleff, *Babe,* 230.

320 "You might suppose": Didrikson Zaharias, *This Life I've Led,* preface.

320 There was one unhappy new note: Ibid.

320 "fresh trace of cancer": Johnson and Williamson, *Whatta-Gal,* 209, 210.

321 "took the bad news": Cayleff, *Babe,* 233.

321 "As far as I was concerned": Didrikson Zaharias, *This Life I've Led,* 232.

321 "In the future": Ibid.

322 "really get going": Johnson and Williamson, *Whatta-Gal,* 214.

322 "So she played in loafers": Author interview with Peggy Kirk Bell. See also Johnson and Williamson, *Whatta-Gal,* 214–15, and Cayleff, *Babe,* 237–38.

322 "Peggy, you've got to be one": Author interview with Bell.

322 A home movie was made: This home movie is located in the USGA archives. Author interview with Rhonda Glenn, who described the film vividly in a wonderful press release written in 2004. See "Babe Didrikson Zaharias — Whatta' Gal," USGA, http://www.uswomensopen.com/2004/press/whatta-gal.html.

323 "I just wanted to see": Author interview with Glenn, who was told about this moment by Bertha Bowen. See also Glenn, *The Illustrated History of Women's Golf,* 131, and Glenn, "Babe Didrikson Zaharias — Whatta' Gal."

323 "I was dying to win": Johnson and Williamson, *Whatta-Gal,* 216.

323 "Shhhh....Babe is sleeping": Joan Flynn Dreyspool, "Subject: Babe and George Zaharias," *Sports Illustrated,* May 14, 1956, available at http://sports illustrated.cnn.com/vault/article/magazine/MAG1069639/index.htm. All the quotes and observations that follow are culled from Dreyspool's amazing profile.

Chapter 23: Greatness and Goodness

328 "That was it": Johnson and Williamson, *Whatta-Gal,* 217.

328 "Babe, she knew": Ibid.

328 "She suspected": Johnson, *The Incredible Babe,* 272.

329 "When George and I": Johnson and Williamson, *Whatta-Gal,* 218.

329 A surprise party: "Cheerful Babe Continues Stubborn Battle against Cancer as 42nd Birthday Nears," June 26, 1956, BDZ, doc. 11.1.8.3. Note that her age is incorrect here and elsewhere.

329 "God bless you": "Tributes from World Over Pour Down on Babe at Birthday Party," June 27, 1956, BDZ, doc. 11.1.8.4. See also Associated Press, "Birthday Party Cheers Mrs. Zaharias, 42, as She Pleads for Cancer Research Fund," *New York Times,* June 27, 1956, 38.

329 "the finest I've ever had": Terry McLeod, "Babe Has 'Happiest Day of My Life,'" *Dallas News,* June 27, 1956, 1–2.

329 Across the ocean: Ibid. See also Associated Press, "Birthday Party Cheers Mrs. Zaharias."

330 "Business as usual": "Babe's Family Gather as She Grows Weaker," August 26, 1956, BDZ, doc. 11.1.8.9.

330 she represented hope: The press coverage during Babe's last summer was filled with hope—often false hope. See "Physicians Report Babe Doing Well," July 15, 1956, BDZ, doc. 11.1.8.7; "Babe's Grit Praised by Physicians," August 1956, BDZ, doc. 11.1.8.11; and especially "Physicians See Much Improvement," September 5, 1956, BDZ, doc. 11.1.8.12a. The last article was published three weeks before Babe's death.

330 But Betty Dodd: Considine, *They Rose Above It,* 105.

330 "If she had been anybody": Cayleff, *Babe,* 238.

330 "This is just a note": United Press, "Golfer Greets Golfer: Note from President Cheers Babe Zaharias in Hospital," *New York Times,* 25.

331 "Mrs. Zaharias": Ibid.

331 "She was flat": Johnson and Williamson, *Whatta-Gal,* 201.

331 "George, I ain't gonna die": "Babe's Fighting Spirit: 'Ain't Gonna Die,'" editorial, *Beaumont Journal,* September 28, 1956, BDZ, doc. 11.1.10.3; "Finally She Had to Lose," *Life,* October 8, 1956, 169.

331 at 6:42 a.m.: "Babe Zaharias Dies; Athlete Had Cancer," *New York Times,* September 28, 1956, 1. See also "Cancer Claims Life of Babe Zaharias," *Beaumont Journal,* September 27, 1956, BDZ, doc. 11.1.9.3.

331 "Babe never really": Johnson and Williamson, *Whatta-Gal,* 203.

331 "She's had enough agony": "Babe Didn't Ask God for Much, Husband Recalls," *Beaumont Journal,* September 28, 1956, BDZ, doc. 11.1.9.5.

332 "Ladies and gentlemen": Dwight D. Eisenhower, Transcript of White House Press Conference, September 27, 1956, Eisenhower Presidential Papers, Dwight D. Eisenhower Presidential Library.

332 The flash across the country: Associated Press, "Woman Athlete Babe Zaharias Dies at 42," September 27, 1956; "Babe Zaharias Dies; Athlete Had Cancer," *New York Times,* 1, 30.

332 Babe Didrikson has finally lost: "Babe Didrikson Zaharias," editorial, *New York Times,* September 28, 1956, 26.

333 "She wasn't ready": Author interview with Peggy Kirk Bell.

333 The funeral service: Memorial service program, BDZ, doc. 11.1.9.10b.

334 Babe's brothers: Notes on Babe Zaharias's funeral, BDZ, doc. 11.1.9.10. See also announcement of memorial services, BDZ, doc. 11.1.9.10a, and notations concerning Babe's burial, BDZ, doc. 11.1.9.11.

334 "She was always just Babe": Associated Press, "Throng Attends Zaharias Rites: Lutheran Service Held in Beaumont, Tex., Church for Famed Athlete," *New York Times,* September 29, 1956, 19.

334 "Know ye not": Ibid.

334 *The loafer has no comeback:* Author interview with Peggy Kirk Bell. The Rice poem, entitled "The Final Answer," was published posthumously in 1955 in *The Final Answer and Other Poems,* ed. John Kiernan, New York: A. S. Barnes.

334 Babe's body was cremated: Announcement of memorial services; Certificate of Cremation, September 29, 1956, BDZ, doc. 11.1.9.10.

335 At Babe's burial: Johnson, *The Incredible Babe.*

335 do everything possible: Associated Press, "Throng Attends Zaharias Rites," 19. George Zaharias is quoted as saying on the day of Babe's funeral that he planned "to erect a large monument at Forest Lawn Memorial Park" to his wife. See also Bill Scurlock, "Babe Zaharias' Trophies to Be Brought Here if Suitable Place Made Available, Mayor Hails Plan for Permanent Display," *Beaumont Journal,* October 1, 1956, 1, 4. George told Scurlock that he "would bring all of Babe's trophies, pictures and mementos to Beaumont provided the city would furnish a permanent place for her sports treasures." Mayor Jimmie Cokinos said, "Beaumonters should be deeply grateful to the husband of this greatest of all women athletes for bringing these things back to Babe's home town. I personally would like to see Beaumonters build a specially designed building in which to place these things — a place always open where the thousands who will want to see them may do so — not only now but for generations to come."

Epilogue: Museum for One

337 And also, now, for you: I have visited the Babe Didrikson Zaharias Museum in Beaumont on a number of occasions. The visit I describe here was on November 17, 2004. I met and first spoke with Helen Caspar on that day and conducted a follow-up phone interview with her on July 18, 2009.

339 You see the path: Hudson, *Women in Golf,* 38.

339 Babe is the only woman: For a list of the top athletes of the twentieth century, see "SportsCentury," ESPN.com, http://espn.go.com/sportscentury/. Babe was ranked number 10.

Bibliography

Abernathy, Francis Edward. *Legendary Ladies of Texas*. 2nd ed. Nacogdoches: Texas Folklore Society, 1994.

Albertson, Roxanne M., and Jean Pekara. "Golden Cyclones, 1931 National Basketball Champions." *North American Society for Sport History: Proceedings and Newsletter* 13 (May 1985). Available at http://www.la84foundation.org/SportsLibrary/NASSH_Proceedings/NP1985/NP1985zd.pdf.

Alcott, Amy, and Don Wade. *Amy Alcott's Guide to Women's Golf*. New York: Penguin, 1991.

Anderson, David L. *The Human Tradition in America Since 1945*. Lanham, MD: Rowan & Littlefield, 2003.

Baker, Aaron. *Contesting Identities: American Sports in Film*. Champaign: University of Illinois Press, 2003.

Bell, Peggy Kirk. *The Gift of Golf: My Life with the Wonderful Game*. Southern Pines, NC: Pine Needles Lodge and Golf Club and the Pilot, 2001.

Bell, Peggy Kirk, and Jerry Claussen. *A Woman's Way to Better Golf*. New York: E. P. Dutton, 1966.

Berg, Patty, and Mark Cox. *Golf Illustrated*. New York: A. S. Barnes, 1950.

Berg, Patty, and Otis Dypwick. *Golf*. New York: A. S. Barnes, 1941.

Burnett, Jim. *Tee Times: On the Road with the Ladies Professional Golf Tour*. New York: Scribner, 1997.

Cayleff, Susan E. *Babe: The Life and Legend of Babe Didrikson Zaharias*. Urbana: University of Illinois Press, 1995.

Collett, Glenna. *Golf for Young Players*. Boston: Little, Brown, 1926.

———. *Ladies in the Rough*. New York: Alfred A. Knopf, 1928.

Congdon, Don, ed. *The Thirties: A Time to Remember*. New York: Simon & Schuster, 1962.

Considine, Bob. *They Rose Above It*. New York: Doubleday, 1977.

Corcoran, Fred, and Bud Harvey. *Unplayable Lies: The Story of Sport's Most Successful Impresario*. New York: Meredith Press, 1965.

Costa, D. Margaret, and Sharon Ruth Guthrie. *Women in Sport.* New York: Human Kinetics, 1994.

Coubertin, Pierre de. "L'éducation des jeunes enfants et des jeunes filles." *Revue Olympique,* October 1902.

Coyne, John. *Golf for Women.* London: Angus & Robertson, 1975.

———. *The New Golf for Women.* New York: Doubleday, 1973.

Crane, Malcolm. *The Story of Ladies' Golf.* London: Stanley Paul, 1991.

Crawford, Ann Fears, and Crystal Sasse Ragsdale. *Women in Texas.* Austin, TX: State House Press, 1982.

Crosset, Todd W. *Outsiders in the Clubhouse: The World of Women's Professional Golf.* Albany: State University Press of New York, 1995.

Dahlberg, Tim, with Mary Ederle Ward and Brenda Greene. *America's Girl: The Incredible Story of How Swimmer Gertrude Ederle Changed the Nation.* New York: St. Martin's Press, 2009.

Darwin, Bernard. *Every Idle Dream.* London: Collins, 1948.

Didrikson Zaharias, Babe. *Championship Golf.* New York: A. S. Barnes, 1948.

———. *This Life I've Led.* As told to Harry T. Paxton. New York: A. S. Barnes, 1956.

Dunn, Betty, and Jackie Pung. *Women's Golf Legend: The Thrill and Heartbreak of an LPGA Professional.* Lincoln, NE: iUniverse, 2005.

Findling, John E., and Kimberly D. Pelle. *Encyclopedia of the Modern Olympics.* Westport, CT: Greenwood Press, 2004.

Foldes, Eva. "Women at the Olympics: A Historical Survey of Physical Education for Women." Fourth Session of the International Olympic Academy, 1964.

Fountain, Charles. *Sportswriter: The Life and Times of Grantland Rice.* New York: Oxford University Press, 1993.

Gibson, Nevin H. *The Encyclopedia of Golf: With the Official All-Time Records.* New York: A. S. Barnes, 1964.

Glenn, Rhonda. *The Illustrated History of Women's Golf.* Dallas: Taylor Publishing, 1991.

Guttmann, Allen. *Women's Sports: A History.* New York: Columbia University Press, 1991.

Hargreaves, Jennifer. *Sporting Females: Critical Issues in the History and Sociology of Women's Sports.* New York: Routledge, 1994.

Harper, William Arthur. *How You Played the Game: The Life of Grantland Rice.* Columbia: University of Missouri Press, 1999.

Hauser, Melanie, Liz Kahn, and Lisa D. Mickey. *Champions of Women's Golf: Celebrating Fifty Years of the LPGA.* Naples, FL: QuailMark Books, 2000.

Haynie, Sandra. *Golf: A Natural Course for Women.* New York: Atheneum, 1975.

Hecker, Genevieve. *Golf for Women.* New York: Baker & Taylor, 1904.

Helme, Eleanor E. *The Lady Golfer's Tip Book.* London: Mills & Boon, 1923.

Hudson, David L. *Women in Golf: The Players, the History, and the Future of the Sport.* Westport, CT: Praeger, 2008.

Ikard, Robert W. *Just for Fun: The Story of AAU Women's Basketball.* Little Rock: University of Arkansas Press, 2005.

Inabinett, Mark. *Grantland Rice and His Heroes: The Sportswriter as Mythmaker in the 1920s.* Knoxville: University of Tennessee Press, 1994.

Jacobs, Linda. *Laura Baugh: Golf's Golden Girl.* St. Paul: MEC, 1975.

Johnson, Thad S. *The Incredible Babe: Her Ultimate Story.* Privately published, 1996.

Johnson, William Oscar, and Nancy P. Williamson. *Whatta-Gal: The Babe Didrikson Story.* Boston: Little, Brown, 1975.

Juergens, Vernon, and Rhonda Glenn. *The Beginners Guide to Great Golf for Women.* Dallas: Taylor Publishing, 1993.

Kahn, Liz. *The LPGA: The Unauthorized Version; The History of the Ladies Professional Golf Association.* Menlo Park, CA: Group Fore Productions, 1996.

Kalick, Rosanne. *Cancer Etiquette: What to Say, What to Do When Someone You Know or Love Has Cancer.* Scarsdale, NY: Lion Books, 2005.

Knudson, R. R. *Babe Didrikson: Athlete of the Century.* New York: Puffin Books, 1986.

Leigh, Mary Henson. "The Evolution of Women's Participation in the Summer Olympic Games, 1900–1948." PhD diss., Ohio State University, 1974.

Leitch, Cecil. *Golf Simplified.* London: Thornton Butterworth, 1924.

Lewis, Beverly. *Golf for Women.* New York: Gallery Books, 1990.

Lipsyte, Robert, and Peter Levine. *Idols of the Game: A Sporting History of the American Century.* New York: Turner Publishing, 1995.

Lopez, Nancy, and Peter Schwed. *Education of a Woman Golfer.* New York: Simon & Schuster, 1979.

Lopez, Nancy, and Don Wade. *Lopez on Golf.* London: Stanley Paul, 1987.

Lucas, John A. "A History of the Marathon Race, 490 B.C. to 1975." *Journal of Sport History* 3 (1975).

Lynn, Elizabeth A. *Babe Didrikson Zaharias.* New York: Chelsea House, 1989.

Marlow, Joan. *The Great Women.* New York: A & W Publishers, 1979.

Messerli, Dr. Fr. M. "Women's Participation in the Modern Olympic Games." Edited by the International Olympic Committee, 1952.

Moran, Sharron. *Golf Is a Women's Game, or How to Be a Swinger on the Fairway.* New York: Hawthorn Books, 1971.

Nash, Jay Robert, and Stanley Ralph Ross. *The Motion Picture Guide, N–R.* New York: Cinebooks, 1988.

Nelson, Byron. *How I Played the Game.* New York: Dell, 1994.

Nickerson, Elinor. *Golf: A Woman's History.* Jefferson, NC: McFarland, 1987.

Oliver, Greg, and Steven Johnson. *The Pro Wrestling Hall of Fame: The Heels.* Toronto: ECW Press, 2007.

Patterson, James T. *The Dread Disease: Cancer and Modern American Culture.* Cambridge, MA: Harvard University Press, 1989.

Pieroth, Doris H. *Their Day in the Sun: Women of the 1932 Olympics.* Seattle: University of Washington Press, 1996.

Puett, Barbara, and Jim Apfelbaum. *Women's Own Golf Book.* New York: St. Martin's Press, 1999.

Rankin, Judy, and Peter McClerry. *Women's Guide to Better Golf.* Chicago: Contemporary Books, 1995.

Rice, Grantland. *The Tumult and the Shouting: My Life in Sport.* New York: A. S. Barnes, 1954.

Robertson, Mrs. Gordon. *Hints to Lady Golfers.* London: Walbrook, 1909.

Sampson, Curt. *Texas Golf Legends: Mildred Ella "Babe" Didrikson Zaharias.* Lubbock: Texas Tech University Press, 1999.

Saunders, Vivien. *The Complete Women Golfer.* London: Stanley Paul, 1975.

Sheehan, Patty, and Betty Hicks. *Patty Sheehan on Golf.* Dallas: Taylor Publishing, 1996.

Simri, Uriel. *Women at the Olympic Games.* Netanya, Israel: Wingate Institute for Physical Education and Sport, 1979.

Smith, Lissa. *Nike Is a Goddess.* New York: Atlantic Monthly Press, 1998.

Stanley, Louis T. *How to Be a Better Woman Golfer.* New York: Thomas Y. Crowell, 1952.

Suggs, Louise. *Par Golf for Women.* New York: Prentice Hall, 1953.

Suggs, Louise, Marlene Bauer Hagge, Beverly Hanson, Jackie Pung, Barbara Romack, Joyce Ziske, and Ruth Jessen. *Golf for Women.* New York: Doubleday, 1960.

Tricard, Louise Mead. *American Women's Track and Field: A History, 1895 Through 1980.* Jefferson, NC: McFarland, 1996.

Vaughn, Roger. *Golf: The Woman's Game.* New York: Stewart, Tabori & Chang, 2000.

Wakeman, Nancy. *Babe Didrikson Zaharias: Driven to Win.* Minneapolis: Lerner Publishing, 2000.

Ware, Susan. *Letter to the World.* New York: W. W. Norton, 1998.

Wethered, Joyce. *Golfing Memories and Methods.* London: Hutchinson, 1933.

Whitworth, Kathy, and Rhonda Glenn. *Golf for Women.* New York: St. Martin's Press, 1990.

Williams, Jackie. *Playing from the Rough: The Women of the LPGA Hall of Fame.* Las Vegas: Women of Diversity Productions, 2000.

Wilson, Enid. *The Babe in Retrospect.* London: B. T. Batsford, 1965.

Woolum, Janet. *Outstanding Women Athletes: Who They Are and How They Influenced Sports in America.* 2nd ed. Phoenix: Oryx Press, 1988.

Wright, Mickey. *Play Golf the Wright Way.* Garden City, NY: Doubleday, 1962.

Oral Histories

Amateur Athletic Foundation Library, Los Angeles, interviews by George A. Hodak
    Evelyne Hall Adams, September 1987
    Jean Shiley Newhouse, September 1987

USGA Oral History Project, Far Hills, NJ, interviews
    Judy Bell, 2001
    Peggy Kirk Bell, 1991
    Patty Berg, 1991
    Angela Ward Bonallack, 1991
    JoAnne Carter, 1992
    Alice O'Neal Dye, 2003
    Mary Lena Faulk, 1992
    Maureen Garrett, 1991
    Rhonda Glenn, 2004
    Marlene Bauer Hagge, 1991
    Betty Hicks, 1991
    Betty Jameson, 1992
    Carol Mann, 1992
    Barbara McIntire, 2001
    Maureen Orcutt, 1991
    Betsy Rawls, 1990
    Barbara Romack, 2004
    Janet Seagle, 1997
    Marlene Stewart Streit, 1992
    Louise Suggs, 1992
    Virginia Van Wie, 1991
    Enid Wilson, 1991
    Mickey Wright, 1991

Index

About the Author

Don Van Natta Jr. has been a *New York Times* correspondent since 1995. Prior to that, he worked for eight years at the *Miami Herald.* He is a member of three Pulitzer Prize–winning teams — two at the *Times* and one at the *Herald.* He is also the author of *First Off the Tee* and the coauthor of *Her Way,* both *New York Times* bestsellers. He lives in South Florida with his wife, Lizette Alvarez, who is also a *Times* correspondent, and their two daughters, Isabel and Sofia.